4.19.19
$ 26.85
AS-14

4/19

HISTORIES
OF THE
UNEXPECTED

HISTORIES
OF THE
UNEXPECTED

HOW EVERYTHING HAS A HISTORY

———

SAM WILLIS & JAMES DAYBELL

Atlantic Books
London

First published in hardback in Great Britain in 2018
by Atlantic Books, an imprint of Atlantic Books Ltd.

Copyright © Sam Willis & James Daybell, 2018

The moral right of Sam Willis and James Daybell to be identified
as the authors of this work has been asserted by them in
accordance with the Copyright, Designs and Patents Act of 1988.

1 2 3 4 5 6 7 8 9

A CIP catalogue record for this book is available
from the British Library.

Hardback ISBN: 978-1-78649-412-2
E-book ISBN: 978-1-78649-415-3
Paperback ISBN: 978-1-78649-414-6

Printed in Great Britain by Bell & Bain Ltd, Glasgow

Atlantic Books
An Imprint of Atlantic Books Ltd
Ormond House
26–27 Boswell Street
London
WCIN 3JZ

www.atlantic-books.co.uk

Everything

HAS A

history

EVEN THE MOST

unexpected

OF SUBJECTS...

... and *everything*

LINKS — TOGETHER

IN

WAYS

unexpected

For Julia and Tors

CONTENTS

ACKNOWLEDGEMENTS

This book is about sharing great research and new approaches to history. Our first acknowledgement, therefore, must go to all of those brilliant historians – professional and amateur – who are writing today and who are changing the way that we all think about the past. You are all doing a fabulous job, and it is one that often goes unremarked and unrewarded. Thank you all for your time, effort, energy and brilliance. We could not have written this book without you.

More specifically we would like to thank those historians who have particularly inspired us with their creative thinking, support and encouragement over the years. Since this book is intended for a wide and general audience we have chosen not to publish with extensive footnotes. We acknowledge our indebtedness to fellow historians in the selected further reading section at the end of the book, which is also intended as a spur to further research for our readers.

We would like to thank the many colleagues and friends who have generously offered ideas, guidance, support and sustenance, intellectual and otherwise: Andy Gordon, Nadine Akkerman, Nick Barnett, Sue Broomhall, Anthony Caleshu, Erika Gaffney, Lee Jane Giles, James Gregory, Daniel Grey, Emma Haddon, Dan Maudlin, Angela McShane, Elaine Murphy, Svante Norrhem, the Lord John Russell, the Worshipful Company of

Glovers, Adam Smyth, Jacqueline Van Gent, Charlie and A. J. Courtenay, Suzie Lipscomb, Janina Ramirez, Phillip Northcott, Darius Arya, James Holland, Michael Duffy, Andrew Lambert, Richard Nevell, Jennie Stogdon, and among the twitterati @HunterS_Jones, @RedLunaPixie, @KittNoir, and @Kazza2014.

Collective thanks are also due to Dan Snow, Dan Morelle, Tom Clifford, Natt Tapley and the fabulous History Hit team for all their support and encouragement, as well as to Will Atkinson, James Nightingale, Kate Straker, Seán Costello and everyone at Atlantic Books.

We would also like to thank everyone (and there are hundreds of thousands of you) who has listened to the podcast or come to see one of our live events and been so charming and enthusiastic.

Most of all, however, we would like to thank our families, young and old, for everything they have done and continue to do, to cope with – of *all things* – a historian in their lives.

But we have created this book for you.

Sam and James
Isca – Escanceaster – Exeter
The Feast of St Eligius – 12 Rabī' al-'awwal 1439 – I.XII. MMXVII – 1 December 2017 '

INTRODUCTION

This book was born from our *Histories of the Unexpected* podcast series, which has provided us both, as professional historians, with more fun and intellectual stimulation than anything either of us has ever done before. It has fundamentally changed the way that we think about the past – and the present – and we hope that it will do the same for you.

The idea is simple. We believe that everything – and we mean *simply everything*, even the most unexpected of subjects – has a history, and that those histories link together in unexpected, and often rather magical, ways.

This book is intended as a journey of historical discovery that tackles some of the greatest of historical themes – from the Tudors to the Second World War, from the Roman empire to the Victorians – but via entirely unexpected subjects.

You will find out here how the history of the *beard* is connected to the Crimean War; how the history of *paper clips* is all about the Stasi; how the history of the *bubble* (and also *cats*) is all about the French Revolution; how the *Titanic*, the nuclear destruction of Hiroshima and Ground Zero are all connected, and what they have to do with Charles Dickens's *Great Expectations*; you will come to understand why the history of *the scar* is so important; why the history of *chimneys* is so charming; why the history of *snow* is so inspirational.

The past to many is still often presented as the study of great men and women, events, wars and revolutions, cultural movements or epochs that move us from the ancient and medieval to the modern world. Some historians privilege different aspects of the past such as religion, society, economics, gender, politics, military affairs or ideas. All of this is useful; it brings different perspectives and insights to our study of the past. However, history as we know and understand it today is exceptionally complex and interconnected, and no one perspective on the past is really adequate in order to unpack it in its entirety.

We hope that *Histories of the Unexpected* will help to bridge this gap between the well-established scholarly embrace of complexity – achieved through mind-bending thought paths and innovative research – and the public appetite for digestible but meaningful and thought-provoking history.

Essentially, we believe that reading about the past in a predictable, linear way is unsatisfactory. History is like a maze; to get the most out of history you need to ramble around it, get lost in it – and then hope you can find your way back to the beginning. That, therefore, is EXACTLY how we have written this book: each chapter links to the next and the last to the first.

Let's begin with your hands, which are holding this book...

·1·

THE HAND

—

The history of the hand is all about…
time travel, medieval magic, cave painting,
royal power, intimacy and grief.

Knock, knock…
Knock, knock…
What are your hands doing? Ours are knocking on the door of your brain. They are waking you up. They are starting a conversation. They are starting *this* conversation – by typing. Yours, presumably, are holding a book or tablet. But how many different ways have you used your hands today? And how many more different ways will you use them before tomorrow? You have presumably got dressed, washed, prepared food, fed yourself, picked up or put down an enormous variety of objects, communicated to yourself by touching or communicated to others by writing, typing or gesturing. Maybe you have shaken hands, waved goodbye, raised your fist in anger or delivered a thumbs-up or 'OK' sign to broker friendship.

Such gestures from the past survive in the present day in a number of forms, but perhaps most powerfully in prehistoric art dating from as far back as 40,000 years ago.

CAVE PAINTING

Hand stencils are a common visual form of prehistoric art. They have been discovered across sites in France, Spain, Africa, Australia, Argentina and Borneo (which are thought to be by far the oldest examples c.40,000 years ago). They were created either by blowing or spraying paint made from charcoal or a pigment called red ochre over the hand, thus creating a type of hand shadow – the most common type of images that survive – or by covering the hand in paint to create a print.

In our evolutionary past the hand was significant because the opposable thumb, fine motor skills and the manual use of tools was a distinctly human characteristic that distinguished *Homo sapiens* from animals. Hands had significance in prehistory in other practical ways: digits for counting, or the hand's span as a rough and ready way of measuring; the height of horses was also measured in hands. It is no surprise, then, that hands were one

Prehistoric rock drawings and handprints in the caves of Cueva de las Manos, Río Pinturas, in the province of Santa Cruz, Patagonia, Argentina.

of the commonest forms of visual expression in our most ancient history. The compulsion to create art, moreover, is one of the few but crucial things that define us as human, along with the ability to think and plan for the future and also (and here is the historian writing) the ability to remember and learn from the past. These hand stencils, therefore, are not just part of the history of art but evidence for the evolution of the modern human mind; they are a chapter of the very earliest history of *Homo sapiens*.

The creation of these images is believed to hold some form of magical or ritual significance and we know that, in some locations, the prints would have been extremely uncomfortable for a person to make on their own, and that other prints would have been impossible to make without help. In these single hand prints, therefore, is some of the earliest evidence of human teamwork. In some locations there are so many hand prints in one place that the artwork would have taken both planning and considerable time. They also show a surprising variety of hand shapes, sizes and patterns. Intriguingly, many have been shown with apparently amputated digits. The belief that the images were accurately depicting hands with missing fingers has now been consigned to the past. Our modern understanding focuses on the way that the hand can be manipulated by bending fingers inwards or downwards – in much the same way as it is for shadow puppetry – to make the hand shadow appear unusual.

This in turn suggests that the fingers were somehow significant in ancient communication. Researchers have even tackled the question of who left these prints and it remains uncertain. Recent work has suggested that three-quarters of the surviving Neolithic hand prints from eight cave sites in France and Spain were likely to have been made by women. This research was itself based on the work of a British biologist who discovered that men and women can be identified by the relative lengths of their index and ring fingers.

A HISTORICAL CLUE

This raises the interesting question of the hand as a historical signpost. Not only can hands be 'read' in history for gender, but also in other, simpler ways for differences in age, race and class related to hand size and the colour and condition of the hand's skin. Workers' hands, for example, are often marked by the signs of manual labour, with calluses or fingers lopped off, an indication of the dangers of work, especially among factory operatives. These might be compared to the pampered hands of the pianist or the history professor, or the clerk's hands stained with ink. One Victorian clerk, Benjamin Orchard, wrote bitterly of his lot in 1871:

> We aren't real men. We don't do men's work. Pen-drivers – miserable little pen-drivers – fellows in black coats, with inky fingers and shiny seats on their trousers – that's what we are. Think of crossing *t's* and dotting *i's* all day long. No wonder bricklayers and omnibus drivers have contempt for us. We haven't even health.

Inky figures were, for the Victorian clerk, a marker of occupation, a stain on their hands that signified their Bob Cratchit-like, lowly place within society.

Hands could be physically distorted, mutilated through agricultural accident or otherwise broken and shapeless through torture. The breaking of hands was one of the techniques of the torturer's trade. In his Latin autobiography the Jesuit priest John Gerard describes his imprisonment in late Elizabethan England, and the torture that he underwent because of his involvement in the networks that surrounded the Gunpowder Plot. His hands were so badly mangled that, at first, he was not able to hold a pen:

I could scarcely feel I had anything between my fingers. My sense of touch did not revive for five months, and then not completely. Right up to the time of my escape, which was after six months, I always had a certain numbness in my fingers.

With broken hands, therefore, he was barely able to write, a clear intention of the torturers: writing was one of the key ways in which imprisoned Jesuits communicated, in secret letters and invisible ink, with the outside world.

Not only could your hands betray you to a historian but also to the law. The 'criminal hand' itself might even be missing – cut off in punishment – or burned as a public branding of criminality. It was a public sign from which it was very difficult to escape. In Tudor England a criminal could escape a death sentence by claiming 'benefit of clergy', in other words saying that they were a member of the Church (a defence that required someone simply to read from a Bible), and they would then be burned on the thumb so that they could not use this legal loophole a second time. When the sixteenth-century English wastrel and serial womanizer Anthony Bourne sent a Frenchman to murder his wife Elizabeth by stabbing her with a dagger, the would-be killer (for the act of violence failed) was identified as a criminal by dint of his being 'burned in the hand'.

Hands are also fascinating for the historian because they age over time – they are a historical document in their own right, as they become marked by signs of ageing, by liver spots, blemishes and wrinkles, and their skin loses its elasticity. One of the most beautiful observations of this is in a painting by the American artist Thomas Eakins (1844–1916) called *The Writing Master* (1882) [*see fig. 1*]. It is the most magnificent observation of a man who has dedicated his life to his hands by a man who has also dedicated his life to his hands, but in a different way. For this artist's father, Benjamin Eakins (1818–99), was a calligrapher and teacher of penmanship. Notice how the light falls so beautifully on the hands of this venerable, professional man at his work. If you were lucky enough to shake Benjamin's hand you would find it cool and soft, like silk.

Here Eakins holds a pen with which he is communicating, but hands have long been an important way of communicating in their own right, and many of the gestures with which we are now familiar – the handshake, the thumbs-up, the V-sign, the salute, the high five, the fist bump – are all embedded with symbolism. Others in history, such as the biting of one's thumb or the flicking of the chin, are less well known and have meanings in distinct contexts that we are still discovering.

GRIEF

Consider the pulling of one's beard. On the west front of Exeter Cathedral in Devon is one of the great architectural features of medieval England. Begun in 1340 and not finished for 130 years, this screen of well over 100 carvings marked the end of a great phase in the building's history when the Norman cathedral (founded in 1133) was rebuilt in the Gothic style. Statues inhabit niches on three rows and all are surrounded by detailed and exquisite carvings of plants, animals and angels. The entire screen covers almost a third of the cathedral's west front. Originally the image screen would have been entirely coloured;

Exeter Cathedral Founded in 1050 in Exeter in the south-west of England and rebuilt in the Gothic style between 1258 and 1400. Notable features include the carvings on the west front, the longest uninterrupted vaulted ceiling in England and an astronomical clock.

what we see now, though still impressive, is but a shadow of the building's former glory – one of the casualties of the Reformation.

All of the medieval statues were carved from local limestone, a perfect material for working but also one which suffers from erosion. A good number of the statues have lost many of their characteristics, but one stands out from all of the others for the quality of its execution as well as the rather odd gesture that it depicts. Here is a man, immediately to the side of the west door, hunched over and pulling at his beard. To our eyes it seems peculiar but in the medieval period we know that this particular gesture was associated with grief. One of the most vivid depictions comes from the eighth-century epic poem *The Song of Roland*, which describes the Emperor Charlemagne coming across the body of his nephew on a battlefield. His reaction was both violent and very public. Surrounded by soldiers 'weeping violently' the emperor 'pulls at his white beard and tears his hair with both hands'.

Charlemagne (742-814) Otherwise known as Charles the Great, during his reign Charlemagne united most of Europe. He was king of the Franks (from 768), the Lombards (from 774) and, from 800, the Holy Roman emperor.

The meaning of these statues in Exeter remains something of a mystery and the identity of each is still debated. There are definitely depictions of apostles, prophets and evangelists and also the kings of Judah. The old man stroking a beard is certainly a king, identified by his crown and royal bearing, and if you are looking for an English king whose entire reign and subsequent reputation was defined by grief, you need look no further than Henry I (1068–1135), whose only son died in a shipwreck in 1120, plunging England into a long and bloody civil war. Accounts say that, on hearing the news, he collapsed with grief. And he never smiled again. It is likely that the statue is of this most miserable of English kings.

This beard-pulling gesture is personal, emotional and instinctive, and it is part of a history of gesture that includes any kind of body movement, from standing, walking and sitting, to kissing, hat-tipping and bowing. The moving human body itself is an unexpectedly valuable historical text.

ROYAL POWER

Within this history, the hand has also played an important part in ceremonies, such as the joining of hands in marriage, or the lifting up of hands in oath taking. One particularly interesting example of this is the 'royal touch', a ceremonial laying-on of hands to cure disease, and in particular a nasty skin complaint known as scrofula. Linked to tuberculosis, scrofula was a disease that caused great lesions on the neck, which resulted from an infection of the lymph nodes. In more advanced cases the masses on the neck would swell and rupture, leaving what was essentially a festering open wound. With the decline of tuberculosis in the second half of the twentieth century, scrofula became less common. Throughout the Middle Ages in England and France it was believed that the royal touch – the laying-on of hands by the sovereign – could cure disease. This supposed ability to cure what became sometime known as the 'king's evil' was connected to the divine right of kings, and popular superstitious belief in the quasi-magical power of medieval monarchy. Anglo-French kings were able to harness popular beliefs to legitimize their rule, with charisma working alongside military and fiscal might to buttress their position.

The earliest mentions of the miraculous healing attributes of the royal touch occur as early as the eleventh century, with

Charles II performing the royal touch; engraving by Robert White (1684)

supplicants often offered 'the royal coin' by members of the monarch's inner circle, which may have guaranteed an audience at this display of supernatural powers. This practice continued into the sixteenth and seventeenth centuries and beyond, with Elizabeth I of England (1533–1603) reputedly laying hands on more than 1,000 of her subjects on a single occasion. The flamboyant French king, Louis XIV (1638–1715), while averse to the practice of touching the infected, saw more than 1,700 sufferers in one day, while the recently restored English monarch Charles II (1630–85) is thought to have touched upwards of 100,000 of his people in these healing rituals, even though they were frowned upon by the Church as a backward superstitious practice. The proximity that it allowed ordinary people to royal personages perhaps survives today in the crowd-pleasing public perambulations by the British royal family or in their regular garden parties.

INTIMACY

The historical significance of the hand is also all about the significance and meaning of the bare or naked hand – as opposed to a hand encased in a glove. The protocols of when it was acceptable to reveal one's hand were influenced by customs of politeness. As a general rule subordinates would go bare-handed in the presence of their social superiors, and women were more likely to be allowed to cover their hands than men. In seventeenth-century England it was customary to have bare hands in the presence of royalty, or when in church, or when at court. It was also deemed good manners to have bare hands when eating or when shaking hands, the bare hand being seen as intimate and friendly unless it was unbearably cold. In seventeenth-century Polish society a subordinate would kiss the hand of a superior. The polite thing to do was for the recipient of the kiss to proffer a bare hand; failure to do so expressed displeasure, as in the case of Ladislaus IV Vasa (1595–1648) who in 1644 held out a gloved hand to one of the burghers of Cracow to kiss, a gesture of the utmost royal disapproval. Bare hands, in short, were a mark of respect.

Historical hands were also 'gendered' – which is to say that men's and women's hands were viewed as being different. Women's fair hands were idealized as sensual representations of female beauty. In his sixteenth-century conduct manual, the Italian courtier and writer Baldassare Castiglione (1478–1529) addresses the subject of women's hands:

> It is the same with the hands; which, if they are delicate and beautiful, and occasionally left bare when there is need to use them, and not in order to display their beauty, they leave a very great desire to see more of them, and especially if covered with gloves again; for whomever covers them seems to have little

care or thought whether they be seen or not, and to have them
thus beautiful more by nature than by any effort or pains.

In popular wedding practices in premodern England it was
traditional for the bride to go bare-handed, which was symbolic
of purity and intimacy, while the bridegroom's hands could be
covered. The eroticism of the intertwining of men's and women's
hands – of the act of holding hands – is explored in *Romeo and
Juliet* (Act I, Scene v) when Romeo, taking Juliet's hand, considers

If I profane with my unworthiest hand
This holy shrine, the gentle sin is this:
My lips, two blushing pilgrims, ready stand
To smooth that rough touch with a tender kiss.

Here Juliet's 'sacred feminine' hand is contrasted with Romeo's
profane and rough male hand – which raises the very important
question of what happens when you cover up a hand, and the
unexpectedly fascinating history of gloves...

GLOVES

———

The history of gloves is all about...
the holy Roman empire, gift giving,
poisoning and manliness.

J ames has a historical glove fetish. It is only a recent thing, but over the last few years he has developed an obsession with gloves – the object that the Germans delightfully call *Hand-schuh* (hand shoe) and the Anglo-Saxons knew as *glof*. Part of this has to do with the intricate beauty of gloves from the past – the skilful leather and silk work, the stunning embroidery and designs – but more than anything it is the tangible and intimate connection that gloves have to the past that is so enchanting. These objects once gloved the hands of those who made history: to study them is the nearest thing to being able to actually touch the past.

THE HOLY ROMAN EMPIRE

Take, for example, this magnificent bejewelled imperial glove, one of a pair that dates from the period immediately prior to 1220 [*see fig. 2*]. Probably made in Palermo in Sicily, it was part of the ceremonial regalia of the holy Roman emperor, and is the most spectacular historical glove that either of us has seen. Think Michael Jackson… only more sparkles. The gloves are made of red silk, and decorated with a dazzling number of jewels, pearls, enamelled plaques (or badges) and gold metal thread. On the front – the palm side of the glove – an eagle with outstretched wings, the emblem of the holy Roman empire, is depicted in intricate goldwork and the detailed patterning continues on the back of the glove, with two birds featured on the cuff. It is possible that the gloves were illustrated by the gifted German artist Albrecht Dürer (1471–1528) in a portrait of Charlemagne (742–814), which now hangs in the Germanisches National-museum in Nuremberg [*see fig. 3*]. At this particular point in history, it seems clear that nothing said imperial power quite like a glove. These ornate bejewelled gloves were part of a coordinated and rather glamorous outfit worn by the emperor, the opulence of which symbolized magnificence, status and grandeur. They would have cost a small fortune to make, the intricate jewel work and embroidery a labour of love by master craftsmen.

SHAKESPEARE

This question of how gloves were made takes us into a glover's workshop, perhaps even that of William Shakespeare's father, John Shakespeare (1531–1601), a glover in Stratford-upon-Avon in Warwickshire. At the time, as well as actually making the gloves, being a glover included preparing hides and tanning leather, a labour-intensive and rather gruesome business, and one which would have formed a significant part of Shakespeare's early life. Unsurprisingly, therefore, references to glove making regularly crop up in Shakespeare's plays and bring to life this curious industry.

In Act IV, Scene iv of *The Winter's Tale*, the characters Mopsa and Autolycus both make reference to perfumed gloves at the sheep-shearing festival; in *Love's Labour's Lost* Biron swears 'By this white glove' (Act V, Scene ii, line 411), while gloves are referred to as gauges issuing a challenge to combat by both Henry V and King Lear. In *The Merry Wives of Windsor* (1602) Shakespeare connects the leather-working tools of the profession to a male character, Master Slender: 'Does he not wear a great round beard, like a / glover's paring-knife?'

The paring knife* was an extraordinary item, a sharp and heavy circular cutting tool with a wooden handle which was used in the strenuous process of preparing skins, whereby the blood, hair and fat would be scraped off prior to the tanning process. Only once the leather had been treated could it then be cut to fit the size and contours of the hand. This heavy-duty and filthy work was generally undertaken by men, with women later employed as embroiderers to add the decorative elements and designs to the leather gauntlet. The industry itself was regulated by the medieval guild of the Worshipful Company of Glovers, first founded in the fourteenth century and still thriving today, as an important part of the ceremony and rituals of gloves and glove making.

* A good example survives at the Shakespeare Birthplace Trust in Stratford.

RITUALS AND RELICS

The glove itself was imbued with ritual and symbolism. Gloves were used for liturgical purposes in Rome from the tenth century, and in other regions even earlier. Often knitted, with intricate embroidered religious designs, these beautiful sacred garments survive in museums throughout the world, testifying to a medieval glove-related practice that continues in the high ceremonies of the Catholic Church today when celebrating solemn pontifical mass, but which, post-Reformation, was

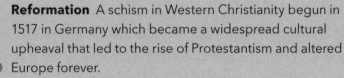

Reformation A schism in Western Christianity begun in 1517 in Germany which became a widespread cultural upheaval that led to the rise of Protestantism and altered Europe forever.

rendered obsolete in Protestant countries.

At the heart of liturgical glove-wearing rituals was the desire to separate the holy from the worldly, to preserve the blessed purity of the host and prevent contamination from 'human' hands. A tapestry originating in the southern Netherlands and dating from 1400–10 depicts several bishops in religious garb, which included gloves, and many examples of such religious gloves survive in museums today. These include an exquisite pair of ecclesiastical gloves held by the Victoria and Albert Museum in London dating from sixteenth-century Spain, knitted out of red and yellow silk wrapped with silver strip, and with the Christian monogram IHS* on the top of the glove.

* *Iesus Hominum Salvator* (Jesus Saviour of Man)

Similarly, gloves played an important part in the ceremonies of the British monarchy. Queens Elizabeth I (coronation 1558) and Elizabeth II (coronation 1952) both had ornate pairs of gloves produced by the Glovers Company to commemorate and play a central part in their coronations, which were worn when carrying the orb and sceptre of state, themselves hallowed objects. Within civic life, mayors and aldermen wore gloves of office, and were often painted in portraits wearing such gloves, which stood as visual testimony of their power. Gloves were also part of a whole series of rituals and ceremonies connected with rites of passage: they were presented to guests at weddings as tokens, while at funerals in the seventeenth and eighteenth centuries pairs of black gloves were passed out to mourners as marks of respect. Gloves clearly fitted into the ceremonial customs of all walks of life.

Gloves associated with famous historical figures, such as monarchs, could assume a sacred status as relics after their owners' deaths. Gloves survive that are purported to have been worn by Mary, Queen of Scots (1542–execution 1587) and Charles I (1600–execution 1649) on the scaffold. Mary's glove was an exquisitely embroidered leather gauntlet, whose pattern features a bird in flight and whose edges are trimmed with silver pendant beads, while King Charles's gloves, which survive at Lambeth Palace Library in London, and date from around sixty years later, were larger leather gauntlets, embroidered with metalwork and edged in silk trim. Charles's gloves are even said to have royal bloodstains from his execution. These gloves have now assumed a status as Royalist relics connected to executed monarchs, which is quite separate from their function as gloves worn by a woman and a man at particular points in time. They clearly demonstrate how gloves can come to mean different things throughout their life cycle: practical gloves worn for protection or fashion could then be given as a gift, passed on as an heirloom, or kept as a treasured relic memorializing their one-time wearer.

> **Lambeth Palace Library** Founded in 1610, it is the library of the Archbishops of Canterbury and one of the main archives for the history of the Church of England.

SEX

The varied meanings of the gloves in different contexts show that what one actually *did* with a glove was important. During the medieval and early modern period and beyond, for a man to strike another man with a glove was to issue an insult or challenge to combat, while for a woman to drop a glove in front of a man, or to be painted with a single dropping glove, was a sign of sexual availability. A wonderful example survives in a portrait of one of Elizabeth I's maids of honour, Anne Vavasour, attributed to John de Critz in around 1605, which depicts her in a highly fashionable embroidered gown, with one glove on and the other one dangling in the fingers of her left hand – a sign of her sexual availability. It is therefore perhaps unsurprising to learn of her chequered romantic life, which saw her enter into an adulterous affair with the queen's champion Sir Henry Lee, and a bigamous marriage in 1618.

The wearing of gloves by a woman at the royal court enabled her to touch another courtier or to dance with a man, and the removal of a glove was a gesture that could be erotically charged, as in the famous glove scene in Thomas Middleton's play *The Changeling* (1622) where Beatrice-Joanna drops a glove hoping that the handsome Alsemero might find it, but instead it is picked up by the detested retainer De Flores; finding this out she casts the other glove down, now wishing to disown both, the first having been touched. De Flores's reply is savagely sexualized, punning on his own hide being tanned, and violating her gloves by forcing his fingers into them:

I know she had rather wear my pelt tann'd
In a pair of dancing pumps than I should
Thrust my fingers into her sockets here.
I know she hates me, yet cannot choose but love her.

Thomas Middleton (bap. 1580–d.1627) Playwright and contemporary of Shakespeare and son of a bricklayer. His plays include *The Honest Whore* (1604), *The Roaring Girl* (1611 with Thomas Dekker), *A Chaste Maid in Cheapside* (1613) and *A Game at Chess* (1624).

GIFT GIVING

The discarding of gloves here represents a rejection of someone detested, and yet the opposite is also true, and there is a distinct history of giving gloves as gifts. Take Elizabethan Tudor England where gloves were intimately connected to the custom of gift giving at the royal court, and are listed in the fascinating New Year's gift rolls. These are wonderful historical sources; 12-foot-long vellum rolls that on one side recorded all the gifts presented to the monarch, and on the other, all the gifts that she gave in return. They thus record not only the elaborate ritualized gift exchange at the heart of Elizabeth's political regime, but also precisely who is in favour in any particular year throughout her reign, since it was an honour to be allowed access to the monarch's person at court. Among the many different kinds of gifts listed are several dozen assorted and bejewelled gloves given to the queen by men and by women. The 1579 gift roll, for example, records the following entry: 'By Mr. William Russell, a paire of gloves, garnished with gold and sede perle'.

Women of the bedchamber were also key figures as political intermediaries, and the delivering of gifts – including gloves – formed an important part of this complex political exchange, as recorded by Frances Lady Cobham in a letter to Lord Burghley which reports that 'her majesty hathe resevyd your gloues and lykethe well of them and wylled me to thanke yow for them', adding that the buttons and silk that garnished them 'plesethe her much'. Many of the pairs of gloves presented to the queen were in fact perfumed, including in January 1578 'By the Lady Mary Sydney, one peir of perfumed gloves, with twenty-four small buttons of golde, in every of them a small diamond'. Perfuming gloves with exotic scents lent the gloves a refined and exclusive edge, but also usefully masked the strong smell of leather.

The fact that Elizabeth received perfumed gloves is particularly interesting as it raises the olfactory problem that historians face of recreating a 'smellscape' of the past. It's certainly nice to know that Elizabeth received perfumed gloves, but it would be *wonderful* to know what that perfume smelled like. Recipes for perfuming gloves appear in manuscript and print throughout the sixteenth and seventeenth centuries, including writer Gervase Markham's heady glove perfume recipe in his *English Housewife* (1615) which was coupled with a notably sexualized recommendation that women should let their scented gloves 'dry in your bosom, and so after use them at your pleasure'.

> *To perfume Gloues*
>
> To perfume gloues excellently, take the oyle of sweet Almonds, oyle of Nutmegges, oile of Benjamin of each a dramme, of Ambergreece [ambergris] one graine, fat Muske two graines: mix them all together and grinde them vpon a Painters stone, and then annoint the gloues therwith: yet before you annoint them let them be dampishly moistened with Damaske Rose water.

POISON

The giving of gifts to the monarch was something done personally, an intimate act that required access to the royal person, which was therefore fraught with security problems because perfume was intimately connected with poison; the glove in Elizabethan England – when access to the queen was strictly

Christopher Marlowe (bap.1564–d.1593) English playwright, poet and government agent. The son of a shoemaker. Stabbed to death in a house in Deptford.

controlled – was a much more effective assassin's weapon than the knife. Gifts of poisoned gloves were not unknown, so much so that they were dramatized in Christopher Marlowe's play *Massacre at Paris* (1593), in which the character of the Old Queene fatally accepts poisoned gloves, remarking

Me thinks the gloves have a very strong perfume,
The scent whereof doth make my head to ache...
... the fatal poison
Doth within my heart: my brain-pan breaks,
My heart doth faint, I die.

Rather than being absorbed through the skin by wearing the glove, the poison was administered through the fumes of its smell. Elizabeth's reign is notable for the almost constant threat of assassination which hung over her. Early in her reign in 1563, draft precautions in the hand of William Cecil, Secretary of State, regarding the 'apparel and dyett' of the newly installed queen warned her not to accept 'Apparel or Sleves' or 'Gloves' from any stranger, lest they 'be corrected by some other fume' – in other words, in case the gloves' perfume was poisoned.

William Cecil (1520/21-1598) One of the most important Tudor statesmen. A page of the chamber to Henry VIII, he became Elizabeth's chief adviser.

MANLINESS

This idea of a history of gloves presenting a danger to their wearer raises the important question of its opposite – the history of gloves providing protection to their wearer and what that can tell us about the culture in which they were made and worn. Gloves were worn for protection in a whole host of activities, each with its own extraordinary history, from the wearing of rubber gloves for cleaning with domestic chemicals to wearing kid gloves – that is to say gloves made out of kid skin for its own peculiar qualities – for protection from flash fires in modern warships. Baseball gloves in particular are a fascinating window into the past because they are now such an icon of the sport, and of America itself, and yet baseball players did not, initially, wear gloves. The game, which has murky origins at the end of the eighteenth century but first became popular in America during the American Civil War (1861–5), was initially played at slow speed and all throwing was underarm. Gradually however, speed, athleticism and the frequency of play increased until, in the 1870s, calluses and broken bones were the mark of a baseball player. They were also, in this post-Civil War era of Industrial Revolution, the mark of a man, a symbol of masculinity. Against this background the glove was adopted for fielding in baseball.

The exact origin of glove wearing in baseball is unclear but it is certain that one of the earliest pioneers was Charles C. Waite, a first baseman for New Haven in Connecticut who wore a glove in a match against Boston in 1875. His glove was a fingerless mitt without any of the modern webbing that characterizes the modern glove but, crucially, it was a light-brown 'tan' colour – the same colour as his skin. Waite chose this colour for the specific reason that it would be difficult for the spectators to see: there is a history of shame in glove wearing, for he chose the colour to preserve his masculinity. He was later queried about his glove by another player, the famous pitcher A. G. Spalding. Waite admitted to Spalding that he was 'a bit ashamed' to wear it which was the reason he had chosen the colour. His attempt to hide his glove failed and he was teased and taunted by spectators and fellow teammates. However, the idea began to gain some traction and, a year or so later, Spalding set up a sports equipment company and began to manufacture and sell baseball gloves. Spalding's reputation helped the glove overcome the stigma and the gloves he sold were almost black; they had transformed from something that was hidden to a proud symbol of the sport, which the baseball mitt came to define, and which challenged American perceptions of masculinity.

PROTECTING THE PAST

But what of the flip side to this history? What of people wearing gloves to protect *the objects they are holding* rather than their hands? This is a question intimately linked with history itself and the practice of being a historian, specifically when handling historical objects, and particularly historical manuscripts.

We have all watched historical documentaries where the presenter leafs through an old book or touches a rare manuscript having donned a pair of white gloves, an image intended to inspire in the viewer a sense of awe in these sacred literary remnants of the past. But gloves are a trick used by the documentary director to instil that sense of wonder when, in the world of archives, it is well known that wearing gloves can in fact be harmful to manuscripts. Experts agree that, instead of wearing gloves, the reader or 'toucher' should wash and dry hands before use, thus removing any oils that could potentially damage the manuscript. Clean and dry hands are infinitely preferable in the majority of circumstances. Wearing gloves when handling books, manuscripts or fragile paper can endanger the item being viewed as it reduces manual dexterity and the sense of touch, increasing a tendency to grab. The gloves' cotton fibres, moreover, may lift or dislodge pigments, inks or other material on the surface and the cotton can snag surprisingly easily on page edges. Gloves do have their place in archives, but only in very specific circumstances – such as the handling of lead seals or old photographs.

The practice of historians wearing white gloves is, in fact, a relatively recent phenomenon dating from the nineteenth century, probably begun by photographers keen to protect negatives from greasy fingerprints. From there cotton-glove use spread to rare book and archives reading rooms. Archivists are now rising up together in their war on gloves. In 1999 the unthinking and widespread use of gloves unleashed a torrent of reaction from specialists. The curator of rare books at Smith College, Massachusetts, wrote: 'I require my readers NEVER to wear gloves of any kind, except when handling photographs. Where is the logic in making the nice people wear an ill-fitting thing which makes them more clumsy and reduces their sense of touch?' It's an important point for any historian intending to 'read' an object, for you must do so with your hands as much as with your eyes, whether it be a glove or a written document, because touch is a profoundly valuable historical tool. The main thing to remember if you are handling documents is that you should wash your hands thoroughly first to ensure that they are rid of all chemicals – which raises the important question of the history of perfume…

·3·

PERFUME

——

The history of perfume is all about…
memory, squid beaks, the Reformation,
cats, napalm and the plague.

———— MEMORY ————

There is an unexpectedly intense relationship between smells and memory. The French novelist Marcel Proust (1871–1922) identified smell as a key mechanism for evoking a remembrance of the past, famously writing in his novel *In Search of Lost Time* (1913)

> But when from a long-distant past nothing subsists, after the people are dead, after the things are broken and scattered, taste and smell alone, more fragile but more enduring, more unsubstantial, more persistent, more faithful, remain poised a long time, like souls, remembering, waiting, hoping, amid the ruins of all the rest; and bear unflinchingly, in the tiny and almost impalpable drop of their essence, the vast structure of recollection.

Think of the different periods in your own lives. What distinct smells allow you to recall early memories? A childhood evoked by a mother's perfume; freshly mown grass; lime groves in Greece; lavender in Provence; or perhaps the smell of the toilet cleaner that scented the lid and bowl as you threw up drunk for the first time as a teenager. Such smell-memories are deeply personal, and trigger associations and meanings from former times.

The reason for this, the scientists of smell tell us, is because tiny olfactory receptor cells in the nose relay information to the brain associated with 'good' and 'bad' smells where they are then stored for later recall. We know this thanks to Richard Axel and Linda B. Buck, the 2004 Nobel Prize winners in physiology or medicine, and their impressively titled research on 'Odorant Receptors and the Organization of the Olfactory System'. The prize committee's official summary explained that

> A unique odour can trigger distinct memories from our childhood or from emotional moments – positive or negative – later in life. A single clam that is not fresh and will cause malaise can leave a memory that stays with us for years, and prevent us from ingesting any dish, however delicious, with clams in it. To lose the sense of smell is a serious handicap – we no longer perceive the different qualities of food and we cannot detect warning signals, for example smoke from a fire.

This then is how we understand smell today, but that under-standing itself has a history – it is the history of how smell has been understood across time, in specific locations and periods. And here the history of smell is related to the history of the senses as connected to the body: touch (the hand), taste (the tongue), hearing (the ears), sight (the eyes), and of course the sense of smell itself (the nose).

HISTORIC SMELLS

The history of perfume, or in other words of smell (the olfactory history of the past), is a challenging one to write, since odours from centuries ago seldom linger. Only in very rare instances do smells actually survive from history, and their rarity gives them a powerful historical pull.

Two significant examples have survived from shipwrecks where the ship has, for one reason or another, been sealed as a time capsule. Henry VIII's warship the *Mary Rose* sank in battle off Portsmouth harbour in the summer of 1545. She sank with such force that her hull was driven deep into the mud of the Solent, which wrapped her in an anaerobic blanket for 437 years. She was raised in 1982 revealing an entire Tudor world. One of the areas of the ship that was preserved forever in the blink of an eye was the surgeon's cabin. In his medicine chest was a collection of jars containing a variety of ointments and other ingredients for medicines, and when the archaeologists first pulled the corks from one of the bottles they were met with the whiff of Tudor menthol.

> **The *Mary Rose*** An English warship launched in 1511 during Henry VIII's reign that became one of the world's most important historic ships. She served for thirty-four years in wars against France and Scotland before sinking off Portsmouth during a battle against the French in 1545. The wreck was raised in 1982.

Another example comes from a shipwreck off Bermuda discovered in 2011. This ship, the *Mary Celestiar*, foundered in 1864, and sealed in her bow were a number of unopened perfume bottles made by the famous London perfumiers Piesse & Lubin (est. 1855). A great deal of historical material survives about these intrepid and ingenious partners who transformed the history of perfume. W. G. Septimus Piesse in particular was a genius who invented the concept of 'notes', a scent scale used to rank the odours of perfume. Rather brilliantly, Piesse described this as an 'odaphone'. Piesse & Lubin created some of the most famous scents of the Victorian period, which reads like a 'greatest hits' of historical perfume and also provides a window into the fascinating question of Victorian marketing strategies.

Ambergris (1873)
Hungary Water (1873)
Kiss Me Quick (1873)
Bouquet Opoponax (1875)
The Flower of the Day (1875)
White Rose (1875)
Frangipanni (1880)
Kisses (1880)
Myrtle (1880)
Frolic (1894)

For all that we know about these men we did *not* know what any of their perfume actually smelt like until the discovery of that Bermudan shipwreck. In 2014, however, science and history collided. One of the perfume bottles was opened, its contents analysed and the perfume was reproduced by the Bermuda Perfumery.

This is not the only example of heritage scientists collecting, cataloguing and understanding historic odours using pioneering methods. The technique used in Bermuda is fabulously entitled 'gas chromatography with mass spectrometric detection', and it has also allowed scientists to collect smells from old books, objects and buildings using carbon sponges that absorb the organic compounds they emit. These are then run through the instruments to produce what is effectively a blueprint of – or recipe for – the chemical components of that particular smell. 'Old book smell', for example, is acetic acid, furfural, benzaldehyde, vanillin and hexanol. This is nothing less than the scent of history itself: the fact that smell has a history may be surprising, but who knew that history *itself* has a smell?

By breaking down smells in this way it is possible to record and then reassemble smells at a later date, which has huge implications for museums and heritage sites, as well as historians interested in odiferous aspects of the past. Think of the potential for recreating the waft of fresh buns from the bakery at the Tower of London in 1078 when it was built. Less appetizing is the potential for recreating other types of stench, though there would be value in it.

What of the smell of gangrene from a wounded soldier during the First World War, or the sewers of Viking Jorvik, or the hideous pits of the tallow chandlers on the banks of the Thames where they boiled up animal bones and fat to make candles?

The Worshipful Company of Tallow Chandlers
A livery company of the City of London founded around 1300 to protect and regulate the trade in tallow, a valuable product made from animal fats and used in the production of tallow candles, oils, ointments, lubricants and preservatives.

Hideous maybe, but it is important. Contemporary records often mention stench, and of the very worst kind. The smell of the burning of human flesh in particular is one that sears itself in the brain. The horrors of Auschwitz or of napalm as remembered in sensory ways are partly connected to the horrors of smell.

A survivor from Auschwitz, Esther Grossman, described the hell-like experience of life in the concentration camp:

> I could never eat a piece of meat because of the smell of burning flesh and hair. We saw the flames, heard the screaming, and smelled the burning flesh and burning hair. All night long we heard screaming. The flames were shooting high, and the whole sky was red.

One can only imagine the horror caused by such a smell, which was so specific to a particular time and place, and is unbearably and indelibly scarred on the human memory of survivors.

PERFUME INGREDIENTS

The recreation of aromas is, in some instances, made possible by surviving perfume recipes. These can be found in a variety of places: herbal manuals, gardening books, religious tracts and accounts of the plague. From these literary sources we are thus able to reconstruct something that is sensory.

A seventeenth-century English recipe book contains the following sweet-smelling recipe for 'A Perfume to Burn', indicating the methods by which perfumes during this period were commonly home-made:

> Take 2 ounces of the powder of juniper, benjamine, and storax each 1 ounce, 6 drops of oyle of cloves, 10 grains of musk, beat all these together to a past with a little gum dragon, steeped in rose or orange flower water, and roul them up like big pease and flat them and dry them in a dish in the oven or sun and keep them for use they must be put on a shovel of coals and they will give a pleasing smell.

Unusual ingredients used for perfume were so well known that they could also be mentioned for comic effect in plays, as in Shakespeare's *As You Like It* (Act III, Scene ii) where a conversation between two characters touches upon the misunderstanding of the shepherd Corin that 'courtiers' hands are perfumed with civet', something that is used to mock his rustic simplicity, but also poke fun at the court. The scene is all the more fun when the shepherd has it explained that civet is, in fact, 'the very uncleanly flux of a cat' – the discharge from a cat's anal glands. Civet, however, really *is* a perfume ingredient – it is a fixative, and that changes the way we should think about this example. Like all good comedy it has its roots in truth and here that truth was twofold: on the one hand there was truth in the fact that the courtiers perfumed their hands; on the other there was truth in the fact that perfume was often made from quite extraordinary, and occasionally deeply unpleasant, ingredients.

Perhaps the most famous such ingredient was, and still is in some modern perfume, ambergris. Scientists still don't know exactly what ambergris is but what they do know is unpleasant enough. Simply put, ambergris is something that forms in the intestines of sperm whales. Sperm whales primarily eat squid, and the discovery in lumps of ambergris of the only hard bits of squid – their beaks, eye lenses and a quill-like organ known as a pen – has led scientists to believe that ambergris is part of a process designed to break down or eject that which cannot be digested. A sperm whale regularly vomits out these tough bits of squid, but occasionally it does not and the beaks and eye lenses pass into its intestines where it begins to form into ambergris. The process, therefore, is the result of an imperfection or failure in a whale's digestive system. In time the mass of squid beaks solidifies, grows larger and eventually acts as a dam, forcing the gut to absorb faeces, which builds up behind it. Exactly *how* the ambergris is then ejected is also uncertain – but it is either excreted or, in the case of particularly large lumps, it blocks the intestine of the whale, causes its death by internal rupture and then only emerges to float in the sea once the whale's corpse has rotted and been torn apart by a million ravenous sea creatures. In every case ambergris is exceptionally rare because it has been estimated that it is only created in one per cent of sperm whales.

Once in the sea the ambergris then goes through another transformation process as it is baked by the sun and drifts semi-submerged in salt water, sometimes for decades. Only then does it become a perfumier's treasure and in that sense it is a deeply historical object – it is one of a handful of things in this world which is only formed by time and which only improves with time. But that history is always lost to us – we have no way of knowing when or where or by which whale it was produced. In that respect it is both historical and utterly ahistorical: ambergris, in short, is a perfect historical conundrum. It is also only ever discovered by chance as it washes up ashore and is stumbled upon by a beachcomber or is hauled aboard a fishing boat in a lobster pot or is even found in the belly of a fish: in 1909 the *Washington Post* described a fisherman discovering a lump of ambergris *inside* a swordfish he had caught off Boston. That piece was then estimated to be worth $20,000 – an uncommon fortune.

Ambergris is valuable not only because it is so rare, but also because it has unique qualities for a perfumier. The first is its unique scent, which humans have tried, and utterly failed, to describe ever since it was discovered. In an 1844 article in the *American Journal of Pharmacy*, it was said to have a 'smell somewhat resembling old cowdung', and the desperate author of an article in the *New York Times* in 1895, literally clutching at straws, described its odour as being 'like the blending of new-mown hay, the damp woodsy fragrance of a fern-copse, and the faintest possible perfume of the violet'. In this difficulty of pinning it down, however, lies some of its magic – for the scent of every lump of ambergris is subtly unique, the result of the process by which each was uniquely formed. Further complicating matters, and providing another reason for its almost magical status, the same sample of ambergris can smell different to different people. The second unique value to the perfumier is that it acts as a 'fixative' – in essence it glues a perfume together and it reduces the rate of the aroma's evaporation. In an age of perfume being made entirely by natural ingredients which were difficult to bind together and could quickly dissipate, such a fixative was essential to the perfumiers' art if they were not to create beauty only for it to vanish.

VERSAILLES

The Palace of Versailles A royal chateau near Paris. Built in 1624 by Louis XIII as a hunting lodge, it was enlarged into a fabulous palace by Louis XIV. From 1682 until 1789 it was the centre of French political power and the location of the royal court.

Once mastered, however, the perfumiers' art was one of exceptional skill that was used to signify wealth, social status and individuality, best explored in the heady realm of Versailles palace in the 1690s, a world stage and home to the 'Sun King' Louis XIV and his court. The gardens, corridors and rooms of this palace were, if contemporary accounts are to be believed, heady with wafting scent. Even the *fountains* at Versailles were scented with fragrance, and the gardens were so strongly perfumed with roses that, according to the diarist the Duc de Saint-Simon (1675–1755), 'nobody could remain in the garden'. So heavily scented was Versailles that it became known as 'the perfumed court'.

We also know that different female courtiers had their own distinct perfumes. The Duchesse d'Aumont (1759–1826) favoured coriander, iris, cloves, sweet flag and nut grass; Madame du Barry's (1743–93) preferred scent consisted of neroli oil,* bergamot,† lavender, grape spirit and rosemary; while Marie Antoinette's perfume known as *Sillage de la Reine* ('in the wake of the queen') was concocted from tuberose,‡ orange blossom, jasmine, sandalwood, iris and cedar. In other words, each of the court women had her own olfactory signature. These were not shop-bought scents, but bespoke and delicate concoctions catering for the olfactory pleasures of the courtiers who commissioned them. The king himself demanded that his apartments be sprayed with different perfumes every day, yet by the end of his life even the slightest scent was said to bring on a migraine, which led to the banning of perfume in his presence.

An important reason for the amount of perfume applied at the French court was to disguise the stink of overdressed courtiers in all their finery. Thus the history of perfume is a history of human aroma which is also intimately connected with the history of cleanliness, bathing and soap, subjects which themselves have interesting and unexpected histories to tell. For many years Europeans considered bathing to be harmful to one's health. With cholera epidemics in the mid-nineteenth century, however, there were attempts to increase access to clean water, systematize rubbish disposal and install effective sewerage systems. Increased bathing decreased the need for strong perfumes to mask pungent odours.

* Produced from the blossom of the bitter orange tree.

† A fragrant citrus fruit.

‡ A plant related to the agave, common in the south of France.

HYGIENE ANXIETY

America in the late nineteenth century experienced what might be described as a hygiene revolution, with urbanites once suspicious of bathing, like their European counterparts,

Try
LISTERINE TOOTH PASTE
it cleans with amazing speed
Price **1/3** per tube.

Often a bridesmaid, but never a bride.

Edna's case was really a pathetic one. Like every woman, her primary ambition was to marry. Most of the girls of her set were married—or about to be. Yet not one possessed more grace or charm or loveliness than she.

And as her birthdays crept gradually toward that tragic thirty mark, marriage seemed farther from her life than ever. She was often a bridesmaid but never a bride.

❉ ❉ ❉

That's the insidious thing about halitosis (unpleasant breath). You, yourself, rarely know when you have it. And even your closest friends won't tell you. Sometimes, of course, halitosis comes from some deep-seated organic disorder that requires professional advice. But usually —and fortunately—halitosis is only a local condition that yields to the regular use of undiluted Listerine Antiseptic as a mouth-wash and gargle.

Being antiseptic, it checks food fermentation in the mouth—a cause of odours. Being also a germicide capable of destroying 200,000,000 germs in 15 seconds, it attacks mouth, nose and throat infections — another cause of odours. Then, it gets rid of the odours themselves, *not* by sub-stituting some other odour, but by really removing the old one. The odour of Listerine Anti-septic itself quickly disappears, so that its systematic use puts you on the safe and polite side.

Obtainable at all Chemists in three sizes . 3-ounce Bottle **1/6**, 7-ounce **3/-**, 14-ounce **5/6.** It has dozens of different uses as a safe antiseptic. Read the pamphlet that comes with every bottle.

End halitosis with

LISTERINE

BRAND ANTISEPTIC

" Kills 200,000,000 germs in 15 seconds."

Advertisement in *The Sketch*, 21 May 1930

now embracing showers, toothbrushes and bathrooms. It is a revealing history because advertising companies assisted by marketing departments played on female insecurities about beauty and attractiveness. It is a history, therefore, which speaks to us of both ruthless bullying by advertising companies and the perception of female anxiety in history. And it is quite shocking.

The first deodorant was invented in Philadelphia in 1888, and marketed as 'Mum' in the sense of 'Mum's the word' or keeping silent in the sense of being embarrassed about smelling bad. This brand of antiperspirant is still found on the shelves today, but at that time it was a rather greasy, waxy cream that was applied under the armpits. From as early as 1912, adverts for the antiperspirant *Odo-Ro-No* tried to convince American women that they smelled bad and that nobody told them about their body odour (which they named BO). A 1930 advertisement from *Sketch Magazine* for Listerine mouthwash, with the tagline 'Often a bridesmaid, but never a bride', suggested that halitosis can lead to women being left on the shelf, marriage-wise, 'as her birthdays creep towards the tragic thirty mark'.

Once this female consumer base had been secured, companies trained their sights on the male consumer, who soon discovered that he was equally challenged by unpleasant bodily odours which might harm his career or chance of financial success – the supposed equivalent anxieties of American men in the first half of the twentieth century. The history of perfume in this respect, therefore, is the invention of the concept of smelling bad. While the wearing of perfume at court was indeed to mask odoriferous odours, what was now new was that the natural musk of the human body was suddenly offensive and repellent, and marketing executives were actively making people feel bad about it, exhorting them to wear deodorant and to wash more often with soap – which brings us to the important question of the history of the bubble...

·4·

THE BUBBLE

—

The history of the bubble is all about...
childhood innocence, despair, the French Revolution,
feats of stamina and ornamental hermits.

TRANSIENCE

There are bubbles everywhere in history, if you just know where to look. They first appear in visual sources in the mid-sixteenth century in woodcut engravings depicting children making and catching bubbles, but they also lie elsewhere, unseen. What is today's leading bubble industry? It is the same as it has been for centuries: bread making. In the baking of bread, yeast blows the microscopic bubbles for us, which allow the dough to rise. How do the blue jay and kingfisher get their colour? The answer is from bubbles in the horns of their feathers which scatter blue light, giving their bodies an almost iridescent sheen. With the exception of a handful of unique examples, including kingfisher feathers plucked and shaped in the eighteenth century into a headdress for a Chinese bride, or Roman bread preserved in Pompeii by the eruption of Vesuvius, no actual bubbles survive from the past, and therein lies their allure. They are objects of extraordinary beauty – radiant in their rainbow-coloured spherical translucence and perfect lightness as they rise on the air – but they are also transient, gone in an instant with a soapy pop, and it is that transience that has made them repeatedly attractive as symbols to poets, authors and artists. Mark Twain in his 1867 travel book *The Innocents Abroad* wrote: 'A soap bubble is the most beautiful thing, and the most exquisite in nature… I wonder how much it would take to buy a soap bubble if there was only one in the world.'

Vesuvius A volcano near the Italian city of Naples famous for the eruption in 79 CE that buried the Roman cities of Pompeii and Herculaneum under tons of ash. The eruption was described in great detail by Roman author and politician Pliny the Younger. The cities, immaculately preserved, were not rediscovered until 1599.

BUBBLES IN ART

What greater challenge, then, is there for the artist than capturing for all eternity something that lasts just a few seconds? One of the most entrancing of bubble images is *Soap Bubbles*, painted in 1734 by the French artist Jean-Siméon Chardin [*see fig. 4*]. He had been fascinated by the challenge of capturing contemporary Parisian childhood play on canvas and drew inspiration from seventeenth-century Dutch artists who had already embraced the challenge of representing the bubble. The image he produced shows a beautifully ringleted boy, neither rich nor poor, bending over a windowsill, using a most delicate straw to blow a most perfect and fat bubble. The light catches the bubble. A younger boy, perhaps a younger brother and just tall enough to peer over the sill, watches from the shadows.

He and the viewer hold their breath, anticipating the moment the air-filled bubble takes momentary flight, only to burst and disappear forever.

Here, apparently, is a moment of innocence and joy in the world, but it has, of course, been influenced and affected by the times in which it was painted and the personal experience of the artist; and therein lies the mystery, for this is not just an image of weightless joy, but of heavy sadness. Chardin painted this as he grieved for the sudden death of his wife and child. The joy he had experienced in sharing his life with them had burst as suddenly as a bubble, as suddenly as *this*, pregnant, bubble. His painting, then, is not a mirror of his idle joy as he merrily drifts around the streets of Paris reminiscing about carefree times, but is a representation of a man in shock, yearning for something fleeting that has been taken away by the capriciousness of the world.

Chardin's painting is also all about the French Revolution. Here is the world of France a generation before the Revolution, so frequently and hauntingly captured by artists in this period as a picture of senseless, superficial frivolity. Here, then, the eyes of the historian can gaze on this image and wonder if this child, and if his children, went on to survive the carnage that was coming. This bubble, therefore, is not just about a boy's joyous moment or an artist's heavy heart, but is about a nation's self-destruction, a great chasm torn in the history of the world.

The painting itself became famous, and we know that Édouard Manet knew of its existence when he painted *Les Bulles de Savon* in 1867. Images of bubbles can be traced right back to the Italian artist Dosso Dossi's painting *Allegory of Fortune* (c.1530), which depicts the classical figure of fortune sitting on a bubble [*see fig.* 5]; Adriaen Hanneman's painting *Two Boys Blowing Bubbles* (c.1630); and Caspar Netcher's painting of a boy blowing soap bubbles dating from 1679. The use of a bubble as a metaphor for human life can itself be traced back to the Roman author Marcus Terentius Varro (116–27 BCE) who began his treatise on agriculture *De Re Rustico* with 'man is a bubble'. Chardin's painting, therefore, also has its own significance in both the broader history of bubbles and the more specific history of bubbles in art.

ADVERTISING

During the nineteenth and twentieth centuries businesses also appropriated images of children blowing bubbles, but this time to sell soap. One of the best images from the history of advertising was the London company A. & F. Pears' famous 1886 advertising campaign that used a painting by the Pre-Raphaelite English artist and illustrator John Everett Millais (1829–96) which depicted a child playing with bubbles. In it the cherubic bubble-blower looks as his bubble rises towards the words 'Pears Soap' [*see fig. 6*]. Here the bubble not only connects to childhood innocence, but also to emerging concepts of freshness and cleanliness, and associations with bathing, personal hygiene and the laundry business of the late nineteenth century.

In the mid-nineteenth century in England an ideology of cleanliness developed that reached the middle classes, and helped peddle soap as a commodity that was connected to respectability. While small-scale soap manufacture dates from the 1780s, it was midway through the next century that it reached mass production. The Pears Soap advert 'Order of the Bath' (a pun on a British order of chivalry of the same name) was aimed at a mass market to encourage regular hygienic bathing. This coincided with the development of piped water infrastructures in European cities, and by the end of the nineteenth century affluent homes in the US and Europe would enjoy hot running water and private baths.

At the heart of these explorations of the bubble is a wonderful history of childhood play and the very act of blowing bubbles, something that is still endlessly entertaining for children and adults and is also beneficial: bubble-blowing is now regularly used as a technique in a variety of therapies. Examples of elaborate clay pipes and plastic bubble-blowers survive today in the collections of London's Victoria and Albert Museum of Childhood.

Yet this was a playtime activity that could easily be improvised with nothing more than a piece of twisted wire and some soap, and was therefore an eminently *democratic* pastime – it was a hobby for everyone, and that accessibility became a defining characteristic of bubble-blowing. In 1918, John L. Gilchrist of Wilkinsburg, Pennsylvania filed one of the earliest patented designs for a 'bubble-pipe' that could 'be cheaply manufactured and in which the parts are so associated that they may be disassembled and cleaned and quickly reassembled by an unskilled person'. Such innovation meant that the innocent charm of playing with bubbles became one of the defining experiences

Woodcut of children blowing bubbles in the sixteenth century

of childhood. That experience itself has a history, as descriptions survive from numerous different times and locations. A wonderful example appears in D. C. Beard's *The American Boy's Handy Book: What To Do and How To Do It* (1882). It contains an entire chapter entitled 'Novelties in Soap-Bubbles', in which he waxes lyrical about bubbles and notes the surprisingly addictive nature of blowing them.

> It is like a beautiful dream; we are entranced while it lasts, but in an instant it vanishes and leaves nothing to mark its former existence except the memory of its loveliness. Few persons can stand by and watch another blowing bubbles without being seized with an uncontrollable desire to blow one for themselves. There is a peculiar charm or pleasure in the very act, which not many who have known it ever outgrow.

Beard goes on to describe a recent trend in 'soap-bubble parties' in which guests, armed with clay pipes, stand around a punchbowl filled with soapsuds and blow bubbles. Prizes were awarded for the largest bubble or for that which flew in the air for the longest period of time, or went the highest. These parties seem to have become quite rowdy. He writes:

> As may be imagined, these parties are very amusing, and everybody at first tries to prevent his or her neighbour from succeeding, until, amid great merriment and confusion, the hostess announces that if her guests expect the prizes to be awarded, a rule must be enacted compelling them to pay more attention to their own efforts and not allowing them to molest each other.

This magic and wonder of bubbles conjures a world of childhood games and play that immediately feels timeless, but it also extends to a grown-up world of play, for it is not just children who have been fascinated by bubbles, but scientists and mathematicians.

ISAAC NEWTON

As elusive objects of beguiling geometrical perfection, extraordinary gifts from nature – and in this the bubble is akin to other wonders of nature, the snowflake, a spider's web or the etchings of frost on a leaf – bubbles have also been obsessed over by scientists for what they can tell us about the natural world, as well as for the scientific challenges they pose. How, for example, would you go about measuring the thickness of a bubble's skin? It is the type of question that allows genius to sing to us from the past. Any idea how to go about it? No. Well Isaac Newton did.

In 1704 he used soap bubbles to study the interference of light and as part of that process he worked out – correctly – that the thickness of soap bubbles actually varies: at their thinnest point they are 1/2,500,000 of an inch thick (or 0.000001016 of a centimetre), or 4,000 times thinner than a piece of paper. It was Newton, in his work *Opticks*, who first described the phenomena that take place on the surface of a bubble, and he used bubbles to develop his famous theory of light, more widely known for his use of prisms to diffract light. The bubble continues to be a subject of intense scientific enquiry, with the Nobel Prize-winning physicist Pierre-Gilles de Gennes discussing soap bubbles and surfactants (compounds that reduce surface tension) in his 1991 Nobel lecture: 'Surfactants,' he wrote, 'allow us to protect a water surface, and to generate these beautiful soap bubbles, which are the delight of our children.'

DETACHMENT

The bubble thus appears throughout history as a fascinating physical object but it also has a significant history as a metaphor: the idea of living in a bubble, being detached from reality, apart from everyday life – something that has had drastic implications for certain politicians and monarchs, cocooned by sycophantic yes-men and oblivious to the moods and sufferings of the people. Even today the 'Westminster bubble' refers to the self-preoccupation of London-based politicians who throng the corridors of power, but are out of touch with the state of the rest of the nation. All significant political power bases – Washington, Berlin, Paris, Tokyo, Beijing, Brussels – have their own bubbles, populated by navel-gazing political elites.

Perhaps the most famous historical example of this comes from Paris in the years before the French Revolution when political opponents of Louis XVI's monarchy focused on what they saw as the uncaring, extravagant and frivolous behaviour of the Austrian-born queen consort Marie Antoinette in the bubble-like palace of Versailles. Her apocryphal reply, when told that the people had no bread, was 'Let them eat cake' (a rough translation from the French 'Qu'ils mangent de la brioche') but it is pure fantasy – a phrase attributed to the French philosopher Jean-Jacques Rousseau in his 1782 autobiography *Confessions*. There is no evidence connecting this phrase to the wife of Louis XVI, but what *is* interesting is that it has persisted across the centuries. It resides in the popular historical consciousness and has been used to vilify the French queen. In many ways, the truth of the matter is of no consequence, since what counted for Republican enemies of the monarchy is that Marie Antoinette could be portrayed as detached from ordinary people – as living in a bubble.

For rulers and political leaders to be detached from the realities of the people they govern and represent is one thing, but at

Marie Antoinette (1755-93) Wife of Louis XVI, she was the last queen of France before the French Revolution of 1789. Widely criticized for her lavish expenditure and opposition to social reform, she was guillotined on 16 October 1793.

different times throughout history, various people or groups have sought to detach themselves from mainstream society, and to create what we might view as their own insular communities or bubbles. Academics caught up in the affairs of the dreaming spires are said to be within the 'Oxford bubble', and similar cloistered institutions such as schools, colleges, clubs and societies can – intentionally and unintentionally – promote a degree of insularity.

HERMITS

Throughout history, certain religious groups have removed themselves from secular life, preferring instead to lead a more ascetic existence away from what they saw as the corrupt complacency of everyday life. The early history of the Christian Church is dotted with examples of pious types who took themselves off to live with little or no contact with the outside world. St Anthony (c.250–355) retired to the Egyptian desert to live as a hermit; Simeon the Stylite (c.390–459) was a Syriac saint who lived for more than thirty years atop a 60-foot pillar; St Columba (521–97) landed on the tiny Scottish Highland island of Iona in 563 with twelve followers and built a church and monastic community.

For most people such acts of asceticism were inspirational, and for many they became a significant tenet of Christianity. From the early medieval period we see the development of Christian concepts of orderly communal monasticism, whereby men (monks) and women (nuns) lived in cloistered environments and rejected worldly pursuits to pursue spiritual lives in monasteries or convents.

Monastic life followed a strict set of principles or rules, as for example the hugely influential early medieval *Rule of St Benedict*. Something of the isolation and atmosphere of such monastic communities is conveyed by the twelfth-century Benedictine abbot William St Thierry describing the French monastery of Clairvaux:

> At the first glance as you entered Clairvaux by descending the hill you could see that it was a temple of God; and the still, silent valley bespoke, in the modest simplicity of its buildings, the unfeigned humility of Christ's poor. Moreover, in this valley full of men, where no one was permitted to be idle, where one and all were occupied with their allotted tasks, a silence deep as that of night prevailed. The sounds of labour, or the chants of the brethren in the choral service, were the only exceptions.

While for politicians living in a bubble can be construed negatively, making them out of touch with the real world, a lack of worldliness was exactly what monasticism was all about: a purity of life and spirit, devoted to prayer and the love of God. Metaphorical bubbles were what made this happen.

Clairvaux Monastery Cistercian monastery in north-eastern France. Founded in 1115 by the French abbot St Bernard and a handful of hardy monks who endured extreme deprivation during the decade of its construction. The original building is now in ruins, but remains the earliest example of the layout of a Cistercian monastery.

The secular version of a monastic life is the 'ornamental' or 'garden' hermit (literally people who would live in your garden), whose bubble was the hermitage, a spartan domestic dwelling where the hermit led a more or less solitary life.

It was during the eighteenth century and early nineteenth centuries that ornamental hermits had their heyday, as figures of interest in country house gardens. Such was the curiosity value in these rustic figures among the social elites of Georgian Britain that people advertised for hermits to come and live in their gardens, almost as visitor attractions. One advertisement placed in the 11 January 1810 edition of the *Courier* was in fact placed by a would-be hermit who sought a hermitage. It read:

> A young man, who wishes to retire from the world and live as a hermit, in some convenient spot in England, is willing to engage with any nobleman or gentleman who may be desirous of having one. Any letter addressed to S. Laurence (post paid), to be left at Mr. Otton's No. 6 Coleman Lane, Plymouth, mentioning what gratuity will be given, and all other particulars, will be duly attended.

Nothing is known of whether this strangely intriguing request was ever answered. However, it appears that, in addition to a roof over his head, the hermit expected to receive a salary or stipend.

A superb description of the hermitage at Sir Richard Hill's Shropshire estate, Hawkstone, dated 1784, provides a vivid picture of the resident hermit, the nonagenarian Father Francis, who lived, we are told, in a

> well-designed little cottage, which is an hermit's summer residence. You pull a bell, and gain admittance. The hermit is generally in a sitting posture, with a table before him, on which

is a skull, the emblem of mortality, an hour-glass, a book and a pair of spectacles. The venerable bare-footed Father, whose name is Francis, (if awake) always rises up at the approach of strangers. He seems about 90 years of age, yet has all his senses to admiration. He is tolerably conversant, and far from being unpolite.

Very few actual hermitages survive today but one superb example can be found in the gardens of Bicton House in Devon. Constructed in 1839, this hermitage is tucked away in a secluded spot in the park surrounded by dwarf conifer trees and heathers, and was restored to its former glory in 2006 by rural craftsmen. Constructed on a slight grassy incline with steps leading up to the front door, the hermitage is built of wood, with a hexagonal pitched roof, while its walls are clad with thousands of 'fish-scale' wooden shingles; and the floor is macabrely fashioned out of deer bones, which were pushed into the earth with their 'knuckle' ends upwards.

Clearly ornamental hermits were figures of some curiosity, but it is rather difficult to reconstruct the lives of these individuals who lived in their bubbles because they left so few historical records. Hermits as reclusive figures that lived apart from society often occupied the dark, out-of-the-way corners – which makes them both fascinating for the historian and also raises the important question of the history of shadows...

·5·

SHADOWS

—

*The history of shadows is all about... eclipses,
the underworld, deals with the Devil, the passing
of time, the universe and shaving.*

SOLAR ECLIPSE

Shadows have a significant place in Sam's own personal history and also in his family history. He remembers vividly when, on 11 August 1999, everything he could see, and a huge amount that he could not see, came under the shadow of a solar eclipse.

A total eclipse of the Sun is an exceptionally rare event. The 1999 eclipse was the first solar eclipse visible in the UK since 1927, and before then there had not been one for 201 years. It is very likely that Sam is the only member of his family who has seen a total eclipse in the UK since 1724 at the earliest. That is quite a claim. How many other experiences on Earth are quite *that* rare? Those lucky few in Cornwall in 1999 are part of a generation marked by the eclipse; they are marked by the shadow of the Moon.

So many first-hand accounts of the 1999 eclipse survive that we know that Sam's actual experience of the eclipse was not unusual. He was luckily positioned on one of the cliffs, in exactly the right part of Cornwall, where the clouds suddenly parted at the moment of eclipse. Colours turned to grey, temperatures fell, and animals started to act as strangely as those flocks of humans, temporarily nesting on vantage points across the English landscape, craning towards the Sun with strange glasses protecting their eyes. Most notably birds fell silent, briefly, and then the gulls swirled in a vortex and flew out to sea, crying at the false dawn.

Such abnormal animal behaviour is one of the most remarked-upon characteristics of the Moon shadowing the Sun; it even has its own history. Observational notes on the total eclipses of 24 January 1544 and 21 August 1560 mention strange bird behaviour, how they 'ceased singing' and, more surprisingly, 'fell to the ground'. Mammals, insects, even plant behaviour during solar eclipses have been studied over time. Ants freeze. During the eclipse of 28 July 1851, at Lilla Edet, Sweden, a swarm

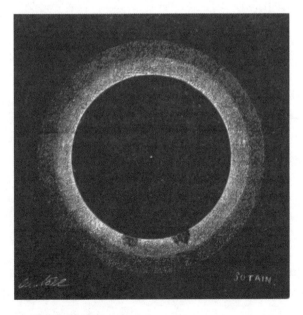

Eclipse of the Sun, 1842, taken from Emmanuel Liais, *L'Espace céleste et la nature tropicale, description physique de l'univers* (1866)

of ants 'which were busily carrying their burdens, stopped and remained motionless till the light reappeared'. They swiftly recovered their equanimity once the shadows cast by the eclipse had disappeared, but interestingly butterflies in the region did not and instead took significant time to readjust even once light had been restored.

The first scientific attempt to study the behaviour of animals during an eclipse was made in 1932 in New Hampshire and Massachusetts in the United States when 498 observations were made by volunteers across the two states. Perhaps the most unpleasant was a woman in Lawrence, Massachusetts, whose 'pantry was greatly infested by cockroaches'; perhaps the most unfortunate was a man in Stony Brook, Connecticut, who was 'molested by mosquitos' for the full two minutes of the total eclipse before they suddenly vanished. Since then the behaviour of animals in both the wild and in zoos has been studied by scientists interested in exploring the phenomena of shadows cast by an eclipse.

DATING

King Yi of Zhou The seventh king of the Zhou Dynasty of China, which lasted longer than any dynasty in Chinese history. The exact dates of Yi's rule are uncertain, however. Historians believe that he either ruled from 899–892 BCE or from 899–873 BCE. The start of his reign is marked by a solar eclipse on 21 April 899.

The written evidence for eclipses is remarkable in its geographical and chronological scope and also in its accuracy. Between 771 BCE and 1368 CE in China alone some 938 solar eclipses were recorded. Aided by astronomers, historians have been able to use the large number of references to eclipses in early written sources to date events and documents. When a description of an eclipse in a known location exists, but there is no actual date given, the calculations can now be made. Thus, for early Chinese history, a text which recorded that 'during the first year of the reign of King Yi, in the first month of spring, the sun rose twice at Zheng' was used to date the start of King Yi's reign to 899 BCE; similarly a description of an eclipse on 'the first day of the last month of autumn' during which 'the blind musicians beat their drums, and the lower-ranked officers and common people bustled and ran about' was used to date the reign of King Zhong Kang, the fourth king of the Xia dynasty, the earliest of the famous Three Dynasties of early Chinese civilization, to 1880 BCE. Before these calculations were made, the earliest known accurate date in Chinese history, calculated and researched by Sima Qian, the great Chinese historian of the Han Dynasty (145 or 135–86 BCE), was 841 BCE, the rise of the Gonghe Regency. Similar calculations have been made to date crucial moments in history from prehistoric Babylon to seventeenth-century Europe. This use of eclipses to establish dates is itself just one aspect of a specific type of history – chronological scholarship – a branch of history that seeks to bring together a myriad of sources to reconstruct timelines, a practice that can be traced back to the French religious leader and scholar Joseph Scaliger (1540–1609). Here, then, the history of shadows is used to unravel history itself.

MESSAGES FROM GOD

The way that our understanding of such celestial phenomena has shifted over time is also fascinating. Shadows cast over the Earth could be understood as profound messages, apparently from the heavens. Solar eclipses have been linked both with the crucifixion of Jesus and the birth of Muhammad. The German Reformation figure Martin Luther viewed eclipses as 'evil omens and portents, as are monstrous births', and noted that they were appearing more and more frequently in the early sixteenth century, which he interpreted as a sign that the end of time was approaching. When the world did not end he treated such predictions with scorn. In 1628, an eclipse of the Moon and the Sun led astrologers in Italy to predict the death of Pope Urban VIII. So spooked was Urban by these celestial portents that he issued a papal bull forbidding any such celestially inspired predictions in the future. Under the guidance of the Dominican friar Tommaso Campanella a series of rituals were performed in a sealed room – candles were lit to represent beneficent planets, music was played, liquids drunk and sprinkled – all in order to offset what were viewed as the evil effects of these portents that cast the Earth in shadow.

Martin Luther (1483-1546) A German theology professor and monk, and a key figure in the Protestant Reformation, Luther opposed many of the teachings and practices of the Catholic Church. In 1521, he was excommunicated by the Pope for heresy, and condemned as an outlaw by the holy Roman emperor.

While shadows cast by celestial forces might be interpreted as omens and signs from above, personal shadows have been understood in interesting ways in various cultures around the world. In Australian Aboriginal culture it was thought that if an enemy captured any article belonging to an individual, it could be used as a charm to harm or cause illness to that person. When departing a camp they were careful to leave nothing behind, and on occasion where they came across items belonging to their own enemies, these were handed to the chief, and great care was taken by Aboriginals not to allow their own shadow to pass over the object for fear of what might happen to them as a consequence.

In the nineteenth century magicians on the island of Wetar in the eastern archipelago of Indonesia claimed they could make a man ill by stabbing his shadow or hacking it with a sword, in the manner of sticking a pin in a voodoo doll. In Greece and Romania during the nineteenth-century superstition held that to bury a man's shadow under the foundations of a house would protect the building, but the man himself would die within a year. Belief in the custom was so widespread that tales circulated of unscrupulous builders enticing people onto building sites, only to surreptitiously measure out their shadow for burial; and in nineteenth-century Romania there are reports of shadow-sellers who plied a trade providing architects with shadows so that they could guarantee the sturdiness of their foundations. In this sense, shadows are tied up with popular superstitions and belief, and were viewed as an extension of the self – akin to a reflection – with mysterious properties that extended from the physical body.

THE SOUL

The ancient Greeks made a link between a person or animal and their shadow, which was a metaphor for the *psyche* or soul. It was thought that a dead person's soul was comparable with a shadow, and that the Greek underworld of Hades was the land of shadows – in other words it was the land of death. It was believed in Greek mythology that anyone entering the sanctuary of Zeus, the god of sky and thunder, on Mount Lycaeus was destined to lose his shadow and die within a year

This idea of a shadow-soul reappears throughout history in

numerous forms. In some Western cultures superstition held that if the Devil could not succeed in winning the soul of a man himself, then he would try to steal his shadow. This is depicted in literary form in the 1814 German novella *Peter Schlemihls wundersame Geschichte* (*Peter Schlemihl's Miraculous Story*), by French aristocrat Adelbert von Chamisso. In it the protagonist Peter Schlemihl is tricked by the Devil, disguised as an old gentleman in grey, into exchanging his shadow for a bottomless purse (Fortunatus's wishing cap among other magical items): 'Pardon, Sir; pardon your most humble servant... I only beg your permission to be allowed to lift up your noble shadow, and put it in my pocket.' On delivering up his shadow, Schlemihl discovers that a man with no shadow is shunned by all society, and spurned by the woman he loves. To be without a shadow is to be distrusted, to be only part human. Reflecting on his error he intones:

> My inward emotion suggested to me, that even as in this world gold weighs down both merit and virtue, so a shadow might possibly be more valuable than gold itself; and that as I had sacrificed my riches to my integrity on other occasions, so now I had given up my shadow for mere wealth; and what ought, what could become of me?

A much-loved more modern interpretation of this idea is J. M. Barrie's *Peter Pan*, who loses his shadow and has to have it sewn back on by Wendy.

Shadows, then, have significant cultural meaning connected to intangible things such as the soul and the afterlife but they are also connected to far more physical things, not least the passage of time.

TIME

When Sam witnessed that eclipse in Cornwall he realized that to stand on Earth is to stand on the face of a massive sundial. The moving of the shadow around him marked the passing of time: ten minutes before there had not been an eclipse, but now there had, and therein lies one of the earliest of chapters in the history of the shadow: it is the history of time itself.

At its most simple, time can be accurately told by placing a stick in the ground and measuring the length of the shadow around midday. When the shadow is at its shortest, that is the precise moment of noon. It is at that exact moment when one's latitude can be most easily calculated by measuring the angle of the Sun against the horizon. Thus the history of the shadow is also intimately linked with the history of navigation, by land or sea.

The principle of using shadows to tell more accurate time rather than just the moment of noon is ancient, and the earliest 'shadow clocks', as they were known, date to 1500 BCE Babylonia. Over the centuries that followed they appeared in a bewildering array of designs and locations. The secrets behind their construction were first widely shared in print in 1570 when the Italian astronomer Giovanni Padovani published a treatise – the ridiculously long-winded *Opus de compositione et usu multiformium horologiorum solarium, pro diversis mundi regionibus, idq(ue) ubique locorum tam in superficie plana* – that included instructions on how to make them.

Even before then, however, the history of the sundial had taken a dramatic step towards democratization with the invention of the pocket sundial. Thereafter, sundials were no longer simply the preserve of the wealthy. We know a surprisingly large amount about pocket sundials because of a single chance event: the sinking of Henry VIII's warship the *Mary Rose* in 1545. When it was raised from the mud of the Solent over 400 years later, archaeologists discovered an entire Tudor micro-world frozen in time inside her hull. Without any doubt some of the most intriguing of the objects that number among the 26,000 artefacts and pieces of timber (as well as the remains of many of the crew) found inside her were the pocket sundials.

These pocket sundials remained immensely popular, as surprisingly late as the nineteenth century, and they came in many forms. One of the most interesting was the 'universal' sundial, a specific type made for merchants, pilgrims and other travellers who might find themselves needing to tell the time in unfamiliar locations and in a variety of latitudes. In order to tell the time in whatever place they were, the traveller needed to consult a gazetteer incorporated into the device, and would then use that information to incline the dial to the right angle to tell the correct time. They were frequently made of ivory and became known as ivory diptych sundials.

One of the finest assemblages of these is held at the Collections of Historical Scientific Instruments at Harvard University. In total they have eighty-two different examples in their collection, each unique and each exquisite. One of the most beautiful was made in Noremburg in 1636. It is the very embodiment of a multicultural and international society of travellers, many of whom dodged beneath the historical radar as itinerants lacking a permanent address and leaving few records. The thirty-two points of the wind rose, which is a graphic tool to indicate wind speed and direction, are labelled in abbreviated German; the winds are named in Italian; a dial shows the length of day and night in both Italian and Babylonian hours, the former system counts twenty-four equal hours starting at sunset, the latter at sunrise; the phases of the Moon are marked in German; there is a gazetteer for the latitudes of twenty-four European cities. There is even a slot for a mini wind vane for the traveller to see in which direction the wind might take them next.

COPERNICUS

Copernican Revolution Led to a new model of the universe, which placed the Sun - rather than the Earth - at the centre of the solar system. The 'revolution' began with the publication of mathematician and astronomer Nicolaus Copernicus's *De revolutionibus orbium coelestium* (1543).

By the sixteenth century, moreover, a crucial change had occurred in the understanding that lay behind the shadow-clock. For millennia the movement of the shadow around the face of the dial was understood to reflect the movement of the Earth – as the centre of the universe – around the Sun. This all began to change in 1514 with Nicolaus Copernicus's work *Commentariolus* and his subsequent 1543 work *De revolutionibus* which demonstrated that the opposite was true – that the Earth, in fact, orbited the Sun. His ideas were followed up by a handful of history's most eminent astronomers. The Danish scholar Tycho Brahe (1546–1601) who significantly improved the observational data upon which Copernicus had based his theory (though he disagreed with Copernicus on a number of factors); the Italian Galileo Galilei (1564–1642) who, with the use of the newly invented telescope, observed that Venus also orbited the Sun, strengthening the Copernican explanation; and Isaac Newton (1642–1726) who explained the physics of orbiting bodies in terms of gravitational attraction. Snug in the history of the shadow, therefore, lies evidence that the brightest stars in our scholarly history spent significant time on this specific type of shadow and in so doing discovered and then explained that the Earth orbited the Sun – which is nothing less than the key to understanding our universe and is one of the most important scientific breakthroughs ever made.

STUBBLE

This history of shadows and the passing of time is also linked to something less significant than the Copernican Revolution but is still fascinating in its own way; it is linked to the history of the 'five o'clock shadow' – that fleck of stubble that develops on the chin of face-shavers towards the end of the day. While designer stubble first became widely desirable during the 1980s – especially if you wanted to look like George Michael or Don Johnson in *Miami Vice* – during the first half of the twentieth century in the United States, the failure to be clean-shaven had associations with slovenliness. This was a marketing dream for those advertising agencies seeking to peddle shaving products. A 1937 US poster advert for Gem Micromatic razors encouraged men to 'Avoid "5 O'clock Shadow"', while boasting of the qualities of their scientifically designed product:

> Stay clean with Gem! Banish '5 O'clock Shadow' – that premature, unsightly stubble which results from inefficient shaving instruments that merely 'top' the beard. A Gem Blade in a Gem Razor guarantees shaves that *stay* shadowless to the end of the longest day!

This advertising campaign was deemed a success and was followed up two years later with a more targeted one that played on male social anxieties. Running with a similar strapline 'Don't let "5 O'clock Shadow" start a whispering campaign', this depicted two attractive women laughing and pointing at an out-of-shot figure whom we can only suppose is both male and poorly shaven. Before advertising the amazing qualities of Gem razors, readers were warned 'Let down a little in your personal appearance and it's just human nature for others to surmise that things aren't so good with you!' This rather surprising history of

Gem razor blade advertisement, USA, 1937

the shadow raises the very important question of the history of the beard...

·6·

BEARS

The history of beards is all about…
murderers, pirates, tax, cowardice, the
Crimean War and the Reformation.

Love them or hate them, beards have a long and fascinating history, one that has seen them grow in and out of
fashion at different times in different locations and always
for different reasons. We are split on the beard front: Sam is a
hirsute pogonophile (yes there is a word for loving beards just
as there is a word for fearing them: pognophobia), while James
is generally baby smooth, at least when he can be bothered to
shave the designer stubble. Our choices are (probably) based
on laziness, exhaustion, vanity, hipster fashion trends, peer
pressure or the preferences of a loved one: beards are not very
kissable. The wearing or not wearing of a beard is for many
nowadays a throwaway thing, though obviously not for all: the
Taliban for example institutes a strict facial hair policy in areas
under its control that forces men to grow long beards or suffer
punishment. In the past, the motivation for wearing a beard
was often linked to significant historical events, which makes
the beard unexpectedly interesting and culturally important for
those who study history.

TO GROW A BEARD OR NOT?

Throughout history societies have both rocked and knocked the beard. The beard enjoyed a particularly popular time in Britain during the late 1850s, but was less in vogue at other times. During the eighteenth century, however, beards had fallen out of fashion within polite Georgian society, and were only worn by ruffians, rustics, the aged and religious men. They were certainly not worn by soldiers, who represented the British empire globally, and were the product of secular Victorian order and authority, training and temperament. Only certain regiments were given special dispensation, and only then to grow moustaches, which became a distinctive feature of their regimental identity. In France, by contrast, members of Napoleon's mounted 10th Regiment of Hussars were known for their trademark side whiskers and moustaches, a trend that travelled across the Channel to Britain in 1806 when the 10th Light Dragoons were renamed the 10th Royal Hussars, and the regiment sported moustaches, while donning furs and feathers. These new hirsute fashions were soon adopted by other British mounted regiments, including the Life Guards and Horse Guards. This was a military trend that spread. In 1854 the British army decreed that no soldier should shave his top lip, following French fashions and the notion that it would create scary moustachioed battle troops, although presumably it also simply made troops look older.

THE CRIMEAN WAR

The beard, however, was still nominally banned in the British army, but that changed in the Crimean War (1853–6). During the siege of Sevastopol in 1854–55, Lord Raglan (1788–1855), the army's commander in the Crimea, relaxed the rules about facial hair, and permitted the troops to grow beards in response to petitions from the soldiers themselves. This not only saved them the tiresome trouble of shaving in poor conditions, but also provided soldiers with a measure of facial warmth in the Crimea's terrible climate. On returning to Britain after the war, these hirsute heroes were greeted with reverence and respect by the public and the beard became a symbol of heroic manhood

Crimea War soldiers, 'Noble, Dawson and Harper, 72nd Duke of Albany's Own Highlanders', Robert Howlett & Joseph Cundall, 1856

which was adopted by civilians. The sight of these bearded troops was so striking that Queen Victoria recorded an entry in her journal for 13 March 1856 describing them as 'the picture of real fighting men... They all had their long beards and were heavily laden with large knapsacks'.

Crimean War (1853-6) Fought between Russia and the allied forces of Britain, France, the Ottoman empire and Sardinia. A variety of causes included the rights of Christians in the Holy Land, which was controlled by the Ottomans. The Russian empire was defeated.

RELIGION

Wearing a beard was and is often closely linked to religion, and it could be either an act of conformity and belonging, or an act of rebellion and rejection. It is official dogma, for example, for Sikhs to grow a full natural beard if they were able – which is known as to practise Kesh – as a sign of respect for the perfection of God's creation. Among Amish communities married men grow beards, but in fact shave their moustaches, which is related to a time when the moustache was associated with the military, and Amish men wished to distinguish themselves as peaceful. In Islamic faiths too the beard was an important part of the religion, with Shia scholars stipulating that beard length should not exceed the width of a fist; trimming beards was fine, but shaving was forbidden. On the other hand, Sunni traditions hold that trimming the moustache is essential. According to the Bukhari and Muslim Hadith collections (or prophetic traditions) the prophet Muhammad stipulated that 'Five things are part of nature: to get circumcised, to remove the hair below one's navel, to trim moustaches and nails and remove the hair under the armpit'. It is striking that in each of these examples allowing one's facial hair to grow naturally was an important part of religious observance.

The beard was even sometimes conceptualized as 'God's work'. Writing in 1653, the English physician John Bulwer considered that shaving not only was indecent, but also blasphemous, 'most inexpiable against Nature, and God the Author of Nature, whose worke the Beard is'. In less overtly religious terms, T. S. Gowing in his *Philosophy of Beards* (1875) accused shavers of 'a deliberate offence against nature and reason'.

For late medieval priests in the Catholic Church the norm was for a clean-shaven appearance, with the exception of certain occasions, such as mourning, when growing beards was allowed but it was adopted by sixteenth-century continental European Reformers, among them Martin Luther. The Reformers' clerical beard was a consciously anti-Catholic gesture, a visible mark of their aggressive rejection of the established Church.

Sixteenth- and seventeenth-century popes did grow beards, as a mark of religious authority. Take for example the great portrait in the Vatican Museums of Pope Sixtus V (1521–90), which portrays him in a striking white beard [*see fig. 7*]. He was a significant figure in the Counter-Reformation (traditionally dated from 1545 to 1648) and this official portrait in particular shows him with a rather severe countenance, his brow furrowed, his lips set firm beneath his white facial hair. During the 1580s, Pope Sixtus shared the world political stage with another bearded ruler in the guise of King Philip II of Spain (1527–98), who throughout his life – judging by his official portraits – wore a beard. In contrast to the rather full white papal beard of Sixtus V – itself a mark of patriarchal wisdom – the Spanish monarch sported a more ordered, closely trimmed beard, more in keeping with the style of beards worn by courtiers.

COWARDICE AND CIVILIZATION

Other societies, however, knocked the beard, and for an extraordinary variety of reasons. The Roman historian Tacitus in *Germania*, his ethnographic account of German tribes, wrote of the Cattans that, for them, the beard was a sign of cowardice, a lack of 'spirit':

> Moreover a custom, practised indeed in other nations of Germany... prevails amongst the Cattans by universal consent. As soon as they arrive to maturity of years, they let their hair and beards continue to grow, nor till they have slain an enemy do they ever lay aside this form of countenance by vow sacred to valour. Over the blood and spoil of a foe they make bare their face... Upon the spiritless, cowardly and unwarlike, such deformity of visage still remains.

In ancient Rome itself the fashion among urban elites was for careful grooming, and being clean-shaven by a barber was the norm. The Roman author and military commander Pliny the Elder (23–79 CE) in his *Natural History* said of the Emperor Augustus (63 BCE–14 CE) that he never neglected the razor and shaved every day. Such urban sophistication was in direct contrast to the unshaven, rugged look of rural rustics.

For Peter the Great, beards were a sign of backwardness, so much so that he ordered Russian men to shave off their beards,

> **Pliny the Elder (23-79 CE)** An early Roman writer, natural philosopher and military commander best known for his encyclopedic *Naturalis Historia* (*Natural History*). Died in the eruption of Mount Vesuvius.

and in 1705 levied a tax on beards in an attempt to make Russia –
in outward appearances at least – more Westernized like its
European neighbours. This was not the first time that beards
had been controlled. In France in 1535 the wonderfully titled
Edict of Beards banned anyone with a beard from entering a
law court, presumably because facial hair was a sign of being
uncivilized: anyone wanting justice before the law needed to
come along clean-shaven.

FEAR

Sometimes the beard was not just something to be despised but
even to be *feared*. This story comes from an early nineteenth-
century 'chapbook', a type of popular pamphlet that was the
forerunner of the mass-market paperback. They often had moral
or religious themes, and some were very alarmist. This example
is nothing less than a horror story about a serial killer, centred
on a man with an extraordinary beard. *The History of Blue Beard;
or, the Fatal Effects of Curiosity & Disobedience* was published in
London around 1805. It concerned a wealthy gentleman with
a blue beard, 'which made him so very frightful and ugly that
none of the ladies in the parts where he lived would venture
to go into his company'. Bluebeard married a young lady who,
initially afraid of his beard, after a while in his company considered it 'not so very blue; and that the gentleman who owned it
was vastly civil and pleasing'. Bluebeard soon has to go away. As
he leaves he tells his wife that there is a room she must not enter
on pain of 'the most dreadful of punishments'. Curiosity gets the
better of her and she finds there unimaginable horrors: a room
filled with the bodies of several dead women.

In her fright she drops the key, which becomes stained with
blood, but she cannot wipe the blood from the key. Bluebeard
then returns, sees the key and knows what has happened. 'Very

well, madam,' he declares, 'since you are so mighty fond of this closet you shall be sure to take your place among the ladies you saw there.' Just as she is about to be murdered, however, her brothers enter and kill him. She then inherits everything.

It is quite some story, and has its own history. By the time that this version was produced it had already been well known for over a century. It originated in France, written in 1697 by the author Charles Perrault who is believed to have based it on ancient folk tales. The principal theme – of the potentially fatal effects of feminine curiosity – is common, as is the more hidden theme of evil having its attractions. The focus on the beard itself is also well known – think of Samson in the Bible for the beard and strength, or Merlin in the tales of King Arthur for the beard and the mysterious, magical realm. In the case of Bluebeard his beard is a symbol of his strength and of the bestial nature within that can never be tamed – but its colour in historical folk tales is unique. It has been explained in a number of ways: the beard is unnatural in colour, therefore the man, being or monster that Bluebeard represents is also unnatural; the blue beard is translucent, empty, frosty, cruel. However it was explained or understood in the past, it is at least certain that the story remained deeply alluring for generations and was retold in various forms by some of history's best storytellers, including the Brothers Grimm and Charles Dickens.

Nor is it the only famous tale of a frightening character with a coloured beard. Another beard whose story has terrified generations of children, but who was a real person and also terrified people in real life, was the pirate Blackbeard.

PIRATES

Tales of pirates began appearing in print in the latter half of the seventeenth century and immediately revealed a passion for piratical adventure among the reading public. In 1724 a compendium of biographies, *A General History of the Robberies and Murders of the most notorious Pyrates*, was published, possibly written by the author and traveller Daniel Defoe. One of the pirates featured was Edward Teach – known as Blackbeard. This chapter, more than anything else, firmly established the name of Blackbeard in pirate history.

Blackbeard Edward Teach (c.1680–1718), aka Blackbeard, was an English pirate who plied his trade around the West Indies and along the eastern seaboard of Britain's North American colonies. He is particularly well known for forming an alliance of pirates and amassing a small fleet. Under his leadership, in 1718 they blockaded the valuable trading city of Charlestown, South Carolina, seizing vessels at will.

After several paragraphs detailing his fearsome adventures almost two entire pages are dedicated to his beard, 'since it did not a little contribute towards making his name in those Parts', and so impressive was it that the author compares it, somewhat surprisingly, to a comet. Blackbeard, we hear, took his name 'from that large Quantity of Hair, which, like a frightful Meteor, covered his whole Face, and frightened America more than any Comet that has appeared there for a long Time'. Thousands of history fans ever since have wondered how a meteor can 'cover a face'. The author continues:

This Beard was black, which he suffered to grow of an extravagant Length; as to Breadth, it came up to his Eyes; he was accustomed to twist it with Ribbons, in small Tails, after the Manner of our Ramilies Wiggs, and turn them about his Ears: In Time of Action, he wore a Sling over his Shoulders, with three brace of Pistols, handing in Holsters like Bandaliers;

and stuck lighted matches under his Hat, which appearing
on each Side of his Face, his Eyes naturally looking fierce
and wild, made him altogether such a figure, that imagination
cannot form an Idea of a Fury, from Hell, to look more frightful.

This was part of a show put on by all pirates. Their goal was not
to destroy your ship and kill your crew but to capture it intact
and to keep their own crew safe. They did this by weaponizing
fear, with the intention of making their victims surrender
without a fight. A pirate's reputation was key to this and they
made themselves distinctive in one way or another – some by
their clothes, some by their flags, some by their actions. Teach

Illustration of Edward Teach (Blackbeard the Pirate); nineteenth-century engraving

did it by consciously cultivating his image as Lucifer himself. He grew and braided his hair and beard and, when going into action, tied small fireworks into it. If you were unlucky enough to be captured by Blackbeard but lucky enough to survive, you would never forget his fizzing, crackling face and that beard which reached his eyes – and you would tell everyone you knew all about it. In this way, this pirate's beard was a calling card, a logo of his brand, and it was a reason to be very afraid.

FEMALE SEXUALITY

Another type of beard feared in the past was that found on the face of a lady, a fear that stemmed from patriarchal anxieties about female sexuality as facial hair on women clearly challenged orthodoxies of how men and women should look. This condemnation of hirsute womanhood – of bearded ladies – received its most trenchant articulation from the seventeenth-century physician John Bulwer, who wrote that 'Woman is by Nature Smoothe and delicate; and if she have many haires she is a monster, as Epictetus saith, and the Proverbe abominates her [A bearded woman must be greeted with stones from a distance].'

One of the earliest references to a 'bearded lady' is found in the travel writing of the French philosopher, Michel de Montaigne (1533–92). It relates to a young fifteen-year-old French peasant girl, Marie-Germain, who, the story goes, was out one day chasing her swine around a field, when she leaped over a ditch in hot pursuit. The anecdote continues that, such was her exertion on landing, a pair of genitals popped out of her body, and subsequent to this transformation she developed 'a big, very thick beard'. She was examined by physicians and later baptized as a man, male genitalia and a beard taken here to signify male gender. Whether Marie-Germain was in fact a man in disguise we do not know, but this story about transsexuality in sixteenth-century France is another example of the fear of beards.

Biologically, beard growth is linked to the stimulation of hair follicles by various hormones, which are more pronounced in certain populations than in others, and in adult males more than in women. Some women, however, have a hormonal condition, labelled hirsutism, which leads to pronounced hairiness, often including the growth of facial hair and a beard. Several members of the family of Petrus Gonzales, who lived at the French and Italian courts during the late sixteenth and early seventeenth century, were afflicted by a rare genetic condition (now known as *hypertrichosis universalis*), which meant that their entire bodies were covered in hair, including the whole of the face. They were studied by scientists and physicians, painted by artists, and many of their unusual portraits survive [*see fig. 8*]. After visiting the family in 1594 the Italian scientist Ulisse Aldrovandi wrote of the young daughter, Antonietta Gonzales, that

> The girl's face was entirely hairy on the front, except for the nostrils and her lips around the mouth. The hairs on her forehead were longer and rougher in comparison with those which covered her cheeks, although these are softer to touch than the rest of her body, and she was hairy on the foremost part of her back, and bristling with yellow hair up to the beginning of her loins.

Woodcuts of two of the daughters and this description were later published after Aldrovandi's death in *Monstrorum Historia* (1642), which was a huge encyclopedia-type volume that catalogued human and animal abnormalities. These unusual hairy sisters were something of a phenomenon, yet, despite the fascination they exerted, they must have evoked a degree of masculine anxiety given that they so challenged the gendered norms of early modern society. The past, however, is populated by similar bearded women, who were often paraded for show and spectacle, and by the nineteenth-century bearded ladies were a familiar sight at circuses and fairgrounds, to be ogled at by paying punters set on witnessing a freak show.

HEALTH

Beards have long been a cause for concern for pognophobes, less for the chequered characters whose visages they disguised, and more for the hygiene anxieties attached to hairs on the chin, or more accurately, round the mouth.

Every child relishes Roald Dahl's 1980 depiction of Mr Twit's food-encrusted beard, which acted as a larder for snacks should he get hungry between meals: 'if you looked closely (not that you'd want to) you would see tiny little specks of dried-up scrambled eggs stuck to the hairs, and spinach and tomato ketchup and fish fingers and minced chicken livers and all the other disgusting things Mr Twit liked to eat.' Children (and adults) also delight in the literary nonsense-monger Edward Lear's 'Old Man with a Beard' (1920), who found that 'Two Owls and a Hen, four Larks and a Wren / Have all built their nests in my beard!'

Edward Lear (1812–88) English landscape painter, illustrator and writer best known for his nonsense poetry and prose, and especially his humorous limericks. His most famous poem is 'The Owl and the Pussycat' (1871).

Amusing, of course, but this fear of beard-originating health hazards has its own history. An article in the New York *Sun* newspaper dated 10 May 1902 ran the headline 'Danger Found

There was an Old Man with a beard, who said, "It is just as I feared!—
Two Owls and a Hen, four Larks and a Wren,
Have all built their nests in my beard!"

Edward Lear's 'Old Man with a Beard', from *A Book of Nonsense* (1846)

in the Beard. Declared by Doctors to be a Carrier of Disease'. It went on to warn of the dangers of long-bearded milkmen stroking germs from their beards downwards into the milk they carried, and of a surgeon who allowed his beard to touch, and carelessly to infect, the wounds of the patients on whom he was operating. This is not just an isolated example from history. It is also backed up by a recent 2015 scientific study by the microbiologist John Golobic, which reports that beards trap feculent particles and harbour more germs than a toilet seat.

It was not always thus, and in the past luxuriant beard growth was a sign of rude health, connected to masculinity as well as virility. The humoral system of medicine, which underpinned Western medical thinking into the 1800s, saw the body comprising four distinct humours: blood, phlegm, yellow bile and black bile, the correct balance of which was a prerequisite for a healthy body. Facial hair was seen as a form of bodily waste, and was thought to be connected to the liver and heat in the genital area. According to the Elizabethan physiognomer Thomas Hill:

The bearde in man… beginnith to appearre in the nether jawe… through the heate and moysture, carried unto the same, drawn from the genitals: which drawe to them especially, the sperme from those places.

In other words, beard growth was healthy, and was connected to male virility and sexual potency.

RESPIRATORS

In the Victorian period beards were celebrated for their health-related qualities, acting almost as masks or as 'nature's respirators'. Indeed, with the Industrial Revolution in full swing, with its noxious air and harmful clouds of dust, what every workingman needed was a lush crop of facial hair to filter out all of these nasties. In 1854, the wonderfully titled Committee on Industrial Pathology on Trades Which Affect the Eyes argued that growing a beard and whiskers did not simply just protect the face, but 'arrest[ed]… the particles of dust and grit by the hair of the beard and whiskers, and thus [relieved] the eyes'. This was presumably a recommendation that applied less well for women who worked under similar conditions. Nonetheless the medical properties of beards as filters that prevented clouds of noxious substances getting into the nose and throat led doctors to recommend growing beards to male patients who needed to protect their voices. This was particularly the case with clergymen, whose stentorian tones were needed for the Sunday sermon. This connection between beards, health and the Industrial Revolution raises the very important question of the history of our environment, and in particular the history of clouds…

CLOUDS

—

The history of clouds is all about… navigation and weather forecasting, the Devil, urine, nuclear war, invisible gases and cholera.

Clouds are easy to take for granted. Unless you are one of those who describe themselves as 'cloud spotters', and take both time and pleasure in studying the sky for the types of clouds that cross it – cirrus, cumulonimbus, cumulus and so on, in an activity which has its own interesting history – you are unlikely to give much thought to them. Those who work outdoors will have a much stronger connection with clouds than those who do not. Thus the modern office worker and farmhand share an experience of the world with the medieval scribe and agricultural labourer: the one desk-bound, the other exposed to the elements and seasons. Today's children (and some adults, to be sure) also experience the timeless activity of lying on one's back and watching the sky for shapes in the clouds. But ask yourself this: Have you… ever *used* a cloud? It might seem an odd question now, but at any date earlier than two hundred years ago it would not have been.

NAVIGATION

For centuries, clouds were used as a means of navigation. Clouds move with the wind. If you know what direction the prevailing wind blows in your particular location, therefore, the movement of the clouds can offer a sense of direction. If they are motionless, however, all is not lost for they can also offer a sense of the direction of the sun, even if the sun is so low as to be below the horizon or obscured by high ground, by reflecting its light in a golden glow on the cloud's underside. Similarly, clouds reflect water and ice with a different colour: they reflect ice with a bright whiteness and water with a dull grey. In that way a blanket of cloud can act as a reflected map in the sky. When at sea, clouds can indicate the presence of land by gathering over high points such as mountains or volcanoes. The sailors' first glimpse of land after a long voyage was, more often than not, a cloud in an otherwise empty horizon. The cloud in this instance was not just a tool of navigation but a reason for hope, an occasion for congratulation, a symbol of achievement.

CAPTAIN COOK

The richest collection of examples of clouds used for purposes of navigation come from the diaries of explorers, perhaps none more fascinating than those of Captain James Cook (1728–79) who circumnavigated the world twice (1768–71 and 1772–75) and was murdered in the Pacific during his third voyage (1776–79). The diaries from his first voyage are evidence of just how significant clouds were to the safety, work and daily life of Cook and his crew. The vast majority of entries include the words 'cloud', 'clouds' and 'cloudy' in reference to descriptions of locations, the weather or even speculations on the presence of a 'southern continent' from New Zealand before he actually discovered the south-eastern coastline of Australia in April 1770. A particularly interesting extract suggests how firmly clouds were established in the minds of explorers as indicators of land but also how willing Cook was to question established lore. When in New Zealand at the beginning of 1770 – this is just before he discovered Australia – Cook considered the evidence for the existence of the southern continent. This included observations made by the Portuguese explorer Pedro Fernandes de Queirós who in 1605–6 led a Spanish expedition across the Pacific in search of new territories. From the 26th parallel of south latitude Queirós 'saw to the Southward very large hanging Clouds and a very thick Horizon, with other known signs of a Continent'. Cook, with the eye of a fellow explorer, respect for his precursor and the suspicion of a historian, doubted this report, claiming hanging clouds and a thick horizon...

> ... are certainly no signs of a Continent – I have had many proofs to the contrary in the course of this Voyage... neither do I believe that Quiros looked upon such things as known signs of land, for if he had he certainly would have stood to the Southward, in order to have satisfied himself before he had gone to the Northward, for no man seems to have had discoveries more at heart than he had.

Elsewhere in his diaries he doubted the observation of his third lieutenant, John Gore, who suspected he had identified land to the south-east of Banks Peninsula in New Zealand from the presence of clouds on the horizon. Cook, in contrast, had the more experienced eye and wrote: 'I, who was upon Deck at the same time, was very Certain that it was only Clouds, which dissipated as the Sun rose.'

These examples suggest that there was a level of expertise that could be achieved when exploring and navigating by cloud sign: it was not a straightforward activity. A far more obvious cloud sign regularly used by Cook was a cloud of smoke created by fire which he repeatedly noted down as the first observed evidence of human habitation in his exploration of Australia.

WEATHER FORECASTING

The main use of clouds, both at sea and on land, was for weather forecasting. Before the barometer (invented in the 1640s) became widespread and scientific weather forecasting itself became widely accessible, generations of sailors, travellers, pilgrims, merchants and shepherds relied on clouds as an indicator of weather conditions. Evidence for this survives in abundance in both oral and written history that is full of sayings, adages and rhymes of lore aimed at predicting tomorrow's fair or foul weather. Cloud-related lore is abundant with sayings such as: 'Clouds without rain in summer indicate wind'; 'Cloudy mornings turn to clear evenings'; 'When the clouds of the morn to the west fly away / You may conclude on a settled, fair day'. The Tudor philosopher Francis Bacon wrote that 'Fleecy clouds scattered over the sky denote storms; but clouds which rest upon one another like scales or tiles portend dry and fine weather', and even the New Testament speaks of the popular adage of a cloud rising in the west foreshadowing rain.

The first attempt to actually explain clouds as a natural

Francis Bacon (1561-1626) English philosopher, statesman, scientist, author and prolific letter-writer. He held major public office, serving as both attorney general and lord chancellor of England, and through his scientific method is known as the father of empiricism.

phenomenon was made by Aristotle in his *Meteorologica* around 340 BCE, a four-volume work that provided the basis for our understanding of the natural world and weather-related phenomena such as earthquakes, thunder and lightning, rain, hurricanes and clouds. A work of philosophy, it was based on empirical observation, and what is interesting in relation to his views on clouds is the way in which they were studied for what they might suggest about natural events – as symptoms were to illness. In a passage on earthquakes, for example, he explains that these were sometimes preceded by 'long-drawn' clouds.

This tradition of observation of the natural world was continued by men like the thirteenth-century philosopher, priest and polymath Thomas Aquinas (1225–74), who was influenced by Aristotelian ideas on clouds, writing

> If, however, we understand by the firmament that part of the air in which the clouds are collected, then the waters above the firmament must rather be the vapors resolved from the waters which are raised above a part of the atmosphere from which the rain falls.

Much of our early understanding of weather and the clouds stemmed from Aristotle, whose text remained influential until around the seventeenth century when many of his ideas were overturned.

CLASSIFICATION

It was during the first few decades of the nineteenth century, however, that the solid foundations were laid that underpinned the understanding of clouds as a way of scientifically forecasting the weather. Here the history of clouds introduces us to the young Quaker chemist and amateur meteorologist, Englishman

Luke Howard (1772–1864), whose ground-breaking work led to the systematic categorization of clouds, and became the basis for an international system. In December 1802, Howard delivered a lecture on the classification of clouds to the Askesian Society, a philosophical group who met fortnightly, and his paper was later published as 'On the Modification of clouds, and on the Principles of their Production, Suspension and Destruction' in *Philosophical Magazine* (1803). Howard used a straightforward classificatory model using Latin terminology – *stratus*, *cumulus*, *cirrus* and *nimbus* – defining three main groups: 'simple modifications (cirrus, cumulus, stratus); intermediate modifications (cirro-cumulus, cirro-stratus); and compound modifications (cumulo-stratus, cumulo-cirro-stratus vel nimbus)'. His ideas gained remarkable international interest and support at the time, so much so that the German poet Goethe praised his work for 'bestowing form on the formless, and a system of ordered change in a boundless world', and even penned a verse in his honour entitled *'Howard's Ehrengedächtnis'*, in which he recognized the importance of Howard's classificatory system for clouds. As well as establishing meteorology as a serious field of study, it has also been claimed that Luke Howard's new vision of the aerial landscape influenced the likes of John Constable (1776–1837) and Samuel Taylor Coleridge (1772–1834) to think creatively about the skies.

Over the course of the rest of the nineteenth century Luke Howard's pioneering work (which itself had built on that of the French naturalist Jean-Baptiste Lamarck) spawned an industry of meteorological investigations by the likes of the Englishmen Clement Ley and Ralph Abercromby and the Swedish meteorologist Hugo Hildebrand Hildebrandsson who were among those who further developed the nomenclature and classification of clouds.

CLOUD ATLAS

One of the chief inventions to emerge from this work was what is known as the 'cloud atlas', in other words a pictorial guide to different cloud formations, which was fundamental not only to the training of meteorologists, but also to the accurate prediction of weather. Hildebrandsson's book *Cloud Atlas* (1890) was followed in 1896 by the first *International Cloud Atlas*, a title that has been in print ever since. This was the product of genuine international cooperation, and included text in English, French and German, alongside the colour plate photographs of different cloud formations – a significant addition, as colour photographs in books were a relatively new development at the time. It was also priced to be affordable, which meant that it was widely used. It was claimed by Alexander McAdie, the author of a 1923 edition of the *Cloud Atlas*, that the rapid development of aviation would 'require and lead to a detailed knowledge of all the secrets of cloud building', knowledge that aided travel as well as our understanding of the natural world.

Photograph of 'mammato-cumulus' clouds in
The International Cloud Atlas (Paris, 1896)

CLIMATE CHANGE

Such knowledge now tends to exist in the world of pub quizzes or in the heads of specialists in the history of navigation, but it was once a key part of the knowledge base of those whose lives and livelihoods depended on the weather both on land and sea. Nowadays our cloud spotting is not entirely defunct, however. If you only ever study clouds once in your life, study them for what they can tell you about climate change. We now know that clouds are a signpost of climate change, a warning written in the sky if only we know where to look. Clouds, you see, have their own history in the sense that they are changing and have changed. Clouds today are not the same as clouds a century ago, perhaps even fifty years ago: they are changing their appearance as the Earth heats up beneath our feet. The latest research suggests that the main area of storm tracks in the middle latitudes of both hemispheres (those zones in seas and oceans where storms travel driven by winds) has shifted towards their respective poles, expanding the areas of dryness in the subtropics, and the height of the very highest cloud tops has increased. In this sense the clouds that we see in our sky are not the natural phenomena that we may assume them to be. Rather, they are now shaped by man and we are living at a key moment in the history of our clouds.

MAN-MADE CLOUDS

Such man-made clouds have a rather macabre history all of their own. During the First World War, the 'gas cloud' put fear in the hearts of infantrymen trapped in the trenches on the Western and, to a lesser extent, the Eastern fronts. The casualties of a gas attack were depicted by John Singer Sargent in his 1919 painting *Gassed* [*see fig. 9*]. Although The Hague Conventions of 1899 and

1907 explicitly forbade its use in warfare, the German chemist Dr Fritz Haber over the winter of 1914–15 at the Kaiser Wilhelm Institute for Chemistry in Berlin developed technology that would engulf enemy troops in a cloud of poisoned gas. His technique was to use highly pressurized canisters of liquid which, when released into the air, would turn into gas. This was first used in April 1915 at Ypres when some 5,730 cylinders of chlorine gas, which had been dug into the ground, were released, sending a faint grey-green cloud of strong-smelling fumes floating across no man's land into the Allied trenches. The impact on this occasion was to clear over seven kilometres of Allied troops, but with few reinforcements and being themselves afraid of the gas, the Germans failed to capitalize on the impact of their attack. What this heralded, though, was the start of a chemical war, with both sides employing clouds of poisonous gas alongside conventional shelling, infantry advances, tanks and air power. Techniques were developed to cope with such attacks, one of which was a makeshift gas mask fashioned out of a urine-soaked handkerchief, which proved reasonably effective against clouds of chlorine gas.

Nonetheless it was the psychological impact of gas clouds that was the true weapon, as epitomized in the English poet and

Wilfred Owen (1893-1918) English poet and soldier, and widely considered one of the most important poets of the First World War. Early in the war he was blown up by a trench mortar and spent two days unconscious, surrounded by the remains of a fellow soldier. He later won the Military Cross. He died in action a week before the armistice. His poems are astonishing for the way in which they show the brutality of the war.

soldier Wilfred Owen's disturbing 1917 poem 'Dulce et Decorum Est' in which he describes a gas attack in verse that stands so starkly against the patriotic perception of the war that was peddled by the government in recruitment posters.

> In all my dreams, before my helpless sight,
> He plunges at me, guttering, choking, drowning.
>
> If in some smothering dreams you too could pace
> Behind the wagon that we flung him in,
> And watch the white eyes writhing in his face,
> His hanging face, like a devil's sick of sin;
> If you could hear, at every jolt, the blood
> Come gargling from the froth-corrupted lungs,
> Obscene as cancer, bitter as the cud
> Of vile, incurable sores on innocent tongues

Elsewhere in the poem the gas itself is described as being a 'thick green light / As under a green sea', which undoubtedly describes the use of chlorine gas on British troops. One of the huge drawbacks of early forms of poisonous gas was that it was eminently detectable: you could smell it and – more importantly – you could see it. In the chemical weapons war of 1915–18, the technological battle then became about the development and manufacture of more effective types of gas, such as phosgene and mustard gas. The use of phosgene gas was pioneered by French chemists and first used in 1915 against German lines. The main advantage of phosgene was that, unlike chlorine gas, it was completely colourless, and therefore a more effective chemical weapon because it was difficult to detect. In the history of chemical warfare, the First World War is thus all about the manufacture of invisible, man-made clouds.

MUSHROOM CLOUDS

A new chapter in the history of man-made clouds arose at the end of the Second World War. Ever since the dropping of atomic bombs on the Japanese cities of Nagasaki and Hiroshima in August 1945, 'mushroom' clouds have dominated our view of total war and the power of modern-day nuclear weapons to annihilate life on earth. 'Mushroom' is the term used to describe the shape of the cloud caused by the power of the blast, as material gathered up from the ground, water vapour, a spherical fireball and blast wave are forced upwards and outwards.

Photograph taken of the atomic bombing of Nagasaki on 9 August 1945

The term 'mushroom' had stuck by the 1950s, but the first observers of nuclear explosions used other words to describe them. Those who watched the 'Trinity Test' of July 1945 reported what they described as a 'multi-coloured surging cloud', 'giant column', or 'chimney-shaped column', a 'great funnel' and even a 'raspberry'. Of Hiroshima, one Japanese witness described what was a 'pillar of black smoke shaped like a parachute', and an eyewitness of the test on Bikini Atoll in 1946 spoke of witnessing a 'cauliflower' cloud. It was at the Bikini tests, however, that a reporter remarked 'the mushroom, now the common symbol of the atomic age'.

Trinity Test The first detonation of a nuclear bomb by the US army on 16 July 1945. It took place in the Jornada del Muerto desert of New Mexico. The bomb was the same design as that detonated over Nagasaki on 9 August that year, the last time a nuclear bomb was used in combat.

So dominant was this distinctive cloud in conveying the horrors of nuclear war during the twentieth century that the Russian newspaper *Pravda* reported that a 'mushroom-shaped cloud' was 'suspended over the future of mankind'. This haunting spectre of the man-made mushroom cloud was a dominant fear during the Cold War period, and indeed is still one that hangs over us today.

DISEASE

This fear of clouds even has its own history. In the nineteenth century, clouds – sometimes 'mist' or miasma – were believed to carry disease and in particular were central to contemporary understanding of the way in which cholera spread. Typical of these sightings of cholera clouds was one incident reported in October 1831 in the northern Scottish fishing village of Nigg, where villagers reported seeing a 'little yellow cloud' that was said to hug the ground. Terror gripped the village as the inhabitants were convinced that it represented the deadly disease cholera, at which point one brave soul armed with a linen sack sought to 'catch' the cloud, securing the neck of the sack with a large number of pins. Noticing that the linen sack used to capture the cloud was in fact changing colour from white to yellow, the quick-witted fellow decided that it was unlikely to hold its deadly contents for very much longer, and therefore buried it in the ground, marked with a stone, which still stands to this day: the 'cholera stone'. This shows how the cloud was used by contemporaries to conceptualize the spread of a lethal, yet invisible, disease. In nineteenth-century thinking, cholera was refigured as an object – a cloud made up of deadly spores which could be seen – which meant in turn that it could be easily and widely comprehended.

This connection between clouds and tiny particles that spread contagious diseases raises the very important question of the history of dust...

·8·

DUST

---

*The history of dust is all about... the invention
of the microscope, the mysterious deaths of
Egyptologists, America in the 1930s,
lost knowledge and the Big Bang.*

Dust *is* history. A physical manifestation of time passing, it changes the appearance of objects as a visible signifier of neglect. Thus years of 'hands-off' care of the rare collections at Knole House in Sevenoaks, Kent, the one-time home of archbishops of Canterbury and Tudor monarchs, took its toll on the ornate and highly valuable seat furniture, which became so encrusted with dust that, according to one National Trust fabric conservation adviser, there was 'an air about them of slumped grey corpses needing the kiss of life'.

Dust can gather on an object, spoiling its appearance and necessitating cleaning, just as it can also mark where an object once stood: it can both cloak and create a dust shadow. It brings with it smells, odorous ghosts of where it has once been: a burning heath, the seashore. It is a constant in human history; humans and dust go hand in hand. Indeed, we now know that dust consists primarily of human skin. Every time you chew you create dust; every time you clap, walk, stand, sit, dress, undress, cough, sneeze, fart or burp, you create dust. Dust, therefore, is intimately linked to the human story – in fact to *any* human story – and our relationship to it, the ways in which we have understood or reacted to it, have also changed over time. Dust, therefore, is not only an unexpected subject for history but also an unexpectedly fascinating and important one.

TININESS

First, consider its size, its tininess. For millennia dust was the smallest thing known to man in a period without precise measurement or calculation. Our understanding of dust, and our relationship with it, was associated with a transformation in science and knowledge of the natural world from the fifteenth century when tools and techniques for observing and measuring the world around us moved from the obvious to the barely visible and then, eventually, to that which was invisible to the naked eye, a trajectory that can be followed to the discovery of the atom and subatomic particles.

This observation of the infinitesimal was first made possible by the invention of the eyeglass, the result of experiments in glass manufacture in and around Venice at the turn of the fourteenth century. After the eyeglass came the telescope and then, in the Netherlands in 1590 or perhaps Italy in 1610, the microscope. Within forty years the Dutch scientist Anthony van Leeuwenhoek (1632–1723) was able to magnify an object 270 times and was the first to see and describe red blood cells. A century later, the Italian Catholic priest and biologist Lazzaro Spallanzani (d.1799) compared the profound importance of his discoveries of tiny worlds under the lens of his microscope with that of Christopher Columbus's discovery of the New World in 1492. Among many extraordinary observations, Spallanzani discovered that even the smallest of living things had parents, a belief which ran directly against the established theory of spontaneous generation. In Spallanzani's understanding of the world we can glimpse both the technology and the intellectual framework of our contemporary understanding of dust, for, if studied through a microscope, it is clear that we humans are the parents of dust.

FEAR OF DUST

This understanding of dust brought with it the slightly alarming revelation that dust consisted primarily of human skin, hairs from humans and animals, and the excrement and enzymes of dust mites, which excrete twenty times a day and produce a new generation every three weeks. These little critters inhabit the dark, humid, warm corners of the home, especially in textiles such as blankets and clothing. They become airborne only when disturbed by movement, and can be troublesome if inhaled. Dust mites are connected to asthma. These charmers also feed on humans' dead skin; thankfully they don't eat us while we're alive. Dust is also comprised of pollen, minerals from soil, textile and paper fibres. None of the ingredients of this dust cocktail, which is itself historical in that it varies from location to location and from period to period, are particularly appealing. Does your skin crawl as you imagine all of the dead insects and excrement you ingest through dust? Ours does, for we, like you, are ever so slightly afraid of dust.

Some past societies feared dust, believing it to be an enemy of civilization, and make no mistake about quite how extreme those beliefs could be. 'Cleanliness' was 'indeed next to Godliness', as the founder of Methodism John Wesley exhorted in a sermon on dress in 1786; dirt, therefore, was next to... what... hell? Moral bankruptcy? For Wesley, dirt was next to the evil of

'Slovenliness' which, in his view, was 'no part of religion'. Cleanliness was certainly a sign of good manners, proof that you had raised yourself above the worker's muck. Running water, light, electricity, education, law, public finance and moral reform are also all part of this chapter on the history of dust. Dust and dirt were dangerous, obstructed progress; the darkness that hid it, or helped to cause it, was the antithesis of the Enlightenment ideal. Light, air, cleanliness, education, manners – these were the ingredients of progress.

John Wesley (1703-91) Church of England clergyman and a founder of Methodism. In 1738 he experienced an evangelical conversion which 'strangely warmed' his heart and led him to form his own ministry.

INDUSTRIAL REVOLUTION

Yet that progress itself, ushered in by the Industrial Revolution, brought with it entirely new forms of dust in eye-wateringly large amounts. In the nineteenth century the nature of dust itself changed with mass production. Coal and brick dust spread everywhere from factories, trains, mines and bulldozers, fired by the engines of capitalism. So too was there a drive to invent cleaning products to remove it, and an increase in the popularity of items such as rugs and carpets to hide dust from view. The study of occupational or 'industrial' disease was born during this period, particularly in the hide, skin and leather processing and papermaking industries, and it became a popular topic for contemporary writers and social reformers.

In his monumental book *Das Kapital*, Karl Marx described the noxious and damaging dust that was generated in rag-picking, part of the industrial process in the production of paper, and the

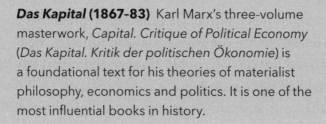

Das Kapital (1867-83) Karl Marx's three-volume masterwork, *Capital. Critique of Political Economy* (*Das Kapital. Kritik der politischen Ökonomie*) is a foundational text for his theories of materialist philosophy, economics and politics. It is one of the most influential books in history.

endless dust produced in cotton mills, which engulfed anyone working under these conditions, including children:

> The atmosphere of the flax mills, in which the children of these virtuous and tender parents work, is so loaded with dust and fibre from the raw material, that it is exceptionally unpleasant to stand even 10 minutes in the spinning rooms: for you are unable to do so without the most painful sensation, owing to the eyes, the ears, the nostrils, and mouth, being immediately filled by the clouds of flax dust from which there is no escape.

Dust became a central focus of the writing of social reformers of the late eighteenth and nineteenth centuries. The Georgian doctor and reformer Charles Thackrah's 1830s investigation across the trades and professions into 'the agents, which produce disease and shorten the duration of life' focused on workers 'whose employments produce a dust or vapour decidedly injurious'. This medical interest in turn led to regulation, and by the end of the nineteenth century printing, flax and linen milling, cotton and clothing manufacture, brass finishing and ivory and pearl button making were all regulated by legislation: our relationship with dust had deteriorated to the point where we legislated against it.

DUST COLLECTING

With such concern over dust there was, during the Victorian period, a whole industry in dust collecting, as depicted in Charles Dickens's novel *Our Mutual Friend* (1865). The Wilfer family home, we are told, was

> in the Holloway region north of London… Between Battle Bridge and that part of the Holloway district in which he dwelt, was a tract of suburban Sahara, where tiles and bricks were burned, bones were boiled, carpets were beat, rubbish was shot, dogs were fought, and dust was heaped by contractors.

Dust, which was effectively synonymous with certain types of rubbish during the nineteenth century, accumulated according to the English social reformer Henry Mayhew (1812–87) in his account of 'the dustmen of London' in 1851 'in houses from a

Victorian dust-sifters. *View of a Dust Yard* (from a sketch taken on the spot), woodcut illustration published in Henry Mayhew's *London Labour and the London Poor* (1851)

variety of causes, but principally from the residuum of fires, the white ash and cinders, or small fragments of unconsumed coke, giving rise to by far the greater quantity'. Dust heaps were separate from dung heaps; the collection of human faeces was the occupation of the Victorian night soil man, rather than the dustman.

Dust had value. It was sifted, collected, sent to dust yards, processed and stored. It was then recycled, and used, among other things, for making bricks. R. H. Horne in his 1850 essay 'Dust; Or, Ugliness Redeemed' described the process whereby

> the fine cinder-dust and ashes are used in the clay of the bricks, both for the red and grey stacks. Ashes are also used as fuel between the layers of the clump of bricks, which could not be burned in that position without them.

Sifting through dust brought with it the prospect of finding hidden treasures: silver, jewellery and other riches that had been mistakenly discarded and that might be resold. There was money in dust. This was the inspiration for Dickens's character, Nicodemus Boffin, the Golden Dustman, whose nouveau-riche status, which is playfully mocked in the novel, came from his success in the dust business. Mr Boffin's prototype was a wealthy philanthropist named Henry Dodd, who in the 1820s set up as a dust contractor, with premises at 14 Pump Row, Hoxton, London. He later established an operation at City Wharf, and held lucrative cleaning contracts for several London parishes, employing hundreds of dustmen and horses. When he died in 1881 he left a fortune of £113,000.

It was, however, a dangerous and unpleasant business. The dust heaps were all populated with the carcasses of dead animals, and it was believed at the time that the heaps were hotbeds of acutely infectious diseases.

Ever since this transformation in the production of dust and our attitude towards it, housekeepers, cleaners and conservationists worry about dust as it builds up over weeks, or days or even hours, but what happens if it builds up over years, centuries, or... *millennia*?

TUTANKHAMUN

This was the question that, for the first time, confronted archaeologists and newspaper editors in the 1920s. The unknown properties of ancient dust concerned the archaeologists because it was they who uncovered Egyptian tombs of unimaginable luxury, including that of the boy king Tutankhamun, who had been buried in 1323 BCE; newspaper editors were intrigued because several of those who had first entered the tombs died in unusual circumstances. At first a 'curse' was blamed, a story that hit the headlines on both sides of the Atlantic. The story was devoured by the public and remains today a popular theme in books and films. Scientists, however, soon began to turn their gaze to the air in the burial chamber and the dust that it had contained. Surely ancient toxic pathogens were responsible. Had insects, mould and bacteria somehow been nourished by the food that the pharaohs were buried with? Did poisonous gases accumulate inside the sarcophagi? There is much here that speaks of the enduring fear of the invisible. Nothing conclusive came from investigations into Tutankhamun's tomb. This dust, it seemed, was not guilty, at least not in this particular instance.

Recent research, however, has shown that archaeologists of all types – not just Egyptologists like Howard Carter who were lucky enough to enter a tomb that had been sealed for millennia – *are* at risk from the past that they study. Bacterial and viral infections can hide in the soil or organic waste they excavate, toxic substances from historic technology can pollute sites, bodies of those who died from disease can still harbour pathogens. Here, then, our fear of a particular type of dust – historical dust – is justified: the past is indeed a dangerous place.

DUST STORMS

Fear of dust is therefore entirely sensible and rational. Over time people have experienced this for very different reasons. House dust triggers allergies; coal dust causes terminal respiratory disease; not to mention the dust from nuclear fallout. Dust storms are a particular feature of arid or semi-arid desert areas, where fine particles of dry sand or soil become airborne and are blown about, sometimes with catastrophic consequences. Large parts of the globe still suffer today from storms of this nature, a phenomenon exacerbated by climate change, but also due to over-intensive cultivation and poor management of dryland regions. Sandstorms are a prevalent feature of the Sahara, and scientists have shown their negative impact on health, connected as they are with respiratory problems and the spread of contagious diseases through virus spores buried in the ground. Dust affects the lives of ordinary people around the world, and impacts local and global economies.

One of the most catastrophic events to hit the United States during the twentieth century was the Dust Bowl of the 1930s, which combined with the Great Depression to bring great hardship to enormous numbers of American citizens in the panhandles of Texas and Oklahoma, as well as parts of New Mexico, Kansas and Colorado. The affected region extended over 150,000 miles of southern plains, and was both a man-made and natural disaster. During the First World War, demand for US wheat to feed the troops rocketed, which led to massive increases in production, as farmers were driven by healthy profits. Responding to this boom in demand and record wheat

Photograph of the Dust Bowl, Dallas, South Dakota, 1936

prices, farmers over-grazed and over-ploughed their lands, aided by the introduction of new petrol tractors, such as Henry Ford's mass-produced and wildly popular Fordson, which dominated the US market. The double whammy of the drought and the Great Depression decimated the wheat industry, which saw prices tumbling to pitiful levels. As the golden acres of wheat dried up and withered in the ground, the expanses of prairie grass which it had replaced were no longer there to anchor the topsoil and prevent it from being carried away by the strong winds that blew across these southern plains. Added to this hardship the region was hit by near biblical plagues of jackrabbits and grasshoppers that destroyed any crops that grew in this harsh landscape.

What is most enduring in the popular historical conscious-ness is the huge dust storms that were experienced across the prairies. These are remarkably recorded for posterity in the many photographs that survive: images of farm buildings, trucks and fences buried in drifts of sand, of enormous blackened clouds of dust that block out the light, of cars trying to outrun the storm as the occupants flee for shelter and safety [*see fig. 10*]. These disturbing events of the 1930s, which displaced so many families, are brought to life in John Steinbeck's magisterial Pulitzer prize-winning novel *The Grapes of Wrath* (1939). In it the Joad family are forced to leave their farm in Oklahoma (though in reality the majority stayed put) where they have lived for years, to move to California to attempt to start a new life. Steinbeck powerfully captures the conditions of the Dust Bowl: 'The surface of the earth crusted, a thin hard crust, and as the sky became pale, so the earth became pale, pink in the red country and white in the gray country', later dramatically describing a dust storm (or 'black blizzard'): 'Little by little the sky was darkened by the mixing dust, and the wind felt over the earth, loosened the dust, and carried it away.'

The impact of these dust storms cannot be exaggerated, both in terms of their size and power, and the destruction they caused. In 1934, the eastern seaboard of the United States witnessed the arrival of a dust storm two miles high that had travelled some 2,000 miles, and left monuments such as the Statue of Liberty shrouded by sand and debris. The very air itself was so charged that it crackled with static electricity. During such storms the environment was permanently damaged along with people's health. An Oklahoman woman interviewed in 1940 described being caught in a dust storm on a day in 1934 at 4 o'clock in the afternoon:

We saw such a huge black cloud [that] just looked like smoke out of a train stack or something. Dust came rollin' over and when it got to the house we was all afraid. We ran into the farmhouse because we thought it was a storm. We lit the lamp, but it was so dark in there that we just couldn't see one another even with the lamp on and we just choked and were smothered.

These were experiences shared by countless numbers of Americans. This is why dust has an important place in the history of America during the early twentieth century.

HISTORIANS

History itself – as a discipline – has long been intertwined with dust. The very act of researching and writing history requires the historian to encounter dust: archives, libraries and muniments rooms are veritable shrines to dust, which accumulates over the centuries on boxes of records, on old books and manuscripts, coating paper and vellum. The role of the historian, then, must be to blow the dust off these literary remains of the past, to breathe new life into it. Such was the approach of the great nineteenth-century French historian Jules Michelet on his first visit to the Archives Nationale in Paris. Writing in the preface to his *History of France* he addressed the nameless dead whose history was in his hands:

> Softly, my dear friends, let us proceed in order, if you please. All of you have your claim on history... And, as I breathed on their dust, I saw them rise up. They raised from the sepulchre, one the hand, the other the head, as in the Last Judgment of Michel-Angelo, or in the Dance of Death.

Examining the riches of the archives he wrote, 'these papers and parchments so long deserted, desired no better than to be restored to the light of day'. Working with old documents – as any historian will testify – necessitates actually breathing in the dust of the past: the dust that has accumulated on historic records, but also the dust of their own disintegration.

Historians encounter dust not simply because documents and books accumulate dust with time, but also because such

Jules Michelet (1798-1874) French historian, particularly famous for his *History of France* (1855). The first historian to use the term 'Renaissance' to describe the period in Europe's cultural history after the Middle Ages.

records disintegrate into dust. Leather-bound rare books post 1880 experience their own form of decay – 'red rot', or 'red decay' – which sees leather that was now increasingly treated by vegetable-based tanning processes simply powdering away. The rare book or manuscript conservator is therefore in an ongoing battle against the disintegration of historical documents into dust. Examining an eighteenth-century account book under the careful supervision of the conservation staff at a West Country record office, James was struck by how fragile historical records sometimes really are. The large folio-sized manuscript volume, which needed to be consulted in a conservation lab, was very badly damaged by damp, so much so that it could only be read with the use of a paper knife to painstakingly turn the pages. The first hundred or so pages were almost impossible to decipher, and were quite literally crumbling to dust. History can only be written based on the evidence that survives, and countless histories are lost to decay. An important part of the history of dust, therefore, concerns the history of book conservation, the preservation of manuscripts and an awareness of the knowledge that has been lost to dust.

BOOKS

The 'dust jacket' – a detachable outer cover to books with folded flaps that secured it to the front and back boards – had almost nothing to do with protecting books from dust. Dust jackets date from the 1830s when books were produced using cloth bindings (and sometimes expensive leather and silk), and were intended to protect books as they left the printers, only to be later discarded. Prior to this, books were sold unbound, and owners then had their volumes specially bound, often in a uniform style. One of the earliest surviving examples is a Bodleian Library copy of *Friendship's Offering* (1829), which is a paper wrapper for a silk-bound gift book. Originally dust jackets were plain, but later on publishers and designers saw the merits of the dust jacket to promote the books, and so began the wonderful tradition of beautifully illustrated book jackets. Ironically, dust jackets are often thrown away, especially by libraries, where hardbacks are stored without them. Large collections of dust jackets are held in libraries like London's British Library and the New York Public Library, and rare examples of dust jackets are collectors' items. A first edition of Sir Arthur Conan Doyle's *Hound of the Baskervilles*, which would normally fetch £3,000–£4,000, sold for £80,000 in July 1998 – because it had one of the original dust jackets.

BIOLOGY

It is sobering to remember that, not only do we produce dust, but we are, in fact, made entirely of dust, and of a very special sort. We now know that everything in us originated from cosmic explosions billions of years ago. Our bodies are literally made up of stardust. We have material in each of our bodies that is as old as the universe and 40,000 tons of cosmic dust falls to Earth every year and is absorbed into our bodies as they change and grow old. Our bodies are in a constant process of decay and regeneration. Cell division is constant – we are literally not the same as we were a few seconds ago. Blink and you are different.

This is an important idea that actually has its own history, most visibly and famously in the Bible and Koran, which teem with references to dust. 'Then the Lord God formed the man of dust from the ground and breathed into his nostrils the breath of life, and the man became a living creature' (Genesis 2: 7), and 'for you are dust, and to dust you shall return' (Genesis 3: 19). The Koran is equally specific: 'Amongst his signs is this, that he created you from dust' (Sura 30: 20).

Ultimately, then, we are all descended from dust, and to dust we will return. We are not 'fixed'. Living is a process, a pattern that can be mapped. Dust, therefore, is less about decay than about circularity, a continuum; it is, in short, about the relentlessness of time passing us by – which raises the very important question of the history of clocks...

·9·

CLOCKS

———

The history of clocks is all about... villages in the Pyrenees, prayer, food, the Reformation (again), icebergs and widows.

Today accurate time is available wherever and whenever we need it and we accept unquestioningly the way that clocks punctuate our daily lives. This makes it easy to overlook their extraordinary history, but consider these questions: How was time measured in the past? And what did time *mean*? How did considerations of time impact on people's daily lives? These issues are fundamental to all historians and even to the discipline of history itself. The relationship that people have had with time has changed markedly over the centuries – and once you realize *that*, the history of clocks opens up an entire, and rather magical, historical world.

—————— SLAVERY ——————

During the Industrial Revolution in the nineteenth century factory workers were ruled by time. In the Victorian factories of the early 1800s it was the foreman's fob watch that structured the daily routines of those in wage servitude, dictating when they rose from their exhausted slumbers, trudged to work, when they ate, worked, even when they relieved themselves and then, finally, when they slept. The clock-watching claustrophobic control of Britain's cotton mills is brought to life in an anonymous address of a Journeyman Cotton Spinner (1818):

> The workmen… are trained to work from six years old, from five in a morning to eight and nine at night… observe the squalid appearance of the little infants and their parents taken from their beds at so early an hour in all kinds of weather… There they are, (and if late a few minutes, a quarter of a day is stopped in wages) locked up until night in rooms heated above the hottest days… and allowed no time, except three-quarters of an hour at dinner in the whole day… The English spinner slave has no enjoyment of the open atmosphere and breezes of heaven. Locked up in factories… he has no relaxation till the ponderous engine stops, and then he goes home to get refreshed for the next day; no time for sweet association with his family…

This is a damning (if polemical) depiction of the impact that clocks could have on the lives of ordinary people. But the world has not always been enslaved by clocks. Once it was guided by the rhythms of the seasonal year. In Europe during the sixteenth century the year began with the first flowers, and the lengthening of the days; it was only those who worked with official documents – lawyers and diplomats – for whom the year began on its official rather than its seasonal date. Rural time was not rigid and regular, but instead marked by vagueness and the cycles of the agricultural year.

TIME IN THE COUNTRYSIDE

Montaillou A small commune in the southern French *département* of Ariège, now in ruins, but during the Middle Ages a hotbed of Cathar heresy. Due to the survival of remarkable Inquisition records for the period 1294 to 1324, we know almost everything about the everyday lives of the 250 inhabitants, from what they ate to their attitudes to sex.

We learn much about the nature of rural time from details of the lives of farmers, shepherds and craftsmen in the medieval Pyrenean village of Montaillou, where people simply did not own clocks and time seems to have been less pressured. We know about how the inhabitants of this southern French hamlet talked about and marked their time from their personal testimonies when interrogated during an Inquisition into heresy by Jacques Fournier, Bishop of Pamiers between 1318 and 1325. Villagers spoke about time with vague expressions: 'a short moment'; a 'brief pause'; and time during the day was referred to by fixed points: meal times, sunset, night or cockcrow. There were of course church bells, which we ordinarily think of as striking out the daytime hours with their chimes, but in Montaillou the bells were only rung at significant occasions like funerals and the elevation of the host, rather than to mark the passage of time on a regular basis. Neither did the villagers work to a fixed and continuous timetable; days were marked by long irregular intervals and most inhabitants almost always found time to stop for leisurely conversations unpressured by the demands of the clock. The standard terminology that we readily associate with time – seconds, minutes, hours, days, weeks, months and years – was not employed as standard. Instead, dates were fixed by references to natural phenomena, such as harvests and agricultural work, and by references to the Christian year, to feast days and saints' days such as St Michael's Day (29 September) or the day of the feast of St Martin (12 November). This was the reality of medieval time in rural Montaillou. The only exception to this vague timetable was the town priest, who alone possessed a calendar and was responsible for keeping track of what day of the year it was.

SALES AND SOULS

In the premodern world merchants and the Church had an interest in time for reasons to do with sales and souls. Keeping track of time was central to the spiritual lives of many Christians* and, just as those in the countryside lived according to 'rural time', those who lived religious lives lived according to 'religious time'.

* Which itself introduces the idea of labelling a date as BC (Before Christ) or, as is now fashionable, as BCE (Before Common Era), and as AD (*Anno Domini*) or, as is now correct, CE (Common Era).

Take for example the Catholic Benedictine monks whose daily routine was ordered by a set of rules collectively known as the *Rule of St Benedict*. Their lives were punctuated by a round-the-clock procession of prayers. The rule, which was composed in Italy around 530, outlined 'How Divine Service Shall Be Held through the Day', explaining,

> As the prophet says: 'Seven times in the day so I praise Thee.'
> Which sacred number of seven will thus be fulfilled by us if,
> at matins, at the first, third, sixth, ninth hours, at vesper time
> and at 'completorium' we perform the duties of our service;
> for it is of these hours of the day that he said: 'Seven times in
> the day do I praise Thee.' For, concerning nocturnal vigils, the
> same prophet says: 'At midnight I arose to confess unto thee'.
> Therefore, at these times, let us give thanks to our Creator

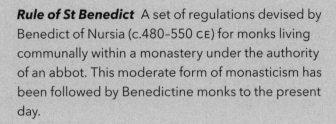

Rule of St Benedict A set of regulations devised by Benedict of Nursia (c.480–550 CE) for monks living communally within a monastery under the authority of an abbot. This moderate form of monasticism has been followed by Benedictine monks to the present day.

concerning the judgments of his righteousness; that is, at matins, etc… and at night we will rise and confess to him…

This *Rule of St Benedict* became the basic template for monastic life throughout medieval Europe, with time very much at the heart of its authoritarian and ascetic code. For thousands of monks over the centuries their time was marked by this unceasing rhythm of prayer.

Within Catholic Christendom church attendance, ceremonial sacraments and confession were routine rituals that structured daily rhythm, not only for cloistered monks, but also for the laity. The deep-seated pious concern for a daily routine of prayer is wonderfully demonstrated by the scores of Books of Hours that survive from the Middle Ages. These devotional manuscript books, which were often highly illustrated, contained a series of psalms and other prayers designed to furnish the owner with structure for his or her daily life. The routine was based on the eight canonical hours extending from Matins, during the night, to Compline, the last prayer before retiring to bed, as well as a calendar of Church feasts. Not only did these volumes function as practical prayer books, but also they were often specifically tailored to the precise requirements of the owner. There is some evidence that they were produced for women, even presented as wedding gifts, and were passed down the family as treasured heirlooms. Owners marked their Books of Hours with personal annotations that included records of events happening on particular dates. On the flyleaf of one Book of Hours belonging to the Derham family of Crimplesham in Norfolk are jottings recording the births of children with astrological precision and devotion: 'Thomas my son was born the xiii day of Januarii the yere of our lorde 1488 on a Tewsday at nyght, between viii and ix: god make hym a good man: that day callid sent hillary ys day [the day called St Hilary's Day].' This annotation, a chance survival over the centuries, shows an awareness of calendrical dates as well as a deep personal impulse to record a key rite of passage in the annals of the family. It also, however, shows an awareness of the specific hour of birth – it is evidence of accurate timekeeping 529 years ago.

THE REFORMATION

The history of clocks and religion is also connected to the Reformation, which brought an increasingly introspective obsession with time. The second half of the sixteenth century and the seventeenth century in Europe witnessed spiritual diarists concerned with the salvation of their souls recording the minutiae of their daily lives. This form of what might be termed 'spiritual accounting' developed after the Reformation as a way of monitoring how one lived one's life as a good Protestant. The deeply pious Elizabethan Yorkshire gentlewoman Lady Margaret Hoby was one of the first Englishwomen to pen a diary.

Her diary recorded the quotidian and rather tedious details (both for her and for us) of a humdrum existence in the north of England. It contains very little in the way of personal feelings or intimate details, and is miles away from the racy memorializing of a diarist like Samuel Pepys. But nonetheless it says something very interesting about her pious obsession with time as a way of accounting for her spiritual life as a good Christian.

Typical of her entries is one dated Tuesday, 28 August 1599, which reads:

> In the morninge, after priuat praier, I Reed of the bible, and then wrought [embroidered] tell 8: a clock, and then I eate my breakfast: after which done, I walked in to the feeldes tell: 10 a clock, then I praied, and not long after, I went to dinner: and about one a clock I geathered my Apeles tell:4: then I Cam home, and wrought tell almost: 6:, and then I went to priuat praier and examenation, in which it pleased the lord to blesse me: and besiech the lord, for christ his sack, to increase the power of this his spirite in me daly Amen Amen: tell supper time I hard Mr Rhodes [her spiritual adviser] read of Cartright [the Puritan, Thomas Cartwright], and sonne after supper, I went to prairs, after which I wrett to Mr Hoby, and so to bed.

Hers was a day structured by prayer, spiritual examination and study and mealtimes. It was in many ways, then, a sense of time that was oriented around the soul and the stomach – rather than the tick and the tock.

OWNERSHIP OF CLOCKS

While church and civic clocks permitted the public keeping of time in England, it is not until the eighteenth century that we see a marked increase in the private ownership of clocks, something that can be measured through probate inventories (which list the possessions of deceased individuals), which are a marvellous source for studying everyday life and the consumption of things. In a comparative survey of Kentish and Cornish households in the seventeenth and eighteenth centuries, it was estimated that, in Kent, only 1 per cent of households owned a clock during the first half of the seventeenth century, but that by the 1740s over

78 per cent of households owned a clock. Cornwall, in contrast, yields only one example of a clock owned by the sampled households prior to the 1650s, and only about 12 per cent of households owning clocks by the mid-eighteenth century. This study shows that, in England, clocks were adopted on a large scale at the turn of the eighteenth century and also that the pattern varied from location to location.

HEIRLOOMS

The presence of clocks in probate inventories is particularly interesting because clocks were often valuable and personal items that could be passed on as heirlooms, or as treasured memento mori of close relatives and friends. Time itself is often a gift that is deliberately chosen to mark passing time; clocks are in their very essence the most historical of objects. Sam's wristwatch was once owned by his great-grandfather, a gift to him (a naval officer and policeman) from his colleagues; James owns a watch passed down to him from his own father that keeps excellent time.

One particularly touching historical example of timepieces as heirlooms is found in the astrological diary of the seventeenth-century merchant and nonconformist, Samuel Jeake (1652–99) of Rye in Sussex. The entry for 3 October 1690 records an intimate account of the passing of his father, Samuel Jeake senior, at about eight o'clock in the evening. The deathbed scene focuses on the final parting of father and son, and Samuel junior describes the moment when his father gave him his watch, saying, 'I deliver you this in name of possession of all that I have which I had not given you before, so that you may be in possession actually of it... ' When Samuel said, 'Farewell, dear Father,' and kissed his dying lips, he answered, 'Farewell, my dear lamb, the lord bless thee, and prosper all that thou undertakest.' In this simple gesture of passing on a watch to a loved family member we glimpse the complex way emotions can be bound up with the timepiece as an object, which in itself acts as an invisible bond between two people.

STOPPED CLOCKS

These examples all demonstrate that, once you give it some thought (and ironically some time), it becomes clear that clocks are not just functional objects, interesting only for their ability to tell the time, but interesting objects for what they tell us about concepts of time, and *that* raises the very interesting question of what happens when a clock suddenly... stops. Particularly so when a clock's function as a timekeeping device has been transformed by an external, unexpected event, into something far more significant.

Usually these events are tragedies. What happened at 03.07 a.m. on 15 April 1912? What happened at 08.15 a.m. on 6 August 1945? What happened at 10.04 a.m. on 11 September 2001? Each of these moments represents an event that resonates through history; each of these precise moments has been captured on the faces of clocks which have stopped; each of these clocks has become the centrepiece of globally significant exhibitions and has therefore had a profound impact on the perception of history for those many thousands who have attended the exhibitions.

TITANIC

The first moment was when Robert Douglas Norman, a second-class passenger on the maiden cruise of the most famous steamship of the day, submerged. Robert was in the water because his ship, the *Titanic*, had hit an iceberg and sunk. The wreck of the *Titanic* was discovered in 1985 at a depth of

3.8km below the surface, and hundreds of items, including numerous watches, have been recovered. Interestingly, they all tell a slightly different time and therefore represent entirely different and personal stories of this renowned disaster. They do not represent the time that the ship sank but the time that the passenger submerged, and the two are by no means the same. Some jumped overboard early on, others struggled into lifeboats as the huge liner was sinking, some were trapped inside, some chose to stay on board until her last dramatic moment when, with her bow deep underwater and her stern saluting the sky for one last time, this enormous steel ship of 46,328 tons split in half like a twig.

Those watches are also a reminder that the sinking of the *Titanic* was a painfully slow event. The iceberg was first spotted at 23.39 and the collision happened only a few minutes later; preparations to abandon ship were not made for another thirty minutes and they lasted for a further forty minutes; the lifeboats started to leave the ship an hour after she struck the iceberg and the last was not launched until 02.05; her final moments came fifteen minutes later, at 02.20, when her bow plunged into the sea and the remaining passengers on board had to jump for their lives. Only a handful of those who were forced to swim in the minus 2 °C water survived. In those moments everyone's watches would have stopped, frozen in time by ice-cold water, the sound of ticking now drowned out by an extraordinary noise created by more than a thousand people in the water. One of the few who survived recalled 'a dismal moaning sound which I won't ever forget; it came from those poor people who were floating around, calling for help. It was horrifying, mysterious, supernatural.' Stopped watches remain among the most valuable of *Titanic* memorabilia bought at auction, and exhibitions of objects from the wreck of the ship that have toured the world have all featured stopped clocks or watches as centrepieces [*see fig. 11*]. For many of the thousands of people who have visited those exhibitions, the story of the *Titanic* has become forever linked with a stopped watch.

HIROSHIMA

The second moment was when Fukuichi Mikamo was killed by a blinding flash of light. His son, Shinji, described it as 'a gigantic fireball. It was at least five times bigger and 10 times brighter than the sun. It was hurtling directly towards me, a powerful flame that was a remarkable pale yellow, almost the colour of white.' The sight was accompanied by the loudest thunder he had ever heard. 'It was the sound of the universe exploding.' He was set on fire. The house collapsed. His skin hung off his body in pieces 'like ragged clothes', the flesh underneath a strange yellow colour, like the surface of a sweet cake his mother would make. Shortly afterwards, localized storm-force winds combined into something like a tornado that sucked up debris. Shinji described it as 'a dark monster'.

This was the experience on the ground of the American atomic bombing of the Japanese city of Hiroshima in which somewhere between 90,000 and 146,000 civilians died. Shinji had been less than a mile from the epicentre of the explosion. In the aftermath of the bombing Shinji and his father were separated, but several months later he returned to the site of his home. There in the rubble he found his father's pocket watch, a smooth silver disc with the shadow of the time forever scarred into its surface. The clock had lost its hands but the heat of the blast had embossed the time onto the face of the watch. For Shinji this was not just a reminder of the explosion that had destroyed his world, it was the moment that he realized he would never see his father again, which hit him 'like another atomic blast'. In 1955 Shinji donated the watch to the new Hiroshima Peace

Memorial Museum. In 1985 it was loaned to the United Nations headquarters in New York for a permanent exhibition, where, in 1989, it was stolen and has never been recovered.

The third moment provides one of the most important exhibits in the Ground Zero Museum Workshop in New York, which was set up in 2005 to bring back to life the 'recovery period' after the al-Qaeda terrorist attacks that destroyed the World Trade Center in 2001. It is a wall clock that stopped when the building it was in collapsed. It is one of the most photographed objects of the museum's exhibition. These stopped clocks are a bridge between history and the present day; they have transformed from a clock that tells the time into a time-portal.

PRESERVING A MOMENT

The recognition of the potent agency of these stopped clocks – the *idea* of the stopped clock – itself has a history as an interesting literary trope, one that has often been associated with mourning. In Britain W. H. Auden's 'Funeral Blues' from 1936, despite its origins as a parody of power, has become a familiar part of the modern funeral service with its wonderful lines:

> Stop all the clocks, cut off the telephone,
> Prevent the dog from barking with a juicy bone.
> Silence the pianos and with muffled drum
> Bring out the coffin, let the mourners come.

But the idea of stopped clocks and mourning is older still. Most famously of all it was embraced by Charles Dickens in 1861 through the character of Miss Havisham in *Great Expectations*, an extraordinary ghost-like person trapped in her own personal prison of time in which her clocks and watches are her jailer.

The book's main protagonist and narrator, Pip, records in

1. Thomas Eakins, *The Writing Master* (1882)

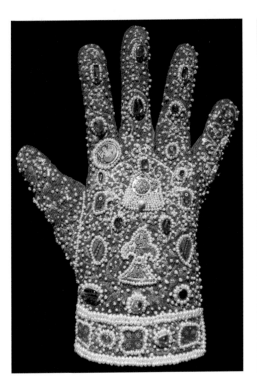

2. Bejewelled imperial glove from Palermo worn by the Holy Roman Emperor, c.1220

3. Albrecht Dürer, Emperor Charlemagne (1511–13)

4. Jean Siméon Chardin,
Soap Bubbles (1733–34)

5. Dosso Dossi,
*Allegory of
Fortune* (1530)

6. John Everett Millais, *Bubbles*
(Pears' soap advertisement) (1890)

7. Portrait of Pope Sixtus V (r.1585–1590)

8. Lavinia Fontana, *Portrait of
Antonietta Gonsalez* (1614)

9. John Singer Sargent, *Gassed* (1919)

10. Photograph of a Texas dust storm, 1936

great detail the moment he realizes that something is really rather wrong with the house that he is in. 'It was when I stood before her,' he writes, 'avoiding her eyes, that I took note of the surrounding objects in detail, and saw that her watch had stopped at twenty minutes to nine, and that a clock in the room had stopped at twenty minutes to nine... It was then that I began to understand that everything in the room had stopped, like the watch and the clock, a long time ago... ' It is soon revealed that 8.40 was the time that, while interrupted dressing for her marriage, Miss Havisham received the letter informing her that her fiancé would not marry her. Her immediate reaction is to freeze the moment in time, even to the extent that she keeps just one shoe on and leaves the other on her dressing table.

Miss Havisham's stopping of the clocks is a desperate measure to suspend time or indeed deny its existence, as if there is a chance that her groom will change his mind and return, but for Pip as an observer the impact is different, for this shows him the past influencing the present in the most profound way possible: the events of the past have shaped the present in denying Miss Havisham a life since her betrayal. Dickens's symbolism has been carefully chosen for its effect. When we meet Miss Havisham she is wearing her wedding dress – 'she was dressed in rich materials – satins, and lace, and silks, – all of white... and some lace for her bosom' – materials that have been deliberately chosen by Dickens for the marriage that they unmistakably symbolize – which raises the important question of the history of needlework...

·10·

NEEDLEWORK

The history of needlework is all about...
abandoned children, racism, murder, invasion
and Heinrich Himmler.

APARTHEID

The history of needlework is extraordinary. It can prick your soul; it can even make you weep.

In 1996 the Truth and Reconciliation Commission (TRC) was set up in South Africa to heal the wounds of a nation trying to deal with the legacy of apartheid. One of the many things it identified was a striking absence of black female voices in South Africa's story. Attempts have since been made to correct this by collecting and archiving the visual memory narratives contained in the women's 'memory cloths' held in the Amazwi Abesifazane (Voices of Women Museum). In these pieces of fabric stitched by female black South Africans, the TRC has been able to capture the testimony of women who suffered under Apartheid, and they record the horrors of their experiences – rape, murder and violence. One example of a memory cloth, worked by Ntombi Agnes Mbatha, depicts a violent scene of a gunman opening fire on her family, and is accompanied by the words,

> In 1992, my husband and I were going into town. Our son of 20 asked us to buy him some shoes. We bought him the shoes, but when we returned home our son was not there and then we heard he had been gunned down. We were so sad...

Harrowing and heartfelt pieces of this nature lay to rest any notion of needlework as a serene domestic task. In these ways, women normally denied access to more traditional forms of historical writing were able to record family and national history in a different form. For them, quilting was nothing less than a form of speech.

This is just one way that, once you really consider needlework, history unfolds in front of you in all of its patchwork complexity. Needlework is a broad term, which denotes the handicrafts of sewing and textile arts, and embraces various decorative forms of sewing from embroidery, quilting and appliqué to knitting, tapestry and weaving. And it's fascinating. Needlework can be considered from the perspective of tools and materials, manufacture and production, skilfulness and form. Needlework was also commissioned, produced, consumed, displayed and passed on, and often the reason we know about it today was that it was preserved for posterity by families, or as exemplars of aesthetic design by museums such as London's Victoria and Albert which, since its first acquisition of a sampler in 1863, has built up a collection of over 700 examples, ranging in date from the fourteenth century to the early twentieth. This means that fabulous examples of needlework survive from the past for us to enjoy and that needlework, if we think about it in a creative way, can open up wide windows into a whole variety of surprising histories.

AMERICAN QUILTS

Consider the history of American quilt making. A form of needlework that has different traditions among Native Americans, slave and black families, and early Americans, it is a practice passed on from one generation to the next, and that continues throughout the United States today, often with different generations of women in the family stitching a bride's quilt for her marriage bed. The politics of communal stitching of this nature lie in the practice of stitching and its design, the passing on of practical skills, the family bonds strengthened in the hours spent stitching together, the emotional symbolism of the quilt as a gift, and the significance of these textile family heirlooms as they passed down the matriarchal line.

Many of these ornate textiles are collected and preserved in the National Quilt Collection at the Smithsonian's National Museum of American History in Washington, DC. Exemplary among these is a quilt dating from the second quarter of the nineteenth century belonging to Susan Strong, who was among the pioneers to come to Richland County, Ohio. A notable feature of this blue and white quilt is its appliquéd and embroidered adaptation of the Great Seal of the United States that sits in the dead centre of the fabric. The US government has used this Great

Seal in order to authenticate documents since 1782, the year that the British American colonies won their independence and the United States of America was born. The appearance of this patriotic motif – a bald eagle with its wings spread – suggests a deep sense of national patriotism, and it is a common decorative design used on many quilts and other objects that survive from the nineteenth century. That this patriotic theme was stitched by a woman is perhaps remarkable, but it also signifies more broadly the way in which needlework of this sort evidences the spread of nationalism throughout the county in the decades after the 1776 Declaration of Independence.

This practice of quilting was strong among slaves and African-Americans, and was a traditional technique practised in African tribes. For these societies, quilts were a way of preserving family histories and events – literally stitching the rites of passage of births and marriages, of place and religion, into the design of the quilt. One such beautifully stitched and unique quilt was made during the years 1885–86 by the African-American female farmsteader Harriet Powers from Clarke County, Georgia. Harriet showed her quilt at the Athens Cotton Fair of 1886, where it caught the attention of the local artist Jennie Smith, who was struck by its originality. It depicted a series of biblical scenes, including Adam and Eve in the Garden of Eden, Cain killing Abel, the baptism of Christ, the Crucifixion, and the Last Supper. The quilt was a remarkable work of art, much valued by its maker, who only later sold it for the price of $5 because she had fallen on hard times.

MALE ANXIETIES

The practice of quilting played an important part in women's contribution to the household economy. During the Renaissance and beyond, however, male commentators often recommended the use of the needle in the home as an antidote to women's 'wayward minds'. In his 1631 volume, *The Needles Excellency*, John Taylor pronounced that women should 'use their tongues lesse and their needle more'. Yet the very art of needlework was itself a minefield for early modern male writers so concerned with policing female behaviour. While, on the one hand, needlework promoted chastity and confined young women within the house-hold, it was also feared that idle minds might stitch inappropriate things that either challenged the male social order, or otherwise filled women's heads with what were seen as romantic notions. What is more, through the public display of 'samplers' – pieces of embroidery worked in various stitches as a specimen of skill – the needle was transformed into a pen, offering an independent form of expression, which some men found threatening. Partic-ularly fine stitching, although clear proof of impressive artistic skill, was even vulnerable to criticism for being time-consuming and expensive – a form of conspicuous and morally suspect consumption. Needlework, therefore, could be dangerous.

LEARNING

Samplers had a complex purpose during the seventeenth and eighteenth centuries in Britain and America. 'Marking' samplers, as the process was known, taught girls basic embroidery tech-niques, combined with literacy and numeracy, skills which were also useful for labelling household linens with simple initials and numbers. More decorative pictorial samplers showcased higher levels of artistic technique and refinement, all of which were transferable skills for housewifery and the marriage market. Superb examples of samplers survive in museums around the world, displaying the techniques and uses associated with this most quotidian form of needlework. One of the earliest extant and highly accomplished and decorative examples held in the collections of the Victoria and Albert Museum dates from 1598 and was produced by Jane Bostocke. It is an example of cross stitch, back stitch and other more complicated stitches, to commemorate the birth of her cousin Alice Lee two years earlier.

Another beautiful example from the same collections, but dating from almost 200 years later, was produced by Mary Ann Body, aged nine. Stitched into it are the words 'Dear mother I am young and cannot show such work as I unto your goodness owe. Be pleased to smile on this my small endeavour. I'll strive to learn and be obedient ever.' Here the sampler, produced as a gift for Mary's mother, functioned as a form of learning which inculcated submissive modes of daughterly behaviour and reinforced social constraints on young girls. This example, therefore, is the opposite of needlework as a platform for subversive self-expression.

Katherine Parr (1512–48) Queen of England and Ireland, and sixth wife of Henry VIII. Known for her Protestant religious devotion, and as a Tudor woman writer. On Henry's death she married Sir Thomas Seymour (uncle of the boy king Edward VI), and became guardian of Princess Elizabeth.

TUDOR POLITICS

Yet it is as a form of self-expression that early modern needlework primarily achieved its significance and potency when it was allied with political and diplomatic ends. As a young girl, Princess Elizabeth, the future Queen Elizabeth I, embroidered New Year's gifts of calligraphic religious manuscripts for her deeply pious stepmother Katherine Parr. In 1544, when the young princess was just eight, she translated Marguerite de Navarre's

The Miroir or Glasse of the Synneful Soul, copying out the poems and prayers in her own hand to produce a manuscript book that she presented to her stepmother [see *fig. 12*]. The cover of the volume was intricately embroidered in blue silk with interlacing scroll work in gold and silver braid. It bore the queen's initials 'K. P.' on the front and carried the handwritten dedication

> From Assherige, the last daye of the yeare of our Lord God 1544... To our most noble and vertuous Quene Katherin, Elizabeth her humble daughter wisheth perpetuall felicitie and everlasting joye.

A second embroidered handwritten book was gifted by Princess Elizabeth to Katherine Parr in 1545, this time a compilation of the queen's own prayers and meditations entitled *Prayers of Queen Katherine Parr*, which was equally decoratively covered. Taken together these two precious needlework volumes not only illustrate the princess's proficiency with needle and thread, but also evidence her political adroitness at such a young age in attempting to align herself with her stepmother and represent her religious humanist learning in translating religious texts.

Mary, Queen of Scots was likewise an inveterate stitcher, and her embroidery was full of ciphered political messages and imagery which betrayed her political identity and ambition. A cushion given to the Duke of Norfolk (1536–72), who was executed for treason under Elizabeth I, depicted a hand pruning a vine and was accompanied by a Latin motto which translates as 'virtue flourishes by wounding'. The message was taken to be that Elizabeth was the barren stalk to be cut away so that Mary could flourish and grow, and the needlework was admissible as evidence at Norfolk's trial. Meanwhile, Bess of Hardwick (c.1527–1608), the Scottish queen's needlework companion during her time of house arrest, used needlework in the form of lavish iconographic tapestries as a mode of self-aggrandizement as she dressed her stately homes like Chatsworth with professionally embroidered depictions of scenes from classical texts.

THE ARMADA

If this use of needlework as a representation of political identity or allegiance has a scale, right at the far end of it are a series of tapestries made in the aftermath of the greatest national crisis of the Tudor era, and one of the gravest the British Isles has ever faced: the Spanish Armada. In 1588 England faced an invasion threat of unprecedented scale. The Catholic king of Spain Philip II plotted to invade England and seize the throne from the Protestant Elizabeth I. To do so he launched an invasion fleet unlike any that had ever been seen in northern European waters. More than 130 ships transported more than 30,000 men. Harried up the English Channel by the Royal Navy, and then scattered by a fireship attack and ferocious battle at Calais, the Armada fell apart and sailed to its own destruction in storms off Scotland and Ireland as it tried to limp home. The failure of the Spanish Armada – interpreted as a successful British naval campaign – was commemorated in needlework. Lord Howard of Effingham (1536–1624), the admiral of the English fleet, commissioned a noted Dutch artist and seascape painter, Hendrick Cornelisz Vroom (1566–1640), to design no fewer than ten *enormous* tapestries, each taller than fourteen feet high and twice as wide, that were then woven in Brussels by Francis Spierincx (1549/51–1630). 'Sumptuous' does these tapestries no justice at all. Each was focused on a grand scene of the campaign and around each border were further details including portraits of the key men. The images were made using gold and silver threads, created by wrapping fine wire around silk. They cost the equivalent of eighty-seven years' worth of wages for a workman in 1590.

Once complete, Howard kept the tapestries for himself but then sold them to the English king, James I, in 1616. Hung in the House of Lords in 1644 they went on to provide the backdrop to some of the most significant events in British history. The history of this needlework, therefore, is multilayered: it includes the event of the Armada itself, the tapestries' creation and then their subsequent life in the national gaze for centuries. During his reign James I brazenly hung them in the banqueting hall to receive the Spanish ambassador and, perhaps surprisingly given their clear associations with monarchy, Oliver Cromwell's administrators renamed them *The Story of 1588* and hung them in parliament during the Commonwealth of England (1649–60). For Cromwell and those who had stood by him at the execution of Charles I and who now led a commonwealth in a world dominated by monarchies, the common theme was of standing strong against hostile powers.

The history of the tapestries does not even end in 1834 when they were destroyed in a fire. Such a magnificent work of art in such a significant national location left an imprint on our historical consciousness which never vanished. A project to bring the tapestries back to life as paintings was begun in 2007 and finished in 2010. The paintings can now be seen in the Prince's Chamber in the House of Lords. Go and see them – for now that you know where to look you can appreciate the hidden history of embroidery disguised in oil and canvas.

1066

This sense of an individual piece of needlework having a history can be further explored through another piece of embroidery with similar links to national identity, monarchy and invasion: the Bayeux Tapestry. The story it tells is well known – that of the Norman Conquest of England in 1066 when William, Duke of Normandy embarked in a large invasion force, landed in Sussex and then defeated King Harold at the Battle of Hastings. That is the *story* of the tapestry, and it is told on the tapestry's front. Modern research, however, has begun to reveal the artefact's *own* history, and that is a story told on its reverse – by the knots on its back. This is one of the beauties of needlework as a historical source; you can reconstruct the creation of the object in minute detail and, in so doing, you can learn a great deal.

King Harold (1022-66) An eleventh-century king who ruled England for only ten months from 6 January 1066 until the Norman Conquest. Killed at the Battle of Hastings fighting the Norman invaders, he died as the last Anglo-Saxon king of England, but the jury is out on whether he was actually shot through the eye with an arrow.

The first thing that a study of the tapestry's back reveals is that it is not a tapestry at all, but an embroidery. A tapestry is woven on a loom whereas embroidery has a 'ground fabric' on which threads are sewn or embroidered to form a picture. From a close study of the techniques involved we also now know that the workers were probably professional embroiderers, all trained to a uniform level with certain minimum requirements of technical accuracy and the economic use of materials. Occasionally the level of skill varies in the depiction of a scene but the standard of workmanship does not. By decoding the order in which scenes were made it is also possible to see how significant forward planning was involved, which is suggestive of an experienced embroiderer overseeing the project and one or more teams working together to realize it.

Much like the Armada tapestries, the Bayeux Tapestry also acquired immense political and propaganda value for the tale that it told – a tale of a successful invasion of Britain by a people descended from Vikings; Napoleon, Himmler and Hitler all lusted after it. It has been stolen, damaged, hidden, discovered, moved, protected, hunted and displayed over centuries, all for what it shows and the way in which it was made.

This piece of needlework, therefore, has had the power to shake the foundations of nations, but another aspect of the beauty of needlework as a historical source is that you can also see in it the most personal, private and emotional of bonds. This is because one chapter in the history of needlework reveals the way samples of needlework could form the most touching links between desperate mothers forced to abandon their babies as a result of poverty, illness or family breakdown had driven them to their wits' end.

ABANDONED BABIES

Between 1741 and 1760 more than 4,000 babies were left at London's Foundling Hospital, which was set up in 1739 by philanthropist Thomas Coram (c.1668–1751) to care for babies at risk of abandonment. When leaving their babies at the hospital, mothers would cut a piece of fabric either from their own clothing or that of the baby to act as a kind of token, which was used by the hospital to identify the child. This was then attached to registration forms, and became part of the hospital records, bound into ledgers.

More poignantly, though, these tokens represent the moment of parting between mother and child, and when combined with the skeletal details in the hospital's biographical ledger, they send whispered echoes of these children down the centuries. A girl named Sarah Barber, for example (Foundling number 2,584), was admitted on 27 October 1756 and is identified by a fragment of an expensive flowered dress dating from about 1750.

She died five years later on 17 March 1761. Similarly, a bunch of four silk ribbons, coloured yellow, blue, green and pink, and tied in a knot, was found on an abandoned girl who became Foundling number 170 when she was admitted on 9 December 1743. The hospital named her Pamela Townley. She died in her third year of life on 1 September 1746. The power of these samples lies not only in their design aesthetic as an inspiration for embroiderers, but in what they tell us about the histories of abandoned children.

These fragments of fabric also form one of the largest collections of eighteenth-century cloth, and are a remarkable source for studying popular clothing patterns and fashions – which brings us to the interesting question of the history of comfort, and in particular, to the extraordinary history of the itch...

·11·
THE ITCH

The history of the itch is all about…
phlegm, penitence, infidelity, syphilis
and gunpowder.

A HISTORICAL MARKER

Have you ever felt that nagging, unprovoked tickle in a hard to reach spot and had the urge to scratch it? Have you ever been bitten by a mosquito, a flea or even bed bugs, or had lice, scabies or threadworms? As a child did you patiently wait while the calamine lotion was applied to your chicken pox spots and obey your parents to resist the temptation to scratch, and scratch and scratch? Or have you ever suffered from any kind of serious dermatological complaint – from eczema, contact dermatitis, urticaria, lichen planus, psoriasis, to syphilis, folliculitis and prurigo – and wanted to scratch at your skin until it was raw and bleeding? James's most haunting historical experience of itching occurred as a teenager in a rural hotel in northern France in the 1980s, where a nocturnal mosquito attack left him looking like the Elephant Man; Sam's itchiest memory comes from the early 1990s and an allergic reaction to chemicals in a Spanish swimming pool which left him hopping for hours, followed by weeks of infected nail-scrape wounds. It happened more than twenty-five years ago but he can remember it to this day. Such peculiar discomfort embeds itself easily in our memory and becomes a historical marker for our lives, but the itch also has its own unexpected history.

UNDERSTANDING THE ITCH

Although an itch is a subjective phenomenon and the symptoms and experience of it in history varied from individual to individual, there were concerted attempts to try to understand and treat it. The medical history of the itch has a long tradition prior to the nineteenth century when the field of dermatology emerged with its modern scientific approach to classification, diagnosis and treatment. While the itch is not easy to find in medical literature before this period – because it did not easily fit into the somatotopic form of medical classification whereby each and every area of the body has a point-to-point correspondence to a specific location on the central nervous system – it is mentioned in ancient, medieval and Renaissance medical manuals in relation to localized diseases or in sections on dermatoses. And what is extraordinary is the way in which the itch was conceptualized as relating to humoral imbalances in the human body.

Corpus Hippocraticum A compendium of ancient Greek medical texts that are connected with the physician Hippocrates, who is known as 'the father of medicine'. Diverse in content and style, it may have been produced by his students and followers.

One ancient Greek medical text, the *Corpus Hippocraticum*, which was compiled from the fifth century BCE, explained that 'leprosy, pruritus, scabies, lichen, vitiligo and alopecia arise from phlegm and are mere blemishes rather than diseases'. Here the itch was explained by humoral pathology – in other words, it was caused by an imbalance of the four different 'humours' of which men's and women's bodies were composed. In this case of itching skin an imbalance of phlegm carried the blame. Phlegm, however, was not the only culprit of the itch. Another entry blames yellow bile for the fire it represented. A serious case where 'serous fluids appeared in the skin. Having coalesced, they became warm and caused itching. Then they erupted like burn blisters caused by fire, and they seemed to smoulder underneath the skin.' The itch was also a way of diagnosing. Another ancient Greek medical text, *Coan Prenotions*, prognosticated that in consumptive patients an itch preceded by constipation boded ill, and that 'in all patients, itching will be followed by black stools, and vomiting'. This understanding of the itch caused by humoral imbalance did not go unchallenged, but nevertheless persisted throughout the Byzantine and medieval periods. The tenth-century Islamic writer 'Alī Ibn 'Abbās al-Majūsī (d.94) (Latinized as Haly Abbas) considered scabies and itching to arise from 'a mixture of salty phlegm with bilious blood'.

Such humoral-based theories of the cause of the itch led to particular methods of healing. One of the remedies for such imbalances was blood-letting, but by no means was this a treatment recommended by all, and one of the fiercest Renaissance critics was the Swiss-born physician and alchemist Paracelsus (1493–1541), who believed that diseases were related to chemical imbalance, and that remedies therefore required a knowledge of chemistry. He wrote 'Whoever aspires to cure and counsel' those afflicted by a skin disease he described creepily as 'the mange' must not use blood-letting, but rather other things, that is: the Arcanes.* Behold what blood-letting be in truth. It is no more than if someone has a scab on his scalp, and scratches it, and it bleeds in the morning, of what use is the bleeding? It is of no use at all, for soon another scab is in its place. Thus, blood-letting is nothing but the bleeding for tomorrow's scabs when a scab has been scratched.

TREATING THE ITCH

As well as such efforts to understand the itch, the centuries are littered with recipes, cures and salves to treat the symptoms of itching. Writing in the sixth century CE Alexander Trallianus recommended that those suffering from scabby, itchy heads should 'Crush rue and alum in honey and use them to anoint the shaven head. When the skin has peeled off, boiled leaves of the olive tree should be applied with honey as a poultice', while a medical recipe book dating from 1680 contains instructions to cure what is described as 'the itch infalable'. This cure, which includes saltpetre – a significant ingredient in gunpowder – and involves the patient standing undressed before a fire and their clothes being boiled, is a somewhat extreme example and was surely created by someone who knew the peculiar and personal torment of an incessant itch.

For the Itch Infalable
Put the 3[r]d part of an ounce of white mercury into a q[ua]rt of spring water with an ounce of salt peter & a small handful of ordinary salt let them boyle together gently an hower & a halfe and as it boyles put in more water to keep the same quantity let the party stand naked by the fire & dab in a rag

wheresoever you se any itch let it dry in & wear stil the same shirt boyle the shirt in an earthn pot that may be broke & break the bottle for tis poison.

There was certainly some increased pressure to cure the itch in this period because it was now considered life-threatening, and John Graunt's *Natural and Political Observations Made upon the Bills of Mortality* (1662) referred to the death of a Londoner in 1648 by 'itch', which took its place as a mortal threat along with lethargy, grief, lunacy, fright and fainting in the bath. One of the most sustained explorations of the itch was Thomas Spooner's *A Short Account of the Itch, Inveterate Itching Humours, Scabbiness and Leprosy* (1718), in which he opined that,

> The itch is a filthy Distemper, infesting the External Parts of the Body universally, but more particularly, the Joints, and between the Fingers, commonly with Pustulous Eruptions raised upon the Scarf-Skin by almost unavoidable scratching, occasioned thro' violent itching of the Parts; from these Pustulous Eruptions, or little Bladders, when broke, there issues a thin Crystalline Humour, which touching any other Part not yet infected, soon causes incessant itching, and upon Scratching, more Bladders to arise.

Prior to the nineteenth century, then, the itch was understood medically in very different ways from how it is understood by professional medics today and reveals generations of changing medical thought and practice. That thought process, moreover, had significant and numerous cultural implications.

COMFORT

The history of the itch, for example, is in one sense about the history of comfort. Consider an itch caused by clothing. Today an itch caused by clothing is a manifestation of unusual discomfort but that sense of what is expected or acceptable in terms of discomfort has its own history. Comfort – or more specifically comfort for the masses – is a surprisingly new idea. Before the Industrial Revolution, before mass access to comfortable material and mass production of that material into clothing, comfort was the preserve of the few; the itch the curse of the many. For centuries the most common fabric, for all classes, was wool, and linen the most popular fabric for undergarments. Cotton was rare but present; there is evidence that it was being cultivated in Pakistan and Egypt 3,000 years ago. Silk was the preserve of the Chinese until sometime around 1 CE when it started to move westwards along the trade routes that would become known as the Silk Roads. One thousand four hundred years later it was being cultivated in Europe. For all of that time, however, and for centuries to come, silk would still remain the preserve of the wealthy. In sixteenth-century Europe silk was an extravagant material used in courtly, military and church life, as recorded by the Lateran canon Tommaso Garzoni (1549–89):

> Is it not clear that silk adorns everything? Is it not silk that adorns the coaches, the carriages, the litters, the maritime gondolas, the horses of the Princes, with trappings, with outfits, with tassels, with fringes, with cords, with cushions, with cloths, and a thousand other beautiful things. Does not silk adorn the banners, the standards, the insignia, the halberds trimmed with brocaded velvet and fringes, the sheathed pikes, the bandoleers, the trumpets, the uniforms of t he soldiers at war? Does not silk adorn the umbrellas,

the canopies, the chasubles, the copes, the pictures, the palliums, the sandals, the cassocks, the dalmatics, the gloves, the maniples, the stoles, the burses, the veils for chalices, the lining of tabernacles, the cushions, the pulpits, and all other things of the Church?

In spite of its opulence, the extent to which there was a wider social dissemination of silk is evident. Giovan Andrea Corsuccio, author of *Il Vermicello dalla seta* (1581) (*The Little Silkworm*), claimed that 'anyone, vile as he may be' was dressed in silk 'so that even the charlatans, if they have no velvet cap or doublet, are not able to draw a crowd of listeners'. Part of the reason for this was the creation of new types of fabric, which were woven using only small quantities of silk and were therefore cheaper and more accessible. Extraordinary physical evidence of this spread of previously luxury materials is revealed in the collections of the London Foundling Hospital. The scraps of fabric that accompanied deserted children that are part of the registration records allow us to glimpse into the fabric history of a particular place and time. These scraps strongly suggest that affordable silk and cotton fabrics were accessible to the lower end of society.

FLEAS

Even for the elite, the removal of the itch was relative. Fleas and lice crawled and bit with little concern for the status of their victim [*see fig. 13*]. In 1664, Elizabeth Pepys, wife of the famed London diarist Samuel Pepys, chided her maid for not checking their bed for fleas, Pepys having woken fearing that he had been bitten in the night. In the end, as he writes, it turned out to be 'only the change of the weather from hot to cold, which, as I was two winters ago, do stop my pores, and so my blood tingles and itches all day all over my body'. Fascinating artwork survives that records this ever-present biting companion, two of the finest examples being the Parisian artist Nicolas Lancret's *A Girl in a Kitchen* and *Women Bathing*, both of which depict women, from opposite ends of the social scale, sharing the same activity of examining themselves for flea bites. One solution for the elite was an ingenious device known as a flea catcher. An intricate ivory flea catcher survives at Louth Museum in Lincolnshire. Measuring about seven centimetres in length, it was designed to be worn around the neck filled with blood, fat or sometimes jam or honey, which were thought to attract and then trap the fleas.

SELF-PUNISHMENT

All of these examples have considered the itch as a curse – something to be removed – but there is also a fascinating body of evidence for those who *welcomed* the itch for the simple fact that comfort could be controlled. The elective presence of the itch, therefore, became a means of self-expression: put on the silk shirt and you feel its smoothness soothe; but put on the *hair* shirt and you feel its coarseness irritate.

The wearing of clothes that deliberately itch has a long history. The cilice – the hair shirt – comes from the name Cilicia, a region of Asia Minor, from which first came a type of goat hair that was particularly rough and itchy and thus perfect for clothes worn by penitents seeking to inflict self-mortification, emulating the suffering of Christ. The evidence for this practice goes back to the second century and it took a variety of forms, and not always focused on an individual. In the late tenth century in the archdioceses of Mainz and Salzburg, public rituals of penitence on Ash Wednesday and Maundy Thursday involved the collective donning of hair shirts.

MORAL JUDGEMENT

For many the itch was more than a welcome or undesirable irritant but rather a sign of something seriously wrong, for it was also a common symptom of disfiguring, life-changing, even deadly diseases – amongst which was syphilis [*see fig. 14*]. The itch, therefore, could also be viewed in moral terms. One of the earliest reports of the spread of an epidemic of syphilis that swept Renaissance Europe was in a letter dated June 1495 by the Italian physician Niccolò Squillaci written on a diplomatic mission to the Spanish court.

> There are itching sensations, and an unpleasant pain in the joints; there is a rapidly increasing fever; the skin is inflamed with revolting scabs and is completely covered with swellings and tubercules, which are initially of a livid red color, and then become blacker... It most often begins with the private parts. I exhort you to provide some new remedy to remove this plague from the Italian people... Nothing could be more serious than this curse, this barbarian poison.

We now know that the 'barbarian poison' or disease of syphilis to which Squillaci's letter refers is spread through sexual activity.

William Hogarth, *A Harlot's Progress*, plate 5 (1731/32)

The connection between syphilis and immorality was particularly pronounced in the Victorian period, but also present in the eighteenth century. Take William Hogarth's engravings of *A Harlot's Progress* (1731 and 1732), which chart the life of Moll Knockabout who arrives in London from the country and embarks on a career as a prostitute. In plate 1, Moll is inspected by a pox-marked brothel keeper on her arrival in the capital, and by plate 5 of the series we are presented with a syphilitic, immoral Moll in the throes of dying.

William Hogarth (1697-1764) An eighteenth-century English painter and engraver. He worked in a range of mediums from formal portraiture to a series of morality satires such as *A Harlot's Progress*, *A Rake's Progress*, and *Marriage à la Mode*.

The syphilitic itch, as a physical and crucially visible result of the immoral behaviour that may have been the disease's cause, therefore became a sort of moral signpost, an opportunity for others to judge: that person is scratching an itch; that person is diseased; that person is immoral, went the thinking.

INFIDELITY

Another common way of associating the itch with sin was through infidelity. One of the most heinous of sins – as far as most world religions were concerned – was infidelity. Throughout history in many parts of the world fidelity within marriage was a bedrock of society, central to patriarchal systems which constrained sexuality. In the second half of the twentieth century the desire to stray within marriage became known as an 'itch', as portrayed in the 1955 American romantic comedy starring Marilyn Monroe, *The Seven Year Itch*, which itself was based on a play of the same name by George Axelrod. Both tell the tale of declining interest in marriage after being married for just a short number of years, the phrase stemming originally from a long-term skin complaint. The story of those who, like Monroe's character, succumbed to scratching that itch of sexual frustration and committing adultery has an important history.

In sixteenth-century England the ecclesiastical courts policed sexual activity outside of marriage, and men and women who were caught committing adultery were publicly shamed, with sexual offenders even being forced to wear placards around their necks on a Sunday outside the parish church, which detailed their deviancy. The wearing of such shameful signs hung round the neck was often accompanied by a formal penance, as in the example of Ursula Shepherd in 1589 whose husband brought a case against her for adultery; the judge awarded a separation, although did not allow either to remarry, but sentenced Ursula to public penance. Her words are recorded by the courts:

> Good people I do here before God and you all confess that whereas I have been a married wife unto Henry Shepherd for the space of twenty years I forgetting god and my duty unto my husband have committed adultery and played the harlot with one Richard Mathewe my servant now of late time. And for the same I am by order of law divorced [i.e. separated to live apart] from my husband and enjoined to do this my penance. And therefore I desire you all to take example by me and do promise hereafter to lead a chaste life and this her penance is to be done upon Sunday next following in the parish church of St Mary Woolchurch in London in service time.

This was shame indeed and experienced in the most public of ways, and it raises the interesting question of how such adultery was discovered – which in turn raises the very important question of the history of holes...

·12·

HOLES

—

The history of holes is all about... sex, spying
and privacy, losing things and lasers.

The unexpected history of holes is all about sex – but not in the way that you might think. It's about the history of privacy, of voyeurism or eavesdropping; it's about the fact that premodern urban dwellings had walls so thin that neighbours living cheek by jowl were able to spy on one another through holes in the walls, to report indiscretions, illicit sexual acts and carnal appetites that crossed the line of what the Church or even local community deemed appropriate. The twentieth-century world of fascism and 'Big Brother is watching you' is not as far as you might think from the tentacles of the pre-Reformation church and the European intelligence states that burgeoned from the Renaissance onwards.

SPYING

In England in 1666, Mary Babb and her brother-in-law Richard Babb were prosecuted for adultery and incest in the consistory court of York, the Church being responsible for the policing of illicit sexual and moral behaviour. Sex outside marriage was strictly forbidden at this time and sexual relationships between close kin was likewise prohibited. Prosecution by the Church courts normally included some form of penance that involved public shaming. This could include standing outside church on a Sunday, clothed in a white sheet on which was written your offence, such as adultery. One such example survives in the Colchester Borough Records in Essex Record Office of a placard worn by one 'Briant Hedd for adulterye with Alyce Samforde wydowe' dated 1584. This ritualized form of public humiliation within the community worked to enforce moral codes of conduct.

The evidence given against the incestuous pair Mary and Richard Babb came from one Elizabeth Tullett, a neighbour. In her deposition she explained that, 'having only a wall betwixt them', how she 'hath several times seen and observed very uncivil passages betwixt them'. On one occasion, spying through a hole in the wall, she observed 'the said Mary Babb pass by the said hole having her clothes and smock pulled up to her breast none being in the house with her' but Richard Babb. On another occasion she describes the pair 'in the very act of adultery or incest in a very beastly manner she the said Mary holding up her hinder parts and having her clothes and smock pulled up above her loins and he thrusting at her behind nine times.' Holes here are not simply orifices, but cracks, slits or crevices through which we can spy and observe. The story continues that the eavesdropper, Elizabeth Tullett, was joined by two others, Mr and Mrs Richard Vintin, who also witnessed the lewd act. Incensed by what they saw, they did 'hastily go into the house' hoping to catch the couple in the act, but upon hearing their imminent arrival Mary and Richard Babb dressed themselves, though when accused of incestuous indiscretions Richard looked 'very pale and shameful' and said nothing.

PRIEST HOLES

Holes also made good historical hiding places for objects or even people. In the aftermath of Queen Elizabeth I's excommunication by Pope Pius V in 1570, the toleration and acceptance of English Catholics was replaced by much harsher measures to fine and imprison known Catholics who obdurately refused to attend the Anglican Church. This was coupled with attempts to capture, interrogate and execute Jesuit priests who were sent to England in increasing numbers to cater to the spiritual needs of Catholics, who were alienated by the kind of Christianity now preached in their local parish churches. Priests were essential to the practical aspects of Catholicism as intercessors with God and they were central to administering the sacraments including the Eucharist during mass. In late Elizabethan England, then, priests were vital in sustaining and catering for Catholics whose religion was formally banned. Driven underground, recusant Catholic practice was centred on the household, and there existed a clandestine Catholic community network (often relying on women who travelled under the radar) which sheltered priests catering for their flocks.

It is in this context that we see the development of priest's holes, hiding spaces built into primarily Catholic houses designed to conceal priests from hunters such as Richard

Recusant Individuals in the sixteenth and seventeenth century in England, Wales and Ireland, who refused to attend Anglican church services. Under Elizabeth I, recusancy laws were passed against English Catholics who publicly held to their beliefs, with punishments including fines, confiscation of property and imprisonment.

Topcliffe who apocryphally travelled with a portable rack for extracting confessions from his victims. Throughout the last decades of the sixteenth century Catholic priests were pursued, hunted down and tortured to betray the networks that spread from continental Europe as tentacles into the counties of England. Over this period, there was a spate of building activity to construct 'holes' or 'hides' in which priests on the run might shelter from the authorities. These constructions, built into chimney pieces, cupboards or bedrooms, ranged from complex systems of interconnected hides to simple cubbyholes in stairways and passages. Adapting an existing feature of a house – a chimney, a space under the floorboards or a gable end – the hide-maker would build a hidden entrance that would prevent it from being detected by the searchers, those representatives of the state who searched out Catholic priests and their would-be harbourers.

One of the best-known specialist builders of priest's holes was Nicholas Owen (1562–1606), an Oxfordshire recusant who was trained as a carpenter and joiner and known affectionately as 'Little John' because of his trade. It was these woodworking skills that were put to such great use in Elizabethan England in building intricate hiding places for Catholic priests in domestic homes, and drew him the esteem of English Catholics. Owen plied this secretive trade in service of the Catholic mission to cater for the spiritual needs of a beleaguered minority for over eighteen years, and worked in cramped and claustrophobic conditions mainly in the dead of night to avoid being detected by the authorities. John Gerard in his *Narrative of the Gunpowder Plot*, probably produced shortly after his appointment as English confessor at St Peter's, Rome in early 1607, wrote that

his chief employment was in making of secret places to hide
Priests and Church stuff in from the fury of searches; in which

kind he was so skilful both to devise and frame the places in the best manner, and his help therein desired in so many places, that I verily think no man can be said to have done more good of all those that laboured in the English vineyard. For, first, he was the immediate occasion of saving the lives of many hundreds of persons…

Owen was noted for his complex hiding systems, often designed with a bolt-hole or hatch to allow the occupants a means of escape. He is thought to have built the 'cat-walk' at Burghwallis Hall in south Yorkshire, which involved a series of hides linked together by an escape passage. Owen was arrested in the aftermath of the Gunpowder Plot in January 1606, and brutally tortured to betray secrets about his fellow Catholics. He died in agony without divulging any information, his guts ripped open by a knife, and according to the priest John Gerard 'his bowels gushed out together with his life'.

LASER SCANNERS

House historians are pioneering new techniques to help us find and understand these hidden spaces. At Coughton Court, a mansion in Warwickshire and home to the Throckmortons, a powerful Catholic family in the Tudor period, 3D laser scanners have been used to map a priest's hole in the tower of the gatehouse that was first discovered in the 1850s [*see fig. 15*]. The scans revealed how the priest's hole was designed as a 'double-blind' – essentially a priest's hole within a priest's hole – the purpose of which was to fool searchers into thinking that they had found the priest's hole they suspected to exist, but that it was empty. Such innovative historical research is ideally suited to the study of priest's holes in historic houses. A number of examples of priest holes still exist in houses around England today, but they are, by definition, difficult to access even if you know where they are. Scans like these, then, allow visitors to visualize and understand the hidden spaces in a building. It is a wonderful example of technology enhancing our understanding of history.

Gunpowder Plot A failed attempt by English Catholics led by Robert Catesby to blow up the Houses of Parliament and assassinate King James VI and I of England and Scotland in November 1605. Guy Fawkes was in charge of the explosives, and the foiling of the plot is celebrated each 5 November by burning an effigy of him on a bonfire.

These hiding places were not simply for concealing people on the run, but also clandestine books and papers. Northamptonshire gentleman and Catholic recusant Sir Thomas Tresham intended to preserve his papers securely, a plan carried out by his daughter, presumably in the aftermath of the 1605 Gunpowder Plot, when the papers were 'bound up in a lynnen cloth [and] sealed up with hard waxe', and then walled up in a closet that stewards' accounts record having been built in 1596. These papers were only discovered centuries later in 1828 when a workman, according to the Historical Manuscripts Commission, pulled down 'a very thick partition wall, in the passage leading from the Great Hall', revealing 'a very large recess or closet, in the centre of which was deposited an enormous bundle'. The building of secret architectural spaces and the walling in of clandestine Catholic books and papers again reinforces the strong link between holes, secrecy and religious belief.

HOARDS

In the hazardous early medieval world it was also common practice to hide things such as personal goods, treasure, loot and coins by burying them in holes in the ground for safekeeping and later retrieval. Violent times led to drastic measures to keep things safe. Think of holes in the ground as the early medieval equivalent of banks, safes or even a shoebox under the bed. These 'hoards' as they are known, along with grave goods – which stem from the medieval practice of burying items and possessions with the deceased – are among the most valuable sources that we have for early societies where written evidence is often limited, patchy and hard to interpret.

One of the finest surviving examples is the Staffordshire Hoard, a dazzling collection of Anglo-Saxon metalwork and silverwork numbering around 3,500 items, which is now owned jointly by Birmingham Museum and Art Gallery and the Potteries Museum and Art Gallery who purchased it for £3.285 million. Discovered in 2009 in a field near the village of Hammerwich in Staffordshire it is a spectacular haul of military paraphernalia and equipment, including helmets and swords of very high-quality workmanship dating from the seventh century. Cumulatively these kinds of finds buried in holes in the ground shed significant light on early medieval societies, their customs and organization, wealth, beliefs and religions, warfare and weapons, as well as family and everyday life.

ACCIDENTAL LOSS

But holes can also be about loss – about things falling out of holes in pockets or bags. The history of this is very important because it leads to subsequent chance discoveries. If, for example, a monk wandering through the fields of King Alfred's Wessex in the ninth century CE had noticed the split in the seam of his pocket or the rat-gnawed hole at the bottom corner of his bag, we would probably not know about the Alfred Jewel, the most important piece of surviving Anglo-Saxon enamelling and gold-smithing known to exist [*see fig. 16*]. It was discovered in 1693 in a deer park in Somerset just three and a half miles from the Isle of Athelney where King Alfred founded a monastery and, quite remarkably, is engraved with the words 'aelfred mec heht gewyrcan', translated as 'Alfred ordered me made'. Believed to be a decorative end to a pointing stick which would have been used to follow words when reading a book, it is possible that it is one of several 'aestels' – staffs – which we know from a written source were sent by Alfred to each bishopric in the kingdom along with his translation of Pope Gregory's book *Pastoral Care*. In the preface of the book he wrote 'And I will send a copy to every bishop's see in my kingdom, and in each book there is an aestel of 50 mancusses and I command, in God's name, that no man take the staff from the book, nor the book from the church'.

This chance discovery has transformed our understanding and appreciation of Anglo-Saxon art. Did it fall out of a hole in a bag or pocket? Our understanding of history is directly shaped by the existence of such holes, themselves usually created by the passing of time. This is the passing of time creating opportunities to influence our understanding of the passing of time – it is history *making* history.

In fact the chance discovery of coins, many of which would have fallen through holes in purses or pockets, has dramatically altered the way that we understand the past, either through the specifics of the information given on the coin – such as the name of an emperor or monarch – or, most commonly, by providing a date to a historical site or particular archaeological layer within that site. One of the most spectacular such chance discoveries is again, curiously, from the Anglo-Saxon period. In 2001 near a footpath on the banks of the River Ivel near Biggleswade in Bedfordshire, a metal-detector enthusiast discovered an immaculate gold coin from the reign of Coenwulf, King of Mercia. This single, unluckily dropped but luckily discovered gold coin is one of the most important Anglo-Saxon archaeological discoveries of the last century.

Coenwulf of Mercia Ruler of the Anglo-Saxon kingdom of Mercia from 796 to 821. His reign was marked by an extraordinary struggle for power between rival rulers. He was challenged in Kent by Eadberht Præn, which led to Coenwulf invading to retake his kingdom, during which period Eadberht was captured, blinded, and had his hands cut off.

The coin is in such perfect condition that it must have been lost within a very short time of being struck, and is one of only eight gold coins to have survived from the 500-year period 700–1250. It is also the earliest of those coins which we are certain was intended for use as regular currency. Very little is known about Coenwulf but he was without doubt a significant figure in the unification of England. He stole the throne from the son of King Offa, invaded East Anglia and Kent and created an empire which stretched from the south coast to the Welsh borders and the Humber. He is shown on the coin as a Roman emperor and the coin bears the Latin inscription *DE VICO LVNDONIAE* (from the trading place of London). This conscious aligning of an Anglo-Saxon king with the Romans – who had abandoned Britain three centuries before – is interesting and important. It shows a keen awareness of history by the Anglo-Saxons and mirrors the behaviour (and currency) of Charlemagne, the monarch and subsequent emperor of the Romans who united most of Western Europe at the same time that Coenwulf united southern Britain. This particular coin, then, speaks of eighth-century continental rivalry and ambition as much as it does of the Anglo-Saxon perception of, and admiration for, their ancient past.

The use and study of such chance-discovered coins by historians itself has a history and can be traced back to the late 1940s when a project in Germany, Funmünzen der Antike (Coin Finds of the Classical Period), registered every ancient coin found within Germany, a method that was soon mirrored elsewhere as numismatics developed as a subfield of archaeology.

BOOKWORMS

Holes, however, are also about loss in another sense: they are about devouring words, the holes made in documents and books by insects and mice. The history of holes, therefore, returns us once again to the very stuff of history – to documents and archives. Bookworms – nowadays a synonym for a bibliophile or a particularly precocious child who is an avid reader – is a fairly capacious term to describe all manner of insects that do, actually, eat books. It includes moths that attack cloth bindings as well as beetles that feast on leather-bound books, and the paper louse which munches on moulds and other organic matter found on poorly treated materials. Medieval books are often found to contain worm holes, and are sometimes destructively riddled with bookworm throughout. The worm having hatched in the wooden boards of the binding emerges and then chews its way through the pages, leaving havoc in its wake. Mice and damp conditions were similarly a problem for maintaining documents, as the Devon yeoman farmer Robert Furze (c.1535–93) described when writing about the plight of the family papers that on the death of his father-in-law, Edmond Roland, passed to his widow Joan. The writings it appears had rather a tragic history: they were stolen by Joan's new husband, and left in a parlous state in a coffer with no lock, which Furze wrote 'in truthe did gretely spoyle the wrytynge', some being eaten by mice, others lost.

Medieval manuscripts produced on parchment – which was made out of the skins of animals such as calves, sheep or goats – frequently contain holes, sometimes caused by cuts produced during the preparation process, when the flesh and hair was torn away from the skin producing a puncture. Preparing parchment as a surface for writing or binding was a delicate and skilful task. Medieval scribes were used to dealing with holes, and tended to merely write around them, or turn them into a decorative feature. An early ninth-century manuscript from eastern France contains a 'through-view' hole, which allows the reader to peer through to the next page to view an animal-head initial, which introduces a dragon into the story [*see fig. 17*]. In other examples scribes or owners attempted to repair holes, either by sewing tears, or in the case of a group of fourteenth-century Swedish nuns they used purple and red thread to embroider over a hole in a religious manuscript in their care.

The history of holes, then, is also all about wear and tear, repair and recycling; holes are about mending and making do, from the darning of socks and the patching of clothes to the ingenious medieval techniques of repairing manuscripts with careful embroidering [*see fig. 18*].

ABUSE

This history of making do and mending transports us to the Magdalene Laundries (also known as the Magdalene Asylums) of eighteenth- to late twentieth-century Ireland, which have been depicted in Peter Mullan's haunting film *The Magdalene Sisters* (2002). The laundries were set up and run by Catholic orders to house 'fallen women', and an estimated 30,000 women went through the doors of these barbaric institutions that confined, controlled and disciplined their inmates who were kept separated from society 'for their own good'. Conditions within these laundries were abominable, and there are widespread reports of mental, sexual and physical abuse. The women were beaten, treated as slaves, denied family contact, even in some instances denied their names, being referred to simply by numbers. The sheer scale of the abuse and the momentum that its uncovering generated, all of which was documented with historical testimony from hundreds of women, forced the Irish state to issue a formal apology in 2013. The Irish prime minister Enda Kenny described the laundries as 'the nation's shame'. Among the menial tasks undertaken by these poor young women was the mending and repairing of holes in bedding to the extent that, for some, the learning and practice of mending linen actually replaced their formal education. This story of incarceration and the endless task of mending the holes in bed sheets brings us to the important question of the history of beds...

·13·

THE BED

---

*The history of beds is all about... portals to
and from this life, fishmongers, privacy,
historical education and empires.*

FIRST WORLD WAR

One of the most striking, and historically fascinating, series of images created by the horrors of mass combat in the First World War is of photographs taken in hospitals in the aftermath of battle. Functional beds, steel-framed and sparse, are set out as if on parade, stationed exactly at right angles to walls, with immaculate pressed sheets and parallel to each other in military rows. They are neat, neat, *neat*: in this period the appearance of bedding was a measure of clinical competence; it was one of the ways in which the quality of nursing was judged. Those beds in the photos which are inhabited contain men who are often unconscious, sometimes rendered slack-jawed by opiates and occasionally heart-breakingly cheery in defiance of their broken or missing limbs, the burns and scalds in their skin, the holes and rips in their flesh.

Look more closely, however, and you will often see that these men are convalescing or dying in unusual historical buildings. Is that a stained-glass window behind the man with his head wrapped in bandages? Is that a medieval timber frame holding up that ceiling? Is that... is that really a... *Rubens*... behind the man with his leg in a cast?

With the war in full flow from the summer of 1914 onwards, existing medical facilities were quickly overwhelmed. Such was the demand for beds that many private residences were pressed into military service to serve as auxiliary hospitals. They included country houses, town halls, Oxbridge colleges, churches, castles – even royal palaces. After the Battle of the Somme, Princess Louise (1838–1939), the sixth child of Queen Victoria and Prince Albert, turned over her apartments in Kensington Palace to hospitalize injured soldiers. Accounts of wounded soldiers in this period are, unsurprisingly, full of their impressions of such buildings. Their hospital bed was a vantage

Great Dixter, Northiam, East Sussex, where a room in this Arts & Crafts house with its celebrated gardens was converted into a hospital ward during the First World War

point from which they could engage with British history, in a way in which many of them would never have experienced before.

One such auxiliary hospital, which gave men a glimpse into a privileged and previously hidden British history, was the hall of the Worshipful Company of Fishmongers in the City of London, the home of one of the oldest of London's twelve ancient livery companies. The company has existed since at least the thirteenth century. In 1914 the Great Hall, with gilded ceiling and walls, was divided by wooden partitions to form cubicles, each containing two beds. Before the war access to this building was strictly controlled, but by the end of the war 800 patients had been treated there and more than 250 operations performed in the makeshift operating theatre. In November 1914 the king and queen even came to visit.

For the men in auxiliary hospitals like this, the collision between their contemporary and historical worlds was a significant part of their lives, experienced either as the surroundings for their recovery or as the stage for their death, and here the bed has another fascinating history, because the bed across time has performed different functions other than simply being the place where one slept. In particular it was often connected to the family lifecycle in the form of the birthing bed, the sickbed and the deathbed. It was the portal into the world, connected to the arrival of new births, as well as the exit point from which people departed this life. Thus the bed, which is so often seen as innately private – often connected with marriage, the conjugal bed and sexual intimacies – was, in fact, a quasi-public space that could be both communal and sociable.

THE DEATHBED

The deathbed in particular was a communal space, functioning as a stage for departing the world, and throughout history there has been much ritual and focus on this key rite of passage. Even today, in this age of medically managed deaths, families gather around the bedside of loved ones in order to comfort them during their final hours. We have both attended bedside vigils and taken part in the ritual of saying goodbye to relatives and loved ones, and our experience has been shared by many in history. The deathbed across the centuries has been an intimate site of family life in the pre- and post-Reformation worlds. In many ways, people living in premodern societies were much better equipped psychologically for dying and preparing for death: religious belief in the afterlife, the ubiquity of death, as well as the rituals that accompanied it, meant that people were more comfortable with mortality.

The deathbed can also give people power and a voice and in many ways is a shared spectacle that is life-affirming and sustaining to those left behind. One of the most remarkable and moving accounts of a deathbed scene is that of the young Elizabethan wife Katherine Stubbes who, in 1590, died at the age of nineteen. Her death was described by her husband Philip in a small pamphlet entitled *A Chrystal Glasse for Christian Women*, first published in 1592, and republished many times thereafter due to its huge popularity. The little volume gave an account of the life and 'godly' – in other words, deeply pious – death of Katherine, and was published to glorify God and so that her example could act as a mirror (hence the title 'glasse') of woman-hood. In other words, it was a work that demonstrated how to be a good Puritan woman and was part of a tradition of similar 'conduct' literature.

Stubbes began by describing his wife's good parentage and

her marriage at the age of fifteen, which was far from typical for the period with most marrying in their twenties. To Puritan eyes she was, in many ways, the consummate wife: godly, obedient, silent and zealous; she was always reading religious works or praying; she never left the house when her husband was away; she was reserved and restrained in diet and dress; and her demeanour towards her husband was deferential and subordinate. And yet in what follows she was anything but a timid little mouse.

A large part of the text deals with her preparation for death, and her final dying moments upon her deathbed. She prophesies her own death after giving birth to their son, but recovers after childbirth, only for God to visit her with a sickness that lasted six weeks when she failed to sleep for more than an hour at a time. Nonetheless, she dealt with her ordeal with patience, never once questioning God. Her final deathbed scene is an extraordinary set-piece of Puritan theatricality.

The pamphlet provides a lengthy description of her illness and death, accompanied by a heavy dose of Puritan teaching. The main act is a confession of her faith, interpreted as the spirit of God speaking through her, which deals with a range of elements of Puritan doctrine punctuated throughout by the refrain 'I believe'. The proclamation of faith is a veritable roll call of godly thought, including rejection of good works as salvation and purgatory, and a belief in predestination and justification by faith alone.

On finishing this catechistic catalogue Katherine fights the Devil, disputing his words of temptation:

She had no sooner made an end of this most heavenly confession of her faith, but Satan was ready to bid her the combat, whom she mightily repulsed and vanquished by the power of our Lord Jesus on whom she constantly believed.

And whereas before she looked with a sweet, lovely and amiable countenance, red as the rose, and most beautiful to behold, now upon a sudden she bent her browes, she frowned, and looked as it were with an angry, stern, austere countenance, as though she saw some filthy, some ugly and displeasant thing, she burst forth in these speeches following, pronouncing her words scornfully and disdainfully, in contempt of him who she spake to.

Satan is then banished by Christ, and in the final moments of dying she is filled with sweet smiling laughter at having beaten off the Devil. The booklet ends praising her example, made all the more impressive because of her tender years: 'The lord giue vs grace to folow her good example'. Katherine's experience shows that the deathbed could accord women, normally marginalized from Church matters, a significant degree of spiritual potency.

TRANSFERENCE OF POWER

In the political life of nations and families too, the deathbed was extremely important, as the death of a monarch or head of a family signalled the passing of the crown, lands or power to the successor or heir apparent. Beds were therefore as much about the transfer of power as their image was a prompt for national mourning.

One of the most striking images from British history of such a crucial moment, when the fate of the nation could turn one way or another, can be seen in a late sixteenth-century painting by an unnamed artist hanging in the National Portrait Gallery entitled *King Edward VI and the Pope*, which depicts the deathbed of that most turbulent and violent of Tudor monarchs Henry VIII. Possibly commissioned during the reign of his daughter, Elizabeth I, it portrays Henry propped up in the royal bed, curtains drawn back, pointing to his successor who sits at his side, his son the boy king Edward VI (1537–53), who went on to rule for just six years after Henry's death.

The young prince is surrounded by members of Henry's council including his uncle Edward Seymour, Protector, Lord Somerset; John Dudley, Duke of Northumberland; and Thomas Cranmer, Archbishop of Canterbury. Outside the window in the top right-hand corner are scenes of iconoclasm, the wilful destruction of holy images, and below Edward at the bottom of the portrait is the pope, slumped over, crushed by 'the worde of the Lord'. The painting, therefore, is a heavy-handed example of royal propaganda, perhaps dating from after 1570 – dendro-chronological dating of the wooden panel on which it is painted dates it to a tree felled between 1574 and 1590 – when the Prot-estant Elizabeth I was excommunicated by Pope Pius V's papal bull *Regnans in Excelsis*, which effectively freed English citizens from loyalty to the queen. The importance here iconographically for British history is that Henry VIII separated from the Church of Rome, and his son Edward was brought up as a Protestant and as such took the country down a particular national religious path which Elizabeth proudly continued.

LUXURY BEDS

The bed depicted in this portrait was a truly grand affair, a lavish four-poster with carvings, canopy and curtains, and richly decorated sheets. Beds themselves came in all shapes and sizes, ranging from the kinds of elegant pieces of furniture that adorned the bedchambers of the high and mighty to more modest arrangements, which might simply be an improvised straw pallet covered with a blanket. Writing in 1577, the Elizabethan traveller and writer William Harrison (1534–93) described the 'delicacy' of contemporary furniture in houses, which included 'joined beds with tapestry and silk hangings', and explained that this was a departure from the past:

> our fathers, yea and we ourselves also, have lain full oft upon straw pallets, on rough mats covered only with a sheet, under coverlets made of dagswain or hopharlots... and a good round log under their heads instead of a bolster or pillow... Pillows (said they) were thought meet only for women in childbed. As for servants, if they had any sheet above them, it was well, for seldom had they any under their bodies to keep them from the pricking straws that ran oft through the canvas of the pallet and rased their hardened hides.

THE GREAT BED OF WARE

The four-poster bed was always a statement of luxury and status. One of the most magnificent examples of this kind of bed-bling is the Victoria and Albert Museum's amazing Great Bed of Ware [*see fig. 19*], a bed so famous in its day that William Shakespeare referred to it in his play *Twelfth Night*, first performed in 1601, and it was also mentioned by his contemporary playwright Ben Jonson (1572–1637). This bed was made around 1590 by the

Hertfordshire carpenter Jonas Fosbrooke as a talking piece, a 'show bed' commissioned for the White Hart Inn, one of the great inns in the town of Ware in Hertfordshire, an easy day's journey of twenty-two miles from London. It then made its way to a series of four other inns in Ware – the George, the Crown, the Bull and the Saracen's Head – before being sold in 1870 to Henry Teale, who purchased it as a tourist attraction for Rye House, Hoddesdon. The bed is famous not only for its unusually large size (it measures an impressive 3.38m long, 3.26m wide and 2.67m high, large enough to accommodate three or four couples!), but also for the intricate wood carvings that decorate it, figures carrying baskets of fruit, representing fertility, as well as architectural scenes with swans. The bed also bears the signs of those who slept in it before it became a museum piece, and discernible on the bedposts and headboards are the signatures and seals of visitors keen to leave their mark on this grand piece of furniture.

CAMPAIGN BEDS

The Great Bed of Ware occupies one end of a scale of beds, organized in terms of their portability, but the other end of that scale, that of temporary 'camp' beds, has its own important and fascinating history. The camp bed – a folding, portable bed – is so called because it is an abbreviation of the word 'campaign'; it is a type of bed that was invented for military use and therefore has a significant history related to both war and empire.

Throughout the eighteenth and nineteenth centuries portable furniture was a key characteristic of European armies. It was believed that standards of comfort for officers serving abroad should approximate those at home, and so travelling with the accoutrements of domestic life became both an important marker of social status and a symbol of empire. Because of this the finest minds in furniture design, including Thomas Chippendale (1718–79) and George Hepplewhite (1727–86), as well as countless ingenious inventors seeking to make a fortune, committed themselves to designing furniture that could be easily carried and assembled without tools.

> **Thomas Chippendale (1718-79)** A Yorkshire-bred cabinet maker and designer, who was born into a family of carpenters. In 1754 he published a highly successful pattern book of 160 engravings of furniture designs, *The Gentleman and Cabinet-Maker's Director*. He became one of the preeminent cabinet makers of the eighteenth century.

Armies traipsed across deserts, mountain ranges and jungles, the desire to carry domestic baggage bloating their size to almost unimaginable proportions. A surviving receipt for a single British officer preparing to travel to Flanders in 1793–5 to fight the revolutionary French included 49 separate items of campaign furniture. It was reported in *The Times* of 2 February 1858 that the baggage of General Sir Colin Campbell (1792–1863), Commander-in-Chief of India, 'extended for eighteen miles, when he came down from Lucknow' – that's almost the distance from Dover to Calais. So popular did this furniture become that it began to be used domestically – for picnics, camping or days out at sporting events and also, in times of peace, for travel or exploration. All types of furniture were made, from chests of drawers to enormous dining tables and bookcases which, with a push here and a fold there, would collapse flat to be eminently portable.

NAPOLEON'S BED

One of the most common types of campaign furniture was the bed, and one of the finest surviving examples of a historical campaign bed belonged to none other than Napoleon.

It is a portable iron bed, made by a locksmith, Marie-Jean Desouches (1764–1828), who described himself as *'serrurier du garde-meuble de S.M. l'Empereur et Roi'* – or 'wardrobe locksmith to HM the Emperor and King'. An ingenious iron frame folding along both its width and length, and held together with hinges and brass rings, allowed the bed to be swiftly assembled and disassembled while retaining impressive stability, and also created a gilt-knobbed frame for a canopy suitable for an emperor and king who once ruled half of Europe and owned forty-seven imperial palaces.

Not only did Napoleon take such a bed on his campaigns, but also, when his empire turned to dust and he was exiled to Saint Helena, a tiny barren rock in the middle of the southern Atlantic Ocean, he took it with him, and it was upon his camp bed that he slept from 15 October 1815 until he died almost exactly six years later, on 5 October 1821, also on the bed. For all of the titles, ermine-lined robes, palaces and treasures that Napoleon acquired in his extraordinary life, his bed is a reminder that he was a soldier to the very end, that his exile was but a temporary chapter that would soon pass. Interestingly the Duke of Wellington (1769–1852), another lifelong soldier and Napoleon's nemesis who defeated him at Waterloo, also spent the last few years of his life sleeping in his campaign bed and, like Napoleon, he also died in it. In a curious way, for both Napoleon and Wellington, their 'temporary' beds thus became a permanent fixture in their lives and they have also become a permanent fixture in history because both beds survive – Napoleon's at Longwood House in Saint Helena and Wellington's at Walmer Castle in Kent.

THE BOER WAR

A key moment in this history of the portable bed is the Boer War of 1899–1902. The war was fought in South Africa between the British and the Boer states, the South African Republic and the Orange Free State. The war was characterized by surprise attacks, rapid troop movements and guerrilla tactics, and the British soon realized that their army in the field was woefully cumbersome. In 1903, Secretary of State for War H. O. Arnold-Forster (1855–1909) declared, 'The British Army is a social institution prepared for every emergency except that of war.' In this new age of the motorcar and motorbike, soldiers travelling with huge quantities of belongings and furniture became a thing of the past. Military beds became purely functional, a place to snatch sleep – which raises the interesting question of the history of what beds were actually used for in the past.

For much of the premodern period, beds were, to our eyes, surprisingly public places because past sleeping practices were notably different from today's. It was common for wives to sleep with female servants when their husbands were away, and it was considered completely normal for two male servants to share a bed as 'bedfellows'. Sleeping, after all, was a sociable activity for many centuries, and the bed was not simply a place for sleeping alone or with a spouse, nor was it simply for sex.

SAMUEL PEPYS

Indeed, for the seventeenth-century philanderer and diarist Samuel Pepys (1633–1703), the bed was for anything *but* sex. Pepys's numerous sexual assignations were in taverns, alleyways and corridors.

His diaries are fascinating for the historian of seventeenth-century sleeping practices and behaviour in and around the bed. For Pepys the bed was a place for talking and for business, unless his numerous entries such as 'lay very long in bed with my wife talking' are to be read as a euphemism. We know, for example that, in the Pepys household, the winter of 1661 was a time for unusual lie-ins. An entry for Saturday, 14 December 1661 describes 'All the morning at home lying in bed with my wife till 11 o'clock. Such a habit we have got this winter of lying long abed.' One wonders why his habits suddenly and significantly changed.

We also know that, after a meeting with Admiral Sir Edward Montagu in October 1660, he shared a bed with Mr Sheply, Montagu's servant, but 'could hardly get any sleep all night, the bed being ill made and he a bad bedfellow' and that, in December 1660, he visited the politician and courtier Henry Jermyn and found him in bed, meeting with a man he presumed was a priest.

For Pepys and his contemporaries, then, the bed took on many functions, though one suspects from his regular, charming but wearisome refrain at the end of every diary entry 'and so to bed' that his favourite one was sleeping, but what went on in his mind while he was asleep is another question entirely – and is one that raises the very important question of the history of dreams...

·14·

DREAMS

—

The history of dreams is all about... demons,
temptation, the rise and fall of empires,
Islam, recipes and spoons.

Experts argue that we all dream a great deal. On average we are supposed to have between three to five dreams every night, with some people experiencing up to seven. The length of dreams can vary from a few seconds to half an hour, with the most vivid occurring during the rapid eye movement (REM) phase of sleep, and they are more likely to be remembered if the sleeper awakes mid-dream. James has vivid memories of recurring dreams from his childhood, which, crucially for a historian, he can actually date because his family moved around a lot, and they are associated with specific places. As a boy he lived in a house with a folly in the garden – a tower with turrets, quite amazing to a seven-year-old. His bedroom window looked onto the garden, and a frequent nightmare involved a floating spectre swooping out of the uppermost window and flying towards him but he always woke in a muck sweat before it actually reached him. Other memorable dreams involved his teeth falling out; being chased and being rooted to the spot; and, more spectacularly, riding high in the air on a magic carpet as it hovered through a wooded landscape. These dreams of his childhood are memorable because they were recurrent; they obviously made such an impression that they have stayed with him for well over thirty years. But how many of our dreams are fleeting and forgotten, never to be recalled?

This is the essence of a real historical problem. Reconstructing the global history of dreams is infinitely interesting and important to the historian. They are a fabulous and unexpected source of knowledge; they are inspired by cultural influences that speak of our daily lives, hopes, fears and anxieties; they are intimate, revealing, and somehow unguarded. Yet dreams are often very difficult to remember and, even where they are recorded – as with much that is unspoken and intangible in history – we are faced with the intractable problem of capturing something that is silent and fleeting, that happens when we are asleep and resides only in fragmentary recollections.

Records of dreams exist in a variety of written forms, from early religious texts to notes taken by confessors and personal diaries. Among the most interesting sources, because of the detail that they provide, are doctors' notebooks.

DOCTORS' NOTEBOOKS

The astrologer, physician and clergyman Richard Napier (1559–1634), who plied his trade as a healer in Buckinghamshire, kept voluminous notes on his patients, including women troubled by terrifying postnatal dreams. Elizabeth Banebury of Fenny Stratford in Buckinghamshire visited Napier three times in 1618 suffering mental disturbances after childbirth. Napier meticulously recorded each of these visits in his notebooks. After his first meeting he recorded that she grew 'mopish' after a bad dream, and later that a 'frightful dream' had left her 'troubled in the mind', which dried up her milk. Following this he noted on 13 March 1618 that she

> hath a child of 9 weeks old which another suckleth. After her childbirth fell with a dream and was frighted as if something lay upon her and since hath been troubled with worldly matters. Over careful of the world. Well in health but much troubled in mind.

Elizabeth appears to have suffered from what we would now diagnose as postnatal depression, and her troubled mental state was manifesting itself in the world of her dreams, which gives a remarkably intimate insight into the psychology of ordinary women from the seventeenth century.

DREAM DIARIES

From as early as the eighteenth century, we witness the emergence of the practice of keeping dream diaries. Noted scribblers-down of remembrances of nocturnal slumbers include the Swedish scientist, philosopher and theologian Emanuel Swedenborg (1688–1772), whose dream journal was discovered in the Royal Library in Sweden in the 1850s and published in 1859 as *Drömboken*. The journal was begun by Swedenborg around 1744, at which time he travelled to the Netherlands and began experiencing vivid dreams, some exhilarating, others terrifying. The notebook allowed him to record these dreams as a form of catharsis, a spiritual exercise that examined his relationship with God. One entry for 17–18 April recounts:

> I had frightful dreams; dreamt that the executioner roasted the heads which he struck off; and for a long time he put the roasted heads one after the other into an empty oven,

which nevertheless was never filled. It was said that this was his food.

Other famous dream-diarists are the novelists Graham Greene (1904–91) and Jack Kerouac (1922–69), the Italian film director Federico Fellini (1920–93) and a whole host of surrealist artists including Max Ernst (1891–1976), René Magritte (1898–1967) and Salvador Dalí (1904–89). The fact that these creative geniuses were working around the same time is no coincidence, for the 1920s saw a remarkable new trend of *using* dreams.

André Breton, the French writer, poet and founder of surrealism, argued in his first *Surrealist Manifesto*, published in 1924, for the value of irrational thinking because of the freedom that it gave the thinker. For the surrealists, dreams had their own reality to which they attributed equal, if not more, value than 'real' life. The surrealists believed that dreams were central, rather than marginal, to human thought, and some of these men went through periods when they were more in touch with their dreams than their waking life.

Dalí even invented a technique by which he could repeatedly access this dream state, thus allowing him to maximize its artistic potential – this was Dalí's way of *farming* dreams, by creating a fertile habitat for them to grow and then being ready to harvest them into his dream diaries. He did this by sitting in an upright chair, holding a spoon over a metal mixing bowl. The idea was that, when sleep took hold, the ensuing muscle paralysis would cause the spoon to drop onto the plate, which would make a clang, thus waking up the surrealist dreamer who would spring into action and record his visions. This technique is one of the reasons that Dalí's notebooks are such magnificent historical sources and particularly prized by collectors.

One of the finest creations from Dalí's dream state is his 1944 painting, snappily entitled *Dream Caused by the Flight of a Bee*

Around a Pomegranate a Second Before Awakening. Here is Gala, Dalí's wife, stretched out, half-consciously dreaming. A fish shoots out of an exploding pomegranate, and out of the fish come two snarling tigers and a bayoneted rifle which, moments later, will wake the sleeping woman by stinging her with its point. It is a vision of an infinitely tiny but dormant moment, the second before waking, the moment that Dalí believed to be the most creative for the brain.

USING DREAMS

The surrealists' fixation on dreams was itself inspired by another interesting chapter in the history of *using* dreams, pioneered by Sigmund Freud (1856–1939). In 1900 he published a major work, the first in the field that we now know as psychoanalysis, entitled *The Interpretation of Dreams*. Often Freud is assumed to have been the father of dream interpretation, but this proves not to be the case at all because, at the start of his book, he meticulously covers the extant scholarship on dreams. He goes on to recount and analyse a number of his own dreams as well as those of some of his patients. In one passage, Freud narrates a dream he had of a one-eyed doctor whom he had not seen for thirty-eight years:

> In my dream I saw a man whom I recognized, while dreaming, as the doctor of my native town. His face was not distinct, but his features were blended with those of one of my schoolmasters, whom I still meet from time to time. What association there was between the two persons I could not discover on waking, but upon questioning my mother concerning the doctor I learned that he was a one-eyed man. The schoolmaster, whose image in my dream obscured that of the physician, had also only one eye. I had not seen the doctor for thirty-eight years, and as far as I know I had never thought

of him in my waking state, although a scar on my chin might have reminded me of his professional attentions.

Throughout the book Freud blends analysis of his patients' dreams with those of his own. Although our understanding of the workings of the mind are now significantly more sophisticated than they were in Freud's early twentieth-century Vienna, the impact of his psychoanalytic theory on twentieth-century history was profound. Put simply, by framing his arguments around dreams, he revolutionized how the Western world conceived of human behaviour for almost the entirety of the last century.

Freud was *the* innovator in the use of dreams for psychoanalysis and therapy but he was by no means the first to see value in the interpretation of dreams. While the historical residue of dreams survives from across history – from ancient Mesopotamia and Egypt, classical Greece and Rome to the present day – what has shifted over time is the way in which dreams have been interpreted. In other words, once recalled and formulated – a process shaped by memory, and of course by language and narrative form – the ways in which past societies have understood dreams is differentiated across time and place.

DIVINE INSPIRATION

In the ancient world, dreams were viewed as messages from the gods, in some cases beings who literally visited dreamers in their sleep. In the Bible the Book of Genesis is simply stuffed with dreams, including Jacob's dream of a ladder that connected heaven and earth, and in the Koran dreams were the conduit for the receiving of revelations from Allah. Native American cultures saw dreams as a channel for communing with their ancestors, and the Ojibwe tribe used 'dreamcatchers' as protective charms.

Ojibwe tribe One of the group of Anishinaabeg indigenous peoples in Canada and the United States, who lived in the Great Lakes region of Michigan, Wisconsin, Minnesota, North Dakota and Ontario. Traditionally they speak Ojibwe, a form of Algonquian language. They fought alongside the French during the French and Indian War (1754-63), but sided with the British during the American War of Independence (1775-82).

Traditionally dreamcatchers were made out of a willow hoop, strung with a woven net or web, and then decorated with sacred feathers and hung over cribs or beds to catch bad dreams as people slept.

In Western Europe, dreams strongly influenced the lives of the early Church Fathers. In 375, the confessor and theologian St Jerome (347–420) had a dream resulting from his Lenten fast which caused him to experience fever and unconsciousness. As a result of the dream, which was fabulously captured on canvas by Matteo di Giovanni (c.1430–95) [*see fig. 20*], St Jerome was hauled before the court of heaven and condemned and whipped for reading pagan writings, which drove him to reject the devouring of classical texts for pleasure. We know about the dream in detail because he describes it in a letter dating from around 384 written to his protégée Julia Eustochium. He reflected:

> I was caught up in the spirit and dragged before the judgment seat of the Judge; and here the light was so bright, and those who stood around were so radiant, that I cast myself upon the ground and did not dare to look up. Asked who and what I was I replied: 'I am a Christian.' But he who presided said: 'Thou liest, thou art a follower of Cicero and not of Christ. For where thy treasure is, there will thy heart be also.' Instantly I became dumb, and amid the strokes of the lash – for he had ordered

me to be scourged – I was tortured more severely still by the fire of conscience, considering with myself that verse, 'In the grave who shall give thee thanks?' Yet for all that I began to cry and to bewail myself, saying: 'Have mercy upon me, O Lord: have mercy upon me.'

Whether or not the dream was 'real' (in the sense of a nightmare or vision) or merely some kind of rhetorical, pious fiction, there is something about it that is undoubtedly revelatory. The upshot of Jerome's dream was that 'I read the books of God with a zeal greater than I had previously given to the books of men'. In this sense, the dream – real or fictional – presents Jerome as a transformed figure, who encourages others to take the Christian pathway.

Dreams were not always the conduit for divine inspiration, and it was during the medieval period that the Church developed a much harsher line on interpreting dreams as malign and evil, as dreams became associated not just with God and ancestors, but with the supernatural. Nocturnal hours when people were asleep were viewed as ripe for visitations from night demons. Martin Luther saw dreams as the work of the Devil trying to insinuate himself into people's lives. 'Satan plagueth and tormenteth people all manner of ways,' he wrote in his *Familiar Writings* on 'The Devil and His Works': 'insomuch that he fooled and affirmeth some in their sleep, with heavy dreams and visions, so that now and then the whole body sweateth by reason of anguish of heart'.

Pre-Freud there was a clear belief in the interpretation of dreams as a form of self-analysis. The physician and author Sir Thomas Browne (1605–82) in his essay on dreams appears well before his time in writing: 'However dreames may bee fallacious concerning outward events, yet may they bee truly significant at home, & whereby wee may more sensibly understand ourselves.

Men act in sleepe with some conformity unto their awaked senses, & consolations or discoureagments may bee drawne from dreames, which intimately tell us ourselves.' On the other hand, the seventeenth-century London artisan Nehemiah Wallington (1598–1658) regularly recorded his dreams, but on the whole dismissed them as 'lying vanities'.

CHILDREN'S DREAMS

Children's dreams are a particularly interesting topic but for the historian they are even more difficult to access than the dreams of adults. For premodern periods it is very difficult to reconstruct the dreamscape of children, except through the mediated prism of their parents. Nonetheless the occasional chance discovery opens up this magical world. Ralph Josselin, the seventeenth-century vicar of Earls Colne, Essex, was an inveterate observer of the quotidian goings-on in his family and household, and in December 1654 he recorded in his spiritual diary a remarkably vivid dream described to him by his son Tom:

> … this morning my son Tom told me his wonderful dream. Jesus Christ in a white robe came into my pulpit while I was preaching, and hugged me, and I him. Then he came to him and put his inkhorn in his pocket and carried him into the churchyard and asked him what he would have. Tom said 'A blessing'. Jesus Christ bade him follow him, and mounted up to heaven…

The extract is remarkable not only in that it permits us access to the dream world of an early modern Essex schoolboy, but also for what it tells us about the boy's own religiosity. The healthy diet of religious instruction administered within the Josselin household no doubt pervaded the nocturnal wanderings of the young mind of Tom Josselin, a boy clearly eager to please his minister father.

DRUGS

Such naturally occurring dreams are, however, only one type of dream. Another type with a significant history is that which has survived today in the phrase 'pipe dream'. Now understood as a metaphor for fanciful, unattainable aspirations, these have their historical roots in the fantastical imaginings brought on by smoking opium. Numerous descriptions of opium dreams survive from as early as the sixteenth century, and, perhaps not surprisingly, they vary in literary quality.

> I am engulfed, and drown deliciously.
> Soft music like a perfume, and sweet light
> Golden with audible odours exquisite,
> Swathe me with cerements for eternity.
> Time is no more. I pause and yet I flee.
> A million ages wrap me round with night.
> I drain a million ages of delight.
> I hold the future in my memory.
> —Arthur Symons (1865–1945), 'The Opium Smoker'

Other fabulous artists, poets and musicians, whose work has been respected for generations, including Samuel Taylor Coleridge (1772–1834), John Keats (1795–1821), Percy Bysshe Shelley (1792–1822), Thomas De Quincey (1785–1859), Frédéric Chopin (1810–49) and Hector Berlioz (1803–69), harnessed the power of their opium dreams.

Opium was consumed in Persia, India and China from ancient times, was known in classical Greece and Rome and was well established in European medicine from the sixteenth century at the very latest. The first book in English to be published on opium addiction – Dr John Jones's *Mysteries of Opium Reveal'd* – appeared as early as 1700. It was after the 1780s, however, that opium first came to the West in serious bulk, and its use in English society was completely unrestricted until the Pharmacy Act of 1868. In that time opium was used in Britain, and elsewhere in the West, freely and largely unselfconsciously. Opium was smoked for escapism and as a response to social pressures, but it was also taken in cough medicine and a host of other remedies. Nonetheless the lives of *millions* of people, for the best part of a century, were coloured, in part, by their experience of opium-tinged dreams or even their experience of life itself *as* an opium-tinged dream.

Opium could be smoked in private but, more commonly, was consumed in public in opium dens. This was the Victorian theatre of dreams. Such a profound impact did these places have on society that hundreds of colourful descriptions of them survive, none more lucid than that of Oscar Wilde, for whom the opium dens in his novel *The Picture of Dorian Gray* (1891) were 'dens where one could buy oblivion, dens of horror where the memory of old sins could be destroyed by the madness of sins that were new'. Such descriptions of domestic opium consumption, which start to appear in the 1860s, are a gift to historians

Oscar Wilde (1854-1900) An Irish poet and playwright well known for his epigrams, plays and novel *The Picture of Dorian Gray* as well as his stories for children. Imprisoned for two years' hard labour in Reading Gaol for his sexuality, Wilde had a phenomenal intellect and photographic memory of everything he read.

for the variety of ways in which they can be used. The fact that so many such descriptions survive, for example, says as much about the efficacy of the anti-opium movement and a new willingness and desire to peer into the dark corners of British life from the 1860s onwards as it does of the actual consumption of opium in dens in that period.

THE OPIUM WARS

A significant portion of the opium consumed in Britain came via long-established overland trade routes from Turkey, but the provision of opium to a global audience was facilitated by the British who grew it in their tropical territories, mostly in India, and transported it to old and new markets worldwide with their massive merchant fleet. The profits they made from it were then reinvested into the empire. Britain even fought two major wars – known in England as the First and Second Opium Wars (1839–42 and 1856–58) – to force the Chinese to open their doors to the opium trade, wars in which tens of thousands of people died and an emperor fled with his ancient palaces on fire: there is a history of invasion, death and cultural destruction in this particular history of the dream.

In this very violent way but also in the years of social disintegration caused by the widespread use of the drug, China certainly suffered from its thirst for opium, but so too did the Indians of the Raj – British India – which produced most of the world's supply right up until the 1920s. The East India Company enforced the compulsory cultivation of opium poppies for decades and in doing so created a human and natural disaster that historians are now only beginning to understand. This is how one chapter in the history of dreams is linked to nothing less than the rise and fall of empires.

INDUCING DREAMS

If smoking opium was an obvious trigger for dreams, the question of how dreams were, and are, created itself has a fascinating history. The dilemma for learned people in the later medieval and early modern worlds was whether dreams were a consequence of supernatural forces or merely originated in bodily disorders. Overindulgence or consuming the wrong kinds of food and drink were increasingly thought to be the cause of a disturbed night's sleep, rather than malevolent forces, a hangover from the more superstitious medieval Church. William Turner, writing in 1568, considered that 'new wine is hard of digestion and breeds heavy dreams'. The seventeenth-century physician Nicholas Culpeper (1616–54) went a stage further, denouncing the medieval Church for peddling ideas of seductive demons. 'The nightmare,' he wrote,

> was supposed by the ancients not to be any real disorder of the body, but to be an effect, or sensation, derived from carnal contact in the night with some evil spirit or daemon during the hours of sleep… absurd as was this doctrine, whole volumes have been written upon it.

Instead, bad dreams were caused by a 'nervous affection', which he believed arose chiefly from indigestion. Overeating and gluttonous consumption too soon before bed were harmful, with 'experts' recommending the avoidance of heavy red meats, but also cheese, and vegetables such as gourds, beans, garlic, cucumber and leeks.

Disturbed nights and demonic temptation aside, our forebears nonetheless apparently loved to dream, and even concocted recipes guaranteed to induce fantastic dreams. In a recipe 'To cause marvellous dreams' the *Secrets of Master Alexis of Piedmont* (1563) advises readers to 'take the blood of a lapwing or black plover and run your temples with it, and so go to bed, and you shall see marvellous things in your sleep', while if you wanted to 'see wild beasts in a dream' it was recommended that you 'take the heart of an ape and lay it under your bed when you go to sleep'.

EROTIC DREAMS

Far more concerning for dreamers of a more religious disposition were the anxieties caused by the immoral and lascivious contents of 'wet dreams'. Such moral quandaries were unpacked by the early Church Father St Augustine in his *Confessions*. His vow of celibacy forbade him from marriage and committing fornication, but he writes 'in my memory, of which I have said much, the images of things imprinted upon it by my former habits still linger on. When I am awake they obtrude themselves upon me, though with little strength. But when I dream, they not only give me pleasure but are very much like acquiescence in the act.'

St Augustine of Hippo (354-430) One of the most important early Christian theologians, philosophers and Church Fathers in Western Christianity. Born in Numidia in North Africa, he was bishop of Hippo Regius (a city in modern Algeria), and his most influential works include *The City of God* and *Confessions*.

The moral questions and anxieties that surrounded such 'nocturnal emissions' have long concerned Christians as a matter of spiritual conscience. Puritan diarists were constantly troubled with the implications of sinful feelings of lust, and what they saw as 'self-pollution'. The vexed question of wet dreams was treated in the periodical literature of the eighteenth century, where it was considered alongside what was seen as the sin of 'onania' in anti-masturbation literature. Contemporaries were worried about how precisely to interpret nocturnal emissions. There was, at the heart of the debate, a dichotomy: on the one hand it was felt that involuntary semination during sleep could hardly be avoided, yet on the other, it was felt that it was encouraged by impure dreams, over which the conscience, even while one was asleep, was believed to exercise some control. One anonymous correspondent to an eighteenth-century periodical wondered whether 'it can properly be term'd Pollution... for a man to ease himself voluntarily of that trouble and stimulus... provided the Action be entirely free from mental impurity'. The advice given considered whether it was justifiable for a man to masturbate rather than risk 'nocturnal pollutions', which might embarrass 'those whose business extends to either Bed or Linnen'.

Dreams of an erotic nature like this created a moral dilemma for pious souls, and in the world of extreme piety it could lead

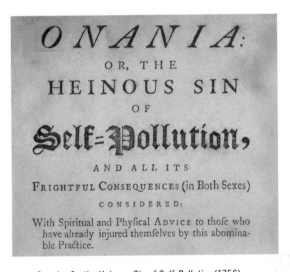

Onania: Or, the Heinous Sin of Self-Pollution (1756)

to acts of fortitude, self-denial and even self-inflicted wounds. One of the most common forms of this was the donning of uncomfortable shirts made of goat hair – which brings us to the important question of the history of hair...

·15·

HAIR

—

*The history of hair is all about… the Duke of
Wellington and the Great Man in history,
memory, love and Arctic exploration.*

A CHANCE DISCOVERY

This history of hair begins with a research trip to Oxford in the
summer of 2015 and several days spent in the Bodleian Library's
majestic Manuscripts Room. James was there calling up endless
collections of papers in the hope of chancing on interesting
documents for a book on the ways in which family memories
are preserved. Leafing through the library's filing system one
afternoon (18 June 2015 to be exact, and this date is important)
revealed a vague entry in the catalogue of the North Family
Papers describing a memory box of miscellaneous objects
connected to Lady Susan North, Countess of Guilford (1771–1837).
The box itself, uninspiringly labelled 'MS North d.68', included
a range of signatures, some regimental lace, a number of printed
books and manuscript notebooks, pressed flowers, cards and –
remarkably – a tiny envelope, which bore the inscription 'Duke
of Wellington's Hair'.

Inside the envelope was a small slip of folded paper labelled 'Duke of Wellington's hair saved by his valet before he died' and, sure enough, inside the folded paper were several strands of silvery white hair. Extraordinarily, the date of this discovery, 18 June, was significant; it was 200 years to the very day since Wellington's famous Battle of Waterloo. It felt to James as if the great man was calling to him across the centuries, so much so, in fact, that he felt a powerful urge to stand up and shout in the cloistered quietness of the reading room, 'Do you know what I have here – Wellington's hair!' Instead, and careful not to sneeze and scatter those precious hairs to the four winds on the reading-room floor, James folded up the paper and put it safely back in the box. Sometimes for the historian, serendipity does pay off, and casting the research net in unexpected places can uncover such hidden historical gems.

Trawling further through the archives it soon became clear that these strands of Wellington's hair were far from being the only locks related to this great British soldier and statesman that survive today. In fact we know that Wellington was discovered almost bald on his deathbed, having been more or less scalped by relic hunters desperate to get their hands on some part of this national hero. In the build-up to his funeral there was a veritable frenzy for Wellingtoniana, with retailers selling 'Duke of Wellington funeral wine' and 'the Wellington Funeral Cake'. Among the most expensive items for sale were locks of his hair, which were advertised in *The Times*. One such advert read 'lady having in her possession a quantity of the late illustrious DUKE'S HAIR, cut in 1841, is willing to PART WITH a portion of the same for £25'. A miniature portrait of Wellington was even produced after his death encased in a gold frame which contained three locks of hair: one taken during his youth, another after his death, and one from his beloved horse, Copenhagen. Copenhagen's hair (and in one instance this famous charger's hoof) is still prized by trophy hunters, and a gold case kept in the National Army Museum in London contains a swatch of it.

The hair of other famous historical figures – such as Napoleon and Thomas Jefferson, and more macabrely the hair of known serial killers, such as the Moors murderer Ian Brady – has similarly acquired the status of relic. Today there is still a healthy market for such items in auction rooms around the world.

One strand of the history of hair, therefore, is all about the Great Man in history, an approach to the past that has glorified the deeds of famous men, shaped by assumptions about the kinds of histories *worth* studying. Such an approach has privileged a form of history that is about kings and queens, high politics, wars and diplomacy at the expense of the rest of history, of ordinary people, of everyday life – in other words, a much more rounded view of history.

The examples presented thus far are all of men's hair, but the preserving of hair as tokens or mementoes of individuals was not restricted to male heads, a case made clear when James gave a lecture on Gertrude Courtenay (d.1558), Marchioness of Exeter, at Tiverton church in Devon. The marchioness was active in the early Tudor period, and is known for her association with the Holy Nun of Kent (c.1506–34), a mystic who was executed for prophesying the death of Henry VIII and his second wife Anne Boleyn. Gertrude narrowly escaped a similar fate by petitioning both Henry himself and his chief minister Thomas Cromwell for clemency. Before James gave this talk, the archivist from nearby Powderham Castle came up to him and said, 'I've got something here that I think you'd be interested in.' And so he was, for what she had with her was nothing less than a lock of hair, reputed to be and labelled 'a lock of Gertrude Courtenay, Marchioness of Exeter's hair'. Presumably this lock of hair had been passed down through generations of the Courtenay family until it reached its resting place in the archives room at Powderham Castle.

LOVE TOKENS

The preservation and sharing of hair belonging to famous people is only part of this curious history, however. During the eighteenth and nineteenth centuries, locks of hair – single pieces, commonly referred to as ringlets, tresses or curls – assumed a deeply personal and emotional significance, and were routinely exchanged between friends and family or as tokens between lovers, especially before a period of separation. Locks of hair were commonly consigned in correspondence between loved ones and family and friends, which is largely where they still survive today within the archives. The seventeenth-century letter-writer Dorothy Osborne (1627–95) begged her lover and later husband Sir William Temple for a lock of his hair to remember him by while they were parted, adding 'Oh, my heart! What a sigh there was there!'

Here locks of hair were cut as love tokens, as a reminder of loved ones when they were physically absent, and it was common practice to keep such locks in lockets on chains around the neck. Occasionally hair was pressed into the seal of a letter to achieve a personal, emotive and intimate gesture, as in the case of a letter sent in the first decade of the seventeenth century by the remarkable Wiltshire gentlewoman Maria Thynne to her mother-in-law Joan. The two had fallen out over Maria's clandestine marriage to Joan's son, and the new daughter-in-law sought to repair relations by sealing in wax a grovelling letter to her with a lock of her own red hair as a token of reconciliation. Here the physical form of the letter communicated emotionally through the meaning attached to wax and hair.

Nowadays, within families, babies' first curls are often kept as keepsakes. This practice has a long history, and superstition held that it was thought to bring good luck. In the National Archives at Kew in London, the mid-nineteenth-century private papers of Mrs R. B. Wylie contain a lock of hair labelled 'Lock of her hair at age of four months', where it is kept among school records and other family papers as a series of mementoes connected to her child. In a period prior to photography, saving hair was a way of marking the birth of a child; nowadays such rites of passage are recorded with digital cameras, plaster casts of hands and feet, tattoos and some modern parents keep locks of hair too.

Locks of hair were also kept during the Victorian period as memento mori of lost family members, and were even fashioned into rings. A particularly interesting example of this survives in a letter to Fanny Knight dated 29 July 1817 when Cassandra Austen informed her niece of the death of her sister, the novelist Jane Austen (1775–1817). As was customary, Cassandra cut several locks from her sister's head before her coffin was closed, and in her letter Cassandra asked her niece how she would best like her lock mounted. Fanny's reply asks for it to be set in a pearl brooch bearing Jane's name and the date of her death. Keeping with the literary theme, a presentation collection of the English Romantic poet Percy Bysshe Shelley's (1792–1822) letters in the British Library contains a lock of his hair within the front doublure – a decorative lining within a book – along with a lock of hair from his wife Mary Shelley, the author of *Frankenstein*. The back doublure holds some of Shelley's ashes. The lock of hair here is therefore part of a collection of personal writings and physical remains that acted as a memorial to this literary figure.

Hair has long been used as a memento, a tangible remembrance of someone gone or separated by distance or by death.

Percy Bysshe Shelley (1792-1822) One of the finest English Romantic poets. His radical poetry and politics meant that he found it difficult to get published during his lifetime, though his work drew great acclaim after his death. Less than a month before his thirtieth birthday he drowned. Some accounts suggest that when his body was being burned a close friend snatched his heart whole from the pyre.

The fact that it was hair that was ordinarily kept rather than something else (nail clippings, dead skin, teeth for example) is interesting in itself, and probably has much to do with the lustre of hair, which one could hardly say of toenails.

SCALPING

In other non-European cultures, the cutting and preserving of hair had distinctly different meanings. One of the most intriguing is the practice of scalping – the act of cutting or tearing part of the human scalp, with the hair attached – as a form of trophy of an enemy. Scalping has a long tradition, which can be traced back to the ancient Greek historian Herodotus's (c.484–c.425 BCE) description of Scythian warriors, and developed independently in different cultures in both Eastern and Western hemispheres. It is often interpreted as part of broader cultural practices of mutilating and then displaying human body parts as trophies. The actual practice of scalping – which involved gripping the hair of the victim, making semi-circular cuts on either side of the part to be taken, then ripping it back, taking with it a layer of the human scalp – is perhaps most widely associated (especially in popular imagination) with Native American Indians, but was, without doubt, practised by Europeans as well. The British Scalp Proclamation of 1756, issued by Governor Charles

Lawrence (1709–60) during a period of skirmishes between the British and the First Nation people the Mi'kmaq, announced: 'And, we do hereby promise, by and with the advice and consent of His Majesty's Council, a reward of £30 for every male Indian Prisoner, above the age of sixteen years, brought in alive; or for a scalp of such male Indian twenty-five pounds, and twenty-five pounds for every Indian woman or child brought in alive.'

The Mi'kmaq A First Nation people indigenous to Quebec in Canada and Maine in the United States. Traditionally they spoke Mi'kmaq, an Eastern Algonquian form of language. Mi'kmaq warriors resisted the British during the French and Indian wars (1755–63), and during the American War of Independence some sided with the British and some with the Americans.

Scalping was part of violent warfare, and scalps might form part of ceremonial clothing. A highly decorative shirt from the Sioux tribe of Dakota dating from the mid-1800s was made of porcupine quill, leather and human hair, the latter standing as testimony of the wearer's bravery and conquests in battle. Scalping must also however be understood for its religious and spiritual importance. Many tribes believed that hair was the locus of enormous spiritual power, a nest for the soul, which made it highly prized. A wool shirt dating from the late 1890s belonging to a warrior from the Crow tribe was decorated with human hair and ermine skins, and warriors were often instructed via dreams to make clothing of this nature that would then aid them in battle.

Some of the most detailed records of scalping come from the American painter, author and traveller, George Catlin (1796–1872), painted and wrote about Plains Indians in their own territory, explaining to white Americans their customs, manners and traditions during the 1830s. As a Christian he found the custom of scalping 'disgusting', but elsewhere depicted the cultural significance it had, not least in his paintings of the scalp dance, a ceremony that narrated the particulars of battle. He also described the lavish dress of a Blackfoot chief whom he painted, which consisted of a shirt or tunic made from deer skins with beautiful embroidering as well as 'a fringe of the locks of black hair, which he has taken from the heads of victims slain by his own hand in battle... and worn as trophies'.

For many, the ordeal of being scalped was fatal, but there are those who miraculously survived the experience to tell the tale. There exists today in Omaha Public Library a 150-year-old scalp belonging to the Englishman William Thompson, an employee of the Union Pacific Railroad, who in 1867 was attacked, shot, scalped and left for dead after an ambush by members of the Cheyenne tribe. Not only did Thompson survive the attack, but

William Thompson's scalped head, 1867

he also managed to recover his severed scalp, which he hoped to be able to have reattached. Alas for him this was not to be the case, but the scalp was kept – which explains its survival and public display today.

MUMMIFIED HAIR

Such scalps and locks have survived *because* of their removal from the temporality of the human body, but in some cases hair has survived from the past because it has remained attached to the body, a body that has been mummified either on purpose as part of burial practices, such as the famous mummies of the Egyptian pharaohs, or by accident of the environment in which the burial occurred. Wet, dry, salty and cold conditions can all lead to the survival of human hair over centuries, sometimes millennia, and even a slight chemical imbalance in the soil and raised levels of chromium or copper can aid its survival.

One of the most stunning examples of survival caused by environmental conditions comes from John Franklin's expedition to the Arctic in 1845 in which Franklin and all 129 of his crew died. From shortly after their disappearance right up until the present day explorers have sought to find traces of the expedition and clues to its fate. Most recently, in 2014 and 2016, Franklin's ships, HMS *Terror* and *Erebus*, were discovered, beautifully preserved time capsules resting on the Arctic seafloor. An earlier discovery which provided a breakthrough in our understanding of the men in Franklin's expedition happened in 1984 when archaeologists discovered the burials of three of Franklin's crew on Beechey Island in the north of modern Canada. Deep-frozen for over a century and a half, the condition of the bodies was quite extraordinary. The colour of their clothing was as bright as it ever was, their skin unblemished and, perhaps most striking of all, their hair was as it appeared on the day that they died. The hair of one skeleton, in particular, fell across his face from a parting on the left. If ever a haircut deserved the adjective 'shock' then this is it: it is like nothing more than a shock of wheat. Brown, straight, dirty, tangled, wild, up, down, left and right, all framing a face in which you can see more than a hint of the man that was. We know from the grave marker that this was Able Seaman John Hartnell, a twenty-five-year-old, and that he had died on 4 January 1846.

Once the bodies were discovered, the scientists got to work, and here the hair itself became a tool for history. Since the late 1850s hair has been used by scientists to help us understand ourselves, though its study was not established as a forensic science for a century more. Because hair grows at roughly 15cm per year it is a peculiarly important resource for the scientist and a particularly interesting tool for the historian. The hair *itself* contains a history; it changes over time and those changes are permanent and visible. Hair, therefore, is a unique type of historical document. A urine test for drug consumption, for example, can tell us if someone has been using controlled substances within the last few hours, but an analysis of a person's hair can tell us about that person's health or lifestyle over a far longer period of time: not only can it tell us if the drug was used but, because it was preserved in the hair at the time and the hair then grew, it can tell us *when*.

In the case of the Franklin mummies, hair analysis revealed that each of the three mummies buried on Beechey Island was suffering from lead poisoning. The issue of lead in the sailor's diet – ingested from food contaminated with lead from the solder of the cans in which it was preserved, or from the lining of the ships' water tanks, or simply from high levels of lead ingested prior to the expedition – thus became an important factor in the investigation into the expedition's fate, to go alongside tuberculosis, starvation, scurvy and the very weather that preserved those corpses so beautifully. Similar analysis of historical hair has suggested that Beethoven, who famously suffered from an appalling list of symptoms including abdominal pain, poor digestion, colic, chronic bronchitis and foul body odours, had raised levels of lead in his body, and that George III, the famous 'mad' king of England, had consumed arsenic, which is certain to have worsened the hereditary condition of porphyria which triggered his mental illness.

George III (1738-1820) King of Great Britain 1760-1820, the third monarch of the German royal House of Hanover. His reign was marked by a remarkable period of warfare, including the Seven Years War with France (1754-63), the American War of Independence and the French Revolutionary and Napoleonic Wars (1793-1815). The latter part of his reign was marked by his mental illness, and a major relapse in 1810 led to the creation of a regency, with his eldest son George presiding as prince regent.

AUSCHWITZ

Hair analysis was even used as evidence for the Holocaust in trials of leading Nazis after the Second World War, including that of Rudolf Hess, the former commandant of Auschwitz. In May 1945 Polish officials dispatched ten pounds of human hair found at Auschwitz to the Institute of Forensic Medicine in Cracow where it was found to contain traces of cyanide and Zyklon, the chemicals used in the Auschwitz gas chambers.

The hair discovered at Auschwitz now serves another, powerful purpose. Nearly two tons of it is on display in the Auschwitz-Birkenau museum. Visitors stand, dumb, taking in the braids, knots, waves, twists and variety of hair colours from snow-white to fiery auburn. In this way hair has become one of a large variety of objects that memorialize the victims of the Holocaust and the victims of war more generally, objects which include shoes, glasses, clothing and luggage from the past, as well as poppies, crosses and even paper clips from the present – which raises the important question of the history of the paper clip...

·16·
THE PAPER CLIP

The history of the paper clip is all about…
the Stasi, Albert Einstein, 'puzzle women',
suffragettes, Nazis and fish sacks.

You may not believe it, but anyone who has read any history at all will have been influenced by the paper clip. It is more than just a history of record-keeping, organizing documents and archiving (which is itself unexpectedly interesting), but is all about the whys and wherefores of 'keeping things together' – and in that lies nothing less than our understanding of the nature of history itself.

THE INVENTOR

The first patent for a paper clip as we know it was granted in 1867 in the United States to Samuel B. Fay, and the type that we all know today, the 'Gem' paper clip, was invented in the UK a few years later, around 1870, and produced by the Gem Manufacturing Company. The Gem design never received a patent and so its origins are still mysterious. Nonetheless, it spawned a whole industry in ingenious designs, which brought us, among other modifications, the Eureka clip (which was made from sheet metal, 1894), the Niagara paper clip (1897), the Clipper clip (1899), the Octo fastener (1901), the Banjo paper clip (1903), as well as the uber-complicated Mogul paper clip (1906), which was the Fort Knox of the paper clip world, guaranteed to avoid any loose papers slipping out.

By 1883, the manual *The Home Library* was championing in the US the efficacy of the paper clip, which was deemed far superior to its predecessor, the pin: 'For binding together papers on the same subject a bundle of letters, or pages of manuscript, the Gem Paper-Fasteners, or McGill's Paper-Fasteners, are better than ordinary pins.' Over those few years from the end of the 1860s there was a veritable revolution in paper-fastening technology which went on to have some spectacular impacts upon history.

—— THE PREHISTORY OF THE PAPER CLIP ——

The first thing to note, however, is that there is a significant 'prehistory' of the paper clip. While the medieval period saw the transition from memory to the written record, it was the Renaissance (from c.1300) that witnessed the true explosion in paper archives alongside the expansion of Church and State, trade and traffic, and all manner of institutions that needed to maintain proper records. Early sixteenth-century Dutch portraits by Jan Gossaert (1478–1532) and Hans Holbein the Younger (1497–1543) depict merchants surrounded by the paper paraphernalia of their trades: bundles of bills, accounts, legal instruments and other documents, correspondence strung on wires or impaled on spikes, papers piled on shelves or pinned to walls. Take for example Holbein's *Portrait of the Merchant Georg Gisze* (1532) [*see fig. 21*] which portrays the London-based Hanseatic merchant Georg Gisze clad in velvet tunic, hat and silk sleeves at a desk, behind which are folded letters in wooden racks with wax seals, a note pinned to the wooden wall above his head, and leather-bound accounts resting on shelves around the room. This was a world of trade and traffic, paper and parchment. In other words, Renaissance filing was very ad hoc, involving a myriad of systems of papers piled into bundles, stored in trunks and boxes – and not a paper clip in sight.

Hans Holbein the Younger (1497-1543) The German-born artist Hans Holbein the Younger is one of the most accomplished portrait painters of the sixteenth century. He is known for his portraits of the court and nobility during the reign of the English monarch Henry VIII, as well as for his magnificent painting *The Ambassadors*, which memorializes two powerful and wealthy diplomats.

One of the pressing concerns for politicians of the period was how to deal with and process the mountains of paperwork that arose from an expansion in bureaucracy, as literacy rates rose and more business was written down rather than being conducted face-to-face. In Tudor England, William Cecil (1520–98), Elizabeth I's chief minister, according to one of his secretaries, drew upon him more than sixty to a hundred written requests in a day, all of which needed to be efficiently dealt with amidst a welter of other pressing concerns, and that was only *his* incoming correspondence. The wider Cecil family was served by a large private secretariat in addition to government clerks. Nicholas Faunt (1553–1608), one of Sir Francis Walsingham's secretaries, outlined in 1592 a series of instructions for the incoming secretary of state that described in some detail the roles and duties of secretaries in a busy government department. Their daily task was

... every morning to set [the papers] in several bundles for the present use of them, and when they grow to be many, those that have been most dealt in and dispatched to be removed into some closet or chest or place, lest confusion or loss of some of them grow through an exceeding and unnecessary multitude of papers as hath been seen in that place.

The prehistory of the paper clip, therefore, is a history of bundles of paper, of chests and boxes, as states and institutions across Europe imposed order on the records they produced, records that became the bread and butter of historians. It is this ordering of paper records, itself an exercise of power, that is so fascinating. What is preserved and filed and what discarded and purged greatly influences the kinds of history and stories we can write.

THE STASI

A leap across the centuries takes this idea of the state control of paper into the heart of post-war East Germany, for the history of the paper clip is also about the Stasi (the East German secret police). The Ministry for State Security (*Ministerium für Staatssicherheit*), more commonly known as the Stasi, was established in February 1950 in order to know simply everything about everyone. This was brought hauntingly to the screen in the 2006 German-language film *The Lives of Others*, which depicts a secret police agent conducting surveillance on a writer and his lover. It gives a microscopic account of the almost obsessive spying of one particular man, but be very clear that this was everywhere in East Germany. Prior to the fall of the Berlin Wall, the Stasi employed some 90,000 full-time staff and 170,000 full-time unofficial collaborators to conduct detailed surveillance and maintain files on almost *six million* of its citizens, using techniques which included surveillance of their homes, interrogations and the interception of mail. Eavesdropping became not only an art form, but also an industry. The infamous 'Department M' used machines to blow hot air to open correspondence and then mechanically seal it again. Files were likewise opened and updated in a systematic way; they were named and labelled, the papers enclosed within the cardboard covers, referenced, grouped and paper-clipped with notes, dates, times and photographs. Perhaps no state in history has made use of so many paper clips in such a sinister way.

When the Berlin Wall came crashing down in 1989, the spying activities of the Stasi were investigated by the West German government. In 1991 this culminated in the Stasi Records Act, which allowed access to the Stasi archives by members of the public anxious to view precisely what records had been kept on them and their family. It is estimated that, every month, some 5,000 people ask to consult former Stasi files and that more than 2.75 million requests have been made to view the files since 1991.

PUZZLE WOMEN

The situation, however, was made all the more complicated because, after the collapse of the Wall, Stasi officials had systematically removed the binding paper clips and then shredded the highly sensitive records they had compiled on the East German population for over forty years. They left behind some 15,000 sacks, which contained an estimated 600 million documents in billions of pieces. So important were these documents, however, that, rather than despair at the impossibility of the task, the authorities had them painstakingly reassembled *by hand* by a workforce of 1,800 women who became known as 'puzzle women'.

This seemingly impossible task is now central to our understanding of the inner workings of the East German state, and these 'puzzle women' are still at work, but are now assisted by technology that uses pattern-recognition algorithms to help piece the tiny fragments together.

WAR CRIMINALS

The paper clip gained huge historical significance in the aftermath of the Second World War when it was used to bind new identities to people. Identity fraud and identity change became an important historical issue both during and after the war as many thousands of people sought to hide their real identities in order to avoid persecution or to escape prosecution for war crimes. This changing of identities became an official state-sponsored activity after 1945 in a US programme which was known as 'Operation Paperclip'. Both a symptom of and influence on the Cold War, its purpose was to resettle thousands of German scientists, engineers and technicians in the US, as a means of denying Germany, Russia and Britain access to intellectual capital that could influence future military capability. This was a form of arms race fought with scientific brains. The Russians had their own such programme – Operation

> **The Cold War** A period of geopolitical tension between the Soviet Union and its satellite states (the Eastern Bloc) and the United States and its NATO allies (the Western Bloc). Avoiding direct military engagement, both sides supported other nations in regional wars. The years witnessed frosty diplomatic relations, a nuclear arms race and widespread fear of Armageddon. The Cold War is thought to have ended either in 1989 when Communism fell in Eastern Europe, or in 1991 when the Soviet Union collapsed.

Osoaviakhim. A significant part of the US operation was to give scientists new identities to allow them to be granted the requisite security clearances they would need to work in the US.

The operation's name was derived from the paper clips which attached the scientists' new identities to their official 'Government Scientist' personnel files held by the Joint Intelligence Objectives Agency. In total 1,600 men and their families were repatriated in this way, including the German-born aerospace engineer Wernher von Braun (1912–77) and many of his team that developed the V-2 rocket. Scientific men of this calibre were key in the arms and space races that characterized the Cold War period.

A parallel programme conducted with Japan saw the US government use its paper clips to give new identities to Japanese war criminals, many of whom had spent the war at a secret base in northern China known as Unit 731, where they used human subjects and vivisection to develop chemical and biological weapons.

This was more than a little morally and ethically ambiguous – some said repugnant – and others claimed (though incorrectly) that it was illegal, that it was conducted by the US War Department in disregard of official US policy. In practice, however, these operations were conducted under an official policy sanctioned by the president.

This history of the paper clip, therefore, is part of the history of human capital flight and can take its place alongside the mass exodus of Huguenots from France after 1685 when Louis XIV (1638–1715) declared Protestantism illegal; the Jewish exodus from Germany before the outbreak of the Second World War, which included such leading names as Albert Einstein; and the 400,000 doctors and academics who have left Israel since the beginning of the Arab–Israeli War of 1948. It is also a chapter in the history of the freedom of information, for when it was

> **Unit 731** A top-secret Japanese biological and chemical warfare research laboratory run by the Imperial Army during the Second World War. Between 1937 and 1945 lethal human experiments were carried out on more than 3,000 men, women and children. Those who conducted the experiments were not tried and punished for war crimes, but granted immunity by the US in exchange for divulging the findings from their experiments on human subjects.

discovered that Nazis and Japanese war criminals had been settled in the US, a legal basis for their deportation was created in the late 1970s that eventually led to the 1998 Nazi War Crimes Disclosure Act which declassified US government records relating to Nazi war criminals in the US. The full impact of these documents has yet to be felt but it is certain to transform our understanding of the post-war world in the West.

FREEDOM FIGHTERS

The history of the paper clip, however, is far more than just a chapter in the history of documents, for that is not the only thing that they have been used to bind together: in Norway during the Second World War the paper clip bound *people* together.

In April 1940 the Germans occupied Norway, a neutral country. The Norwegian king and the government escaped to London and civil rule was assumed by the *Reichskommissariat Norwegen* – the Reich Commissariat of Norway. The Norwegian Jews that had not escaped were transported to concentration camps. Nearly half of the country's industrial output was immediately seized by the Germans and Norway lost almost all of its pre-existing trading partners. Basic commodities vanished. People began to starve. In these fraught circumstances, the paper clip became a symbol of solidarity and of subversive national identity, a way for Norwegians to make a veiled protest about their Nazi-infested world. Students at Oslo University began to attach paper clips to their lapels and to fashion accessories from paper clips, such as paper clip bracelets. It was a gesture with complex motivation. Importantly the paper clip was cheap, accessible everywhere, attachable to almost anything, and because it was malleable and easy to bend it was easily customizable – the perfect object to use as a symbol visibly to bind thousands of people together in common cause.

It showed, in a peaceful yet subversive way, unity and national solidarity in the face of the German occupation and also a measure of national pride. Symbols clearly linked to the Norwegian royal family had already been banned along with other badges or pins depicting national symbols: the Nazis were well aware of the desire to demonstrate resistance among the populations of the countries they subjugated.

It was also, curiously, the result of historical ignorance. It was then widely, and incorrectly, believed in Norway that the inventor of the paper clip was the Norwegian Johan Vaaler (1866–1910). He certainly was an inventor of *a* paper clip and he did register patents in both Germany and the US, but he did so in 1901 and his designs were never manufactured. With a single loop, they were unlike the Gem paper clip we know today and which the Norwegians used as their symbol of Nazi defiance. Nonetheless the belief that Vaaler was the inventor of the paper clip survived long after the Second World War. There is even a monument built in honour of him in 1989 in Sandvika just outside Oslo, but it shows the Gem paper clip – someone else's design. Part of the history of the paper clip, therefore, is the history of the value of historians in identifying mistakes.

SOLIDARITY

The Norwegians' subversive use of the paper clip certainly worked to galvanize national sentiment. A vigorous resistance network was formed and they had significant military successes, not least the sabotage of the Nazi nuclear programme by targeting its heavy water production site at Vemork in 1942–44. The Germans clocked what was going on with the paper clips and banned them, along with other secret symbols of Norwegian national identity and resistance that they had identified, including the – oh-so-innocent – bobble hat. If you want to learn more, a visit to Norway's excellent Resistance Museum in Oslo will guide you through this fascinating period of the country's history.

The history of the paper clip, therefore, is also part of the history of symbols of solidarity, which range from the stitching of a 'broad arrow' into the clothing of suffragettes, a visual link to women's prison uniform that was marked with broad arrows, to the modern use of safety pins as a symbol of solidarity against racism, religious persecution or homophobia. The paper clip was also chosen, in 1998, by schoolchildren in the small Tennessee town of Whitwell as the object with which to create a monument commemorating victims of the Holocaust. A German railcar was filled with 11 million paper clips (to represent the murder of 6 million Jews and 5 million Roma, Catholics, Jehovah's Witnesses, homosexuals and other groups), while a further 11 million paper clips were fashioned into a sculpture representing the 1.5 million children exterminated by the Nazis. Begun as a way of encouraging tolerance and understanding of diversity within the world, the paper clips project became a worldwide cultural phenomenon. Inspired by the Norwegian example, tens of millions of paper clips were received over the duration of the project, and it featured in a 2004 documentary film of the same name, *Paper Clips*.

PRESERVATION

Not only is the paper clip a boon for historians by grouping things together, it also causes them immense problems. Having worked in archives collectively for the best part of forty years, we have witnessed the widespread use and misuse of paper clips, now degrading, their rusty residue colouring and decaying the documents that they clipped together. Over time, the paper clip can destroy as well as it can preserve, and part of its history is the story of the damage that it can do to historical records, and it must take its place alongside staples, binder clips, pins and rubber bands as a historian's nemesis. Part of *that* history is the very long history of the careless handling of historical documents. Examples are endless, and with every one, years of knowledge have disintegrated, but one of the most striking comes from the seventeenth century and the farcical story of the journey made by the records of the Court of Wards and Liveries.

This was a court set up in 1540 during the reign of Henry VIII to administer feudal income that arose from wardship (when a minor inherited land). When it was dissolved in 1660 the court's records – a goldmine for historians for what they tell us about attitudes towards the family – were stuffed into sacks and left to decay in a 'hell-like fish cellar' near Westminster Hall. In 1708 a House of Lords committee visited the fish cellar and described in angry terms what they discovered: '... they found a great number of books and papers lying upon the floor in the greatest confusion and disorder... the lead being stolen from the top of the roof, and the windows broken, the rain has corrupted and destroyed many of these papers.'

More than 200 years later, many of these documents are too unstable to be examined, and those that can be read almost disintegrate upon being touched, leaving nothing but a fine red dust on one's clothes. One message of this chapter for the reader interested in historical research is very clear: beware paper clips, past and present. The best method for preserving documents is to place them in individual acid-free folders inside archiving boxes, but of course this presents profound problems of space where vast bodies of materials survive. Among the world leaders in this field of conservation are the archivists at the Bodleian Library, who would blanch at the sight of a rusty paper clip on a document under their care and who have pioneered a remarkable new way of preserving fascicles (individual manuscripts) which is simply brilliant for storing correspondence – which raises the important question of the history of the letter...

·17·

LETTERS

——

The history of the letter is all about…
secrecy, the Royal Navy, marriage, castration
and, of course, eggs. Yes, letters are intricately
connected to the history of eggs.

etters – by which we mean written correspondence – are an exceptionally rich historical source that has been around for millennia. We have evidence of the existence of letters, though not the letters themselves, from ancient Egypt as early as 1388 BCE. Their contents touch upon almost every aspect of the past, but they are also fascinating *objects* in their own right. They are a means of communication, a record of handwriting, evidence of transport systems and of paper manufacture. Most importantly, however, they reflect the culture in which they were produced: they are a mirror to the soul of their age. The answer to the question 'how do you *read* a letter?' is not, therefore, as straightforward as you might think and the result – the information they can provide for historians – can be quite astonishing.

THE LOVE LETTER

Perhaps the most intimate form of letter and one with which many of us can identify is the love letter, a tradition of letter-writing that has a remarkable history. It is a form that can be traced back to the twelfth century, to the deeply personal and heartfelt, and yet intellectually complex letters exchanged between Peter Abelard (1079–1142) and Héloïse d'Argenteuil, which are among the literary gems of the medieval world.

Theirs was a relationship that was doomed. Peter Abelard was a medieval French scholastic philosopher, and one of the leading theologians of his age. Abelard entered the household of Fulbert, secular canon of Notre-Dame Cathedral, where he fell in love and began a clandestine affair with Fulbert's niece Héloïse, a woman remarkable for her erudition in Latin, Greek and Hebrew. As a result of the affair Héloïse fell pregnant, and gave birth to a son Astrolabe.* The couple married under rather strained circumstances, with Héloïse resisting at first, then refusing to acknowledge the union publicly, and being sent to live her life as a nun. Abelard was punished by Fulbert, who arranged for him to be beaten up and castrated for his perceived mistreatment of Héloïse, after which Abelard himself entered a monastery.

* Named after the scientific instrument used for observing heavenly bodies.

It was at this point that the pair engaged in their correspondence, which dealt with the tensions between romantic love, chastity and the monastic life. In a letter to Héloïse, Abelard wrote:

> To forget, in the case of love, is the most necessary penance, and the most difficult. It is easy to recount our faults; how many, through indiscretion, have made themselves a second pleasure of this instead of confessing them with humility. The only way to return to God is by neglecting the creature we have

adored, and adoring the God whom we have neglected. This
may appear harsh, but it must be done if we would be saved...
After such a revenge taken on me you could expect to be
secure nowhere but in a convent.

These were far from everyday letters exchanged between ordinary people, but were intellectual exercises written in Latin to
debate ideals of love as it was perceived in the lovers' unique
historical context and position: they are a type of love letter that
could only have been written in one place and at one time.

Other examples survive of women penning love letters from
the medieval period and beyond, including those of Mary Deane
who, in 1600, was imprisoned in Bridewell Prison in London for
adultery, and communicated with her lover in a form of secret
code she had learned from her mother. Unable to crack her
code, the Bridewell authorities arranged for her to be whipped
and deported to Scotland.

THE ABILITY TO WRITE A LETTER

These fascinating examples of love letters are important because
they expose two significant modern assumptions about letter-
writing: first, they include letters written by women, and secondly
they were written by the authors themselves. The ability to write
letters for much of history before the sixteenth and seventeenth
centuries was confined to a relatively select group of Church
and government officers, merchants and scholars, and mostly
men. Moreover, letters were largely employed for formal and
official purposes and most were dictated, and thus penned by
secretaries and scribes.

In the sixteenth century we see a shift in letter-writing ability
and activity, with rising levels of lay literacy and an increasing
tendency for individuals to write for themselves, rather than

relinquish the task to an amanuensis. It is during this period that we witness the development of women's letter-writing. What distinguishes Tudor women letter-writers from their medieval forebears is the degree to which they were able to write for themselves, a skill that facilitated women's self-expression and control over their own affairs and relationships – in other words writing letters gave women a degree of female agency unfettered by male constraints. It is little surprise that, in the Tudor period, the likes of Anne Boleyn, Lady Jane Grey and Princesses Mary and Elizabeth were brought up as competent letter-writers, pushed by politically ambitious families who saw the benefit of such skills for women in power and positions of influence.

FEMALE LETTER-WRITERS

One of the most exceptional female letter-writers of the turn of the sixteenth century is a gentlewoman, Maria Thynne (c.1578–1611), the daughter of George Touchet, Lord Audley, and his first wife, Lucy. Maria – or Mall as she was known to her family – spent time as a maid of honour at the court of Elizabeth I, before marrying Thomas Thynne, the heir of a Wiltshire gentry family who were involved in a long-term feud with Maria's mother's family. This has led some scholars (wrongly in James's opinion) to see this match as one of the sources for Shakespeare's play *Romeo and Juliet*.

Throughout her surviving letters Maria emerges as a highly intelligent, opinionated, clever and very witty correspondent. She came from a rather unconventional aristocratic family. Her siblings led unorthodox and bizarre lives, reflecting unorthodox and bizarre personalities: her brother Mervyn Touchet, who became second earl of Castlehaven, was beheaded in 1631 for charges of sodomy and rape, and her sister Eleanor Davies was a prophetess who was arrested and sentenced to Bedlam, the infamous London psychiatric hospital, for pouring tar over the altar at Lichfield Cathedral.

Maria married relatively young, and in the early years of her marriage she appears rather frustrated by the limited role in estate management permitted her by her husband, expressing herself in a letter to be both sorry and ashamed 'that any creature should see that you hold such a contempt of my poor wits, that being your wife, you should not think me of discretion to order (according to your appointment) your affairs in your absence.' In other letters she openly mocked the rigid behavioural norms for women at the time, on one occasion bemoaning the fact that she was not in London with her sisters, but at home 'talking of foxes and ruder beasts'. After August 1604, when Thomas was knighted, Maria wrote to her husband:

> Mine own sweet Thomken, I have no longer ago than the very last night written such a large volume in praise of thy kindness to me, thy dogs, thy hawks, the hare and the foxes, and also in commendation of thy great care of thy businesses in the country, that I think I need not amplify any more on that text, for I have crowned thee for an admirable good husband with poetical laurel, and admired the inexpressible singularity of thy love in the cogitations of *piamater* [meaning 'tender mother', presumably she was pregnant], I can say no more but that in way of gratuity, the dogs shall without interruption expel their excremental corruption in the best room (which is thy bed) whensoever full feeding makes their bellies ache...

Obviously feeling deserted in rural Wiltshire, she chides her husband, whom she thinks treats her no better than an animal, and writes that she hopes that their dogs shit (or rather more poetically 'without interruption expel their excremental corruption') in his bed for his failing to show her enough love.

Throughout her correspondence Maria pushes the boundaries of what was expected of a Tudor wife, subversively playing with the ideal of the obedient, dutiful and loving spouse while simultaneously pouring out expressions of love to her 'own sweet Thomken'; in one rather steamy and sexually assertive letter she looks forward to him 'rising up' (rendered in doggerel Latin) when they are in bed together on his return.

Even more explosive are Maria's letters to her mother-in-law, Joan Thynne, a woman who was less than keen on her son's wife, had known nothing of the wedding, and had then tried to annul it in the courts. Their relationship – as relationships between in-laws can indeed be – was at best somewhat strained, and at worst plainly abusive, and it can be viewed through a correspondence lasting several years, written in the wake of Maria's clandestine marriage.

Aware of her mother-in-law's great displeasure and the need to placate her, Maria wrote several apologetic letters to Joan, in which she sought reconciliation and at the same time maintained her innocence, having married Thomas with good intentions. 'If I did know that my thoughts had ever entertained any unreverent conceit of you (my good mother),' she wrote in September 1601, 'I should be much ashamed so impudently to importune your good opinion as I have done by many entreating lines, but having been ever emboldened with the knowledge of my unspotted innocence.' The letter itself contains a lock of Maria's red hair under the seal, material testimony of the writer's apparent desire for conciliation.

The situation changed on the death of Joan's husband in 1604, when Maria and her husband inherited the family lands; Maria – not Joan – was now mistress of Longleat House, a shift in social position that dramatically altered the balance of power between the two women. The only correspondence between them that survives from this time, when Joan moved away from

11. The pocket watch of 27-year-old Robert Douglas Norman, who perished in the *Titanic* disaster. The hands are rusted at seven minutes past three, presumably when he entered the water.

12. The embroidered front cover of Princess Elizabeth's translation of Marguerite de Navarre's *The Miroir or Glasse of the Synneful Soul* which she presented to Katherine Parr in 1544.

13. Hand-coloured etching by Thomas Rowlandson entitled 'An old maid in search of a flea' (1794)

14. *The Syphilitic* (1496), engraving by Albrecht Dürer

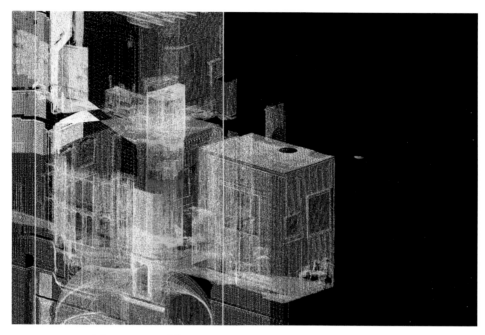

15. 3D laser image of the priest hole at Coughton Court, Warwickshire, produced by researchers at the University of Nottingham.

16. Jewelled terminal of aestel – the Alfred Jewel (871–99)

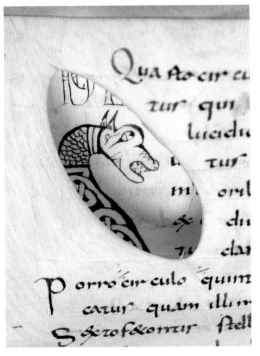

17. Dragon image in a ninth-century manuscript

18. Holes repaired by nuns with embroidery in a fourteenth-century manuscript

19. The Great Bed of Ware, c.1590

20. Matteo di Giovanni (c.1430–1495), *Dream of St Jerome in 375* (1476)

21. Hans Holbein the Younger, *Portrait of the Merchant Georg Gisze* (1532)

Longleat to live at Caus Castle, is a rather striking letter from Maria, which is devoid of the deference and subservience of her earlier missives. Written in response to Joan's complaints about the way in which Maria was neglecting the gardens of Longleat, the letter goads her by saying she'd turned them into a 'porridge pot'. The letter then openly and brutally insults her mother-in-law, describing her as an 'odious' and 'corpulent' grandmother who she suspected 'soiled' her land with her own 'manure'. Particularly waspish here is the pun in the final sentence on what she will 'leave behind' her:

> Now, whereas you write your ground put to basest uses, is better manured than my garden, surely if it were a grandmother of my own and equal to myself by birth, I should answer that odious comparison with telling you I believe so corpulent a Lady cannot but do much yourself towards the soiling of land, and I think that hath been, and will be all the good you intend to leave behind you at Corsley.

Maria had a clear penchant for epistolary scatology.

SECRET LETTERS

Most of the letters mentioned here were sent quite openly, by letter bearers or carriers or, once it had been formed in the mid-seventeenth century in England, by the postal service, which dramatically altered the regularity and security of mail. There were, however, letters that were covert, which needed to be secretly conveyed to prevent their contents falling into the wrong hands. Novel techniques have been used across the centuries in conjunction with codes and ciphers to have letters secretly conveyed. Letters were carried sewn into collars, sleeves or other clothing; they were hidden in trunks, pots, barrels and staffs. The famous Babington Plot letters, which were integral in the downfall of Mary, Queen of Scots in 1587, were conveyed in a barrel stopper, only to be intercepted and used as evidence by Elizabeth I's spymaster, Sir Francis Walsingham.

The Babington Plot A plan to assassinate Elizabeth I in 1586 and put Mary, Queen of Scots on the throne. It was uncovered by the interception of a letter by Mary, approving the assassination, to the Catholic gentleman Anthony Babington, a chief plotter.

One of the most ingenious techniques for hiding a letter was detailed in Johannes Jacob Wecker's encyclopedic *Eighteen Books of the Secrets of Art and Nature* (1660), which taught 'The way to write in an Egge'. Such a trick, he wrote, required one to

Grind Alum very fine a long time with vinegar, and draw what forme you will upon the Egg-shell, drying it in the hot sun, put it three or four days in brine or sharpe vinegar, when it is dryed, rost it, when it is rosted take off the shell, and you shall sind the letters written upon the hard white. Hence ariseth another, you must wrap the egg in wax, and with a pin make letters upin the wax, where the letters are, fill it up with moysture, and let it steep in vinegar twenty four houres, take off the wax, and the shell after that, and you shall read the letters upin the egge.

This, then, is how the history of letters links to the history of eggs and raises the important question of what, actually, *is* a letter? The history of covert correspondence shows us that it certainly does not just have to be a piece of paper inside an envelope. In exceptional circumstances – in urgency, haste, under pressure

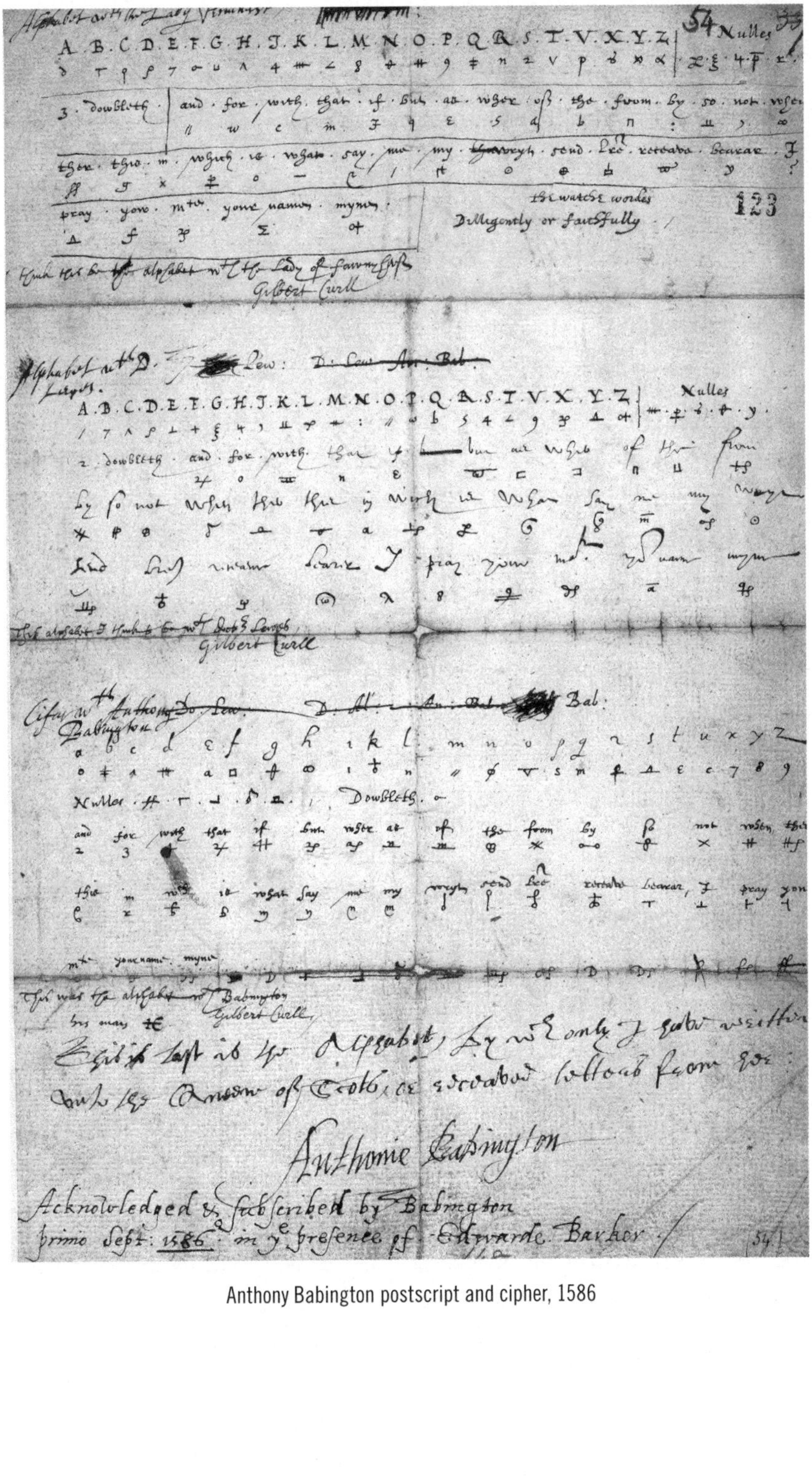

Anthony Babington postscript and cipher, 1586

or while imprisoned – letters were penned on other materials at hand. The Tudor woman Elizabeth Wetherton, for example, wrote to her mother on a fragment of printed breviary with plainsong notation, presumably because paper was in short supply.

The history of the letter, then, is tied up with secrets, codes, spies and espionage, which often involved intricate government systems to intercept, decipher and act upon intelligence gathered in this manner, as in Elizabethan England. At Versailles, the palace of the vainglorious and somewhat paranoid Louis XIV, the French king had all of the incoming and outgoing mail of his courtiers intercepted and read by a special *cabinet noir* – 'black cabinet' – a group that had been set up much earlier under Cardinal Richelieu. Based in Paris, this *cabinet noir* was effectively a crack team of manuscript specialists and cryptographers trained in the dark arts of surveillance. One of the techniques that they specialized in was being able to open letters locked with seals in a way that was undetectable.

SEALS

Before the gummed envelope appeared towards the end of the nineteenth century, letters were enclosed in a folded sheet of paper that was sealed with wax – either beeswax or shellac, a resin secreted by the lac bug, found in India, which is much harder than beeswax. The sealing of a letter at its most straightforward was very simple. A letter would be folded horizontally to form an oblong, the two ends of which would be then tucked inside each other. Wax would then be melted and applied within the seam of paper, and a seal (in the form of a signet ring, or a fob or desk seal) would be pressed onto the wet wax to impress an authenticating design, for example a heraldic coat of arms, or a badge of office. More personal seals show an immense diversity of designs, including bird and animal motifs, various devices, emblems and mottoes, as well as rebuses or visual puns on the owner's name or profession. One particularly poignant personal seal belonged to the Scottish politician and diplomat Sir Robert Moray (1608–73). Made when he was a widower, it featured a winged Eros shooting an arrow towards a heart, and carried the inscription of 'Vne sevlle' or 'one alone' beside an altar, symbolic of his bereavement.

The seal's security system was simple: if the seal was tampered with or broken you'd know that your letter had been intercepted. There were various methods known at the time to bypass these seals, which was a much trickier process than simply steaming open a gummed envelope and resealing it. We know about these methods from a cryptography manual written by a sixteenth-century Italian polymath called Giovanni Battista Della Porta. In *De furtivis literarum notis* (1563) he outlines several ways of opening a letter and counterfeiting a seal, including instructions to: 'Melt Sulphur, and cast it into powder of Ceruse, while it is melted. Put this mixture upon the Seal, but fence it about with paper or Wax, or Chalk, and press it down. When it is cold, take it off, and in that shall you have the print of the Seal.' The key here was to use some form of chemical compound to take an impression of the seal, then to remove it and replace it when done with reading the letter. In this way it was possible to unseal and reseal a letter so that it seemed unopened.

Giovanni Battista Della Porta (c.1535–1613) An Italian scholar and playwright with particular interests in occult philosophy, astrology, alchemy, mathematics, ciphers and cryptology. He was known as the 'Professor of Secrets', and his most famous work is *Magiae Naturalis* (*Natural Magic*).

It appears that courtiers knew that this was going on. Elisabeth Charlotte of Bavaria (the wife of Louis XIV's brother), when writing to her German cousins, warned that just because

> letters are properly sealed does not mean anything; they have a material made of mercury and other stuff that can be pressed onto a seal, where it takes on the shape of the seal... After they have read and copied the letters, they neatly reseal them and no one can see that they have been opened.

In such an 'information state', the letter was no longer simply a means of communication between two people but, thanks to master cryptographers and the interception of mail, these intimate epistolary exchanges between courtiers allow us to observe the political fault lines of absolute monarchy.

STEALING MAIL

An alternative to reading others' mail was simply to seize it, read it, and not give it back – a practice that has its own history. Perhaps the largest archive of seized letters in the world is in the National Archives in Kew, London, because that is where the archive of the Royal Navy is kept, and if any institution in all of history had both the opportunity and means to intercept letters on an industrial scale, it was the Royal Navy. In this archive are letters to and from naval officers, muster books, ships' logs, and so on, a vast array of material amounting to millions of pages covering five centuries of British sea power and a seemingly endless series of wars. A key era in that history was the extraordinary global expansion of the British empire from the mid-seventeenth century onwards, and in the archive is a category of document described as 'intercepted mails and papers'. It comprises correspondence seized from enemy ships by the English state during the period 1652 to 1811 and includes somewhere in the region of 100,000 documents. These documents are pan-European, transatlantic and global in their reach, written to professional colleagues and rivals, as well as family and friends abroad, and therefore reflective of a unique kind of relationship – that which is lived at a distance.

One of the most remarkable features of this archive is that much of it still remains unopened, some of it even intact in its original postbags: here are love letters that never reached their destination; news that never arrived; letters of condolence or invitations that to this day remain sealed, both the sender and recipient having long departed this world. It is history trapped in history, and a fascinating phase in the story of these letters will begin when they are opened by researchers and the light of the modern world falls on their contents for the very first time.

——— THE DUTCH POSTMASTER'S TRUNK ———

One of the most extraordinary recent chance finds relating to unopened letters is the discovery of a Dutch postmaster's trunk containing approximately 2,600 letters sent to The Hague from all over Europe between 1689 and 1706 [*see fig xx*]. None of these letters was ever delivered, and 600 of them have never been opened. Prior to the invention of the postage stamp, payment for delivery was the responsibility of the receiver rather than the sender, and it is therefore highly likely that these undelivered or 'dead' letters were kept in the hopes that they would eventually be claimed and the postage paid for – the trunk was in fact nicknamed 'the piggy bank'.

The team of scholars at Leiden, London and MIT behind the research project want to preserve the original letters intact as a monument to the past, and therefore have pioneered new techniques to read the letters without actually opening them.

A detailed knowledge of how letters were folded has enabled the 'letterlocking project' to team up with scientists to uncover their secrets. High-tech X-ray photography is used to take thousands of images of the insides of the letters and a software program reassembles the letters line for line as they would have been written down centuries before. In this case reading other people's mail doesn't require it to be opened in the first place and those secrets contained in the postmaster's trunk bring us to the important question of the history of the box...

·18·

BOXES

——

The history of boxes is all about…
skips, memories, the Second World War,
floating milk thermometers and
being buried alive.

The history of boxes is not so much about the box itself than what you might put in it. At least one of us still has, in a special memory box under his bed, the shoes (red snake-skin, if you're interested) that his wife was wearing the time they first met, not to mention memento boxes for both of his children containing almost every scrap of paper connected to their existence from the moment they were born. Some of us were born pack rats, hoarders of paper like the medieval Paston family of Norfolk, whose letters and papers survive in such abundance; or the famed seventeenth-century London diarist Samuel Pepys who kept so much material and ephemera that he now has his own library at Magdalene College, Cambridge; or the seventeenth-century Verney family from Buckinghamshire, who seem to have kept *absolutely everything*. Others purged, threw away or discarded, and by these actions their lives are now lost to the historical record. All of this is related to the history of the box, as a way of preserving, filing, collecting and, above all, creating memories of the past.

THE BOX IN THE SKIP

Luck is so often the ally of the historian in his or her quest to uncover the past. It is the only way of describing a chance discovery that happened a few years ago, a discovery that in itself is remarkable, but which could be echoed hundreds of times around the country. The story begins with a house clearance, a skip, a box, and an email to a history professor – namely, James.

The email from a final-year undergraduate history student asked if the professor was available to meet to chat about ideas for a dissertation topic that focused on what the student described as 'a collection of letters in his care'. A time was agreed upon, and at that first meeting the student produced what appeared to be an old shoebox, only slightly less wide and covered in green velvet fabric with braiding. His father, the student said, owned a skip company, and this box had been found in one of his skips after a house clearance. Not quite knowing what to make of the box, his father passed it to his historian son to see what he thought of it. Once opened, the box revealed several hundred items of correspondence dating from the Second World War between one Miss Helen Dare and George Tweddle, a soldier who was away fighting on the Continent, and who would later become this woman's husband.

The box, discarded and found by chance in a skip, presumably on the death of Helen Tweddle (née Dare), was nothing less than a 'memory box', which housed the love correspondence between her and her beloved from when they were parted during the early 1940s. Countless such correspondences must have been conducted in this period, many of which have found their way to the archives of the Imperial War Museum in London or local record offices, while others are doubtless in private hands, hidden under beds, in attics or at the back of wardrobes in boxes of precisely this kind, the boxes acting as repositories of memories of past lives, past relationships, past loves and longings. As generations slowly but inevitably disappear we have a duty to preserve these boxes and these memories, to tell the histories of those generations that have gone before.

POWDERHAM CASTLE

Museums and archives around the world hold boxes of varying types and sizes, from Helen Tweddle's memory box to trunks, cabinets, coffins and sarcophagi and display cases: they are unexpectedly integral to both the study of history and the way that history is experienced or absorbed by the public. This is most clearly revealed by a rummage around the beautiful Powderham Castle near Exeter, the ancestral home of the Courtenay family, earls of Devon since the fourteenth century.

Powderham Castle Situated on the banks of the River Exe and home to the Courtenay family. Built in 1406 as a fortified manor house, it was besieged in 1455 during the Wars of the Roses and in 1645 during the English Civil War when it was a Royalist garrison. It underwent significant rebuilding during the eighteenth and nineteenth centuries.

In the castle archives are myriad boxes acquired across centuries for differing purposes of archiving and preservation, and they are a delight to explore: you simply have no idea what you will discover inside.

As one would expect of any muniments room that has been carefully ordered, documents are neatly housed in boxes and searchable by finding aids and catalogues; box files contain archivists' notes relating to the collection; and early printed books are housed in specially made protective boxes, constructed precisely to fit individual volumes as snugly as possible. A small cupboard contains the religious paraphernalia from the castle's chapel, including boxes of ceremonial equipment: a small shell-shaped box containing a small bowl for use in christenings, another holding a chalice. Alongside these is a small wooden box, simply labelled 'Prayer Books' 'Family', with the word 'old' in brackets. In it are contained dozens of tiny personal books of prayers dating from the late eighteenth to nineteenth century, many of which are annotated with the names of the owner, the person who gifted them, and the date they were presented. Remarkable among these books – which themselves attest to the personal piety of the Georgian and Victorian generation of Courtenays – are thin 'finger prayer books' which, as the name suggests, are no bigger than an index finger. Such thumb-sized tomes could easily be slipped into a pocket for easy reading on the go. Another two piles of family prayer books are contained in old ammunition boxes, probably chosen for their sturdiness.

The archives also include an iron box-like canister measuring over a metre in length, which contains the original Powderham Tithe map dating from 1839, and there are several memory boxes containing the treasured personal effects of a number of members of the family, items and trinkets that were kept for sentimental reasons. One of these, belonging to 'Cousin Betty Somerset', contains rather unexpectedly a device called a 'floating dairy thermometer'. Quite why this contraption ended up in the house's archives is something of a mystery. These Powderham boxes are used to archive, to protect and preserve documents and objects that either have sentimental meaning to the family, or else are important as documentary and legal records, and they are characteristic of this kind of private archive all over the world.

Elsewhere in the castle are boxes housed in storage rooms

brimming with uncatalogued historical items – boxes that historians describe as 'wild archives'. Each male member of the Courtenay family was bought a trunk when he went off to boarding school. The trunk bore his initials and they survive today with the contents of their owners often still intact – a time capsule of personal effects relating to the male generations of this aristocratic Devon family. One such trunk, found off the castle's 'haunted landing' and up a spiral staircase, is full of letters, photos and, bizarrely, two oddly shaped horns. Elsewhere in the house is a box that contains a late Georgian lap-desk – a sort of mobile writing desk – which itself contains letters that, once unwrapped, are found to contain locks of hair.

It is ecstasy for a historian to chance on untouched collections in this way, to be one of the first to uncover the stories they contain, an infectious and utterly consuming reaction the French philosopher and historian Jacques Derrida (1930–2004) described, from first-hand experience, as 'archive fever'.

THE ENGLISH CIVIL WAR

While it is the contents of boxes that are so fascinating and the quest for unopened boxes so addictive, the boxes themselves can also have an interesting story to tell. A cabinet belonging to a woman called Hannah Smith (b.1642) survives today in the Whitworth Art Gallery at the University of Manchester. Elaborately decorated, it is a small upright desktop chest with miniature doors, drawers and a lock.

Such items of furniture were associated with the safe-keeping of secret correspondence and were specifically manufactured for storing documents. One of the remarkable features of this cabinet is that, tucked inside it, is an autobiographical note by the owner. Titled 'The yere of our Lord being 1657', it tells that, in 1654 when Hannah was eleven years old, she went to Oxford, when she began working on her cabinet, and then finished it in London in 1656. More remarkable still is the intricate embroidery on the outside of this box, which – according to the note – she accomplished herself. Hannah was in Oxford at a time when it was a Royalist stronghold during the Republican Commonwealth, and it was at this point that she completed her work on the box.

Republican Commonwealth (1649-60) The period after the execution of Charles I when Britain and Wales – and later Ireland and Scotland – were ruled as a republic. Between 1653 and 1658 Oliver Cromwell acted as 'Lord Protector', but refused to accept the crown and become 'King Oliver'.

The box is made of wood, finely worked, and onto which was mounted an intricate embroidered pattern of silk, metal thread, spangles and seed pearls beautifully stitched onto silk satin and canvas. The embroidery on the box's lid shows the biblical story of 'Joseph in the pit', a representation from the Book of Genesis of a man being left to die. Elsewhere on the box is a sun, partly hidden by cloud, a lion and a leopard, as well as a hidden crowned head. Analysis of these images, which are well-known symbols of kingship, might be taken as evidence that Hannah was in favour of the restoration of the monarchy. The box, therefore, was not only a repository for secret writings, but also a vehicle for coded political messages.

THE PLAGUE

As we have seen, boxes have significant stories to tell. Another type of box that is particularly interesting for the history it reveals is a box for a (hopefully dead) human: the coffin. Coffins have their own long and fascinating history that runs as far back as the oldest timber sarcophagi of ancient Egyptian mummies (around 2500 BCE).*

Historical light has recently been shone on the curious history of coffins by the enormous excavations directly under London for Crossrail, a 73-mile railway line dissecting London along its east–west axis. The excavations have transformed our understanding of both British and world history over millennia. To date 10,000 artefacts have been discovered spanning 55 *million* years of history. In 2012 archaeologists discovered a mass grave by Liverpool Street Station, near the old Bedlam burial ground where some 30,000 Londoners were buried between 1569 and 1738.

Three things made this mass grave particularly interesting. The first was that a nearby grave marker recorded the year – 1665. This was the year of the Great Plague, when some 100,000 people, or a quarter of London's population, died within just eighteen months. The second was that the bodies all appeared to have been buried on the same day; this was not just a mass burial site, but evidence of a mass single-event interment. The third was that the bodies were all buried in wooden coffins. The coffins themselves were thin, evidence of significant pressure on the coffin-making trade and hasty construction, but it was the presence of the coffins, when death was so rampant, which so struck historians, for it presented a different vision of life during the Great Plague than one which has survived in some well-known written sources.

Some contemporary writers wallowed in the death that surrounded them, their accounts focusing on the extremes of the sights and emotions of London and Londoners, none more so than Daniel Defoe (1660–1731), one of the most famous contemporary writers and author of *Robinson Crusoe* (1719). Three years after *Robinson Crusoe* was first published, Defoe wrote about life in London during the Great Plague, presented as an eyewitness account under the initials 'H. F.'. Defoe was just five in 1665 but he based his account on the memory of family members and in particular on the diary of his uncle, Henry Foe. Among the many descriptions of life in London was this particularly lurid account. He described a man, gripped by hysterical grief, following a cart containing his wife and several of his children:

> The cart had in it sixteen or seventeen bodies; some were wrapt up in linen sheets some in rags, some little other than naked, or so loose that what covering they had fell from them in the shooting out of the cart and they fell quite naked among the rest.'

Other accounts of London during the plague also emphasize a sense of chaos. In August of that year the diarist Samuel Pepys had a nasty fright on his way home. He recorded 'To my great trouble I met a dead Corps, of the Plague, in the narrow alley, just bringing down a little pair of stairs', adding 'I shall beware of being late abroad again.'

The discovery of the coffins at Liverpool Street, however, have highlighted an alternative narrative of the plague year, one in which, although Londoners were caught up in unimaginable horror and forced to deal with mass death, they did so with noticeable care for the dead, coffining the corpses and, if there was sufficient room, aligning them east–west, as per Christian tradition. In fact, the sense that one gets from the Crossrail discovery is not one of chaos but one of order – an order born of experience. The 'Great Plague' of 1665 borrowed its title from the Great Plague of 1625 in which over 40,000 Londoners died, and between the two were other deadly seventeenth-century plague years, notably in 1640, 1646 and 1647. These boxes are the most powerful reminder that one of the things that makes us human is that we are the only species that cares for its dead.

BURIED ALIVE

The looming threat of such mass death could create significant psychological anxieties and one of these was the fear of being buried alive. This remains a phobia today but in the past it was far more widespread, particularly in periods of pandemic and before widespread education in scientific medical technique.

This fear of premature burial led to the development of a particular type of box in the eighteenth century: the 'safety coffin'. This was usually a coffin with a bell or other type of signalling device, which the unfortunate but revived person could operate from inside his or her coffin. Other types included glass windows where the corpse could be observed for signs of life. The first recorded example of the safety coffin comes from 1792 when the paranoid Duke Ferdinand of Brunswick (1735–1806) designed a coffin with a window and breathing tube. He also made certain that the coffin and tomb in which he was buried were locked rather than permanently sealed. He was then buried with keys to the locks both to his coffin and his tomb in a pocket in his shroud. Even as late as 1896 the fear of being buried alive persisted and William Tebb (1830–1917), a social reformer otherwise concerned with vaccination, funded the London Association for the Prevention of Premature Burial, and in 1905 wrote a book entitled *Premature Burial and How It May Be Prevented*. In it he recorded some 219 cases of 'near' live burial, as well as 149 actual cases of live burial, 10 cases of live dissection and 2 cases of awakening while being embalmed. It includes the following heart-stopping (and heart-starting) story taken from the *Journal de Rouen* of 1837.

> Cardinal Somaglia was seized with a severe illness from extreme grief; he fell into a state of syncope, which lasted so long that the persons around him thought him dead.

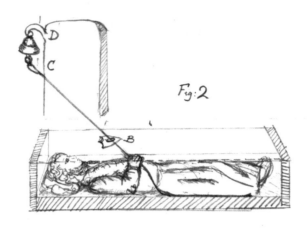

Early sketch of a Victorian safety coffin using a bell attachment

Preparations were instantly made to embalm his body, before the putrefactive process should commence, in order that he might be placed in a leaden coffin, in the family vault. The operator had scarcely penetrated into his chest, when: the heart was seen to beat. The unfortunate patient, who was returning to his senses at that moment, had still sufficient strength to push away the knife of the surgeon, but too late, for the lung had been mortally wounded, and the patient died in a most lamentable manner.

Another quoted story tells the sad tale of a six-year-old boy who was

Discovered during the removal of remains from a village cemetery to a new one at Philadelphia, in which the arms were bent over the skull, one leg drawn up, and the other bent across it in such a way as to show that the little fellow, twenty years before, had been hurried to the grave whilst still alive.

This, then, is just part of the fascinating history of the box which ranges so widely across human history. Make sure that your things – your family memories, your letters, objects, photographs, mementoes – are preserved properly in acid-free archive boxes, which can be purchased cheaply online or picked up from your local record office. Keep documents flat, and protect everything from light and dust, warmth, cold, wet or insects. Do not, ever, put them in a skip, only to be discovered by chance, like that memory box at the start of this chapter, even if such discoveries might make a historian's day. And pray that you do not wake to find yourself facing the fear of being buried alive, which raises the very important question of the history of courage...

·19·

COURAGE

—

The history of courage is all about… gin, stomachs, speeches, the First World War, feminism and shipwrecks.

The history of courage is enormously rewarding, but one must be careful with it – for it is a slippery customer. Courage takes several forms today and has taken several forms in the past; it is connected to personal physical and mental strength, honour and morality, but is also something that can be learned and ingrained. It can even be manufactured.

TYPES OF COURAGE

The history of warfare is an obvious place to start for a history of courage; it is teeming with such stories, but if you look closely it is clear that there are different *types* of courage on show. From a broad perspective, there is the courage of refusing to abandon fallen colleagues in the heat of battle, just as there is the courage of taking responsibility for leadership in seemingly hopeless situations; more specifically there is the courage of going over the top at the Somme in 1916, of running at the sound of a whistle towards a hail of machine-gun fire; and there is the courage in charging on horseback at Balaclava with the Light Brigade in 1854 towards the waiting guns. There is, of course, the courage in holding your ground against such a charge, of standing in the face of horses galloping at thirty miles an hour. At the Battle of Vienna in 1683 at least 3,000 armed and armoured men on horseback charged the Ottoman lines in the largest cavalry charge in history, an unimaginable ordeal. A magnificent description of a relatively late cavalry charge (there were several even in the Second World War) survives from the pen of none other than Winston Churchill who fought as a troop commander in the 21st Lancers during the Anglo-Egyptian war of 1896–98. The charge happened at the battle of Omdurman near Khartoum in the Sudan. The British horsemen suddenly found themselves facing a closely formed unit of Dervish warriors. And they charged – 'As a rider tears through a bullfinch,' wrote Churchill. He continued:

> the officers forced their way through the press; and as an iron rake might be drawn through a heap of shingle, so the regiment followed. They shattered the Dervish array, and, their pace reduced to a walk, scrambled out of the khor on the further side, leaving a score of troopers behind them, and dragging on with the charge more than a thousand Arabs. Then, and not till then, the killing began; and thereafter each man saw the world

Battle of Vienna (1683) Fought to relieve Vienna from an Ottoman siege. A coalition of Christian states led by John III Sobieski, the King of Poland, routed the Ottoman forces and led to a subsequent counter-attack into Ottoman territory. It marked the end of the aggressive expansion of the Ottoman empire in the Mediterranean world which had begun with the conquest of Constantinople in 1453.

along his lance, under his guard, or through the back-sight of his pistol; and each had his own strange tale to tell.

He went on to consider the nature of a cavalry charge with the experience of an eyewitness, his own unusual insight and his wonderful way with words:

> Stubborn and unshaken infantry hardly ever meet stubborn and unshaken cavalry. Either the infantry run away and are cut down in the flight, or they keep their heads and destroy nearly all the horsemen by their musketry. On this occasion two living walls had actually crashed together. The Dervishes fought manfully. They tried to hamstring the horses, they fired their rifles, pressing the muzzles into the very bodies of their opponents. They cut reins and stirrup-leathers. They flung their throwing-spears with great dexterity. They tried every device of cool determined men practised in war and familiar with cavalry; and besides, they swung sharp, heavy swords which bit deep.

MORAL COURAGE

Such courage of facing a cavalry charge is not only to be found on the battlefields of history. Unarmed and unmoving, in 1913 the suffragette Emily Davison (1872–1913) stood her ground in front of galloping horses on the racecourse at Epsom until she was run down by the king's horse. This was a courageous act undertaken for the cause of women's suffrage, rather than courage generated by machismo, military training and codes of loyalty. While the courage of feminists could lead to direct action of this nature – chaining themselves to railings and smashing windows – it was also underpinned by a strong sense of ideological or moral courage. This was a case argued by the writer and pioneering modernist Virginia Woolf (1882–1941) in her polemical work, *A Room of One's Own* (1929). Musing on the fictional character of Shakespeare's sister, she wrote:

> my belief is that if we [women] live another century or so –
> I am talking of the common life which is the real life and not
> of the little separate lives which we live as individuals – and
> have five hundred [pounds] a year each of us and rooms of our
> own; if we have the habit of freedom and the courage to write
> exactly what we think; if we escape a little from the common
> sitting-room and see human beings not always in their relation
> to each other but in relation to reality… then the opportunity
> will come and the dead poet who was Shakespeare's sister will
> put on the body which she has so often laid down.

Her ideas struck at the heart of patriarchal society, and argued for the financial independence of women and the importance of female access to education as a route to creative, social and intellectual freedom. 'Lock up your libraries if you like,' she wrote 'but there is no gate, no lock, no bolt that you can set upon the freedom of my mind.' The courage of one's convictions, to stand up against oppression, to speak up for what is right, to work towards social and political change, this is courage indeed, and its history is recorded across civilizations.

WHISTLEBLOWERS

These particular examples of first-wave feminism are linked with the courage of speaking out, a type of courage with a contemporary relevance. Today one of the forms of courage with which we are most familiar is the courage of recognizing and telling the truth, seen in the form of whistleblowing – standing up against 'the man' for what is right. While it may feel like a modern phenomenon connected only to figures like Edward Snowden who, in 2013, revealed the existence of global surveillance programmes involving numerous democratic governments; Chelsea Manning who, in 2010, exposed American misconduct during campaigns in Afghanistan and Iraq (2004–9); Daniel Ellsberg who, in 1971, revealed American political decision making relating to the Vietnam War; or 'Deep Throat', the code name of the informant who revealed Republican involvement in a break-in at the Democratic National Committee headquarters in Washington (the Watergate Complex), leading to the fall of President Richard Nixon; speaking out publicly against illegal or unethical practices has a surprisingly long history. The earliest written evidence for the rewarding of whistleblowers is, amazingly, 1,300 years old, and comes from seventh-century England in a declaration of King Wihtred of Kent (620–725 CE): 'if a freeman works during [the Sabbath], he shall forfeit his [profits], and the man who informs against him shall have half the fine, and [the profits] of the labour'.

The earliest written evidence for protecting whistleblowers in America comes from over a millennium later. In 1777 officers of the Continental Navy – the navy that had been created by the American Colonies to fight against Britain in the American War of Independence – revealed the torture of British prisoners by none other than the naval commander, Esek Hopkins. In a petition to the new Continental Congress, ten sailors and marines described how they were unhappy with the way that Hopkins had 'treated prisoners in the most inhuman and barbarous manner'. Hopkins retaliated, filing a libel suit against the men. Congress retaliated in turn, passing a law stating: 'it is the duty of all persons in the service of the United States, as well as all other inhabitants thereof, to give the earliest information to Congress or any other proper authority of any misconduct, frauds or misdemeanors committed by any officers or persons in

the service of these states, which may come to their knowledge.'
Hopkins was suspended and Congress paid $1,418 to cover costs
associated with the whistleblowers' defence.

DUTCH COURAGE

In this history of courage, therefore, lies the history of citizen
law-keepers speaking out against those who have broken the
law. Such courage that has been *en-couraged* has a history all
of its own. 'Dutch courage' – bravery induced by drinking –
is, in etymological terms, specifically linked with battle even
though the use of alcohol to ease the nerves was by no means
restricted to war. One possible explanation for its derivation is
that it comes from the use of Dutch gin (or genever) by English
soldiers fighting with Dutch allies on the Continent against the
French King Louis XIV during the Thirty Years War (1618–48).
As an English colloquialism of Dutch origin – different from
'going Dutch' (sharing something equally or paying for oneself)
or 'Dutch uncle' (someone who gives frank advice) – it distinctly
came to refer to drinking spirits rather than beer as a means of
stiffening one's resolve.

The calming effects of alcohol consumption were widely
understood by military commanders whose troops needed artificial courage in the face of adversity. Sailors in the Royal Navy
were given a daily ration of spirits (brandy until 1655, when it
was replaced by rum) and an extra tot was often allowed before
battle and, if available, before undergoing significant surgery –
in which case it acted to boost courage as well as dull pain. As
the British fleet approached the combined French and Spanish
fleet at the Battle of Trafalgar in 1805 the crew of Nelson's HMS
Victory were all issued with half a pint of wine. Similarly, in the
British army ranks at Waterloo (1815), many regiments distributed brandy among the troops before battle.

Rum-drinking caricature: 'Come Youngster – Another Glass
of Grog Before You Go On Deck' (1840)

During the First World War, it was decided over the harsh
winter of 1914–15 to issue troops serving with the British Expeditionary Force with a rum ration to stimulate courage. These
were distributed twice a week, and daily for those on active duty
in the trenches. While medical opinions were sharply divided
on the effects of alcohol consumption on combat troops, Colonel
J. S. Y. Rogers, the medical officer to the 4th Black Watch,
considered, 'had it not been for the rum ration I do not think
we should have won the war. Before the men went over the top
they had a good meal and a double ration of rum and coffee.'
Rum rations were also used during the Second World War, but
were more strictly controlled; and cheap or free beer was widely
available for US troops on military bases in Vietnam during the
Vietnam War (1955–75), possibly more for morale than courage.
The negative sides to all this were high levels of alcohol abuse
and alcoholism among troops, which had a notable medical and
personal cost. Many doctors felt that military life encouraged

a culture of heavy drinking which for some led to addiction. A *British Medical Journal* report from 1916 concluded that consumption of alcohol was 'prevalent and excessive among the recruits'.

NAZI SOLDIERS

It was not just alcohol that was used by state militaries to enhance the performance of their armed forces. Drugs were also supplied, designed to stimulate courage chemically. One of the first coordinated attempts to produce performance-enhancing drugs for military purposes was by Nazi Germany during the Second World War. Vast quantities of the amphetamine-based stimulant Pervitin (commonly known today as crystal meth) were mass-produced and supplied to the *Wehrmacht* to help the Third Reich win its blitzkrieg. Invented in a Berlin-based laboratory in 1938, Pervitin soon came to the attention of German military doctors, who saw the huge potential of a wonder drug that increased alertness, physical stamina and courage. During the few months between April and July 1940, some 35 million tablets were shipped to the German army and navy. Use of these drugs was widespread by German troops. A letter written by the Nobel prize-winning German author Heinrich Böll in May 1940, when he was a young soldier in the German army, asked his family for further supplies of the addictive drug: 'Perhaps,' he wrote rather desparately, 'you could get me some more Pervitin so that I can have a backup supply?', and on another occasion, 'If at all possible, please send me some more Pervitin.'

In 1944 Germany was developing an even more powerful superdrug, D-IX, which had so impressed scientists that it was manufactured and issued to troops. Tests on concentration camp inmates found that subjects could march in a circle for up to ninety kilometres without rest while carrying a heavy backpack. The end of the war terminated production of the drug, so it was never truly tested throughout the German *Wehrmacht*. What is striking, though, is the degree to which performance-enhancing drugs of this nature are used by some modern-day militaries to stimulate a kind of chemical courage that is accompanied by robot-like endurance and ultra-violent ferocity. During the second half of the twentieth century, too, Vietnam War American troops had easy access to amphetamines, and a member of a long-range reconnaissance platoon, Elton Manzione, recalled a navy commando saying that the drugs 'gave you a sense of bravado as well as keeping you awake. Every sight and sound was heightened. You were wired into it all and at times you felt really invulnerable.'

SPEECHES

Another stimulus to courage is aural rather than alcoholic, and is connected to the high-flown rhetoric of motivational speeches. Throughout history words from inspirational historical figures have persuaded people to perform great feats of courage, whether it be Martin Luther King's famous 'I have a dream' speech, Winston Churchill's 'We shall fight them on the beaches' speech, or even Elizabeth I's speech to the troops on 18 August 1588 at Tilbury during the Armada campaign when she stirred the nation to arms with the rallying cry:

> I know I have the body but of a weak and feeble woman; but I have the heart and stomach of a king, and of a king of England too, and think foul scorn that Parma or Spain, or any prince of Europe, should dare to invade the borders of my realm... by your obedience to my general, by your concord in the camp, and your valour in the field, we shall shortly have a famous victory over those enemies of my God, of my kingdom, and of my people.

The speech was pure Elizabethan theatre, spectacular in its pageantry and ceremony. On the morning of 18 August the queen left London by royal barge, travelling to Tilbury closely guarded by her royal bodyguards the Gentlemen Pensioners, all of whom were dressed in their finery of highly polished armour and feathered helmets. On reaching Tilbury Fort, she was greeted by an escort of 2,000 infantry and 1,000 cavalry, before addressing the 17,000-strong force assembled there clad in a man's armoured breastplate. What is more remarkable, though, is that the authenticity of this most famous of speeches from the last of the great Tudor monarchs has been called into question. It is highly likely that these were not, in fact, the exact words that Elizabeth uttered on this day, but rather those rewritten and repackaged for propaganda purposes. The representation of Elizabeth having the 'stomach' of a king is important, because of its connection to courage: to have the stomach for something is to have the courage for something.

Real or rewritten, the passion of such speeches motivated nations and people to acts of courage, persuaded them to take up arms to defend their homelands, families and ways of life, and to challenge those who sought to dominate and oppress them. In the words of Shakespeare's Henry V: 'Once more unto the breach, dear friends, once more; / Or close the wall up with our English dead!'

MEDALS

A further part of the history of courage encouragement is the history of the recognition of courage in the form of a medal, whether to reward acts of military courage and bravery, or to celebrate those who acted courageously in day-to-day life as civilians, and they are surprisingly valuable sources for the historian.

The history of awards for military courage is ancient and dates back to the Roman empire in the form of *phalerae*, a bronze, silver or gold disc that would be mounted onto the staffs of a legion's standard. Evidence for these discs survives in numerous forms. One of the finest representations of a Roman soldier wearing his honours comes from a gravestone, c.9 CE, now in the Bonn Museum [*see fig. 23*]. This man, who we know from the inscription was Marcus Caelius, son of Titus, was from Bologna and a centurion in the Legio XVIII, the eighteenth legion of the Imperial Roman army. He died aged fifty-three in the Varian War and is shown proudly wearing several military decorations including four *phalerae*. In 1978 no fewer than seven were found buried together in a bronze pot in Lupu, Romania. Imagery on surviving *phalerae* are varied, and those from Lupu are particularly fascinating for their depiction of Dacian women who appear only on very rare occasions in ancient material culture, a powerful reminder of the value of medals as historical sources.

The most famous American gallantry medal, the Medal of Honor, was first awarded in 1863 and has only been presented 3,517 times since; the most famous British gallantry medal, the Victoria Cross, was first awarded in 1857 and to date has only been given out 1,358 times. Both of these are interesting examples of originally conceived and designed medals. By no means is this the case for many other medals, however, and the gallantry medal awarded by the Nazis in the Second World War, the Iron

Cross, is an excellent and fascinating example of a medal with a history.

THE IRON CROSS

In 1939 Hitler settled on the Iron Cross as his award of choice for valour. It was originally a symbol associated with the Teutonic Knights but became known to Hitler because of his service in the First World War (he was a dispatch runner on the Western Front) when Kaiser Wilhelm II had also issued the Iron Cross as an award for valour. But during that war it had actually been an award of the Kingdom of Prussia, just one part of the German empire. It had also been used by Wilhelm's grandfather, Wilhelm I, during the Franco-Prussian War (1870–71) but its origins lay even further back in time, during the German campaign against Napoleon in 1813–14: it was then that Frederick William III of Prussia established the Iron Cross as a decoration for valour. Hitler therefore deliberately chose a medal for valour in 1939 that was already

The Iron Cross 1st Class of the Napoleonic Wars,
in its original form of 1 June 1813

deeply rooted in Germanic history and culture, but at the same time it needed updating for his purposes and in March 1939 he officially rebranded the Iron Cross as a *German* decoration, his acknowledgement of the centrality of the Prussian army to the *Wehrmacht* and thus to the German Reich itself.

This valour medal, therefore, was already a medal with multiple histories, but Hitler also subdivided the Iron Cross award into five distinct levels. The highest, the Knight's Cross with Golden Oak Leaves, Swords and Diamonds (*mit Goldenem Eichenlaub, Schwertern und Brillanten*), was only ever awarded once: to Hans-Ulrich Rudel, a pilot who single-handedly destroyed 800 vehicles of all types including 519 tanks, and achieved numerous direct hits on bridges, important supply routes and several ships. By the end of the war he had flown an unmatched 2,530 missions, in which his plane was shot down or he crash-landed more than thirty times. In February 1945 his right leg was blown off by an anti-aircraft shell but he managed to land the plane and six weeks later was flying again with a partially healed stump, a prosthesis and a clever counterweight to help operate his steering rudders. This particular military medal for valour, therefore, is unique because it was created once and awarded once, which gives it a unique place in the history of medals.

Civilian gallantry medals came later than their military counterparts. There are several different types, but among the rarest in Britain is the Edward Medal, awarded to both men and women, initially for miners and quarrymen and later for dockworkers and railwaymen, who risked their own lives to save those of their fellow workers.

—— THE WHITEHAVEN MINING DISASTER ——

The stories of those awarded the Edward Medal are little known but the few that have survived are inspiring. In May 1910 workman Hugh McKenzie found himself faced with a terrible fire at the Wellington Pit in Whitehaven, Cumbria. The fire had followed a terrific explosion. It was feared – correctly, they later discovered – that many of the miners survived the initial blast but were entombed, alive, by debris. The fire, meanwhile, roared into life and burned furiously. Of the original shift of 143 men, only 7 survived. The youngest to die were only fifteen years old. Many families lost more than one family member. The local community was transformed. Of those resident in Whitehaven, 85 women were widowed and 260 children lost their fathers. McKenzie was one of 64 men awarded the bronze Edward Medal after the disaster, the largest number of medals ever given for a single incident. The *London Gazette* published the following account of the men's heroism:

> Right through the night and all the next day, rescue parties were at work trying to reach the workings where the missing men were entombed, but it was extremely difficult, the atmosphere dense. Some of the timbering in the mine was on fire while the only means of ventilating the portion of the pit where the men were trapped was entirely cut off. At the pithead there were heart-rending scenes. Women, with children, in pain and anxiety waited for news of their loved ones. Many of them stayed at the pithead all night and the whole of the following day refusing to leave for rest or refreshment and a number collapsed, worn out by their vigil.

What makes the story even more poignant are the chalked messages found shortly afterwards on the mine's walls, left by those miners who survived the first blast.

ANIMAL COURAGE

By 1943 gallantry awards were issued in Britain to animals, and to date no fewer than sixty-seven animals have been awarded the Dickin Medal, including thirty-one dogs, thirty-two Second World War carrier pigeons, three horses and one cat. Before that time owners found other ways of remembering and commemorating especially courageous animals. In 1824 W. Ellis Gosling commissioned the pre-eminent animal painter of his time, Sir Edwin Landseer, to paint a portrait of his dog, Neptune, a Newfoundland – a breed that was then famed for their lifesaving ability at sea. Neptune is shown on the shore, on the verge of leaping into action [*see fig. 24*]. Gosling framed the painting in oak taken from the hulk of HMS *Temeraire*, a huge warship that had fought at the Battle of Trafalgar (1805), and he included a plaque likening Neptune's sense of duty to that of Nelson's sailors.

Perhaps, however, one of the most interesting things about the history of courage is that, for various reasons, we have often been willing to see it when it is not necessarily there: the history of courage can be the history of false courage, or of courage misidentified in the historical record.

SHIPWRECKS

Consider the shipwrecks of the *Birkenhead* in 1852 and the *Titanic* in 1912. The *Birkenhead* was a troopship built of iron and powered by steam-driven paddle wheels, which sailed from Portsmouth for South Africa, where the troops aboard were to take part in the Xhosa Wars. Also aboard were 600 of the soldiers' wives and children. The vessel struck an uncharted rock near the small town of Gansbaai. She attempted to move astern off the rock but struck it again hard, enough to split her in two. Unfortunately there were insufficient boats for all of the people on board. The women and children were prioritized and placed in the ship's cutter, a small boat for ferrying the crew to shore.

If you believed what was reported in the newspapers, which very quickly covered the event, you would think that the British soldiers stood calmly in rank while the ship sank under them and the women and children were pulled to safety, far away from the powerful vortex that the giant ship created. These accounts ensured that the soldiers became famous as the exemplars of courageous behaviour in hopeless circumstances. The wreck of the *Birkenhead* came to be one of the most enduring stories of Victorian military heroism, and it is even believed that the German emperor, Kaiser Wilhelm II, had accounts of it read to his troops during the First World War as an example of manly courage.

Our understanding of behaviour during shipwrecks, however, means that we no longer accept at face value the nationalism and patriarchal attitudes that coloured such accounts. We now know that the men of the *Birkenhead* were threatened to stay as they were; we know that their immobility was not the spontaneous act that generations believed it to be, nor was it followed by all men there.

Similarly, the sinking of the *Titanic* in 1912 became known as another fine example of the 'women and children first' type of heroism and courage. But we now know in great detail what happened in the hours between the ship striking the iceberg and her final loss and, unsurprisingly in such a situation, the reality is complicated. 'Women and children first' appears to have happened on one side of the ship but not on the other; some men leaped onto lifeboats full of women, endangering all aboard, while others brawled on deck to get access to the lifeboats; some men, once in lifeboats which were not full, refused to row back to survivors treading the freezing water; and some women refused to be given space in a lifeboat if it meant leaving their husbands, brothers, fathers, cousins, nephews and male friends on the ship. This complexity was matched in other shipwrecks. Even if 'women and children first' was practised, in most instances it actually meant the captain's family, followed by ladies, followed by white Christian women and children – and then the rest.

MOUNTAINEERING

Courage was everywhere in the past just as it is everywhere now, but much of it is lost to history. There is the courage of asking someone out on a date, the courage of going to school every day, of going into hospital, of facing intimidation on a daily basis even if it is only you who knows this fear. Historians have a responsibility to ensure that such private stories of courage are never lost to history.

One such story of private courage relates to the numerous volunteers who faced perilous heights and dangers when attempting mountain rescue before the founding in 1950 of the First Aid Committee for Mountaineering Clubs. Its formation followed several serious accidents, which pushed rescuers to test their courage in extreme conditions. In the 1903 Scafell disaster in the Lake District, four climbers fell to their deaths, and in 1928, an accident in the Peak District saw a climber fall 40 feet and break his skull. The courageous efforts of a relay of volunteers to stretcher the climber down to safety ultimately saved the man's life, although his leg needed amputating several months later, but this episode nonetheless paved the way for the formation of the Mountain Rescue service – which raises the very important question of the history of mountains...

·20·

MOUNTAINS

—

The history of mountains is all about…
freedom, prejudice, vendetta, elephants
and the absence of history.

———— FRANKENSTEIN ————

Dr Victor Frankenstein was fascinated with mountains. In Mary Shelley's 1818 novel *Frankenstein*, her protagonist finds himself in the French Alps. He wonders at his environment in a splendidly Romantic way – he is, after all, a man of his time. Climbing on the Montanvert Alpine glacier, he found that the experience 'filled me with a sublime ecstasy that gave wings to the soul, and allowed it to soar from the obscure world to light and joy'. Suddenly, however, the weather changes and Frankenstein finds the mountains haunting, Gothic in their desolation and looming threat. Mont Blanc is described as having an 'awful majesty' (can anyone sense the lurking presence of the monster here?!).

Frankenstein's trip to the Alps captures perfectly the contradictory nature of mountains that has always influenced human history: simultaneously captivating in their beauty and enormity of scale, but equally terrifying and dangerous. They have both the capacity to uplift the soul and inspire greatness yet also heighten an awareness of one's own insignificance. His fictional experience of mountains is a common one in history. Indeed, mountains occupy a special place in the 'deep history' of the world.

The slowness with which mountains change makes them a fascinating subject for historians interested in the deep structures of the past, and the long-standing, imperceptible but slowly changing relationships between people and the world around them. Throughout history they have acted as a physical, political, social and cultural barrier; they have been a natural resource to exploit (think gold rushes and mining); a terrain to conquer and tame; a wilderness to explore and enjoy. 'Mountains come first,' wrote the brilliant French historian Fernand Braudel (1902–85) in his magisterial study *The Mediterranean and the Mediterranean World in the Age of Philip II* published just after the Second World War. What Braudel was concerned with, above all, was the impact that geography had on past societies, and in particular the impact that the mountain ranges of the Pyrenees and the Alps had on the landlocked Mediterranean Sea.

——— MOUNTAIN FREEDOM ———

The mountains of the Mediterranean world during the sixteenth century were in fact all about freedom, what historians can identify as 'mountain freedom'. The sociopolitical structures that stifled the plains and the towns with the tentacles of government and bureaucracy found it much harder to permeate the lofty heights of mountain settlements, with their treacherous roads and passes, many of which were rendered impassable during snow-laden winter months. Feudalism did not work in the mountains; there was no embedded nobility, no rich, well-fed clergy, nor did the arms of the *gendarmes* (or paramilitary police officers) extend into mountaintop hamlets.

In sparsely populated, high-altitude areas, inhabitants were able to defy authority. Local customs were strong, with each village and canton acquiring its own way of ruling, generally through the village elders.

In such areas, unpenetrated by feudal concepts of justice, such as in Sardinia, Corsica and Albania, a culture of vendetta and banditry flourished that has continued into the present day. In Corsica the main haunts of the bandits were between Tor and Mount Santo Appiano in the wilderness regions. One infamous Corsican bandit was Capracinta of Prunelli whose father was condemned to the galleys in the early nineteenth century, which led his son and some of his relations to head into hiding from where they could escape justice and launch attacks to avenge their relative. They descended from the mountains to kill personal enemies, soldiers and spies, and on one occasion even captured the public executioner and executed him! In 1820 Capracinta was also reputed to have headed into the region three times from his mountain hideaway to attempt to kill his mother-in-law 'because she had denounced him to the troops'.

MOUNTAIN TIME

The geographical barrier of the mountain created a kind of a physical or cultural barrier between those societies and the 'broad movements of history': in other words they were societies preserved in aspic. Indeed, in the vague rural time of the turn-of-the-fourteenth-century Pyrenean village of Montaillou it has been argued by modern historians that history itself was almost absent from village culture, that it existed in an 'island of time'. Such isolated villages were, in a sense, *history-less*, as they had no ways of conceptualizing or recording anything but the most recent past. The remoteness of life experienced in medieval and early modern southern European mountain villages was a common feature of mountain life globally – from the Andes in South America to the Himalayas in Asia. Communications between mountain communities and the rest of the world have, throughout history, been limited, and low levels of literacy and formal learning similarly restricted written forms of communication and privileged oral modes of interaction, news and gossip.

This has led to a relative dearth of written historical material relating to mountain societies. To some extent this gap is filled with oral history traditions, such as in the remote mountainous regions of Albania, where oral traditions passed ancient customary law and memory from one generation to the next. An early twentieth-century account of a conversation with a clansman from the northern Albanian village of Thethi is particularly revealing of the ways in which traditions and memory operated in non-literate cultures:

> I am an old man, and I have seen that when men go down to the cities to learn what is in books they come back scorning the wisdom of their fathers and remembering nothing of it, and they speak foolishly, words which do not agree with one another. But the things that a man knows because he has seen them, the things he considers while he walks on the trails and while he sits by the fires, these things are not many, but they are sound. Then when a man is lonely he puts words to these things and the words become a song, and the song stays as it was said, in the memories of those that hear it.

DISAPPEARING CULTURES

The uniqueness of mountain geography, therefore, can threaten the survival of cultures. One of the most powerful examples today, in which we can actually map the slow disappearance of a culture and yet still see that culture clinging on for dear life, is in the Zarafshan mountains of Takjikistan. Here are the remnants of the Sogdians, a civilization whose kingdom, Sogdiana, dominated a large area of Central Asia for more than a millennium, from the sixth century BCE until the eleventh century CE. The Sogdians were, above all, traders, and in those years their language, a form of ancient Persian, dominated trade along the Silk Road. The Sogdians were the middlemen of that trade, and if the Silk Road had a 'soundscape' it would be the merry babble of haggling in Sogdian. Such trade routes were the nervous system of civilizations, carrying oral traditions along their pathways.

The kingdom of the Sogdians now survives in the physical bodies of some 1,500 people who still inhabit the Yaghnob Valley, deep in the Zarafshan mountains. These people, known as the Yaghnobi, are all that remains of the Sogdians. Their language is a direct descendant of the Sogdian language. They took to the mountains in the tenth century CE as their society began to fragment under the pressure of Islam as it spread from the west. For the Sogdians the mountains were a place of refuge where they could escape fragmentation and destruction at the hands of the hostile and invasive culture of the Arab caliphate that swept through Central Asia from the eighth century. And it worked. Today, however, the very isolation that saved them is now killing them, stifling the lifeblood of this noble people [*see fig. 25*]. Their culture is dying out, life seeping after a killer blow struck by another hostile and invasive culture, this time the Soviets. In the 1970s the entire Yaghnobi population was forcibly relocated to the Zafarabad region and it was not until the late 1980s that they started to move back to their valley. So, yes, their language is a direct descendant of Sogdian and the children are taught it in their makeshift classrooms, but we now know that only 30 per cent of its vocabulary actually survives and that Yaghnobi elders have forgotten Sogdian poetry and culture. To listen to the Yaghnobi speak their language, therefore, is to listen to one of the most ancient and important languages in the world, but it is to listen to its death throes – it is the sound of a language dying in a mountain refuge that has become a prison.

MOUNTAIN FOLK

Historians have come to learn a great deal (but by no means enough) about the Yaghnobi from modern research programmes that have seen researchers embedded for short periods with Yaghnobi families; it takes such physical proximity and interaction to get under the skin of mountain histories. For the historian, the innate problem in reconstructing the cultural history of the mountain lies in the fact that, more often than not, it is told by non-mountain dwellers. The paucity of record-keeping in the mountains, combined with widespread illiteracy, means that we know almost nothing from the hands of the mountain dwellers themselves and almost everything from the perspective of literate elites in the towns and plains – the land of bureaucrats and archives. Under such conditions mountain people are frequently characterized either as clowns or as criminals. The nineteenth-century French writer Stendhal described peasants from the Sabine Hills outside Rome venturing down into the lowlands on Ascension Day:

> They came down from their mountains to celebrate the feast day at St Peter's... They wear ragged cloth cloaks, their legs wrapped in strips of material held in place with string cross-gartered; their wild eyes peer from behind disordered black hair; they hold to their chests hats made of felt, which the sun and rain have left a reddish black colour; these peasants are accompanied by their families of equally wild aspect.

The rustic simplicity, rural costume and local dialects are described by travellers and writers as sentimental caricatures; while those who came down from the mountains to the plains for work, for special occasions or due to land pressure, tend to enter the records when they transgress laws and end up in the courts. In neither case is the depiction of the people of the mountains satisfactory. The geographical barrier of the mountain is thus replaced by one that is social and cultural.

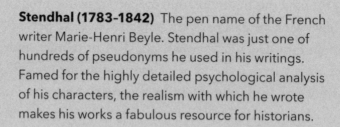

Stendhal (1783-1842) The pen name of the French writer Marie-Henri Beyle. Stendhal was just one of hundreds of pseudonyms he used in his writings. Famed for the highly detailed psychological analysis of his characters, the realism with which he wrote makes his works a fabulous resource for historians.

THE ROCKY MOUNTAINS

Occasionally, however, stories of the trials and tribulations of mountain life do survive and they are rich historical sources. Two remarkable and contrasting accounts, for example, survive of life at the turn of the nineteenth century in the Rocky Mountains of the United States, penned by the indefatigable writer Isabella Bird (1831–1904), whose *A Lady's Life in the Rocky Mountains*, a travelogue of her journeys, was first published in 1879. Similarly, Elinore Pruitt Stewart's (1876–1933) *Letters of a Woman Homesteader* was printed in 1914, recounting in a series of letters the period of her life spent living on a homestead in Burntfork, Wyoming.

Isabella Bird's is an outsider's view of life in the mountains, Pruitt Stewart's a first-hand account of what it is like actually to live there. With both writers there is a tendency to romanticize for picturesque effect for a popular audience. Bird, in describing a journey near Long's Peak in Colorado, wrote: 'The mountains "of the land which is very far off" are very near now, but the near is more glorious than the far, and reality than dreamland.' Struck by 'mountain fever' she comes across a 'very trim-looking log cabin' and is regaled by a fellow countryman, Welshman Griffith Evans, who in the evening light thought that she was 'Mountain Jim, dressed up as a woman!'.

Isabella Bird (1831-1904) A nineteenth-century English explorer and naturalist who spent time in America, Australia and Asia, Bird was the first woman to be elected to the Royal Geographical Society. Her voluminous correspondence and numerous travel books are a treasure trove for historians. Her works include *The Yangtze Valley and Beyond* (1899), *Journeys in Persia and Kurdistan* (1891) and *Among the Tibetans* (1894).

Meanwhile, in a letter to her friend Mrs Comey in December 1912, Elinore Pruitt Stewart described the mountain life as she actually experienced it:

It is true, I want a great many things I haven't got, but I don't want them enough to be discontented and not enjoy the many blessings that are mine. I have my home among the blue mountains, my healthy, well-formed children, my clean, honest husband, my kind, gentle milk cows, my garden which I make myself. I have loads and loads of flowers, which I tend myself. There are lots of chickens, turkeys, and pigs, which are my own special care. I have some slow old gentle horses and an old wagon. I can load up the kiddies and go where I please any time.

These two accounts remind us that mountains were sites of travel and exploration as well as places to inhabit. Such rugged outdoor conditions on the frontier of civilization required a particular kind of human grit, a tenacity and fortitude for survival. In both of these instances we have examples of remarkable women for whom mountain life was a challenge and adventure, and allowed them to assume immensely active roles that were not necessarily expected of ordinary women during the period. Mountain life therefore allowed women to traverse the restrictive gender norms of their age.

THE APPALACHIAN TRAIL

This question of living in the mountains is also linked to the New Deal, the pump-priming economics of Franklin Delano Roosevelt (1882–1945), which sought to kick-start the American economy in the slump that followed the Wall Street Crash of 1929 and to prevent a recurrence of the Great Depression. A central plank of the New Deal was the funding of a wide range of public-works initiatives. Within this economic and political climate the Civilian Conservation Corps was formed, a public-work relief programme that created manual-labour jobs for young unmarried men and led to conservation and development projects across the country from bridge and road building to flood control and forestry work. During this period many of the formal trails that traverse these mountain ranges were created, including the famous Appalachian Trail. A rich photographic record of this work survives, including the building of the Miry Ridge Trail at Gatlinburg, Tennessee by a team in 1934 or 1935. Such efforts saw the taming of the mountains and the opening up of the American 'Great Outdoors' for mainstream recreation.

HANNIBAL

This idea of 'taming' mountains has its own history. Moments of their conquest have become historical honeypots, whether it is Junko Tabei (1939–2016), in 1975 the first woman to climb Everest, or Hannibal (247–183/1 BCE) crossing the Alps in 218 BCE. Hannibal's expedition is particularly interesting not only because he took an army over the mountains but also because he did so with thirty-seven elephants. Here the contrast between the mountains and the natural environment of the elephant – an animal we might assume to be more at home on plains and in jungles – makes the achievement stand out. It becomes a story, therefore, about a man taming both the animate and inanimate natural worlds at the same time.

In practice, however, elephants are rather good in mountains. They cleverly use their trunks to test the reliability of unfamiliar ground, are able to walk very narrow ledges and are particularly useful at clearing paths through heavy snow. Moreover, Hannibal's elephants were not the type that we might immediately assume them to be, based on our concept of elephants in zoos, safari parks or the wild. Hannibal, we think, took with him North African forest elephants, which were smaller than their Indian counterparts, and now extinct.

Hannibal's true achievement was not that he took elephants across the Alps but that they survived the journey. Wild elephants eat for approximately *sixteen hours* every day, or around 300–350lbs of food (the weight of about fifty-five bricks). With no natural food to hand, Hannibal's elephants would have been fed from the supplies of pack animals. They would all have suffered badly from malnutrition. Yes, they survived the journey across the Alps, but of those thirty-seven elephants who survived that particular journey, only *one* survived the subsequent crossing of the Apennines – a journey, which has, unsurprisingly, been forgotten to history.

Throughout time mountains have stood as monumental geological formations across the landscape, impacting on our world in innumerable ways, as great physical reminders of our heritage and connections with former times which are just as powerful as man-made structures that we more readily associate with human history – which brings us to the important question of the history of chimneys...

·21·
CHIMNEYS

—

The history of chimneys is all about...
smuggling, evil fairies, child labour and –
of course – Father Christmas.

——— CORNWALL ———

Anyone who has made the summer pilgrimage to Cornwall by car cannot but be intrigued by the old chimneys that litter the landscape of Britain's south-west peninsula. These archaeological remnants of the past are seared in our childhood memories of holidays spent in St Ives, Padstow, Mousehole and Polzeath. Old chimneys seemed to be everywhere, making the landscape sing of its history. The first historic chimneys you come across on a journey to the West Country are the remains of mining buildings, and there are simply hundreds of them in various states of repair. Together they are one of the most visible, and unavoidable, signposts of the past. Their height and the predominantly barren moorland or clifftop landscapes in which they were built makes them visible for miles. Like a child raising a hand in class they demand attention. 'Come and see me!' they cry. 'Come and find out what I am!' The contrast between the straight lines of an industrial brick chimney and the otherwise entirely natural wild environment in which it is set prompts a series of questions as one traverses the Cornish hinterland. What on earth is that massive chimney doing there? Why was it built in that way, and in that location? How has it survived until the present day?

These imposing structures, which feature so prominently across the backbone of this part of England, are a powerful reminder that the history of mines and mining in the West Country is not forgotten [*see fig. 26*]. The 'Cornwall and West Devon Mining Landscape' is now a World Heritage Site, and takes its place in the UK alongside Stonehenge, Canterbury Cathedral and Blenheim Palace, and worldwide alongside the Taj Mahal, the Acropolis and Machu Picchu as one of the world's most important historic locations.

COPPER AND TIN

These industrial chimneys reflect a time when Britain was at the forefront of global mining technology, in particular the mining of copper and tin, and when those raw materials had a profound influence on the rise and fall of empires. In the late eighteenth and early nineteenth century this small region produced two-thirds of the world's supply of copper, at a time when huge sheets of copper were used to protect the hulls of sailing warships from weed, barnacles and the teredo worm, a giant, voracious type of woodworm, which burrowed into the bottoms of ships, fatally weakening their structure. The copper gave the ships smooth, strong hulls, which made them faster and longer lasting. Tin was also in high demand for, among many other things, the manufacture of cans in an era when the science and technology of food preservation was rapidly changing, and both copper and tin were used in the manufacturing of brass and bronze. The need to produce enormous quantities of these vital metals in turn led to innovation in the mining industry in the West Country, particularly in the use of steam engines. From 1800, mines in West Devon and Cornwall began to operate a new generation of high-pressure steam engines producing pressure at 40 or 50 pounds per square inch – roughly ten times what had gone before which allowed the miners to operate at far greater depths because the new steam engines could pump out the water which gathered so far down. Those steam engines, built for mining in Cornwall, went on to power the Industrial Revolution across the UK and the world.

Yet these majestic monuments to an industrial past have a darker story to tell. The human cost for these technological advances was paid for by the ordinary miners who undertook the back-breaking work in cramped and often sweltering conditions. Air quality was shockingly bad, with miners developing chronic respiratory and other severe health-related problems. One miner from the Cornish village of Gwennap in the late nineteenth century recalled regularly coughing up phlegm as 'black as ink'.

SMUGGLING

These derelict monuments of mining heritage, however, are not the only type of chimney in Cornwall worthy of celebration. There is another type, of which the best example in the world is in the old harbour of Falmouth, once one of the most important ports in England for its large, deep-water and safe harbour, the last that any vessel westward-bound from the English Channel would pass. Located on the corner of a small lane leading to the harbour, and, attached to the Falmouth Customs House, is a chimney known as 'the King's Pipe' [*see fig. 27*]. This chimney shares one important characteristic with the mining chimneys, and that is its power to generate and encourage historical curiosity. It does this by being a perfectly normal, square, tapering, brick-built chimney but, rather than being located where you might expect to find a chimney – on or near a roof – it is built on the ground. Everything about it looks wrong so, rather like the mining chimneys, it poses the questions: What am I, and why am I here? The answers open up an entirely different historical world.

The Falmouth King's Pipe was built at some point around the 1740s for the destruction of contraband tobacco. It is one of several such pipes built at important ports around the British coastline: Liverpool, London, Whitehaven and Llanelli being among the others. It is the earliest surviving example. The history of this chimney, therefore, is all about smuggling, customs and excise, taxes, crime and punishment, and empire-building in the eighteenth century. From the mid-seventeenth century English monarchs committed their country to a near-endless series of wars that crippled the treasury. The national debt grew and the burden of its maintenance fell on the public. An astonishing variety of goods were taxed, including beer, salt and malt among other commodities.

This taxation led to an explosion of smuggling and a corres-ponding drive by the government to control it. One of the means by which they did this specifically in relation to the smuggling of tobacco was, once a shipment had been seized, to burn it in public. The seized tobacco was put into the hearth of the great King's Pipe chimney and burned. Enormous clouds of black smoke would have filled the Falmouth sky. 'The King', passers-by would say, 'is having a smoke today.' Indeed he was, and by doing so and in such a visible fashion, he was demonstrating to everyone, for many miles around Falmouth both inland and out at sea, that the customs men had enjoyed a success in their war against the smugglers. The Pipe therefore demonstrates the use of the landscape by the British state as a means of commu-nication and public control – it fits into the same history as the gibbeting of pirates, the hanging of outlaws, the burning of witches and the impaling of heads on Traitors' Gate at the Tower of London. This chimney is also an important chapter in the history of illicit trade; as a physical object, it fills in the gaps of our economic history that is written from official accounts. It is a chimney that gets us closer to the truth.

> **Traitors' Gate** A gate in the riverside curtain wall of the Tower of London, built by Edward I (1239-1307). Prisoners entering the Tower were brought by barge along the Thames, under London Bridge, where the heads of traitors were displayed on pikes.

LUCKY DISCOVERIES

Not all chimneys were used for destroying things. In November 2016 a group of builders were renovating a fireplace in Aberdeen. They noticed that the chimney was blocked, presumably to stop a draught. The blockage seemed to be a bundle of rags but when it was removed and unwrapped it was clear that it was something rather more special. It was, in fact, an enormous map of the world, over two metres long and more than a metre and a half wide. It had been produced in the early 1600s by the Dutch engraver Gerald Valck, and is one of only three engraved copies known to exist [*see fig. 28*]. Rightly prized by historians following its discovery and restoration by the National Library of Scotland, it would also, once, have been highly prized by its owner. Such maps were exceptionally rare and exceptionally expensive. It would have been the talking point of a house, of a street, of a city, but at some point in its life it came down in the world, condemned to languish in a chimney-tomb. What a story that map could tell, if only it could speak.

And by no means is this the only example of the chimney acting as an archive for documents. One of the earliest such documents to survive is from 1610, a letter from John Southwell of Bareham to his son-in-law, advising on an annuity and property in Canterbury that was lodged irretrievably in a shaft of the chimney, presumably on the father-in-law's death. Such early documents are exceptionally rare, but from the nineteenth century onwards increased literacy meant that a bewildering range of handwritten items was deposited in chimneys. An excavation of the Malthouse in Earl Soham, Suffolk, in 1985 revealed a collection of letters and receipts on a spike, as well as accounts and assorted religious books. Newspapers – always useful to historians for their dates – were also often used as draught excluders. A copy of the *News of the World* from 18 August 1850 found in a chimney in Thorndon, Suffolk, may indicate when a family left their home, discarding various items up the chimney. Letters too were thrown into fires in response to the commands of the sender to 'burn this letter'. In some cases, the draught of the chimney sucked the discarded correspondence to safety instead of fuelling the fire of their destruction.

FATHER CHRISTMAS

Chance has also left us with one of the most interesting types of letters to be discovered in chimneys: children's letters to Father Christmas. For historians, they are a joy. 'I want a baby doll and a waterproof with a hood and a pair of gloves and a toffee apple and a gold penny and a silver sixpence and a long toffee,' wrote the breathless Alfred or Hannah Howard in October 1911 before placing their letter in the fire and it being whisked to safety, for eighty-one years, on a tiny ledge inside the chimney of their house in Dublin. Such letters are magical because not only do they record a list of material objects, but a child's hopes and,

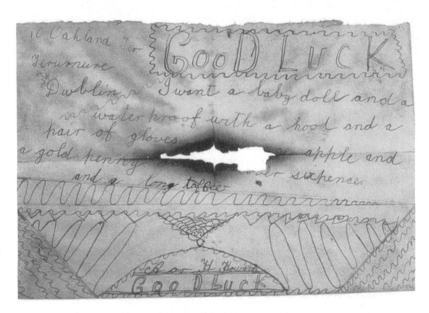

Children's letter to Father Christmas by Alfred or Hannah Howard in October 1911

sometimes, their fears. The lesson of all of this is never to take your chimney for granted: take a look inside – you just never know what it might reveal.

These letters to Father Christmas raise the very interesting question of people – or spirits – going into, up or down chimneys. We are all familiar nowadays with the improbable notion of Santa climbing down the chimney, whether it be from Dr Seuss's Grinch crawling serpent-like down the chimneys of Whoville, Raymond Briggs's beautiful illustrations in his 1973 *Father Christmas* book, or the traditional festive song 'When Santa Got Stuck up the Chimney'. The chimney as a portal into and out of the home is linked to other Christmas traditions: the hanging up of stockings and the posting of Christmas letters, not to mention the burning of the yuletide log. But *how*, you may ask, did Father Christmas and the chimney become so inextricably linked in popular Christmas traditions?

Many of the popular characteristics of the modern-day Santa stem from Clement C. Moore's now classic (and allegedly plagiarized) 56-line American poem, "Twas the Night Before Christmas', which was written in 1822 and first published anonymously in the Troy, New York *Sentinel* on 23 December 1823 under the earlier title of 'A Visit From Saint Nicholas'. It is here that we first meet the 'chubby and plump... right jolly old elf':

> He spoke not a word, but went straight to his work,
> And filled all the stockings; then turned with a jerk,
> And laying his finger aside of his nose,
> And giving a nod, up the chimney he rose...

A precursor to this poetic version of the chimney-climbing St Nicholas in the US was Washington Irving's expanded 1812 *Knickerbocker's History of New York*, which included a new reference to St Nicholas 'rattling down the chimney' himself, rather than dropping down the presents. It was literary representations such as these that shaped the notion of what was later to be dressed up as Santa Claus in North America.

Washington Irving (1783-1859) An American author, historian and diplomat, Irving was America's first internationally bestselling author. Famous for *Rip Van Winkle* (1819) and *Sleepy Hollow* (1820) and biographies of Muhammad and George Washington.

VISITING SPIRITS

These romantic accounts that proliferated across the Atlantic probably stem from earlier European traditions. The chimney in European folklore was associated with the supernatural, as entry points into the home whether for good or evil, and within the

Christian world it was sometimes connected to winter celebrations. In Greece and Serbia, *Kallikantzaroi* or Christmas goblins were believed to live underground for most of the year, surfacing to slip down chimneys during the twelve days of Christmas in order to wreak havoc. While in Italian folklore an old woman named Befana (sometimes referred to as the Christmas Witch) delivered gifts to children on the eve of Epiphany (6 January), slipping them into shoes left by the fireplace. Earlier depictions of St Nicholas associate him with dropping gold coins down the chimney, which in sixteenth-century Holland similarly led to the tradition of children placing their shoes on the hearth on the eve of the Feast of St Nicholas, then awaking in the morning to find them filled with presents and sweets. These earlier chimney-related traditions no doubt passed into usage in the US through patterns of migration.

This belief in people, things or objects coming up and down chimneys also meant that the hearth, or fireplace, became a highly significant location within the home and became places where a whole variety of objects were concealed, from cat skeletons to shoes. These 'spiritual middens' (basically rubbish sites) have a long history that can be traced to the Bronze Age, and are different places around buildings where objects or animal remains are lodged to ward off evil spirits. Such historical oddities, which are still regularly uncovered in historic buildings around the British Isles, allow us to peer into a fascinating world of popular superstition.

Chimneys in practical terms were open to the elements, and therefore the perfect point for malevolent supernatural forces to enter the household, which made the fireplace and hearth extremely vulnerable places. Folklore is full of magical beings who enter via the chimney. In Scotland and England, brownies entered the household at night via the chimney to perform domestic tasks, while in Gaelic tradition a cautionary nursery tale warned of a bogeyman figure called a bodach, who came down the chimney to snatch away naughty children. The chimney was thus a liminal space between the natural and supernatural worlds, a space that needed guarding. In order to ward off various goblins, fairies, witches, sprites and demons, old shoes were used as protective talismans. An extraordinarily large cache of over 100 shoes was discovered in the seventeenth-century National Trust farmhouse Gelli Iago in Snowdonia National Park – a find that speaks of something more than the careless loss of property.

CLIMBING BOYS

Santa, witches, sprites and demons are not the only beings to have spent time in chimneys; they were, for many thousands of children in the eighteenth and nineteenth centuries, a place of work. Soot in enormous quantities gathered in both industrial and domestic chimneys and had to be regularly cleaned away by chimney sweeps, or more often than not by the apprentices or 'climbing boys' whom they employed for the dangerous task of clambering up chimneys. An 1817 'Report from the Committee of the... House of Commons on the Employment of Boys in the Sweeping of Chimneys' outlined the hardships faced by these boys, many of whom had been stolen from their parents or taken from workhouses, and described the bruises and burns that many of them suffered in their work which would take months to heal. The committee reported that

> the deformity of the spine, legs, arms, &c. of these boys, proceeds generally if not wholly, from the circumstance of their being obliged to ascend chimneys at an age when their bones are in a soft and growing state; but likewise, by their being compelled to carry bags of soot and cloths, the weight of which sometimes exceed 20 or 30 pounds, not including the soot,

the burden of which they also occasionally bear for a great length of distance and time; the knees and ankle joints become deformed, in the first instance, from the position they are obliged to put them in, in order to support themselves, not only while climbing up the chimney, but more particularly so whilst coming down, when they rest solely on the lower extremities, the arms being used for scraping and sweeping down the soot.

The Victorian reformer Henry Mayhew described the plight of such young boys prior to parliamentary reforms in his 1851 book *London Labour and the London Poor*: 'The sufferings of many of the climbing boys were very great. They were often ill-lodged, ill-fed and ill-clad, forced to ascend hot and narrow flues, and subject to diseases – such as the chimney sweep's cancer – peculiar to their calling.'

The sufferings of these 'climbing boys' are a distinctive theme of William Blake's poetry, including his verses 'The Chimney Sweeper' and 'London', which heaped criticism on the Church for what he saw as their turning a blind eye to this evil. These chimneys were sometimes no more than seven inches square, which made them incredibly tight to climb, not to mention the awkward bends and turns that needed to be navigated. Progress upwards in these conditions could be slow, so much so that the boy below might stick pins into the feet of the one above (burning straw served the same function) in order to hasten his ascent.

Perhaps one of the most terrifying aspects of this life was the prospect of getting trapped in a chimney, unable to get out.

William Blake (1757–1827) An English poet, painter and printmaker, widely considered one of the most significant romantic poets.

Among the frequent accidents described by Mayhew was 'being jammed or fixed, or, as it was called in the trade, "stuck", in narrow and heated flues, sometimes for hours, and until death.' He recounts the story of one poor wretch who, in March 1813, found himself lodged in a chimney and replied to his master's calls, 'I cannot come up, Master; I must die here.' Efforts were made to save the boy by knocking a hole in the chimney in order to drag him out, but his burns were so great that he later died.

This, then, is the darker side of the history of chimneys, which are usually associated with warmth and light, with stories and conversation around the fireplace and memories atop the mantelpiece. And with such sad stories to tell the chimney brings us to the very important question of the history of tears...

·22·

TEARS

—

The history of tears is all about…
the emotional control of the sexes, crocodiles,
phlegm, learning to speak and the Olympics.

T he history of tears is peculiarly varied. It is all about when
to cry and when not to cry, and whether those tears spring
from joy, grief, loss, upset or some other, perhaps uniden-
tifiable, emotion. The history is beautiful in its complexity: it
might even bring a tear to your eye.

—— WHEN TO CRY ——

The question of when tears are expected and when we are
expected to keep a stiff upper lip is one with which we can all
easily identify. It is a theme that is explored in *L'Étranger* (1942),
the novel by the French philosopher Albert Camus (1913–60),
that doyen of existentialism. In it the protagonist, Mersault,
shocks the French authorities in his Algiers hometown because
he is unable to cry at his own mother's funeral. In recounting the
events around his mother's death he reports how he had

... 'shown insensitivity' the day of Maman's funeral...
I probably did love Maman, but that didn't mean anything.
At one time or another all normal people have wished their
loved ones were dead... The director [of the funeral home]...
said that I hadn't wanted to see Maman, that I hadn't cried
once, and that I had left right after the funeral without paying
my last respects at her grave.

What makes Mersault psychologically odd to our eyes is his lack of tears: it's his inability to show emotion at the right times. This, after all, is a scene about a son burying a mother – a child burying a parent – perhaps one of the most significant emotional crises there can be with the exception of its counterpart: a parent burying their child. As such it is a powerful plot device that brings the history of their relationship into sharp focus. What must have happened, we ask ourselves, to so shatter, or perhaps freeze, this son's feelings for his mother, or his ability to express those feelings if, indeed, they are those feelings of loss and mourning we might expect?

Read one way, this story is a reminder that emotions are complex and personal and bound up with history, but also it encourages us to consider the wider context of a specific place and time, in this case Algiers in 1942 when it was under the control of Nazi Germany and Vichy France and on the point of being invaded by the Allies in Operation Torch, one of the largest military operations in history: that, surely, was enough to

Operation Torch An invasion of French North Africa by Allied British and American forces in November 1942. A highly significant but often overlooked Allied operation because the principal enemy was the French.

play with anyone's emotions. Attitudes towards tears at funerals, however, have varied geographically in the past, just as they vary today.

WAILING

Many cultures throughout history – including some Islamic and Sikh traditions – forbade wailing out loud at funerals, whereas the natural flow of tears, which was uncontrollable, was a culturally acceptable expression of grief.

Nonetheless there were societies where open wailing was more acceptable. Within early Islamic cultures women played an important social role in mourning by wailing for the dead. In 641 or 642 women gathered to wail for the deceased hero and companion of Muhammad, Khālid ibn al-Walīd, with many of them shrieking in ululation, scratching their cheeks, drawing blood, tearing their hair and even ripping at their clothes to bare their breasts. Such actions at the time roused condemnation among some religious leaders as uncivilized behaviour, and yet even today similar practices are traditional among Ethiopian tribes.

The art of women's keening – the performing of a lament at wakes and funerals – was prevalent in Irish society from the pre-Christian period to the early twentieth century where women led communities in public expressions of grief. This was a tradition (also present in Scotland) which included the recital of elegiac poetry, combined with raucous wailing cries.

Khālid ibn al-Walīd (585–642) Also known as 'Drawn Sword of God', Khālid fought in over 200 battles and is widely considered one of the finest military commanders in history.

POLICING GRIEF

In the thirteenth and fourteenth centuries in the Italian states, on the other hand, many communities actually forbade public expressions of grief and in some places a distinction in what was acceptable in terms of public grief was made between genders: it was more socially acceptable for women to grieve than for men, since women were considered more emotional and prone to spontaneous emotional outpourings. Immoderate emotional outbursts by mourners, such as tearing one's hair or clothing, scratching at one's face, or loud public wailing and crying were met with fines. In certain locations there was a policing of the 'scale' of female grief – according to an unspecified acceptable quantity of tears. In 1624, Lady Frances Howard, reacting to the death of her husband Ludovic Stewart, Duke of Lennox, allegedly cut off all her hair and performed 'divers other demonstrations of extraordinary grief'. This was far removed from the modest trickle of tears expected as a sign of respect.

In some cases, professional mourners, usually women, were paid to cry ritually, and they would shriek and wail to encourage others to weep. These people are mentioned in ancient Greek plays, and were commonly employed throughout Europe until the beginning of the nineteenth century. The contemporary practice was brought to life in the 2003 award-winning Philippine comedy *Crying Ladies* that revolves around the lives of three women who are part-time professional mourners for the Chinese-Filipino community in Manila's Chinatown. The Chinese use professional mourners to help expedite the entry of a deceased loved one's soul into heaven by giving the impression that he or she was a good and loving person, well loved by many. The practice also continues today in Africa.

If weeping at a funeral is at least acceptable to us, it is worth considering which social occasions or indeed which locations are no longer expected to be a theatre of tears, for the locations where we might expect to cry or be expected to cry have changed over time, and one of the most interesting of these, believe it or not, is art galleries.

Crying in art galleries is a behaviour that has changed. Simply put, we used to be moved to tears by art on a regular basis, but now we are not. There are countless historical descriptions of people crying at art. This extract from the memoirs of the Danish-French Impressionist painter Camille Pissarro (1830–1903) recalls the reaction to a painting by Jean-François Millet of a male acquaintance by the name of Hyacinthe Pozier in 1887. He recounts that his friend

> greeted me with the announcement that he had just received a great shock, he was all in tears. I thought someone in his family had just died. Not at all, it was *The Angelus*, Millet's painting, which had provoked this emotion. This canvas, one of the painter's poorest, a canvas for which in these times 500,000 francs was refused, has just this moral effect on the vulgarians who crowd around it: they trample one another before it!

There is a long history of crying before works of art, a phenomenon that is little seen now. The reasons for this change are not very well understood. Has the constant immersion of visual stimuli via TV, computers, tablets and smartphones anaesthetized us to the power of art? Some paintings still do elicit a strong emotional response. Why do religious paintings move people of faith to tears? Why does the work of some artists – like the

American abstract expressionist Mark Rothko – generate tears more than others? Why do some people cry and others *faint*? Fainting in galleries used to be such a particular and common reaction for it to have its own name: 'Stendhal Syndrome', after the French author. Stendhal described his experience of fainting at the Basilica of Santa Croce (opened 1442) in Florence when, for the first time, he saw the magnificent frescoes by the thirteenth-century Florentine artist Giotto [*see fig. 29*]. Crying in galleries, therefore, is not only an interesting chapter in the history of art but also is an interesting chapter in the history of extreme emotional responses to art.

CHILDREN'S TEARS

These examples have considered adult tears, but what of children? And what, specifically, of babies? One of the most hotly debated historical issues is that of infantile tears, a theme that resonates with modern-day parents via conflicting attitudes towards 'controlled crying', a parenting technique developed by maternity nurse and author Gina Ford in 1999. Ford argued that a baby left to cry will learn to comfort itself. Millions of parents swear by it; millions of others claim it damages a child's development. Interestingly, our approach to this has a history.

As all modern parents know, different types of cry in infants (relating to basic needs, anger and pain) are central to the ways in which babies communicate in the months before their speech begins to develop. In sixteenth- and seventeenth-century

England, too, crying was seen as a part of the natural physiological development of the child. Here they followed ancient Greek medical teaching from Hippocrates (460 BCE–370 CE) and Galen (130 CE–210 CE) that was based on theories of bodily humours, which saw the human body as composed of a mixture of four humours: black bile, yellow or red bile, blood and phlegm. Men and women (and indeed infants) were thought to be composed of a different humoral balance, which influenced gendered behaviour and characteristics. Disease and illness were caused by an imbalance of humours, the cure for which was to purge the body of excess liquids. In this model, infants were viewed as warm and moist with flexible bodies. It was believed that crying was fundamental to ridding the infant body of excess fluids that resulted from being born in the womb in a mixture of phlegm and moisture.

This all began with the baby's first tears, and crying was seen as a sign of a healthy baby. The midwife Jane Sharp in her *The Midwife's Book* (1671), the first to be authored by a woman, advised: 'you may suffer the child to cry... for it is better for the brain and lungs that are thus opened and discharged of superfluous humours, and natural heat is raised by it.' Excessive

Frontispiece of Jane Sharp's *The Midwife's Book* (1671)

crying after the first few days of an infant's life was, however, treated with more concern, since constant bawling was thought to be harmful – damaging to weak infant bones that were still, it was thought at the time, sodden with moisture. Sharp wrote, 'too much crying will cause rheums to fall', in other words a watery discharge from the eyes and nose (as with a cold), 'and oftentimes the child will be broken bellied by its overstraining'. A remedy for this damaging of bodies was swaddling, the practice of cocooning infants in tightly wrapped layers of fabric to prevent them from moving and hurting themselves. The swaddling of young babies continues today as a way of ensuring well-being and a good night's sleep, although recent studies of swaddling connected to sudden infant death syndrome (SIDS) have challenged its efficacy in older, more mobile babies, and warned of the potential dangers.

EXPLAINING TEARS

As this suggests, scientific understanding of the function and biological basis for tears has changed over time. The Hippocratic and medieval view of tears as a way of purging excess humours from the brain is a far cry from current medical explanations of tears; these are now understood to be generated when a neuronal connection is made between the lachrymal gland – the tear duct – and those areas of the human brain connected with emotion or pain. Scientists and psychologists thus view tears as a response to pain; as an outlet for tension and relief; and, most interestingly, as a non-verbal form of communication designed to elicit a response from others. It has taken highly intelligent adults centuries to realize this: perhaps we should simply have asked a baby.

The concept of tears as a form of communication opens up the question of 'strategic crying', of tears employed as an emotional weapon on – if we were to take an entirely random example of which James has no personal experience – a doting father wrapped round the little fingers of his two charming, yet disarmingly cunning daughters, whose faux tears pull at the paternal heartstrings like nothing else. Modern-day parents are too soft by half. The very public display of tears has long been part of the politician's stock-in-trade: think of Bob Dole's blubbing on the campaign trail in 1996 when he was introduced by former president Gerald R. Ford, or when, in 2008, Hillary Clinton was campaigning against Barack Obama in the Democratic primaries and welled up in a New Hampshire diner as a way of showing a more 'personal side'. Revealing this more emotional side of oneself as a politician, especially a female one, is extremely risky, for as Clinton remarked: 'If you get too emotional, that undercuts you. A man can cry – but a woman, that's a different kind of dynamic.' Historically, too, political figures have willingly and calculatedly wept for oratorical effect. Even the seventeenth-century regicide Oliver Cromwell was not above shedding tears in public for the good old cause that motivated the fight against parliament, and which led the Royalist Sir John Reresby to write of him: 'Tears he had at will, and was doubtless, the deepest Dissembler on Earth.'

CROCODILE TEARS

Such fake tears have been known for centuries as 'crocodile tears'. The phrase originates in an ancient belief that crocodiles shed tears while consuming their food – that they were publicly weeping for the animals they were killing. The earliest references to this appear in a collection of proverbs attributed to Plutarch and were more widely spread in the English language by Sir John Mandeville who wrote his excellent *The Travels of John Mandeville* at some point between 1357 and 1351. He stated:

In that country and by all Inde be great plenty of cockodrills, that is a manner of a long serpent, as I have said before. And in the night they dwell in the water, and on the day upon the land, in rocks and in caves. And they eat no meat in all the winter, but they lie as in a dream, as do the serpents. These serpents slay men, and they eat them weeping; and when they eat they move the over jaw, and not the nether jaw, and they have no tongue.

Plutarch (46-120 CE) A Greek historian particularly known for his work *Parallel Lives,* a history of famous Greeks and Romans, an outstanding historical source on the ancient world. Still, historians believe that as much as two-thirds of Plutarch's works have not survived.

Crocodile tears likewise appear in Edmund Spenser's (1552–99) Elizabethan epic poem *The Faerie Queene:*

As when a weaiie traveller, that strayes
By muddy shore of broad seven-mouthed Nile,
Unweeting of the perillous wandring wayes,
Doth meete a cruell craftie crocodile,
Which in false griefe hyding his harmeful guile,
Doth weepe full sore, and sheddeth tender tears:
The foolish man, that pities all this while
His mourneful plight, is swallowed up unawares,
Forgetfull of his owne, that mindes another's cares...

The phrase has been used in literature for centuries, not least by Shakespeare, when Othello convinces himself that his wife is cheating on him: 'If that the earth could teem with woman's tears', he mopes, 'Each drop she falls would prove a crocodile';

The Faerie Queen (1590) Written in the late sixteenth century by Edmund Spenser, it is one of the longest poems in the English language and a complex allegory of contemporary life told through the activities of several English knights.

in other words, Othello rages (quite mistakenly it turns out) that Desemona's tears were fake ones.

Artists have also seized on the image of crocodile tears for centuries as a powerful metaphor for hypocrisy. One of the finest visual renditions is a cartoon by the American artist Bernard Gillam (1856–96) from 1884 which shows the American general Ulysses S. Grant courting Jewish voters by crying crocodile tears over the persecution of Russian Jews, when Grant himself had been responsible for a 'General Order' twenty years earlier during the Civil War in which he had expelled all Jews from the Confederate States.

We now have a better understanding of why crocodiles produce tears when they eat. Scepticism about the idea of crocodilian remorse first appeared in print in 1700 at the hand of the Swiss physician and naturalist John Scheuhzer, who wrote: 'The foundations and substance of this famous old tale are so feeble that today we would be well advised to do without it.' However, no serious work was undertaken until 1927 when the brave George Johnson studied crocodile tears by applying a mixture of onion and salt to the dry eyes of four, probably enraged, crocodiles. It was only as recently as 2007 that a serious study sought a scientific explanation for the question of why crocodiles produce tears. The research offered several interesting answers, one of which proposed that the tears might be a by-product of the noises (huffing and chuffing, hissing and wheezing) that crocodiles make when they eat, which forces air through their

THEN AND NOW.—1862 AND 1882.

ORDER N° 11,
BY. U.S. GRANT.
1862.
EXCLUDING
JEWS—
FROM THE
ARMY.—

MEETING
CHICKERING
HALL
SYMPATHY
FOR THE
PERSECUTED
JEWS
IN RUSSIA
VS GRANT.

ARMY ORDER N° II—1862 JEWISH VOTE 1884

"OH, NOW YOU WEEP, AND I PERCEIVE YOU FEEL
THE DINT OF PITY. THESE ARE GRACIOUS DROPS."

Bernard Gillam cartoon from 1884 depicting American general
Ulysses S. Grant courting Jewish voters by crying crocodile tears

sinuses and makes the tears flow. It is convincing, if a little disappointing, that crocodiles are not remorseful killers. Mournful or not, a part of this history of tears, then, is the history of our understanding of animal optics – and, perhaps, the history of our lack of understanding of animal emotions.

A CHRONOLOGY OF CRYING

It is even possible to unify our historical understanding of tears and bring it together into a sort of chronology. In the medieval world, the mystic and visionary Margery Kempe (c.1373–c.1438) wept uncontrollably when worshipping God. In her *Book of Margery Kempe*, which she dictated, she described herself in the third person: 'Sometimes she wept very abundantly and violently out of desire for the bliss of heaven, and because she was being kept from it for so long.' In the sixteenth century there is more evidence of such weeping at prayer, and the Catholic

Church in particular was soaked in rituals of crying, whereas Protestants on the whole were altogether uneasy with public displays of emotion.

During the eighteenth-century age of sensibility – which began to place greater value upon emotional and aesthetic influences – public weeping was again publicly acceptable to the British, only to be punctured by the horrors of the French Revolution, after which public displays of emotion were viewed as childish, effeminate and dangerously foreign.

What emerged during the nineteenth century instead was the development of what has become known somewhat collo-quially as the British 'stiff upper lip', a rather masculine code of behaviour linked to militarism and empire that conditioned men to suppress their emotions.

IS IT OK FOR MEN TO CRY?

This brings us to the important question of whether or not it is OK for men to cry. In the modern day, despite the rise of the 'new man' and the public and ritualized outpouring of grief that accompanies celebrity deaths and disasters, men are statistically much less prone to crying than their female counterparts. A study conducted in the 1980s by the biochemist William H. Frey found that on average women cry 5.3 times a month compared with men who cry 1.3 times a month. Historically there has always been a strong inverse correlation between crying and masculinity. For the seventeenth-century English philosopher Thomas Hobbes (1588–1679), crying was a sign of weakness; it was a feminine pursuit, indulged in by women, babies and the powerless in society.

As we have seen, though, manly tears were not always frowned upon. It always depends, of course, on the type of tears one sheds. Tears of self-pity and fear were those of the coward and the weak and were always condemned, whereas tears of compassion or bereavement, if moderate, were sanctioned. Above all, though, spiritual tears were the best, and there is a long tradition of penitential weeping, remorse for one's sins and tears of gratitude for Christ's saving grace. Medieval bishops were forever crying as part of their devotions. It was reported of Gundulf, Bishop of Rochester (1077–1108), 'O when he prayed with what tears did he wash the Lord's feet!... How bitter were his sobs in remembering his sins! Who has not seen his eyes wet with tears?'; and Thomas Becket reportedly 'prayed alone until he was filled with the miracle of tears'. Tears in many cultures, however, were the antithesis of what stood for masculinity. Men were supposed to be tough and rugged, ferocious and intimidating, courageous and strong, which raises the very important question of the history of lions...

·23·

LIONS

—

The history of the lion is all about...
sinking warships, the Thirty Years War,
American populism in the 1900s
and rubbish dumps.

THE LION KING

On the afternoon of 10 August 1628, towards the end of a Stockholm summer, the stunning *Vasa* warship set sail before crowds of onlookers. She was the most expensive, most ambitious ship ever built for the Swedish navy, commissioned by the Swedish king Gustavus Adolphus (1611–32). She was built of a thousand trees, carried sixty-four guns and her masts were 50 metres tall. Four hundred and fifty soldiers and sailors filled her decks. Most striking of all, however, was her decoration: *hundreds* of the most magnificent, ornate and gilded technicolor sculptures covered almost every inch of her hull.

She was to be the flagship of the Swedish navy, specifically built for the invasion of a foreign country – Poland; she was a symbol of Sweden's military greatness, a floating representation of the technical capability, artistic skill, imperial ambition and military strength of an entire country. She cost a little over 5 per cent of Sweden's *entire* GNP to build.

Her name came from the Vasa dynasty of Swedish kings, founded in 1523 but, even more personally, Gustavus Adolphus had been the driving force behind her construction, and the intricate carvings with which she was decorated point to her royal connections. Nowhere was this more clearly signalled than in her figurehead, which was carved into the shape of a pouncing lion, an image closely connected to the king, who was known as 'The Lion of the North' or, in German, *Der Löwe aus Mitternacht* – 'The Lion of Midnight' [*see fig. 30*]. The strength of that symbolism is particularly potent today because it can be felt first-hand. In one of the worst of all maritime tragedies, the *Vasa* sank on her maiden voyage and has since been raised, intact, out of the mud of Stockholm harbour. The *Vasa* museum where she is now on display is one of the world's finest museums of any type.

Gustavus Adolphus earned his nickname from neighbouring countries for his role in leading Sweden to become a great power during the Thirty Years War. The *Vasa* was built during the Polish–Swedish War of 1626–29 when Sweden became dominant in the Baltic region and Gustavus was a constant and significant presence on the battlefield. This was a king who wanted to be seen to embody the character traits of a lion – its strength, ferocity, its dominance – and his lion device appeared frequently on military armour and paraphernalia connected with him. He also wanted consciously to link himself with the German legend that the Baltic would be saved by a white lion from the north.

THE KING OF BEASTS

The lion was an obvious choice for any militaristic monarch and by no means was its use restricted to Gustavus's mid-seventeenth-century Sweden. The lion, as 'King of the Beasts', has long been associated across Asia, Africa and Europe with royalty and power, symbolizing stateliness, bravery, strength, ferocity and valour, though it was not unique as a symbol for royalty and power, which could also be represented by the bear and boar.

As with Gustavus Adolphus, the epithet 'lion' as a mark of royal bravery was attached to many a medieval warrior king, including Henry the Lion (1129–95), known in German as *Heinrich der Löwe*, Duke of Saxony and Bavaria; William the Lion, King of Scots from 1165 to 1214, a legendary figure who gained attention recently because Senator John McCain and former US President Barack Obama both claim descent from this Scottish king; Robert III, Count of Flanders (1249–1322), known as 'The Lion of Flanders', or *De Leeuw van Vlaanderen*; and, perhaps best known to an Anglophone readership, 'Richard the Lionheart' or *Richard Coeur de Lion*, the crusading king Richard I of England (1157–99). Richard was known by the nickname 'lion' or 'lionheart' throughout his lifetime because of his legendary acts of bravery and military prowess. Writing of the period when Richard was a prisoner in Germany, having been captured returning home from the Third Crusade, the French chronicler Guillaume le Breton (1165–1225) considered that Richard 'spoke so eloquently and regally, in so lionhearted a manner, it was as though he were seated on an ancestral throne at Lincoln or Caen.'

HERALDRY

The heraldic device of a lion dates back to the earliest development of heraldry in the twelfth century, and the device of three lions *passant-guardant*, the royal arms of England which adorn the kit of English sporting teams, can be traced back to Richard I, who may, some historians think, have borrowed it

Left: The Howard shield, with a demi-lion of Scotland, which is pierced through the mouth with an arrow; *Right:* Device of three lions *passant-guardant*, the royal arms of England

from his father. It is far more common in heraldic use than the eagle, which was preserved as an imperial device, and the lion became increasingly associated with chivalry. There are even examples of slain lions in heraldry, such as those connected with the English aristocratic family the Howards. At the Battle of Flodden in September 1513 English forces defeated the Scots in the largest land battle between the two kingdoms, and James IV of Scotland was killed on the battlefield. The Howard family, already close to the English king, were instrumental in the English victory and Thomas Howard (1443–1524), Earl of Surrey, was lieutenant-general of the army of the north. In the aftermath of the battle, Howard was created Duke of Norfolk, and his son Thomas (1473–1554), who was then lord admiral, was created Earl of Surrey. Both were granted lands and annuities and the

Battle of Flodden (1513) Fought in the northern English county of Northumberland, the Battle of Flodden was a decisive English victory over invading Scottish forces led by James IV. It was the largest battle ever fought between England and Scotland.

Howard arms were augmented in honour of Flodden with an escutcheon bearing the lion of Scotland pierced through the mouth with an arrow.

Such association between rulers and lions is still very much alive today and lions appear on the coat of arms of many countries, including Finland, Norway, the kingdom of Scotland, and Sweden. It is also an ancient Judaeo-Christian symbol, and the Lion of Judah is the coat of arms of Jerusalem.

PET LIONS

Lions – the actual animals – were even a coveted possession to be owned by monarchs; after all, a peasant might own a chicken, but only a prince might own a lion. In 1235 the English king Henry II (1216–72) was presented by the Holy Roman Emperor Frederick II with three 'leopards' – believed to be lions – representing the three lions of the English coat of arms. Henry was so taken with his gift that he decided to start a zoo at the Tower of London which became known as the Royal Menagerie and existed for more than 600 years. In 1252 the lions were joined by a polar bear and in 1255 by an African elephant. Recent scientific analysis of artefacts discovered in the Tower have added some depth to our knowledge of lions held there. In 1930 two skulls were discovered in the castle's moat, the only big-cat remains yet discovered from medieval Europe, and have now been identified by DNA specialists at the University of Oxford and the Natural History Museum in London as belonging to male 'Barbary lions', a distinctive lion then found in North Africa with a huge, dark mane.* One dated from 1280–1385 and the 'younger' of the two from 1420–80, and both died at just three to four years old.

By no means was this just an English tradition. In 1648, when the Swedes captured Prague at the end of the Thirty Years War, they captured a real lion, perhaps held as a heraldic symbol of

* The last known Barbary lion in the wild was shot in 1942 in the Atlas Mountains of Morocco.

the Czech territory. When it was taken back to Stockholm it became a huge attraction until its death in 1663, with crowds drawn by the popular spectacle of watching it fight other animals. Louis XVI of France (1754–93) is also known to have kept lions; and most recently, and perhaps most famously of all, Haile Selassie (1892–1975), Emperor of Ethiopia, kept pet lions with the distinctive dark and shaggy mane of those that once prowled the menagerie of the English medieval kings. Descendants of Haile Selassie's lions, now believed to be genetically unique survivals, can be seen today in Addis Ababa zoo.

POPES AND POLITICIANS

Leo the Great (400–61) One of the most historically significant popes and a great source for historians as more than 100 of his sermons survive. Leo is famous for meeting Attila the Hun in 452 and convincing him not to invade Italy.

And it was not just monarchs who wanted to be associated with lions. Since Leo the Great in 440 CE, thirteen popes have taken the papal name Leo (which is Latin for lion), and several early Christian saints adopted the name, including St Leo of Bayonne (died c.900), St Leo of Catania (d.785), and St Leo of Montefeltro (d.366), presumably because of its associations with the characteristics of strength and fortitude. It has also been popular for politicians. The current ruling family of Syria, the Al-Assad family, derives its surname from the title 'Asad', meaning 'lion' in Arabic, a name which was formally adopted in 1927 when Ali Sulayman al-Wahhish (1875–1963), the grandfather of President Bashar Al-Assad (in office since 2000), changed his name to Ali Sulayman Al-Assad. During the Indian independence movement in the first quarter of the twentieth century, the collo-quial nickname 'Lion of Punjab' was given to the Indian freedom fighter Lala Lajpat Rai (1865–1928). The name which was plucked from the eighteenth-century Sikh leader Maharaja Ranjit Singh (1780–1839) who became known as the Lion of Punjab for his successful wars against the Pashtuns and the creation of a Sikh state which at its height stretched from the Khyber Pass in modern Afghanistan to the Thar Desert of Rajasthan in the Indian subcontinent, a powerful beacon of Indian independence at a time when the majority of the continent was British.

It is in this history of the association between national leaders, politicians and lions that we find another fascinating and entirely unexpected chapter in the history of the lion, a history that is the direct antithesis of the lion as a ferocious and mighty ruler, a king of beasts: this is the history of the lion as a coward.

THE COWARDLY LION

There is one instance of a cowardly lion that dominates all others in Western history, and that is the much-loved character in *The Wizard of Oz*, the book written by L. Frank Baum in the late 1890s that was turned into a stage play and then a film watched by millions in the 1930s. The book itself had sold three million copies by 1956. The story of Dorothy and her search for the way home along with the Tin Man (with no heart), Scare-crow (with no brains), the Cowardly Lion (with no mettle) and her little dog, Toto, has become one of the most famous fairy tales ever written. If you have read the book or seen the film, as no doubt you have, you have certainly wondered at the fantas-tical collection of characters and locations. As well as Dorothy's motley companions, we have witches, magic slippers, a yellow brick road, Munchkins, a green city, a very peculiar wizard and countless other bizarre things. What *on earth* is going on here!

The answer, in fact, lies almost everywhere that you look in the story, but it took until 1964 – that is, sixty-four years after it was first published – for anyone to work it out. The man who had that stroke of genius, who was suddenly able to see things in this magical story that no one had ever seen before, was a historian and teacher from the Midwest of America named Henry M. Littlefield (1933–2000). He realized that one of the clues to the code was the identity of that paradoxical giant feline, the cowardly lion, which leads us to the complexities of American politics at the turn of the nineteenth century, when America was moving from a pastoral past to an exciting, and frightening, industrial future.

In 1896 American politics was dominated by one issue, one movement, and two people. The issue, known as 'the financial question', concerned how America should create and circulate its currency, a debate which had been simmering, and sometimes raging, since the American states had won their independence from Britain in 1782. The movement, known as populism, was led by disenfranchised 'plain' folk – farmers and workers – seeking the representation they felt they had been denied, and the people at the head of the movement contested the presidential election of 1896: the Republican William McKinley and the Democrat William Jennings Bryan.

Bryan, three-times Democratic nominee for president (and three times failure), was known to be one of the finest orators of his, or indeed of any age, of American politics. Like a lion he commanded attention, indeed he *demanded* attention, both with the resonant boom of his voice and the magical words he would weave. In particular, his speech at the 1896 Democratic National Convention has been heralded by historians and journalists as one of the single most significant speeches in American political history. At the time it was described as 'hypnotic' and 'magnetic', extraordinary words of praise for any politician. Moreover,

William Jennings Bryan cartoon, 'WHO CARES FOR THE CHORUS. The Dog Which Barks Doesn't Bite', *Rocky Mountain News*, 15 August 1896

unlike any politician before him, he travelled thousands of miles to personally meet, entertain and campaign to the public, travelling more than 18,000 miles in the 1896 election alone. For a politician, his celebrity was unprecedented.

If any politician has ever deserved the title 'lion' it was Bryan, and it was not lost on political cartoonists of the time, nor was the fact that the word lion and the name Bryan rather fabulously rhyme.

Bryan was the one great voice of those who supported the belief in silver, rather than following the gold standard, as a monetary solution to the financial question. His subsequent depiction as a 'cowardly' lion relates to his failure, in the 1900 presidential election, to stand up for the views of the populists as he had so vociferously in the 1896 election while at the same time refusing to support America in the short-lived but painful Spanish–American War of the summer of 1898, which dominated the headlines and absorbed the attentions of politicians. To many of his previous supporters his behaviour reeked of nothing less than cowardice.

Here, then, is a leading US politician represented in *The Wizard of Oz* and suddenly, if viewed in the context of American politics of the 1890s, the subtext of the story begins to make sense. Dorothy's slippers, in the original story, were silver and not ruby. She wears them to walk down the yellow brick road, and finally discovers that the answer to all of her troubles lay in her silver shoes. Here is the debate, acted out by Bryan and McKinley, over the value of silver in comparison with the yellow bricks of a gold standard. Here silver solves all of Dorothy's (and America's) economic woes. The Tin Man is the factory worker condemned to lose his humanity and morph into a machine as technology takes hold; the Scarecrow is the farmer of the Midwest, ridiculed in the contemporary press as being 'muddle-headed'; the Wizard is the president, or perhaps any president from this era – no magician, but a normal man who can give each person what they desire; the Emerald City is Washington where he resides and is the colour of money itself, the 'green-back' dollar of contemporary paper currency; the Wicked Witch of the East represents the industrialists and bankers of the capitalist urban east coast holding the west under their spell; the harmless Toto represents the teetotalling Prohibitionists who were an important part of the pro-silver coalition; and what was Oz itself if not an abbreviation of 'ounce', one of the key issues in the monetary debate being the price of silver in relation to gold, measured in ounces at a ratio of 16:1.

These examples, intricate as they are, barely touch on the complexity of Baum's extraordinary creation. The entire book is a window into American politics, a parable of the complexities and contradictions of contemporary cultural concerns of the late 1890s, and the key that unlocks it is that 'cowardly' lion.

LION HUNTING

This chapter in the history of the lion, therefore, is about political satire, American economics and the presidential election of 1896. It is not, however, the only chapter in the *cowardly* history of the lion; another fascinating example comes from a chance discovery in a roadside rubbish dump outside the city of Tucson, Arizona in 1987. In that rubbish dump, discovered and searched through by a professor of environmental biology at the University of Arizona, were the letters of an American dentist by the name of W. S. Lackner, and it just so happened that this dentist was also a lion hunter.

The 'lions' he was particularly interested in were not strictly lions, but cougars, a type of puma or panther: *Felis concolor*, the largest of the small cats from the same genus that contains the domestic pussycat. They have always been known in America, however, as mountain lions. These big cats have been native to North America for at least a hundred thousand years; our relationship with them is but a blink of an eye in their animal memories. Nonetheless it has been sufficiently shocking and unpleasant for mountain lions to eternally regret that they ever came into contact with humans.

The chance discovery of Lackner's archive brings this to life. Here are letters organizing hunts, advertising hunts, celebrating kills, bemoaning and recounting failures, discussing the breeding of dogs for lion hunting and their desirable attributes, letters about hunting licences and so on – a wide window into a lost world, a period in which humanity was hell-bent on the utter destruction of mountain lions.

Some Native American tribes revered the mountain lion but, ever since the arrival of Europeans onto the American continent, they have been hunted to near extinction. Motivation for their hunting has varied across time and location, but originally it was intricately linked with European farming methods. Husbandry of crops and domestic animals required control of the environment, and that meant control of predators such as mountain lions. For some it became a sport and for others it became a source of income either by claiming bounties for the heads of lions, which began to be offered in the 1850s, or through a parasitic relationship with the hunters. One letter found in the rubbish dump, dating from June 1936, illustrates this particularly well.

6/24/36

Dr W. S. Lackner,
79 No. Stone Ave.
Tucson, Ariz.

Dear Dr Lackner,
Thank you for your shipment of the two Mountain Lion hides. Our charges for tanning these hides will be $7.50 and $8.50 respectively – one being larger than the other.
 Do you plan to have these skins made into full head open mouth rugs? If so, we would be pleased to do this work for you...
Yours very truly,
JONAS BROS

By / Colaman Jonas

Here the Jonas Brothers are pushing their services as skinners and tanners of mountain lion hides. These lions were big business. Between 1907 and 1977, 68,000 were killed by hunters, and an unknown quantity of them by hunters lacing dead animal carcasses with poison. By the 1920s they were exterminated from most states east of the Mississippi.

Coloman Jonas, a famous big-game hunter, with the pelts of 'killers of three continents' ahead of the Denver Post–Glenwood Springs Lion Hunt that took place in March 1932

It is in a published article written by Lackner, however, that this specific section of the lion's history turns us back to the question of cowardice. In 1936 Lackner wrote an article for *Outdoor Life* magazine in which he described a recent hunting trip. Mountain lions, he wrote, were 'gangsters of the animal world, the criminals and destroyers, and the sooner we get rid of them the better'. He then went on to celebrate the fact that he had killed four: '... I ended their careers of deer killing and general outlawry.' Elsewhere he described them as 'bloodthirsty killers and arrant cowards' and again 'the most cowardly of predatory animals'.

By no means was this derogatory opinion of the mountain lion Lackner's alone; indeed, we have good evidence that it was widespread, even from the pen of a former American president.

After hunting in the Grand Canyon for mountain lion in 1913, Theodore Roosevelt wrote describing them as 'the destroyer of the deer, the lord of stealthy murder, facing his doom with a heart both craven and cruel'.

The origin of the lion's perceived 'cowardice' and its 'craven' nature is unclear but perhaps lies in the way that the animal was – and is – hunted. Still today mountain lions are chased with packs of special dogs until they run up into a tree to hide, when they are cornered, surrounded, and shot. Lackner wrote of it with relish: 'The sight of the old deer murderer, perched like some malignant tabby, in a tree with the clamouring dogs below, then the kill, with a great tawny lion tumbling from his perch into the snarling pack...'

In this vision of animal 'cowardice' lies a history of hunting to near extinction, which is unhappily shared by other predators such as the wolf and grizzly bear. The good news is that the mountain lion is now making its way back into the wilderness of North America; the bad is that hunting mountain lion is still legal in no fewer than ten American states and two provinces of Canada.*

Who knew that such a fascinating history of lions could be uncovered in a rubbish dump? It is just another wonderful example of passing discoveries changing our perception of history – and it raises the far broader, and very important, question of the history of rubbish...

* Arizona, Colorado, Idaho, Montana, Nevada, New Mexico, Oregon, Utah, Washington and Wyoming, and the Canadian provinces of Alberta and British Columbia.

·24·

RUBBISH

—

The history of rubbish is all about… truth,
secret habits, fixed wrestling matches in ancient
Egypt, sweets and political discontent.

The history of rubbish is about what people choose not to remember or cherish, but instead to throw away and discard – an activity that is in many ways the *opposite* of history. A rubbish tip, in essence, is the antithesis of an archive. That does not make rubbish uninteresting to the historian, however. In fact, quite the opposite is the case: it's fascinating.

——— WHAT IS DISPOSABLE? ———

In one sense the history of rubbish is what people in the past viewed as disposable, unimportant and ephemeral. What once were practical or treasured items can become irrelevant or irksome, even loathed for what they represent: a shopping list of little purpose once the groceries have been bought; a things-to-do list that loses its importance once the tasks have been completed; a love letter from an ex never read again after that rotting relationship has itself been consigned to the dustbin of history. Such items can therefore tell us a great deal about their past, the people they interacted with and the circumstances of their destruction – and sometimes they can have an immense impact upon our understanding of history.

Consider the death in 1617 of Edward Talbot, eighth Earl of Shrewsbury, who died without male heirs and thus ended the direct male line of succession of his branch of the family. This meant that large parts of his landed estates passed to the sixth Duke of Norfolk along with a massive cache of papers relating to the Earls of Shrewsbury. Norfolk had little interest in these papers, made no effort to care for them and during the Civil War they degenerated.

RESCUED LETTERS

In 1671 they were found by the antiquary Nathaniel Johnson mouldering away, unattended in a hunting lodge. He wrote

> at severall tymes, from amids the multitudes of waste papers, and the havock that mice, ratts, and wet, had made I rescued these letters, and as many more as I have bound up in fifteen volumes, and have more to gett bound.

In this instance, papers that had been neglected and become rubbish for one person were then rediscovered by another – and significantly a person with an interest in writing history. Once again, therefore, they became valuable for the story that they told about the noble Talbot family, the Earls of Shrewsbury, a hereditary title dating back to 1074 when it was awarded to Roger de Montgomery, one of William the Conqueror's principal aides and counsellors.

Such a discovery is a jackpot for historians but an understanding of the value of rubbish is also a key foundation of archaeology. Indeed, one of the reasons that we know so much about preliterate and ancient civilization is because of the material remains that survive of those past societies and cultures that can be reconstructed from the detritus of their day-to-day lives. In combination with intentionally stashed hoards and burial goods, rubbish is one of the only reasons that we know so much about the ancient world.

—— 500,000 FRAGMENTS OF PAPYRUS ——

One of the most astonishing chance finds that uncovered the secrets of an ancient civilization occurred in 1895. A team of archaeologists, including the papyrologist Bernard Pyne Grenfell, and his friend Arthur Surridge Hunt, began digging at an ancient rubbish dump near to the Egyptian city of Oxyrhynchus, about 100 miles south-west of Cairo. Their excavations unearthed (strictly speaking 'unrubbished') over 500,000 fragments of papyrus manuscripts dating from the first to the sixth century CE, at a time when this area was part of Roman North Africa. The collection became known as the Oxyrhynchus Papyri and is, without doubt, one of the most culturally valuable archaeological discoveries ever made.

Among this treasure survive literary works, correspondence, accounts, legal documents, tax receipts and some vellum documents [*see fig. 31*]. There are fragments of verse by Greek poets Pindar, Alcaeus and Sappho; fragments of Euclid's *Elements*; lost work of the Roman historian Livy; as well as a lost gospel that tells of Jesus exorcizing demons from possessed men. More unexpectedly there survives an account of a teenage wrestler dating from around 12 BCE, who was managed by his father and agreed to lose a match in return for a bribe: match-fixing has a remarkably long history.

> **Euclid's *Elements*** A mathematical treatise of thirteen separate books written by the ancient Greek mathematician Euclid in Ptolemaic Egypt c.300 BCE. It is one of the most important works in the development of modern science and widely considered to be the most influential textbook ever written.

The site was excavated over a number of decades with scholars from around the world clamouring to be part of the exciting discovery. Something of the atmosphere that surrounded the dig is evident in a letter from the noted British Egyptologist Flinders Petrie to Hunt written in 1922. 'We are in the old palm grove', he wrote,

> & much papyrus found. I am buying up all I can get, especially every scrap of uncial [a type of script written entirely in capital letters] literary; feeling my way as to values by not always offering enough for Byzantine accounts &c. There are three or four literary pieces of 100 words or so. As these are bought, we shall have all to London. Would you be open to looking over all the pieces & giving us – as a matter of business – a report on them in June? There is St Louis University rampant to get some to edit, but if you wish to publish any piece specially I hope you would do so... I hear that the best papyri are found

about 20 feet down in the high mounds. We shall not try to do anything exhaustive, but rescue a little of the architecture & plans before they all vanish.

Not only does Petrie's letter convey something of the wonder experienced during this kind of excavation, but also the scramble among rival Egyptologists to get their hands on the papyri, and the lucrative local market for their sale and purchase.

—— PAINSTAKING TRANSCRIPTION ——

What is even more remarkable about this collection of half a million manuscripts is that the majority are little more than fragments, exceptionally hard to read, and requiring patience and painstaking skill to piece together, translate and ultimately transcribe and edit in printed volumes; and yet this work is moving ahead effectively: historians have become very good indeed at working with such rubbish.

Some of the most intact documents were translated and edited in published volumes as *The Oxyrhynchus Papyri* (an impressive 82 volumes were produced between 1898 and 2017), but this constitutes just over 1 per cent of the surviving papyri. A huge amount remains to be done. In this instance, however, help is at hand in the guise of 250,000 volunteers across the world, who are part of the University of Oxford's 'Ancient Lives' Project. This collaborative research project makes use of sophisticated computer software programs to reassemble dispersed papyri fragments and then makes images freely available for volunteers to transcribe and translate, letter by letter, word by word, line by line.

This is an endeavour in the spirit of the original *Oxford English Dictionary*, which was compiled from 1858 largely by submissions posted in by avid readers around the world. The first edition was published thirty *years* later. The work on the Oxyrhynchus Papyri is similarly slow and time-consuming, but invaluable and somehow magical – a global project conjuring immense value from what was once just rubbish.

──── DELIBERATELY HIDDEN HISTORY ────

Historians love rubbish too because in amongst the orange peels, rusting tin cans and rotting fish skeletons is evidence – if you know where to look for it – that allows us to peer beneath the masks we all wear for the outside world. One of the enduring challenges of the historian is to find out what *actually* happened in the past, rather than what our predecessors would like us to believe happened, and rubbish can help us do that. History is, in many ways, a game played by those in control of the archives: they choose what is important to keep, and discard what, in their eyes, is disposable. The bonfire, shredder or delete button are all part and parcel of the way in which people shape the archives that they leave and edit the narratives of the past that they wish successive generations to read. Consider the presidential libraries of almost all of the former presidents of the United States. These archives are funded by politically motivated donors with the sole purpose of preserving the legacy of a powerful individual. The historical record then is partial, fragmentary and often intentional in its bias.

Rubbish, on the other hand, is what gets set aside, either because it is viewed as ephemeral and unimportant, or – and this is key – because it is exactly what people did not want others to see or history to judge. The past is full of historical figures whose papers were either destroyed, purged or highly edited in order to present them in a favourable light. The same is true of governments. It recently came to light that British officials destroyed thousands of incriminating documents that revealed shameful and horrific acts and crimes committed during the final years of the British empire. In 1961, after instructions from the then Secretary of State for the Colonies Iain Macleod, documents that 'might embarrass Her Majesty's government' were systematically destroyed in order to prevent them falling into the hands of post-independence governments. Additionally, many thousands more were flown back to Britain where they were locked away in a secure facility by the British Foreign Office, long after the 'Thirty Year Rule' which permitted them to be declassified and open for public viewing. This secret, high-security archive only came to light in 2011 when a group of Kenyans claiming to have been tortured and detained during the Mau Mau Rebellion in the 1950s won the right to sue the British government, which led to promises from the Foreign Office to release more than 8,800 files from thirty-seven former colonies. The truth of what really happened in the past lies in uncovering what we were not supposed to see, and an examination of rubbish helps us do just that.

Rubbish, then, is related in a roundabout way to truth, in that the things that you throw out are the things that you do not want people to know about. In this sense, rubbish is about secrecy and keeping things hidden, and it can be much more revealing about everyday life in the past – life that travelled under the historical radar – than can other documentary sources that reveal things on a surface level.

CONTRABAND

This way of looking at the past is particularly useful when considering the consumption of goods or commodities that were frowned upon by society, and reflected badly on the person who consumed them. The history of legal or cultural 'contraband' varies enormously across time and geographical region, but to our minds banned substances or commodities included tobacco, drugs, fast food, pornography, contraceptives, crisps, sweets or alcohol. In rubbish we can see a history of secret consumption, whether it is sweet wrappers tucked behind an old bedhead or into a bedroom air vent where a child has gorged in secret, or bottles of booze stashed away from prying eyes by a guilty alcoholic.

A recent archaeological excavation of a site in Israel has transformed our understanding of life at an army base during the First World War. The site that was excavated was near the city of Ramla, which was secured in November 1917 by soldiers of the Egyptian Expeditionary Force on their way to capture Jerusalem. They remained there for nine months. The written historical evidence for these men at that location consists largely of dry official administrative accounts, of soldiers moving from A to B, of equipment and expenses, but the archaeological evidence most definitely is not. Excavators found the men's rubbish tip, and it contained *hundreds* of bottles, 70 per cent of which contained alcohol: wine, beer, gin and whisky. The army base at Ramla, it seems, was something of a party town. Rubbish, therefore, can be a useful corrective to the official documentary evidence, permitting a glimpse at the underbelly of army life in the early twentieth century.

MEMORIES

If such discoveries represent the embarrassment of certain types of rubbish, which reflect unfashionable, antisocial or unhealthy habits, in another way rubbish tells us a good deal about the cultural everyday of the past. Consider the things that we take for granted, that we view as disposable, that we throw in the bin: old newspapers and magazines, fliers, posters and tickets from concerts and shows, adverts, packaging and wrappers,

22. Seventeenth-century trunk belonging to the postmasters of
the Dutch city of The Hague – Simon de Brienne and his wife Maria
Germain – containing 2600 unopened letters dating from 1689–1706.

23. Gravestone of Marcus Caelius, son of Titus, wearing his medals,
c.9 CE. He was from Bologna and a centurion in the First of Legio XVIII.

24. Sir Edwin Landseer, *Neptune, a Newfoundland Dog, the property of W. E. Gosling Esq* (1824)

25. Sam Willis in the Zarafshan mountains with the Sogdians in 2015.

26. Wheal Coates, an abandoned Cornish
tin mine, near St Agnes, Cornwall.

27. The King's Pipe, Falmouth

28. Conservation at the National Library of Scotland of the seventeenth-
century Dutch map that was found stuffed up a chimney.

29. Giotto Frescoes in Santa Croce, Florence, thirteenth century

30. The lion figurehead on Gustavus Adolphus's *Vasa* warship, which sank in 1628.

once-loved toys and games. In other words, we are talking about objects, things and texts that are seen as transient and throw-away, but that shed important light on the material world of popular culture and the quotidian existence of ordinary people in the past.

Museums do a wonderful job in preserving the rubbish that might otherwise be thrown away. An excellent example of this is the Victoria and Albert Museum of Childhood in London, which is a cornucopia of child-related objects evoking a deep sense of childhood memories. Among the collections of antique prams, dolls and doll's houses reside countless toys from our childhoods – action figures, Lego sets, Meccano – all in their original boxes. These toys that would otherwise have been thrown away allow us a glimpse into the world of childhood play across the centuries.

Rubbish defined in this way is also a trigger for memories. There is a nostalgic fondness for certain types of rubbish that triggers associations, a fondness which can be used to do a great deal of good. Consider sweets. What activity are you usually doing when you hold a sweet wrapper in your hand? The answer is chewing, or sucking, the sweet that was, moments before, in the wrapper. There is probably an explosion of taste going on in your mouth, sugar rushing through your blood, your brain lighting up with pleasure, and all of this with a sweet wrapper – just a piece of plastic rubbish – in your probably sticky hand.

Harnessing exactly this moment, which is, more often than not, also wrapped up with childhood memory, researchers at Nestlé, a Swiss confectionary company set up in 1905, have recently placed an enormous selection of sweet wrappers from the 1920s online with the specific intention of triggering happy memories and discussion from those who suffer from dementia. They have created a 'Reminiscence Pack' from their archive which brings together tin labels, posters, photographs, even one of the earliest Rowntree's Fruit Gums boxes, and is being used, among others, by the UK-based Alzheimer's Society in activities organized for those with dementia and their carers [*see fig. 32*].

SWEETS

This undoubtedly is a new technique in contemporary psychiatry but one wonders how long the pattern of associating fond memories with sweets goes back: we know that humans have consumed sweets since at least 8000 BCE and our understanding of the manufacture and trade in sweets from the Middle Ages onwards is now impressive. The history of sweet-wrapping is just one part of that history but it, too, is progressing and there are some fine collections for historians to work with. One of the most fascinating is the Joseph Downs Collection of Manuscripts and Printed Ephemera held at the Winterthur Library in Delaware, which includes 198 distinct lithographed, hand-coloured French candy wrapper images dating from the second quarter of the nineteenth century.

From a study of this collection we now know that in nineteenth-century France sweets were wrapped in newspaper, but that that changed around 1820 when pictorial wrappers were sold by confectioners to swaddle their goods. One contemporary account noted how complex this became:

> There is a great demand for these articles in France, particularly on New-year's day; and the various envelopes in which they

Winterthur Library, Delaware One of the most important resources for the study of American history, with a collection of around 85,000 objects and more than 500,000 manuscripts and images.

are put up, display the usual ingenuity of this gay and versatile people: fables, historical subjects, songs, enigmas, jeux de mots, and various little gallantries, are all inscribed upon the papers in which the bon-bons are inclosed, and which the gentlemen present to the females of their acquaintance.

These wrappers both protected food and entertained their customers before becoming just another piece of rubbish, tossed into the gutter.

RE-USING AND RECYCLING

Another way of considering history though rubbish is to consider the quantity of rubbish that is, or has been, produced by people tossing useless items away. The majority of the world today is a disposable society, driven by capitalist urges to produce and consume. Technology moves so quickly that consumers are presented with new models to purchase on a bewilderingly regular basis, with marketing gurus generating dissatisfaction and demand, while production teams build into their consumables a short and limited lifespan that requires people to consume more and more. It is often cheaper to buy something new and to throw out the old rather than to have it repaired. There is a strong sense, however, that in the past much more effort was made to mend and make do, to recycle, reuse and repurpose.

This is certainly true of printed ephemera during the sixteenth and seventeenth centuries. This was a period when paper was a relatively expensive commodity, beyond the everyday means of an ordinary labourer. The pages from printed almanacs after they had been used were often repurposed for a whole variety of uses, including to paper walls, write notes, fill holes in shoes and even to line pie dishes. A copy of a seventeenth-century book of natural history by the writer John Jonston (1603–75), held in the archives of Merton College, Oxford, was, unusually, bound in a paper wrapper initially intended to protect quires of paper while in transit.

───── WHEN MONEY BECAME RUBBISH ─────

During the hyperinflation experienced by Weimar Germany between the end of the First World War in 1918 and 1924, as Allied reparations began to bite, even money itself became worthless, considered as disposable: in other words, money became rubbish. So extreme was the financial crisis during these post-war years that, by November 1923, the US dollar was worth an extraordinary 4,210,500,000,000 German marks. Under these circumstances banknotes themselves were recycled, for their purchasing power was zero, and even to carry enough notes around required a suitcase or cart. With a market value of zilch, enterprising Germans found enterprising uses for their worthless currency, such as papering the walls with notes or using rolled-up bills to light stoves. Children even made kites out of money. Under the right circumstances, then, almost anything can be considered rubbish.

Money kite made out of banknotes during hyperinflation in Weimar Germany, 1922

THE WINTER OF DISCONTENT

The opposite of this type of recycling – embracing rubbish for what it can do for us – is to *fear* rubbish, in particular to fear what great piles of it can represent. This was most visible in the UK during the Winter of Discontent of 1978–9 when James Callaghan's Labour government clashed with the trade unions and the dustmen went on strike. Rubbish piled up on the nation's streets, including in London's famous Leicester Square, which became a haven for rats and disease. Such was the public horror at the state of London's streets that numerous

Rubbish left piled up outside a post office in central London during the Winter of Discontent

and powerful images were taken at the time and have survived, usually of Londoners continuing their daily business, in their smart clothes, walking past buzzing shops, but in the shadow of mountains of rubbish. Just months after this photograph was taken in central London an election was called; Callaghan lost and a Conservative government under Margaret Thatcher would utterly transform British society in an uncontested eighteen years of power – power that in some senses was achieved through the public's fear of rubbish as a symbol of social and political disorder.

POMPEII

But where has that fear or anxiety over rubbish come from? Humans used to be surrounded by rubbish. We know from excavations of the Roman city of Pompeii that the Pompeiians threw much of their waste and filth – butchered, charred animal remains, broken pottery and building material – among the city's tombs and cemeteries.

For many years, from the late nineteenth century when this pattern was first observed, this behaviour was considered to be a sign of a city falling into social chaos – why else would you abandon the maintenance of your tombs and graveyards, how could you *possibly* treat the dead with such disrespect? It was seen by a generation of historians as a sign of malaise eating into the heart of the Roman empire itself. We now know, however, that at the time that the rubbish was thrown into the graveyards and among the tombs, Pompeii was thriving. Rather than being the activity of citizens under intense economic stress, it was the activity of citizens in a booming, buzzing city. It reflects the Romans' comfort with living alongside tombs as much as it does their comfort with living alongside rubbish, for the tombs were also often placed all along the city's streets. The rubbish, moreover, was not just in and around the tombs, but piled up along the city walls, outside homes, in streets and alleys, on the floors of houses. Most of us in Western society consider town and city cleanliness to be one of the fundamental tenets of civilization and piles of rubbish to be a symbol of social and economic disintegration, but in Roman Pompeii, and elsewhere in the ancient and medieval world, it was part of everyday life.

——— STREET LEVELS IN NEW YORK ———

For millennia we lived with rubbish, we lived beside it, we even lived *on* it, something that is most eloquently illustrated by the history of street levels. We know that the street level of ancient Troy rose almost five feet per century because of the accumulation of rubbish. Similarly, street levels in today's New York are anywhere between six and *fifteen* feet higher than they were in the seventeenth century. Refuse collection did not, in fact, begin in a systematic way in London until 1846, though it was not until 1875 that it was made compulsory for every household to deposit their rubbish in a dedicated container – a bin. By 1895 these practices had spread across the Atlantic and reached New York, all driven by a desire for social reform. Rubbish was dirty, dirt led to disease, and disease led to economic weakness, social unrest and poverty. Therein lies our modern anxiety about piles of rubbish, an anxiety that in turn has driven environmentalism and our growing awareness of the human impact on our planet, its inhabitants, our environment and our climate – which raises the very important question of the history of snow...

·25·

SNOW

—

The history of snow is all about... tattoos, DNA, bacchanalian excess, the Boston Massacre and cruelty to cats.

Historians love snow. We love it not simply because of a historical fascination with its ethereality, nor simply for the ways in which past societies have understood snow, and developed traditions and practices associated with it – sledging, snowballs, snowmen, skiing and snow angels to name a few. Historians also love snow for the secrets that lie there beneath its cold white carpet waiting to be discovered – if only we know where to look.

─── THE SCYTHIANS ───

Without snow our understanding of the past would not be as rich as it is, nor would our collections of historical artefacts be so dazzling. Because of snow, for example, we now know all about the ancient Scythians, a civilization of warriors so terrifying that the Greek historian Herodotus wrote of them in the fifth century BCE: 'None who attacks them can escape, and none can catch them if they desire not to be found.' These tribes occupied territory from the edge of China to Greece and the Black Sea via Siberia from the ninth to the third centuries BCE, and we know more about them than any other nomadic tribe of the period because so much of their culture has been preserved by snow and ice. Weapons, jewellery, household goods, even perishables such as food – and the remains of Scythians themselves – have survived, all protected for millennia by the natural deep freeze of the Siberian permafrost. In addition to finds such as a bag of cheese, a gold plaque, a false beard and a collapsible table, perhaps the most remarkable survival is a Scythian tattoo, which is inscribed on the skin of a warrior found beneath the snow [*see fig. 33*].

In a climate where it was imperative to keep covered up and warm, such tattoos were rarely seen, hidden beneath layers of clothing and furs. Yet with the passage of time we are able to decode the meanings of ancient tattoos in a way that was unimaginable for previous generations of scholars. The tattoo depicts part of a tiger with menacing claws, and was discovered in a tomb at Pazyryk in the Altai mountains of Siberia, along with four other heavily tattooed bodies. The tattoo of a fierce beast on the torso represents the bravery of warriors in the face of an awesome predatory foe.

Snow in this sense acts as an enormous archive of past civilizations, not only for the Scythians, but also for other peoples and cultures that thrived in conditions of ice and snow. This means that our knowledge of societies that live in such landscapes – often on the margins of the liveable world, often particularly hardy, often with unique cultures that have developed in isolation from others – has begun to grow faster than it ever has before.

WAR IN THE DOLOMITES

We also are beginning to discover more about moments when those who are *not* used to such wintery conditions venture into them. Snow in the Trentino region in the far north of Italy, for example, has preserved a battlefield from the First World War where Italian and Austro-Hungarian troops fought at heights of 12,000 feet and at temperatures as low as –22°C. This was the first time in history that such large-scale battles were fought at such high altitudes. The achievements of these soldiers, in terms of both engineering and endurance, were extraordinary. On Marmolada, the highest mountain in the Dolomites, Austrian soldiers built an immense complex of tunnels, dormitories and storerooms deep under the drifts of snow.

After the war the enormous amount of equipment that had been carried up into the mountains became a lure for men, economically crippled by the war, who braved the journey due to the value of scrap. This is a tale of heroism and endurance which is matched only by those who risked their lives to dive on submerged wrecks in the aftermath of the war for the scrap value of those leviathans lurking in the deep. The highly dangerous nature of this work in the mountains was recalled much later in life in an interview with the 92-year-old former salvager Giacinto Capelli:

> We brought a mallet with us and would pound the bomb at a very precise point so that the casing would break away... If we made a mistake, the powder left inside could have exploded in our faces. It was such hard work. We went back down the mountain with as many as 70 kilos [150 pounds] on our backs. But there was no work in the village, and salvagers made good money. The first time I came home with 320 liras, my father jumped for joy, crying, 'Now we can have polenta all year long!'

This forgotten chapter of combat in the Dolomites during the First World War and scrap-hunting in its aftermath is becoming well known now for a very particular reason: our world is warming up, forcing glaciers like these to reveal their frozen secrets. Global warming, therefore, is making the historian's relationship with snow more relevant than ever. In the Dolomites, machines, corpses and structures of this unique front line are emerging from the snow, changing forever our understanding of the experience of war in that particular location at that particular time.

This is also happening elsewhere where areas once impenetrable because of snow are now accessible, and 'glacial archaeology' has become a discipline in its own right. Intrepid archaeologists working at both poles are uncovering remarkable historic material – flora, fauna, and remains of human material culture – which is helping to create detailed pictures of the historic polar landscapes across time. Archaeologists have unearthed middens (rubbish tips) in Greenland from the society that predates the Eskimo and Inuit, dating from 2500 BCE; Iron Age burials in the Altai mountains in Russia; 500-year-old Incan child mummies in the Andes; and prehistoric Caribou hunting sites in Norway, Canada and Alaska.

GENETICS

The richness of snow as evidence for historians lies in the hidden histories *inside it* waiting to be discovered. In 1999 the body of a young man was found frozen in the Yukon Territory of Canada. He was wearing a cloak of gopher or squirrel skins, and carried a walking stick, an iron knife and a spear-thrower. He was somewhere between 300 and 550 years old, a relative youngster for such ice discoveries, and ten times younger than the Iceman, found in the Ötztal Alps in 1991. His relative youth,

Ötzi Iceman An exceptionally well-preserved mummy of a man who lived around 3,300 BCE. Discovered in 1991 in the Ötztal Alps on the Austrian–Italian border.

however, made an interesting DNA exercise possible, and he was found to share DNA with no fewer than seventeen indigenous people living in the region. The locals named him '*Kwaday Dan Ts'inchi*' which translates as 'long-ago person found' and if one thing is certain in the coming years we will find more such people worthy of the title 'long-ago person found', and also more modern people to link their lives with – it is one of the most exciting promises of our historical world.

ESKIMO HISTORIES

We in the West are also becoming increasingly aware of the history that not only lives in the ice itself, but also in the minds of the people who have lived in the snow. Nowhere is this clearer than in the story of the disappearance of the Arctic explorer John Franklin in 1845. Franklin was last seen by Europeans in late July 1845 when two captains of whaling vessels saw his ships in Baffin Bay, near the entrance to the Northwest Passage. It was not, however, the last time that he or his crew were *seen*. In their desperate bid for survival Franklin and members of his party crossed paths with local hunters and, over the centuries that followed, other Inuit came across material culture associated with the expedition. The value of the Inuit tradition of oral history – their techniques of carefully caring for and preserving folk memory over generations – has been instrumental in piecing together the story of Franklin, his men and his ships, particularly so in the search for HMS *Terror*.

Nine years after Franklin disappeared, the Irish explorer

Sir Francis Leopold McClintock recorded the first evidence of Franklin's men taken from the Inuit. He was told that one of Franklin's ships had been driven ashore in an area known as Ootgoolik, between Reilly Island and the Royal Geographical Society Islands. In the 1860s an American explorer, Charles Francis Hall, then heard from an Inuk who had come across the ship, had even been aboard and had seen the corpse of a large man, fully clothed and smelling badly. He noted that the ship had since sunk but that her masts were left sticking out of the water. An almost identical story was then told to another explorer, Lieutenant Frederick Schwatka, in his expedition of 1878–80. At some point between 1994 and 2008 the story was heard again from an Inuit elder called Frank Analok on Victoria Island.

In spite of this testimony, however, Europeans hunting for Franklin's ships had searched elsewhere for their remains, using the location where the ships had first been abandoned as a guide, even though the Inuit testimony suggested that the ships had perished elsewhere. Finally, in 2016, an Inuk mentioned that, seven years earlier, he had seen a mast sticking out of the ice while exploring on snowmobiles and it was his testimony, given credence by modern historians searching for the wreck, that finally led to the discovery of HMS *Terror*, confirming the Inuit story that it had at some point been moved from the original location of its abandonment, a discovery which is now forcing historians to reconsider our traditional understanding of the Franklin expedition: it is now a distinct possibility that some of the sailors even tried to sail home.

Snow is being increasingly acknowledged as one of the great preservers of the recent as well as the ancient past; the oral histories and folk memories of those who live in the snow are a rich, and relatively untapped, historical resource – and the depth of that knowledge is not to be underestimated. Of all the Inuit testimony collected over the years by those searching for the Franklin expedition, the most remarkable was taken by the American journalist Charles Francis Hall in 1861. He discovered that, not only had the Inuit carefully preserved memories of the Franklin expedition of 1845, but also of Sir Martin Frobisher's expedition of 1576 – almost three *centuries* earlier.

Snow has so many intriguing stories to tell, but it is also a fascinating historical subject in its own right, from the science of the snowflake to the cultural meaning of snow. Its uses and meanings are many and varied across time and across cultures and, in a unique and interesting way, those uses and meanings are often contradictory: snow can nurture by providing water but it can kill by removing heat and light; it can bury or it can reveal; it can prevent travel by blocking roads or tracks or it can permit travel by providing a surface on which to sledge, ski or skate; snow days are a boon for children given the chance to frolic and have fun, but are detrimental for an economy where production is reduced by absenteeism. Snow as a climatic phenomenon has always had an important impact on societies and cultures in the past.

SNOWY MEMORIES

One aspect of the history of snow is connected to the history of weather and climate, and here we do not simply mean the seasons, or regions of the world that are snowbound, but rather the ways in which snowfall and temperatures have varied over time. It is a peculiarly personal subject for both of us. As a child, Sam can remember his grandmother Patricia Willis (1921–2014) talking of ice-skating when she was a child on a lake at the site of the ancient Roman town of Verulamium (modern St Albans) during the late 1920s or early 1930s. It is likely she was recalling the winter of 1927–8 which saw some of the heaviest snowfalls in Britain of the twentieth century, or perhaps the winter of

1933, one of the coldest on record, in which some areas of the country witnessed forty-eight hours of continuous snowfall. Sam remembers being baffled by the concept of a lake freezing thickly enough in southern Britain for children to skate on it; it was a powerful moment when the immediate past seemed inconceivably foreign, and was made so by something as apparently reliable and unchangeable as the climate.

The winter of December 1978 and the early months of early 1979 was one of the worst in recent memory, with record temperatures well below freezing, and huge snowdrifts. It also happened to be the year of the Winter of Discontent, with its widespread strikes. James at the time lived in the seaside town of Hornsea on the Yorkshire coast, and remembers his father making a daily commute to Hull during these winter months, with a shovel, warm blankets and flask of hot coffee in the boot of his car. Driving home one day in the snow, Daybell senior's car got stuck, and he had to dig it out, which was preferable to the plight of the other cars that remained there overnight, and were ploughed into by the snow-plough as they attempted to clear the roads at first light.

THE BRITISH ICE AGE

Historical periods of intense cold have varied from millennia to a matter of months. The last glacial period or 'ice age' in Britain ended approximately 10,000 years ago and the subsequent absence of ice made the British Isles permanently habitable for the first time in history – before then Britain had been inhabited and then abandoned in numerous cycles as the ice thawed, refroze and re-spread. Even within the subsequent pattern of permanent habitation, however, are periods of intense cold, which severely affected all aspects of life. In northern Europe the period c.1550–c.1750 was known as a 'little ice age' when it was so cold that canals, rivers and harbours all froze over. Severe winters were also experienced in North America during these years, especially the cold winter of 1607–8, when ice was spotted on the shores of Lake Superior by the French navigator Samuel de Champlain (c.1574–1635). Europe experienced a bitingly bitter winter during 1407–8, which, although it lasted only a handful of months, still froze rivers, split trees and decimated bird populations. We know about these cold periods because of documentary accounts of the climate and weather conditions, paintings of winter scenes, and even a small number of historic century-long temperature readings.

Such climatic conditions ravaged the European peasantry, bringing hypothermia and hunger; while in the Alps the encroachment of glaciers even destroyed villages. Conditions were so bad that in the seventeenth-century Alpine villagers ate bread made with a mixture of flour and ground nutshells. The harsh climate led to changes in clothing and dress, with hats and gloves donned all the more frequently and knitted under-garments worn to keep out the cold. The period also saw the development of fireplace hoods and enclosed stoves as new ways of insulating the home.

Temperatures throughout this period were frequently cold enough for canals and rivers to freeze, which encouraged pastimes such as skating, as well as winter fairs. In London the Thames was known to freeze over so frequently that there are records of 'frost fairs' taking place. The first to be recorded in London was during the winter of 1607–8, which was reported in a printed pamphlet of 1608 entitled *The Great Frost. Cold Doings in London*. The frontispiece, a printed woodcut illustration, depicted London citizens engaged in sports and pastimes, drinking and trading on the ice. A later fair of 1683–4 was described by the celebrated diarist John Evelyn: 'Coaches plied from Westminster to the Temple, and from several other stairs

Woodcut and account of the London Frost Fair of 1608, thought to be the first

to and fro, as in the streets, sleds, sliding with skeetes, a bull-baiting, horse and coach races, puppet plays and interludes, cooks, tipling and other lewd places, so that it seemed to be a bacchanalian triumph, or carnival on the water.' The 'little ice age' of the sixteenth to eighteenth centuries prompted a cultural explosion in art. Frost fairs, ice skaters and snow scenes were frequently depicted in paintings of the period such as the winter landscape of Pieter Brueghel the Elder, typified by the iconic *The Hunters in the Snow* (1565).

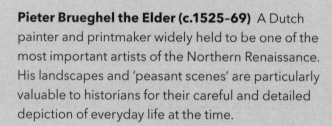

Pieter Brueghel the Elder (c.1525-69) A Dutch painter and printmaker widely held to be one of the most important artists of the Northern Renaissance. His landscapes and 'peasant scenes' are particularly valuable to historians for their careful and detailed depiction of everyday life at the time.

DANGEROUS SNOWMEN

Images like this are powerful reminders that, whoever you are, and whenever you lived, snow is beautiful and yet it is beguiling; it is serene yet sinister, fun yet ferocious. Nowhere is this more apparent than in the winter pursuits of making snowmen and snowballing, which are at once innocent and charming as well as dark and dangerous.

The phenomenon of building a snowman, replete with hat, scarf, coal for eyes, carrot for a nose and twigs for arms, is something that millions of people have indulged in, as children and adults. This image of a snowman has entered the popular imagination and has been playfully represented over the years in pictures, postcards and advertising as well as in literature and film, most famously in Raymond Briggs's wonderfully illustrated

book and film *The Snowman* (1978), which is a tender-hearted tale of a small boy whose snowman magically comes to life, or the slightly less enchanting animated American equivalent *Frosty the Snowman* (1969), which is based on the drawings of *Mad* magazine cartoonist Paul Coker, Jr. (b.1929).

While such 'Snowmen' are well known to modern readers, they have a long history, and can be traced back in documentary evidence to the medieval period, where an illustration of what has been interpreted as a snowman appears in the margins of a Book of Hours held in the Koninklijke Bibliotheek in The Hague, Netherlands and which dates from around 1380. It is depicted with rather a forlorn look, as its snowy buttocks are scorched by the fire that burns beneath it [*see fig. 34*].

In this instance, behind the innocent fun of depicting a snowman can be seen something far more serious – something even with a political edge. The fact that this snowman is wearing a Jewish-style hat is suggestive of a covert anti-Semitic message. There is far more to this than an idle, marginal doodle, therefore; it is a fascinating reminder that, in the past, snowmen have represented more than merely childish ice sculptures or targets for snowball practice.

During the High Middle Ages and Renaissance snowmen were built as effigies to perform a range of social and political functions. The cold winter of 1510–11, for example, led the citizens of Brussels to build a huge number of snowmen all over the city. Around 110 individual snowmen and 50 separate 'scenes' expressed the *Brusseleers'* contemporary hopes, fears and frustrations in an entertaining sort of way. Among the characters depicted in snow were folklore figures such as the wildman, unicorn, mermaids and the sea knight, as well as scenes showing current events. These covered a huge variety of themes – religious, political and local to those that contained explicit sexual and even scatological imagery.

A number of contemporary accounts of the snow festival survive in chronicles of the period, but a lengthy ballad penned by the Brussels poet Jan Smeken has ensured that we have a remarkably detailed knowledge of these snowmen and snow scenes. One of the more sexualized sculptures could be found in Rozendal, the red light district of the city, which depicted a prostitute completely naked, with breasts and genitalia sculpted to attract attention, and a 'dog... ensconced between her legs'. Of the more scatological, the poem describes a snow cow that delivered 'turds, farts and stinking'; a defecating centaur; a '*manneken pis*' fountain depicting a small boy urinating into the mouth of a drinker; and finally a drunk drowning in his own excrement.

Alongside these popular, uncouth bacchanalian images were more traditional biblical and classical scenes. It is clear that the whole city joined in the festival, even the patrician elites. A snowman in the shape of Hercules was erected outside the residence of Philip of Burgundy (1464–1524), the bastard son of Philip the Good and commander-in-chief of the Netherlands. According to Smeken, Philip personally assisted in building this mythological figure with whom he identified, and was probably assisted by his court painter, the Netherlandish artist Jan Gossaert, who had already completed several nude paintings of Hercules for his master.

The 1511 Brussels festival of snow illustrates the intriguing

Philip of Burgundy (1464-1524) An illegitimate son of Duke Philip the Good, he held positions of power as Admiral of the Netherlands and Bishop of Utrecht. Professionally he was ineffective and unproductive, but culturally was a great patron of the arts. In particular he was a protector and supporter of the prolific Dutch scholar Erasmus (1466-1536), and patron of the Dutch artist Jan Gossaert (1478-1532).

complexity of meanings associated with snowmen, a far cry from the 'jolly happy soul' that we know from the *Frosty the Snowman* song of 1950.

SNOWBALL FIGHTS

A similar duality can be found in snowballing, which is so readily associated with childhood play, but which can also take on a more sinister guise. The tradition of throwing snowballs must be as old as human contact with snow, although documentary records of snowballing are much more recent. Among the first visual images of a snowball fight is a fresco dating from around 1405–10 depicting a January scene at Castello del Buonconsiglio, Trento, Italy, of two small huddles of people joyfully hurling snowballs at each other outside the castle gates [*see fig. 35*]. Another splendid example survives in a manuscript copy of the medieval handbook of health *Tacuinum Sanitatis* (c.1390–1400), which shows a man and women throwing snowballs at each other, the man appearing to take most of the punishment.

There are even many descriptions of soldiers playing at war by having snowball fights (or snowball 'matches', as only British soldiers during the First World War could describe them). One of the best survives in the memoir of a Confederate officer, D. Augustus Dickert, recorded during the American Civil War. Dickert describes in great detail a large-scale snowball fight that took place between Confederate troops during the winter of 1862–3. 'The troops,' he wrote, 'delight in "snow balling", and revelled in the sport for days at a time. Many hard battles were fought, won, and lost; sometimes company against company, then regiment against regiment, and sometimes brigades would be pitted against rival brigades.' He goes on to describe a particularly competitive fight between the South Carolina regiment and the Georgians, which details the rather mean treatment of combatants unfortunate enough to be taken 'prisoner'. 'When some', he wrote,

> more bold than the rest, ventured too near, he was caught and dragged through the lines, while his comrades made frantic efforts to rescue him. The poor prisoner, now safely behind the lines, his fate problematical, as down in the snow he was pulled, now on his face, next on his back, then swung round and round by his heels – all the while snow being pushed down his back or in his bosom, his eyes, ears, and hair thoroughly filled with the 'beautiful snow'.

The tongue-in-cheek 'beauty' of the snow remarked upon here reinforces the idea of the purity and whiteness of snow, which blankets the landscape, preserves the past in its freezer-like vastness, but which holds a darker, more dangerous side beneath the beguiling crystalline surface – and there is much historical evidence for a more malign side to this winter activity.

The Boston Massacre of 1770, for example, was started by a rogue snowball. After the British passed the Quartering Act of 1767, which forced Americans to house British soldiers in their homes, tensions became fraught. Things came to a head one winter's night in the centre of Boston when a crowd of Americans taunted a British soldier, which led to the hurling of snowballs. The soldier was joined by his comrades, but things got nasty when one of the soldiers was hit by an ice-packed snowball. The response of the targeted – and now humiliated – soldier was to fire into the crowd, an act followed by a volley of shots from his fellow redcoats. Once the smoke had cleared it revealed that ten people had been shot, five of them fatally. This spiteful little confrontation which snowballed into a massacre became one of a handful of notorious events which were instrumental to the outbreak of the American War of Independence.

DYLAN THOMAS

The brilliant Welsh poet yet cantankerous inebriate Dylan Thomas (1914–53) reminds us that soldiers were not the only living creatures to be bullied by snowballs. *A Child's Christmas in Wales* (1955) is a must-read for everyone at Christmas and forms part of James's numerous yuletide literary rituals. A semi-fictional auto-biographical account of a young boy's experience of Christmas in Wales during the first half of the twentieth century, a time of year when, according to Thomas, it 'was always snowing', one of the most memorable passages describes two young boys waiting in the snow, armed with snowballs. The snow, we are told

> is white as Lapland, though there were no reindeers. But there were cats. Patient, cold and callous, our hands wrapped in socks, we waited to snowball the cats. Sleek and long as jaguars and horrible-whiskered, spitting and snarling, they would slink and sidle over the white back-garden walls, and the lynx-eyed hunters, Jim and I, fur-capped and moccasined trappers from Hudson Bay, off Mumbles Road, would hurl our deadly snowballs at the green of their eyes. The wise cats never appeared.

The wanton mischievousness of these boys, sketched in a moment of Welsh poetic genius as 'Eskimo-footed arctic marksmen', reveals a centuries-old history of mistreatment of animals – which brings us to the very important question of the history of cats...

·26·
CATS

—

The history of cats is all about...
cruelty, superstition, empire, the Devil
and the French Revolution.

CRUELTY

One crucial chapter in the history of cats is all about cruelty. For a large part of the last millennium cats were far from the pampered pets of the present day. For centuries cats were mishandled and mistreated. Their fur was pulled to make them scream and yowl, they were burned and tortured, and occasionally even ritually shaved. In sixteenth-century France, cat abuse was so endemic that it entered the language: to '*faire le chat*' (literally 'play the cat') was used to describe a vast range of violence perpetrated on cats. It is, in fact, quite extraordinary how cruel to cats we have been throughout large periods of our history. To understand this dark side of humanity's relationship to cats, however, the historian must first consider the lighter, purry, side.

In earlier periods, cats occupied a more privileged place. Archaeological evidence suggests that the domestication of cats may date from as early as 12000 BCE, since cats were being buried in graves in the Near East. Clearly these were distinct from the kinds of larger, feral cats that roamed the wild and would have made rather poor house guests. Excavations in Cyprus – an island, meaning cats would have had to be introduced – pinpoints the taming of cats to around 9500 BCE. Interestingly, cats were much later arrivals on the domestic scene than their canine cousins. Dogs were domesticated much earlier by premodern peoples because of their usefulness in hunting. As societies became more settled and less itinerant, agriculture developed along with the storage of surplus crops. It was in these conditions that the cat assumed an unrivalled usefulness, as a mouser, to protect valuable grain from rodent scavengers.

SACRED CATS

Domestication is of course different from our modern-day cat obsession in which cats can sometimes seem to occupy roles as surrogate children and spouses. To describe someone as a 'cat lady' (interestingly there is no male equivalent) is to suggest an unhealthy relationship with felines, and conjures up images of someone who is rather kooky and prone to self-neglect. This intense attachment to cats has its historical precedents, with cats attaining a rather hallowed status in former times. In ancient Egypt they were sacred [see fig. 36]; the Egyptian goddess Bastet was depicted with the head of a cat, and anyone prosecuted for killing a cat was sentenced to death. Vast cat cemeteries survive from this period, including Beni Hasan, which was discovered in 1888 and contained some 300,000 mummified cats. These offerings to Bastet demonstrate the 'cult of the cat' in the ancient Egyptian world, and the remarkable status they occupied within it.

The historical heyday for cats continued into the Roman world, where they were also revered. In Roman thought cats were a symbol of liberty, and early Roman art depicts domesticated cats, including from Aquitaine a first- or second century engraving of a young girl holding a cat. The limestone around the niche of the dome is broken and so the name of the girl is lost; the only surviving name is LAETVUS, just above 'PAT'. A sensible guess is that this is the first name of her father – PAT being short for PATER, the Latin for father. It is a wonderful engraving. It was customary for the deceased to be depicted with things that were familiar to them in life, and here she is with

This funerary stele, now preserved in the excellent Musée d'Aquitaine in Bordeaux, was erected at some point in the second century CE

the animals she loved: a cat and a cockerel, which is playfully biting the cat's tail. She holds the cat like a child would today – with a firm grip under the forelegs and an utterly joyful and innocent lack of concern for the animal's comfort. This is not just an engraving of a cat – it is perhaps the earliest convincing depiction of a child with a *pet* cat.

PETS

A lucky discovery and some clever archaeology has also recently offered us a window into the relationship between humans and cats in this era. In 1997, in a well in the grounds of a Roman villa in Dalton-on-Tees in North Yorkshire, a large collection of animal bones were found, including those of a cat. Subsequent investigation identified horrific injuries to the left-hand side of the animal, perhaps the result of being kicked by a horse or maybe run over by a cart or chariot. The entire top of the thigh-bone from the hind limb was missing. What was particularly interesting, however, is that there were also signs that the limbs had healed and were subsequently used again. A possible and convincing conclusion is that the wounded animal was cared for and fed as it healed, even though its life as a working cat – a mouser – was clearly over. These bones, therefore, are quite possibly the earliest evidence of a pet cat in Britain.

This is just one example of the archaeology of pets which is, itself, an interesting branch of archaeology; new discoveries are changing the way that we think about the relationship between humans and animals. For example, we tend to interpret the remains of cats as companion animals because that is the role that they fulfil today but we are starting to think that other animals fulfilled a similar role in the past, in particular jackdaws, whose remains are frequently discovered in medieval towns in northern Europe. The jackdaw is a common scavenger, but it is

Ship's cat on HMS *Encounter* during the Second World War

also intelligent, at home in the city and the countryside, makes a good companion, bonds with humans and readily adapts to domestic life: it is more than possible that such birds were once our daily companions as much as cats are today.

The Romans are credited with introducing the domestic cat from Egypt to Europe, and this link between empire and cats is itself significant. Cats are, of course, connected to the histories of empire and colonization; their dissemination around the world was linked to trade, discovery and conquest. Ships' cats are integral here, as omens of good luck and, with the added advantage of their being able to catch rodents, their story is linked to the spread of cats through maritime passages. It is no surprise that when the *Mayflower* set sail on its journey in 1620 cats numbered among her passengers, or on board Ernest Shackleton's ship *Endurance* on his doomed trans-Antarctic expedition of 1914–17.* They remained a significant presence on ships of the Royal Navy until 1975 when all pets were banned from naval vessels. The two world wars are particularly full of stories of ships' cats, including 'Unsinkable Sam', the ship's cat of the

* The cat, 'Mrs Chippy', was shot along with all of the expedition's sled dogs once the ship had become trapped in the ice.

German battleship *Bismarck* which survived her sinking in May 1941 when over 2,100 of her crew of 2,200 did not; and 'Jimmy', the ship's cat of HMS *King George V*, the dreadnought battleship and flagship of the 2nd Battle Squadron which played such a central role at the Battle of Jutland of May 1916. Jimmy survived this battle, the greatest clash of battleships in history, but minus one of his ears.

SCARE CATS

This link between cats and luck, or cats and superstition, is by no means restricted to the maritime world. Builders, conservators and archaeologists are occasionally faced with unexpected feline discoveries that attest to this. This is the phenomenon of walled-in cats, mummified cats and scare cats – ancient cats which are discovered inside hollow walls, under floorboards, in attics. It is believed that some of the cats located underneath buildings are often placed there as a type of foundation deposit or votive offering – a superstitious gesture to bring good luck. They are not the only animals so used: this is part of a broader history of animal deposits and votive offerings with particular reference to buildings. During excavations at Roman Pompeii, for example, a deposit of cremated cockerel bones was discovered beneath the foundations of a house, perhaps to bring good luck (it clearly didn't work).

When cat remains are discovered inside the walls of buildings, however, they are often deliberately posed, and sometimes with a bird or rat in their mouth or cowering beneath their raised paws. These are believed to have functioned in a similar way to scarecrows. Fabulous descriptions of such discoveries survive in the historical record.

- In the rood of a fourteenth- or fifteenth-century house, to the south of the parish church in Little St. Mary Street, Bridgwater. This cat was of ebony colour, its mouth open in a 'snarling' way, and its forepaws raised defensively as if striving to fight off an enemy.
- Cat with two rats, found beneath sixteenth-century woodwork in a house in Borough High Street, Southwark, London. It holds in its jaws a rat, which appears to be struggling to escape, with its legs extended, its mouth wide open and its tail erect. Another rat, beneath the cat's forefeet, writhes upwards as if to bite its captor.
- Cat and rat, found when the organ of Christ Church Cathedral, Dublin, was moved from the roodscreen to the transept during the restoration of 1872–8. 'Desiccated bodies were found behind the organ case in a dry and leathery but undecayed condition, and were posed in a glass case, so as to form a sort of tableau.'

Here is not just a history of cats being used as scare cats, but a history of people *discovering* scare cats – it is a history of people wondering at, and occasionally being frightened by, the past.

HERETICS

If, at times, people have been frightened by cats, there is plenty of historical evidence that cats have been frightened of humans; indeed, it's a wonder that they still put up with us at all. Venerated throughout much of the known ancient world and beloved in our own age, the intervening centuries provide an unexpected hiatus, which saw cats lose their scared and protected status. The medieval period witnessed the demonization of cats, which become known as the familiars of witches and as manifestations of the Devil. Superstitions connected to black cats in particular were rife, and ill omens followed when a black cat crossed one's path. Throughout the mid to late medieval period cats (as embodiments of the Devil) were associated with heresy and diabolical acts, and a threat to good Christians, as this twelfth-century description of the behaviour of a group of heretics demonstrates:

> About the first watch of the night... each family sits waiting for the silence in each of their synagogues; and there descends by a rope which hangs in the midst a black cat of wondrous size. On the sight of it they put out the lights and... hum with their closed teeth, and draw near to the place where they saw their master [i.e. the black cat, which was often supposed to represent the Devil], feeling after him and when they have found him they kiss him. The hotter the feelings the lower their aim: some go for his feet, but most for his tail and genitalia. Then as though this disgusting contact has unleashed their appetites, each lays hold of a nearby man or woman and enjoys him or her as much as possible.

The importance of the cat figure here, and its prominent role in this orgiastic descent into anarchic carnality, highlights the changing status of cats, from sacred to demonic.

The malign nature of cats stemmed from their connection with witchcraft: woodcuts and paintings from the late medieval period onwards depicted witches with their cats, and witches themselves were thought able to transform into cats. The classic punishment for such sorcery was meted out to innocent felines, with cats having their tails cut, their ears clipped, their legs smashed or their fur torn or burned on the assumption that such acts of violence would in fact break their malevolent power. Within the home, cats were the focus of social anxiety: they smothered babies while they slept and were associated with sex. In sixteenth-century France popular tradition held that girls eating cat stew might give birth to kittens. Another tale speaks of one girl who sold her soul to the Devil for pretty clothes, and on her death a black cat jumped out of her coffin.

SATIRE

This cruelty to cats was not restricted to the medieval period. Throughout early modern French society cats played a key role in popular culture. During the topsy-turvy *carnival*, in which social norms were subverted in a controlled manner to release pent-up tensions, cats were used and abused for satiric effect. Their fur was pulled to make them yowl at cuckolds; they were burned as part of religious rituals, and in Reformation London a cat was shaved to look like a priest. Cats were always to hand and useful for social and cultural traditions and rituals, in a way that other animals were not. 'You cannot make charivari [a loud, public ritual of mocking] with a cow,' writes the modern-day historian Robert Darnton. 'You do it with cats. You decide to *faire le chat*.'

Cruelty to cats and animals more generally in eighteenth-century London was famously depicted by William Hogarth (1697–1764) in his quartet of engravings, *The Four Stages of Cruelty* (1751). The first two of the series depict the protagonist Tom Nero and others unleashing barbaric acts of cruelty on various animals, among them cats. In the first scene a group of youths are depicted inflicting harm: blinding a bird, tying a bone to a dog's tail, with another having an arrow pushed up its

William Hogarth, *The Four Stages of Cruelty*, plate 1: 'The First Stage of Cruelty' (1751)

anus, and stringing kittens up from a lamppost. In his *Autobiographical Notes*, written in the 1760s, Hogarth claims that these images were created 'in the hopes of preventing in some degree that cruel treatment of poor animals'. Such cruelty provided the impetus for the founding in Britain during the early nineteenth century of the Society for the Prevention of Cruelty to Animals (which later achieved royal status as the RSPCA in 1840 at the grace of Queen Victoria), and a spate of new laws, including the Cruelty to Animals Act of 1835 which prohibited bear-baiting and cock-fighting and protected cattle, bulls, dogs, bears, goats and sheep. Note, however, that it did *not* protect cats. In fact it was not until 1876 that the Act to amend the law relating to Cruelty to Animals first mentioned cats as domestic animals, and specified that experiments 'calculated to give pain shall not be performed without anaesthetics on a dog or cat.'

THE FRENCH REVOLUTION

A parallel history of cats, which is also connected to cruelty, is in fact all about the French Revolution. In Robert Darnton's brilliant book *The Great Cat Massacre* (1984) he takes us to Paris during the 1730s, in particular to a print shop in the Rue Saint-Séverin and the world of two badly treated and downtrodden apprentices, Jerome and Leveille. The pair lived in squalid, freezing conditions; they received daily abuse from their master and the journeymen in the workshop; and they were fed on scraps from their master's table or cat food too unappetizing for normal consumption. Their condition was made all the worse by the fact that they were woken almost nightly in their garret by the noise of alley cats caterwauling in the street below. All of this was in direct contrast to the prosperity and relative comfort of their bourgeois master and mistress, and the latter's pampered feline pet *La Grise* (the grey).

Unhappy with their lot, the apprentices decided to take matters into their own hands and sought to turn the tables on their social superiors by embarking on a series of acts that ended in the ritual massacre of dozens of Parisian moggies. On one particular night one of the boys crept onto the roof and, stationing himself outside his master and mistress's bedroom window, began to howl and meow so loudly and in such a tortured manner that neither of the occupants could sleep. He returned on several consecutive nights to repeat the ordeal, by the end of which his master, thinking that the cats were bewitched, ordered his apprentices to round them up and get rid of them. His wife of course ordered them to spare *La Grise*, her favourite.

Thus empowered by their master, the apprentices were joined by the journeymen and, armed with broom handles and other tools, they sought to round up as many cats in the neighbourhood as they could lay their hands on, beginning with *La Grise*, whose spine they smashed with an iron bar. Afterwards they caught and bludgeoned any cat within sight, climbing over rooftops and depositing the broken and injured bodies in sacks, which were dumped in the workshop yard. What followed was a mock trial, in which cats were accused of crimes including witchcraft, pronounced guilty and summarily executed on a makeshift gallows. Interrupted in their exploits by the mistress and master, the workers were chastised and threatened for their behaviour, but as they left the workers fell about laughing and re-enacting the entire episode in burlesque fashion, which they then repeated on multiple occasions.

While there is nothing funny about the bloody butchery of dozens of alley cats, that in many ways is not really what this story is about. For the historian, the trick here is really getting the joke: it's about understanding the past on its own terms. In this unique set of historical circumstances what is it that makes this saga funny? One way of seeing this episode in French cultural life is as an early form of workers' protest, some fifty years before the revolution of 1789. What it shows is the fertile ground for the kinds of political ideas that were to ignite French society, the surprising part played by cats in exposing the social tensions at the heart of daily life, and their ritualized role in subverting the traditional order of the *Ancien Régime*.

At the heart of this story is a tension between workers prepared to maim and kill cats, and the bourgeoisie for whom cats were cherished pets: this is how the history of cats is, in one sense, all about the French Revolution, a period in the history of

Ancien Régime The undemocratic political and social system that governed France from the late Middle Ages until the French Revolution in 1789.

France that can also be explained through the lens of gestures and emotions. The experience of the guillotine and the Reign of Terror, which saw mass public executions, is seared on the historical memory of the nation, and at the heart of this history lies a story about screams, hysteria, facial composure and defiance – which raise the very important question of the history of the smile...

·27·

THE SMILE

—

The history of the smile is all about...
the French Revolution, insanity, Caribbean
colonies, gang warfare and slavery.

How many different smiles do you have? A reasonable guess for most of us would be somewhere around ten: a spontaneously happy smile, a sad smile, a reluctant smile, a grin, the smile that comes with laughter, a nasty smile or smirk, a fake smile, a suppressed smile. No doubt from your experience of friends, family and colleagues you could add more to this list. Smiling, in short, is an extremely complex form of emotional expression and for the historian it is important to realize that the purpose and effect of each smile is deeply influenced by the life that you live now and the life you have lived in your past: by no means is the smile timeless. Because of this, the smile is a fascinating historical topic.

—— MADNESS ——

The smile in eighteenth-century France is particularly interesting; it is connected to the history of dentistry, Enlightenment sensibilities and the terror of the guillotine during the French

Revolution. Taken together, these influences led to what has been described by historians as a 'smile revolution'.

In the *Ancien Régime*, the act of smiling was widely associated with rustics, harlots, the insane and the demonic. The most wonderful examples are depicted in portraiture of the period, including Dirck van Baburen's depiction of a prostitute in *The Procuress* (1622) or Franz Hals's *Malle Babbe* (1633–35) [*see fig. 37*], which depicts a 'crazy' – '*malle*' – woman, with a pewter beer tankard with an open lid, and a raucous open-mouthed smile on her face. Historians understand her to be an alcoholic or mentally ill. She sits also with an owl on her left shoulder which some have suggested represents a familiar – that the woman being represented was considered a witch.

Whatever the explanation, the lurid smile suggested someone who was troubled or on the margins of society. More lewd is the terrifically energetic Dutch painting *The Laughing Violinist* (1624) by Gerrit van Honthorst [*see fig. 38*], which depicts a musician with twinkling eyes and a full-faced and almost audible wide, beaming smile, which is accompanied by a sexualized gesture of an arm and clenched fist, unmistakably phallic. The canvas communicates its message even more sharply when one recognizes that it was meant to hang to the right of a companion portrait, *Young Girl Counting Money*, showing a young, smiling courtesan with a low-cut top, a magnificent feathered headdress, baroque earrings, who is delicately, suggestively, holding the edge of a coin between her thumb and forefinger and, crucially, looking over her left shoulder – and thus directly at the violinist.

POLITENESS

Toothy grins were hardly appropriate within polite society, as the contemporary commentator Jean-Baptiste de La Salle reminds us in his fabulous – and eye-opening – treatise *Rules of*

Decorum and Christian Civility (1703). The manual was intended for the 'use of the Christian schools', and was aimed as a school-room guide for good manners and politeness. It was extremely well known during the eighteenth century. In it he writes:

> There are some people who raise their upper lip so high or let the lower lip sag so much that their teeth are almost entirely visible. This is entirely contrary to decorum, which forbids you to allow your teeth to be uncovered, for nature gave us lips to conceal them.

Jean-Baptiste de La Salle (1651-1719) The patron saint of teachers, de La Salle was a priest and educational reformer. He dedicated his life to the education of poor children. He was made a saint by Pope Leo XIII in 1900.

In this he follows an earlier conduct writer Antoine de Courtin (1622–85) who reflected that 'bad teeth spoil the mouth and smell foul for those to whom we are talking'. De La Salle, though, considered that: 'It is uncouth to keep your lips too tightly shut, to bite them, or to keep them half open. It is intolerable to pout or to make a face. What you must try to achieve is to keep your lips together, lightly and without constraint.' Behind these French codes of politeness, then, lay some quite practical requirements. Indeed, the reason why the courtiers at the palace of Versailles kept their lips tightly fastened, and were painted with serious expressions, was not simply a matter of elite refinement, but rather because of their appalling dental hygiene.

SUGAR AND EMPIRE

Part of the reason for this was the consumption of sugar, which decayed or completely destroyed their teeth. Blackened stumps and slackened gums were never a good look, especially in the fabulously fashionable court of the Sun King. The history of the smile in the court of Louis and elsewhere in Europe, therefore, is linked with the expansion of global empire, and in particular with the acquisition of Caribbean colonies by European powers to provide land to grow the sugar; the creation of a slave economy to provide manpower to sow, harvest and manufacture it; a merchant marine to provide the necessary shipping to transport the sugar, people and all of the living essentials required to establish and run a successful foreign colony; and a navy to protect both the colony and the merchant marine that served as its umbilical cord back to Europe. In the lack of smiles in Louis's court, therefore, we can see the presence of the French maritime empire and everything that it implied, which began with the colonization of parts of the South American coast in 1624, land that became French Guiana. The Caribbean islands of St Kitts followed in 1625, and then Guadeloupe and Martinique in 1635, which became major locations of sugar manufacture.

The Sun King The name given to the French King, Louis XIV (1638-1715), who reigned from the age of four for seventy-two years, the longest reign in European history. Some historians believe he gave the name to himself, others that he was called it by his subjects. Louis regularly used the sun as his personal emblem.

DENTISTRY

Those troubled by painful gnashers during the first half of the eighteenth century in Paris had no other recourse than to visit a local tooth-puller. One such brutish individual who plied his trade on the Pont Neuf was Le Grand Thomas, a man famed for his tooth-extracting abilities, so much so that his legend entered popular song and entertainment. His portrait depicted him plying his trade, and carried the caption:

> Our *Grand Thomas*, beplumed in glory,
> The Pearl of Charlatans (or so's the story).
> Your Tooth aches? You need never doubt
> *Le Grand Thomas* will yank it out.

Accompanied by musicians and a cart topped with the sign of a smile – a large tooth – Le Grand Thomas represents a branch of dentistry that was far more gruesome than professional dental surgery and, indeed, a public spectacle. What could be more entertaining, if you embrace its *Schadenfreude*, of watching someone else having a tooth hoicked out?

So popular a figure was he that a character was based on him in the 1743 French play *Le Vaudeville*, in which he delivered the following wince-making lines:

> Beware the lure of windy exaggeration
> Which doctors use – for our assassination.
> Tho' I, Thomas, am tongue-tied in truth
> At least I can help with the ache of a tooth.
> I pull it right from the root.
> Crack! Right from the root.

These brute-force techniques of extraction did nothing for the set of a smile, but in a curious way the sufferer's plight could raise a smile in an audience.

By the mid-eighteenth century, however, changes in the protocols of politeness and artistic taste combined to make the gentle softness of a smile acceptable. The smile revolution is connected to new ideas of Enlightenment sensibility that put emotion – with the smile at centre stage – at the heart of what it was to be human. Novels such as the English author Samuel Richardson's *Pamela: Or, Virtue Rewarded* (1740) and *Clarissa: Or, the History of a Young Lady* (1748) had romantic characters who smiled 'sweetly', and William Hogarth stated in his book *Analysis of Beauty* (1753) that the 'lines that form a pleasing smile about the corners of the mouth have gentle windings, but lose their beauty in the full laugh', adding that he loathed 'excessive laughter' which 'gives a sensible face a silly or disagreeable look'.

Part of the reason for this new smile was new dentistry techniques. With the rise of specialist *chirurgien-dentistes* during the eighteenth century, dental work moved from the pavement to private consulting rooms. It was during this period that we see the emergence of formal diplomas for dental surgeons, and the publication of the first medical dental encyclopedia in 1728, the surgeon Pierre Fauchard's *The Dentist, or Treatise on Teeth*. As a result of these developments pearly white teeth became a realistic aesthetic to aim for, aided by the marketing of a wide range of paraphernalia connected with teeth: the toothbrush, toothpicks, mouthwash and, of course, lipstick – which now even *emphasized* the smile.

THE REIGN OF TERROR

The history of the smile took a menacing turn when the smile revolution now merged with a real revolution – the French

Revolution. During the Reign of Terror, that bloody period just after the establishment of the First Republic in September 1792 and the fall of the tyrant Maximilien Robespierre (1758–94) in July 1794 when the guillotines rose and fell in a seemingly endless cycle, the theatre of revolution was public execution. Some victims screamed. The king's mistress Madame du Barry, for example, screamed so loudly at her own public execution that she could be heard on the other side of the River Seine. According to the executioner Henri Sanson she was hysterical: her teeth chattered with fright and she 'cried as I have never see anyone cry'. Others, however, embraced the smile as a powerful symbol of resistance and political defiance by affecting controlled and brave smiles as they mounted the scaffold. These became so well known that they were given a name: 'scaffold smiles'. One of the most notable examples of fortitude before the guillotine was that of the French statesman and minister Guillaume-Chrétien de Lamoignon de Malesherbes who also defended the French king during his trial. Executor Sanson remarked of Malesherbes that he died 'with the smiling steadfastness of a sage and the calm that comes from a conscience at ease with itself'. The controlled smile of bravery was the ultimate form of silent defiance of the revolutionary regime but the revolutionaries made sure they had the final word: for many of those unfortunates, their smiles were quite literally wiped off their faces, as severed heads were put on public display with straw stuffed in their mouths.

Madame du Barry (1743-93) A courtesan and official mistress of Louis XV of France, du Barry is one of the most famous victims of the Reign of Terror during the French Revolution. She was guillotined in 1793 for helping refugees flee from France.

ELECTROCUTION

The nineteenth century saw further major changes in the history of the smile and in particular in our understanding of the physical mechanics of the smile. This science behind the smile led to the creation of some of the most extraordinary photographs ever taken. The man responsible for these pictures was the French scientist Guillaume Duchenne (1806–75). Duchenne committed a lifetime of work to understanding the physiology of facial expressions. The technique he pioneered involved stimulating the facial muscles with electricity. Most striking of his numerous works was the 1862 book *The Mechanism of Human Facial Expression* in which he argued that facial expressions could not only be 'read' but were a window into 'the soul of man', and he believed that facial expressions were – in a wonderful turn of phrase – 'gymnastics of the soul'. His work on the smile was particularly important and created a debate about the face as a means of coded expression, which we are still struggling to understand.

Duchenne demonstrated that there was a difference between a false smile and a genuine smile – the emotion of 'frank joy', in his words – and that the difference lay in the engagement of muscles around the eyes (the orbicularis oculi muscle) along with the muscle which raises the corner of the mouth (the zygomatic major muscle). He believed that the zygomatic muscle 'obeyed the will' but that the orbicularis oculi, which he described as 'the muscle of kindness, of love, and of agreeable impressions', was only 'put in play by the sweet emotions of the soul'. A marvellously gifted scientist and observer, Duchenne might also have been a poet. His work was quickly picked up by none other than Charles Darwin (1809–82) who took it seriously, conducted his own experiments by showing Duchenne's photographs to others and asking how they interpreted the expressions, and added his own amendments to Duchenne's

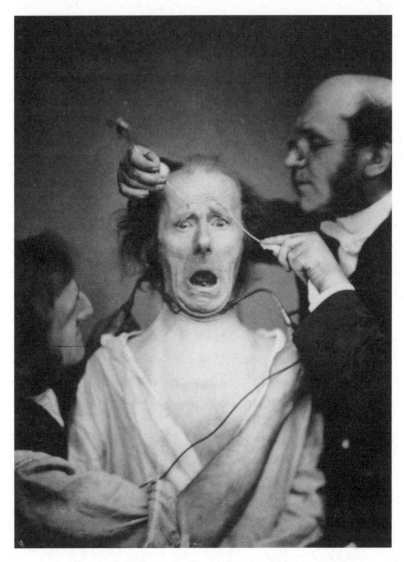

Facial experiments by Guillaume Duchenne (1806–75), using electrostimulation

theory. The study of the mechanism of human facial expression, and in particular of smiling, continues to this day and involves such techniques as precise facial measurement while being told jokes or watching comic films – now there's fun research. It also raises the interesting question of whether or not people were willing to demonstrate by smiling that they *are*, actually, having fun: the hiding of natural smiles, you see, also has a history.

ABRAHAM LINCOLN

The distinction between natural and easy smiles and formal composed facial expressions is most eloquently revealed by the various surviving photographic portraits of the American president Abraham Lincoln (1809–65), the earliest of which dates from 1846 when he was thirty-seven, and the last from just a few weeks before his assassination, in 1865. Lincoln is a unique photographic subject for numerous reasons, but two are particularly important for the history of the smile. The first is that Lincoln was the first American president born in the photographic era and became the most photographed American of his day; and the second is that several photographs of him survive with an unmistakable smile in his twinkly eyes and behind his closed lips. This is extremely unusual for photographic portraiture in the mid-nineteenth century. The long exposure times required by the primitive camera technology made smiling difficult. Perhaps more significant, however, was the stigma associated

Left: Photograph of Abraham Lincoln smiling by Alexander Gardner, 5 February 1865.
He was shot two months later; *Right:* Abraham Lincoln, 'Gettysburg Portrait', 1864

with smiling at the time. In the words of the American writer Mark Twain (1835–1910), a contemporary of Lincoln's, in a letter to the *Sacramento Daily Union*, 'A photograph is a most important document, and there is nothing more damning to go down to posterity than a silly, foolish smile caught and fixed forever.'

In the mid-nineteenth century, levity was by no means a virtue for any politician. One contemporary journalist declared that he was simply unable to

> take a real personal liking to the man [Lincoln]… owing to an inborn weakness for which he was even then notorious and so remained during his great public career, he was inordinately fond of jokes, anecdotes, and stories.

But this was even more the case for Lincoln in the 1860s who, as leader of the northern Union states in the American Civil War, was fighting to rid his world of the horrors of slavery. For such a man in such a time, a photographic portrait required the gravest expression possible and that is exactly what Lincoln provided for his most famous portrait of all, known as the 'Gettysburg Portrait'.* The image was taken by the Scottish photographer Alexander Gardner in his Washington studio on 8 November 1863, just a fortnight before Lincoln delivered what became known as his most famous speech, the Gettysburg Address, a passionate appeal for human equality given four months after the crucial Union victory at the Battle of Gettysburg. It was taken to provide the sculptor (and anti-slavery activist) Sarah

* It is interesting that this portrait was not well known at all at the time but only surfaced from the Gardner archive to subsequent widespread acclaim as the finest Lincoln portrait in 1909.

Battle of Gettysburg (1863) A significant victory for Union forces and the bloodiest battle of the US Civil War which saw more than 23,000 men killed or injured on both sides. The Confederates never fully recovered and lost the war.

Fisher Clampitt Ames (1817–1901) with source material for a bust that had been commissioned for the US Senate collection and which now sits in a niche outside the senate deputy majority leader's office. It was a picture taken, therefore, of a man who was consciously concerned about his appearance.

This image however is particularly powerful because of its contrast to the lighter studies of Lincoln which also survive and which show a man revelling in a secret source of humour. Taken together this group of images reveals a man capable of a thousand subtle expressions, and perhaps in that ability lay his popular appeal. His secretary, John George Nicolay (1832–1901), certainly knew it as a feature of the man. He wrote of the 'despair' of every artist who undertook Lincoln's portrait shortly after his nomination to the presidency. 'They put into their pictures,' he wrote,

> the large, rugged features, and strong, prominent lines;
> they made measurements to obtain exact proportions; they
> 'petrified' some single look, but the picture remained hard and
> cold. Even before these paintings were finished it was plain to
> see that they were unsatisfactory... The picture was to the man
> as the grain of sand to the mountain, as the dead to the living.
> Graphic art was powerless before a face that moved through
> a thousand delicate gradations of line and contour, light and
> shade... from grave to gay, and back again... There are many
> pictures of Lincoln; there is no portrait of him.

Historians still wonder at (and argue over) the enigma of Lincoln's character as revealed in his photographic portraits, but one thing is for certain: he is the first American president (and quite possibly the first American) whose sense of humour, which he was as willing to turn on himself as on others, was revealed by a smile captured on camera.

RAZOR GANGS

While the smile is intimately related to humour and happiness, there is also an alternative history of the smile that is more sinister, linked to the violence of razor gangs in Glasgow during the 1920s and 1930s, with their penchant for inflicting facial wounds. Historically the south side of Glasgow was infamous for its violent gangs, especially the notorious Gorbals slum district on the bank of the River Clyde. By the late nineteenth century, industrialization had caused great overcrowding and appalling living conditions, and the Gorbals in particular experienced high levels of unemployment, peaking in the early 1930s. It is in this context that gangs flourished during the interwar years. A fictionalized account of life at this time can be found in the novel *No Mean City* (1935) co-authored by H. Kingsley Long, a journalist, and Alexander McArthur, an unemployed worker.

Gang rivalries were fuelled by sectarian hatred as the once-Protestant city of Glasgow saw an influx of Irish Catholic workers during the nineteenth and early twentieth century, exacerbating tensions within the city. Gangs such as the Bridgeton Billy Boys, the Norman Conks and the South Side Stickers were divided along sectarian and territorial lines, and the violence was perpetrated on rival gang members as a way of defending territory and inflicting lasting injuries on their enemies, although their victims also included members of the general public.

In the 1930s the policeman Percy Sillitoe was brought in to deal with the menace, having gained experience in handling similar problems in Manchester. Sillitoe had cut his policing teeth in the paramilitary forces in South Africa and Northern Rhodesia, before becoming chief constable of Chesterfield, then of the East Riding of Yorkshire. During this period he transformed the local police force and dealt with the city's numerous violent gangs, which gave him the experience that was desperately needed in gangland Glasgow. His success in Glasgow contributed to him being awarded a CBE in 1936 and a knighthood in 1942, and in 1946 he was appointed to be director general of MI5. His tactics in the Scottish city involved recruiting large Highlanders and rural men who enjoyed a fight, and encouraging them to get stuck in, and while they were ultimately successful, they battled against a regime of ultra violence perpetrated by the gangs.

A horrific injury associated with these gangs was the 'Glasgow smile' (closely related to the 'Chelsea smile'), which involved cutting the victim on both sides of their face from mouth to ear, leaving a wound which scarred in the shape of a smile – which brings us to the important question of the history of the scar...

·28·

THE SCAR

---

*The history of the scar is all about... duelling
and male honour, female beauty, slavery,
the English Civil War and Nelson's ego.*

I t is easy to take our skin for granted but it is a thing of wonder.
It is the body's largest organ; it protects us from damage,
infection and dehydration; and it reproduces itself around
every thirty days. It is, therefore, in a constant state of change,
though that change is usually imperceptible. One moment when
changes become visible, however, is when a wound is healing,
or a scab is forming or falling off. This is the process by which
scars are created. Only the most minor of lesions do not produce
a scar on the human skin. This means that the scar is a gift to the
historian because it allows our bodies to be 'read'. Each scar, you
see, tells a story, and so our skin itself holds memories; in other
words, skin acts as a historical text. This observation in itself is
interesting but we must take it further, for our skin documents
a particular type of history. It does not record everything, but
rather it records moments of drama, moments of pain that are
quite literally inscribed onto flesh through injury or illness, as
a result of medical procedure, or as scarification – scars marked
intentionally onto the skin.

OUR SCARS

We could tell you a story of our lives through our scars. *If you are squeamish, look away now.* Here, on Sam's shins, is where he ran through a glass door in 1983, peeling the skin to the bone; here on the webbing between his thumb and forefinger is where Sam forced the breech of an air rifle shut in 1986, loading his skin, as a pellet in the chamber, ready to fire; here between his eyes is where he landed from the crown of an apple tree in 1989, his head successfully proving the existence of gravity like Newton's apple. On James's left cheek is a small scar from a childhood sword fight (using a bamboo cane); the scar on the middle finger of his right hand is where experimenting with a new penknife went wrong, the blade closing on him as a guillotine of reproach; and of course there are other tiny scars from falling off bikes, chicken-pox and tuberculosis injections. Each individual scar is a story of a time, of a place, of a (usually irresponsible) pattern of decision making. Some scars are more visible than others, which means the story of those scars has been told more often; others are hidden, covered up for various reasons. Life stories told through scars are skewed towards the dramatic end of those events which caused skin to scar: there is historical bias to be avoided in the reading of scars.

None of the memories of our self-inflicted scars are particularly fun to relive. They are, however, nothing compared to the loss of limbs or organs in unimaginable trauma. It is all very well saying that the skin is a historical text, but that is not to assume that the reading of that text is in any way straightforward. On the contrary, it is a process that is unavoidably mixed with intense emotion. It is unsurprising that, over time, this use of a scar for storytelling has become a literary device, introduced for dramatic effect or narrative exposition. In the 1968 film *Hang 'Em High* how did Clint Eastwood get that horrific scar around his neck? He had survived a lynching by a posse who believed he had stolen a herd of cattle. In *The Dark Knight* (2008) how did Batman's Joker get the scars on either side of his mouth? They are cuts – a Glasgow smile (see page 358). In the film the Joker actually gives two versions of how he received his smile. In the first, having watched his father attack his mother with a knife, his father inflicts the wounds on his son to force his son to smile with the line 'why so serious?'; in the second he inflicts them on himself when his wife is scarred in similar fashion by gangsters and he wants to show her that he doesn't mind about her scars. The original Joker in the *Batman* comic book had a rictus smile and bleached skin caused by falling into a vat of acid. And most famously of all, how did Harry Potter get the lightning bolt scar on his forehead? He survived a killing curse from Lord Voldemort.

SLAVERY

The scars of history are sometimes literally carved onto human skin, as reminders of the horrors of the past perpetrated by barbaric and unjust regimes. None are perhaps more horrific than the scars inflicted on black slaves in the United States during the late eighteenth and first half of the nineteenth century. Slaves were regarded as property to be bought and sold, and faced strict laws and punishments. They were not allowed to vote, marry, move about freely or own property, and legally they could be whipped, starved, mutilated and tortured. While the treatment of slaves varied across the US, punishments and physical abuse were widespread. The savage cruelty with which physical violence was administered is described in slave narratives such as Solomon Northup's 1853 memoir *Twelve Years a Slave* or Harriet Jacobs's 1861 memoir *Incidents in the Life of a Slave Girl*. It has recently been explored in film and fiction, as with Quentin

Tarantino's 2012 blaxploitation movie *Django Unchained*, and Colson Whitehead's 2016 novel *The Underground Railroad*.

One of the most famous images of barbaric cruelty administered to an African American slave is a photograph of Gordon (or 'Whipped Peter'), depicting the terrible scarring on his back from repeated whipping. In March 1863 Gordon escaped from his Louisiana plantation, which was owned by John and Bridget Lyons. He was on the run for ten days, during which period he rubbed his body with onions in order to hide his scent from the dogs hunting him down. Eventually he reached safety, arriving at the Union camp in Baton Rouge, where he attained his freedom (although he was later captured by Confederate troops, tortured, and escaped a second time). After his arrival at the camp, he was given a medical examination on 2 April 1863, which revealed the severe scarring on his back. During this examination he is reported to have recounted how he came by his scars:

Ten days from to-day I left the plantation. Overseer Artayou Carrier whipped me. My master was not present. I don't remember the whipping. I was two months in bed sore from the whipping and my senses began to come – I was sort of crazy. I tried to shoot everybody. They said so, I did not know. I did not know that I had attempted to shoot everyone; they told me so. I burned up all my clothes; but I don't remember that. I never was this way (crazy) before. I don't know what make me come that way (crazy). My master come after I was whipped; saw me in bed; he discharged the overseer. They told me I attempted to shoot my wife the first one; I did not shoot any one; I did not harm any one. My master's Capt. John Lyon, cotton planter, on Atchafalya, near Washington, Louisiana. Whipped two months before Christmas.

The testimony, it was declared, represented 'The very words of poor Peter taken as he sat for his picture'. It was apparently at the time of his examination that Gordon was photographed by the itinerant photographer William D. McPherson and his business partner J. Oliver. The photograph captures him in a seated position, stripped to the waist revealing his scarred back

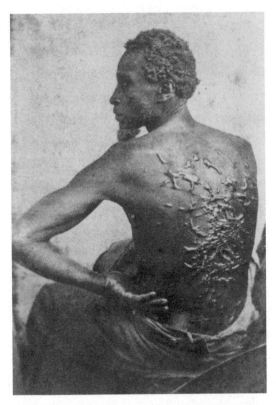

William D. McPherson and his partner Mr Oliver's photograph of the African American slave Gordon (or 'Whipped Peter'), 1863

to the camera, with his head turned nobly in profile. The image was turned into a *carte de visite* (a small photograph the size of a visiting card), and received wide circulation, including being published in *Harper's Weekly* in a special Fourth of July issue. An article in anti-slavery newspaper *The Liberator* from June 1863 described receiving the photograph, and the profound significance it had: 'his stalwart body bared to the waist... Scarred, gouged, gathered in great ridges, knotted, furrowed, the poor tortured flesh stands out a hideous record of the slave-driver's lash.' The power of the photograph was to bring the slave scar to the attention of the public, to use it as a visceral image in the fight for the abolition of slavery.

━━━━━━━ HORATIO NELSON ━━━━━━━

Diaries, letters home and medical notes give historians glimpses into the minds of men and women coming to terms with their scars, but one of the most extraordinary comes from the (left) hand of Horatio Nelson. In a quiet moment during a period of peace before the Battle of Trafalgar, Nelson's mind wandered to his physical condition. He wrote a list of 'Wounds Received by Lord Nelson', characteristically naming himself in the third person, as if observing so many bruises on a peach. The list reads:

> His Eye in Corsica [He was blinded by shrapnel]
> His Belly off Cape St Vincent [He received a 'fist-sized' hernia]
> His Arm at Tenerife [His right arm was amputated]
> His Head in Egypt [A scalp wound that peeled a flap of skin off
>   his skull]

He then added, perhaps ruefully, perhaps proudly, perhaps modestly, 'Tolerable for one war'. This was a man, diminutive in stature, frail and sickly, who collected and cherished his battle scars and wore them like medals. For Nelson they were nothing less than the currency of leadership and loyalty. His scars said, most eloquently, 'I have fought, I have survived, I am selfless, I am your leader, follow *me*.' His were scars that did not dominate him; quite to the contrary, he gave them value, he drew power from them.

DUELLING SCARS

For some men, scars were a mark of honour, a declaration of masculinity. During the nineteenth century duelling scars (or *Schmisse* in German) were popular among the young men of the landed gentry of the Austrian and German states, who were members of university duelling clubs or *Studentcorps*. Count Otto von Bismarck (1815–98), the flamboyant Prussian statesman and first chancellor of Germany, was a keen duellist during his time at the universities of Göttingen and Berlin. While at Berlin, he joined the Corps Hannovera, a kind of student association cum drinking club – the modern-day equivalent of which might be the US college fraternity – and was reputed to have fought twenty-five duels in his first year. A fellow student at Göttingen described his physical appearance, including 'an enormous scar, the relic of a recent duel', which 'extended from the tip of his nose to the edge of his right ear, and has been sewed up with fourteen stitches'. Bismarck was said to have rubbed salt into the wound to exacerbate his scar and make it more pronounced. Martial honour was one of the core values of the Prussian land-owning *Junker* class to which the young Bismarck belonged, and sporting a magnificent scar was a badge of honour. Some young men might bear scores of scars won across a career of duelling while others, who wanted to be part of the culture, even self-inflicted scars with their own razors or paid doctors to cut them with scalpels.

These scars of nineteenth-century Germanic duellists – intentional, proud, markers of manly honour – are just one example of scarification as an important form of expression, a practice that is visible throughout history in numerous ways: as a tribal ritual, as a product of self-harming or as an extreme form of body art. Scars, as with tattoos, piercings and brandings, are a way of communicating meaning to the world in a very public way. Indeed, the great anthropologist Claude Lévi-Strauss (1908–2009) viewed the body as a surface that was awaiting culture to be imprinted upon it. Scarification can be achieved in numerous ways through cutting, branding, removing layers of skin, and even by packing clay or ash into a wound to create a distinctive 'raised' scar. Scarification tends to be more visible on darker skin than tattoos, and is one of the reasons that it was widely performed by tribes across Africa as markers of community, to denote rites of passage and transitions to different life stages. In West Africa facial scarification was used to denote

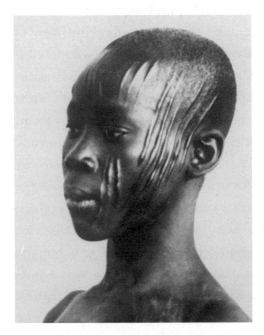

Young African man with facial scarification, c.1930

family and groups, and on women to mark stages in their life process; certain kinds of scarring also made them more likely to be good marriage partners, since scarring demonstrated their capacity to deal with pain, and therefore produce offspring.

SMALLPOX

What distinguishes these forms of African tribal scarification is that they are public and on display, in contrast with many Westerners' attitudes to scars, which is to keep them hidden or covered, and here the history of the scar connects to notions of female beauty. While in African cultures scars were associated with beauty, fertility and womanliness, in most Western cultures facial or bodily scarring was feared as a blight upon female beauty. Early in her reign, in October 1562, Elizabeth I of England contracted smallpox, a disease that was known to badly scar the face and body; so seriously was she affected with the disease that it was feared it would take her life. Fortunately, Elizabeth survived the illness with minimal scarring, but far less fortunate was the lady-in-waiting Lady Mary Sidney who nursed the queen during her illness and contracted smallpox herself, and was badly disfigured as a result. The effect of the scarring is recorded in spectacularly unsympathetic terms by Lady Mary's husband, Sir Henry Sidney, in his *Memoir of Service in Ireland*:

> When I went to Newhaven [Le Havre] I lefte her a full faire Ladye in myne eye at least the fayerest, and when I retorned I found her as fowle a ladie as the smale pox could make her... the skarres of which (to her resolute discomforte) ever syns hath don and doth remayne in her face, so as she lyveth *solitairilie sicut Nicticorax in domicilio suo* [like a night-raven in the house].

BEAUTY PATCHES

Here the smallpox scar was an impediment to beauty. Throughout history in the West visible imperfections – such as moles or birthmarks as well as scars – were covered up, often with a beauty patch, a practice that first originated in the Roman empire. The practice was common in sixteenth-century Europe as a way of concealing scars caused by smallpox and syphilis. Black patches made of silk or velvet cut into various shapes (hearts, stars and diamonds) were popular during the sixteenth and seventeenth century, and were carried around in ornately decorated patch boxes that could be kept on your person. The vogue for such accessories drew scorn from English Puritan members of parliament in 1649 when they brought before the House of Commons a bill banning 'The Vice of Painting and Wearing Black Patches and Immodest Dresses of Women', a bill that was never enacted.

Men could also seek to mask disfiguring scars with various accessories, a direct contrast with those ostentatious Germanic duelling scars. The seventeenth-century nobleman Henry Bennet, first Baron Arlington (1618–85) and later secretary of state under Charles II, was injured fighting on the Royalist side during the Civil War. During a skirmish at Andover in 1644 he

Puritans A group of seventeenth-century English Nonconformist Protestants. Dissatisfied with the English Reformation, they sought to 'purify' the Church of England from what they saw as corrupting and superstitious Catholic practices. Originating in England, their uncompromising beliefs were transported to the Netherlands and across the Atlantic to New England as they sought to escape religious persecution.

received a wound on the bridge of his nose, and took to covering the resulting scar with a black plaster. It was thought that he did so to emphasize his loyalty to the Royalist cause and was openly mocked for it. In the aftermath of the First World War, many soldiers suffered from having had their faces blown off or melted, and we see the development of incredible techniques to rebuild and mask the horrible disfigurements of these men. And it was a challenge unlike any that had been faced before. Sir Harold Gillies, who was at the forefront of this surgery, noted that: 'Unlike the student of today, who is weaned on small scar excisions and graduates to harelips, we were suddenly asked to produce half a face.' One of the techniques was the fabrication of masks, made from plaster casts of the patient's face, a method developed by Francis Derwent Wood, a prolific and talented sculptor. Too old to enlist, Wood adapted his skills and volunteered to help burns victims shorn of confidence by their facial disfigurement. Such was the demand that an entire section of the

Captain Francis Derwent Wood RA puts the finishing touches to a cosmetic plate made for a British soldier with a serious facial wound, which was inflicted during the First World War

Third London General Hospital became the 'Masks for Facial Disfigurement Department', which the British soldiers, with their distinctive war-weary humour, called the 'Tin Noses Shop'.

SCARRED BUILDINGS

It is not only humans that bear scars; our modern world is surrounded by physical remains that are, one way or another, scarred, and in exactly the same way as marks on our skin, those scars in timber, brick, stone or concrete tell a story and have profound historical value, such as the bullet holes that still scar the German Reichstag building, as distant echoes of the battle for Berlin during the Second World War. The value of these kinds of scars is twofold. On the one hand they are a window into a particular event, but also they are a reminder that buildings must be read as a kind of structural palimpsest – a historical document that itself has multiple layers of writing upon it.

One of the most powerful examples of this lies in British churches. What, you may ask, is a church other than a place of worship? It rather depends who you are asking and when you asked the question. If you were asking it in 1643 in Devizes in Wiltshire, or in Farndon in Cheshire, the answer would be 'a military stronghold'. This was the second year of the English Civil War and the country was alive with conflict between the two opposing sides, the Royalists and Parliamentarians. Both sides looked to churches. They were strong, built with sturdy stone; they had stout timber doors and few windows; they had spires, which provided an eagle's view of the surrounding countryside and nests for snipers. They were, in short, ready-made military emplacements.

It was not uncommon for churches to become the centres of battle or the centres of military power in an area. One of the most thought-provoking examples is Malmesbury Abbey in

Wiltshire, one of the most significant seats of European learning in the eleventh and twelfth centuries. But five hundred years after the current abbey was completed, Malmesbury found itself at a strategic crossroads of the English Civil War (1642–51) because it was located halfway between the strongholds of Bristol and Oxford. Malmesbury changed hands no fewer than five times during the war and its identity changed from a seat of learning, scientific endeavour, tolerance and godliness to one of prejudice and violence. Seek out the south-facing wall to the side of the main porch and you will find it scarred with holes from musket fire, for this is the execution wall where prisoners of war were shot.

CASTLE SLIGHTING

A particularly interesting type of scars on buildings were those made deliberately on British castles, a process that was known as 'slighting'. The idea behind it was simple – to visibly damage a building that was once an enemy's stronghold – but the motivation was surprisingly complex. In some cases, it was done to reassert control and authority over a rebellious subject; in others, it was done to prevent the castle being used as a stronghold against you; and in the aftermath of the English Civil War it was carried out as a means of subverting the 'old order' by destroying the literal and figurative structures of their power base.

Thus, in 1173, Henry II slighted Framlingham Castle in Suffolk to punish the Earl of Norfolk who had rebelled against his rule; in 1314 the Scottish king Robert the Bruce destroyed the castles at Edinburgh, Roxburgh and Stirling to prevent them from being used against him; and in the aftermath of the Civil War numerous castles, such as Kenilworth, Corfe and Pontefract, were destroyed by the Parliamentarians as they were closely linked with the Royalists and were expressions of their power and wealth.

The techniques used varied from site to site and according to period. Sometimes the fortifications were simply taken down by hand, with teams of labourers chiselling away at the stone and carting it off to reuse elsewhere; on other occasions siege weapons were used as a dramatic show of strength, with trebuchets and cannon hurling rocks and iron shot to smash the walls and towers. The use of gunpowder as an explosive on its own was rare because of the expense. Sometimes, as in siege warfare itself, walls and towers were undermined: tunnels would be dug and supported with timber joists like in a mine, and then burned. Sometimes the towers and walls came crashing down but sometimes they did not; the result was often a wall or tower, cracked and leaning dramatically. One of the finest examples of this comes from Corfe Castle in Dorset where the south-west gatehouse and western curtain wall, semi-collapsed, leans at an impossible angle [*see fig. 39*].

A powerful symbol of lost power and political turmoil, this castle's leaning walls also raise the important question of the history of the lean...

31. Oxyrhynchus Papyrus 52. Report by Aurelius, Didymus and Silvanus, public physicians, to Flavius Leucadius, a senior municipal official, stating that they had visited the daughter of Aurelius Dioscorus and found her suffering from wounds caused by his house falling down.

32. British advertisement for Rowntree's Clear Gums, 1929

33. Scythian tattoo of fabulous beasts on the skin of a child's arm from Barrow 2 at Pazyryr, Altai, Russia, fifth century BCE.

34. Snowman in the margins of a Book of Hours (c.1380)

35. Fresco depicting a snowball fight in January at Castello Buonconsiglio, Trento, Italy (c.1405–1410)

36. The Gayer-Anderson Cat, an ancient Egyptian statue of a cat dating from 664–332 BCE and now held at the British Museum.

37. Franz Hals, *Malle Babbe* (1633–1635)

38. Gerrit van Honthorst,
The Laughing Violinist (1624)

39. Corfe Castle in Dorset was partially scarred or demolished (slighted)
during the English Civil War, giving the walls a distinct lean.

40. The Shambles, York

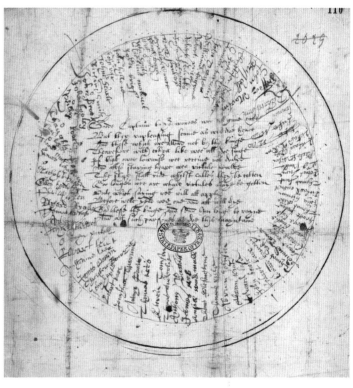

41. Sailors' round robin, 1620s

·29·
THE LEAN

The history of the lean is all about…
urbanization, pensioners,
disability and extortion.

DIAGON ALLEY

The Shambles in York is one of the best-preserved medieval streets in Europe and a real-life version of Harry Potter's Diagon Alley, a hidden and windy little lane full of hustle. In York the timber-framed buildings crowd into each other in the narrow space, casting long shadows even with the sun at its height. They lean up the street, down the street, into the street and even over the street [*see fig. 40*]. Space, light and air are at a premium both inside and outside the buildings. Every building is full of dark, cramped and wonky corners. The cobbled street itself slopes. No lines anywhere are horizontal, no lines are vertical; *everything* leans one way or the other. The buildings have grown organically cheek by jowl over the centuries, rather than being planned on some orderly and uniform system. The Shambles was first mentioned in the Domesday Book in 1086 but many of the current buildings date from the late fourteenth to fifteenth centuries. Formerly known as the Great Flesh Shambles, it once thronged with butchers' shops, with as many as twenty-five packed into these cramped back lanes until 1872, mixed up among residential dwellings.

Similar streets can be found dotted around Britain and Europe today, where the medieval core of cities and towns is still intact. In Stockholm's Gamla Stan (or old town) is to be found Mårten Trotzigs Gränd, a narrow tapering alley that at its narrowest point is a mere 90 centimetres wide, so narrow that if you stand in the middle of the street you can touch the walls on both sides, and the magnificent medieval centre of the German town of Rothenburg ob der Tauber in Bavaria has such alleys almost everywhere you turn.

MEDIEVAL ARCHITECTURE

This unusual form of architectural lean cannot be explained by the loss of building and architectural skills in the medieval world after the disintegration of the Roman empire. The leaning aspect was, in fact, an intentional part of vernacular architecture: one only needs to look at the inspiring edifices of medieval castles or Romanesque and Gothic buildings to realize the immense skills that underpinned medieval construction. Medieval masons are known to have used various tools for ensuring that straight lines could be achieved where required, including the level and the plumb rule, which have a long history.

While subsidence may accentuate particular angles, medieval timber-framed buildings in urban spaces were built using a technique called jettying, whereby each floor was constructed to stick out a bit further than the one below, and it is this which gave buildings the appearance of leaning. Constructing houses where the upper floors overhung the lower was an advantage where space was limited. It was also practical, since it sheltered lower floors from the elements, and in engineering terms it also made sense as the jettied wall counteracted forces in the joists, pushing together for strength. In medieval York and elsewhere this meant that the homes of merchants and craftsmen had characteristically long, narrow plots, with the gable end of the house facing onto the street. Nonetheless, such houses were still capable of displaying the wealth and status of their owners. Number 7, The Shambles (dating post-1450), for example, had grand crown posts for its front gable, to signal its exclusiveness or what might have been described as 'kerb appeal'. Timber-framed buildings were also remarkably flexible, and could go through a series of alterations, both internally as well as externally, with new rooms added, others divided and repurposed. It was, however, exactly this form of organic growth that further contributed to the seemingly haphazard and higgledy-piggledy look of streets like York's Shambles.

DISEASE

In the centre of the Shambles' cobbled street, moreover, is a large gutter where waste would once have flowed – and what waste that would have been. The Shambles was a common name for a meat market, which was, in effect, an open-air, city-centre slaughterhouse. The central gutter was not just for rivers of rainwater but for rivers of blood. Temporary dams of guts and offal mixed with human waste, which despite sewerage systems and public latrines was simply dumped in the streets to make reservoirs of filth. This quaint medieval street so beloved by tourists, therefore, would once have been an open sewer of the worst kind.

Such close, crowded and corrupt conditions were directly responsible for regular outbreaks of disease – the reason that half of England's population died from plague between 1348 and 1350, figures which take no account of those who died from tuberculosis, cholera, dysentery or leprosy, all of which thrived in filth. In some locations the streets and buildings became seen as the culprits. In France during the sixteenth century, jettied buildings were banned in Rouen in 1523 and Angers in 1541. The lean was thus a contributing factor to the spread of disease.

PARIS

These were the conditions that urban planners of the eighteenth and nineteenth centuries sought to eradicate, and nowhere is the programme of 'improvement' more obvious and more interesting to the historian than in Paris, where the city was blighted by disease, overcrowding, and squalor. In 1845 Victor Considerant, the French social reformer, wrote:

> Paris is an immense workshop of putrefaction, where misery, pestilence and sickness work in concert, where sunlight and air rarely penetrate. Paris is a terrible place where plants shrivel and perish, and where, of seven small infants, four die during the course of the year.

In his eyes, this was a festering city. What's more, these narrow Parisian streets lent themselves to revolution since, in such crowded conditions, it was a simple task to raise barricades and block roads.

Between 1853 and 1870, in the aftermath of the 1848 Revolution, Paris became a construction site unlike anything the world had ever seen as the civil administrator Georges-Eugène Haussmann (1809–91) waged war on the city's medieval buildings. The numbers are extraordinary still: the project lasted for seventeen years; he knocked down 12,000 structures; the new buildings, boulevards, railway stations, parks and fountains he

Rue de Rivoli, 1855, the first boulevard built in Paris by Haussmann

built cost Napoleon III some 2.5 billion francs, the equivalent of around €75 billion in today's money; a new aqueduct was built which increased the amount of fresh water brought into the heart of the city from 87,000 to 400,000 cubic metres of water a day. He imposed on Paris a grid system, with streets running north to south and east to west, dividing up the ancient medieval city into new sections, which created twenty *arrondissements*, or administrative districts. He took down an entire shambled city of dark lanes and leaning buildings and replaced them with those broad, straight boulevards and long lines of uniform buildings and parks that we immediately recognize today as Paris. Although he is not without his critics, Haussmann's Paris became a model for urban design throughout European capitals such as Madrid, Stockholm, Rome, Brussels, Barcelona and Vienna, and was even influential in America – in New York, Chicago and Washington, DC. By removing the medieval lean, therefore, Haussmann not only altered the design and feel of many of our great cities and the health of generations of their inhabitants, but shaped the modern world.

Elsewhere our medieval cities have vanished for different reasons: the exquisite Hanseatic port of Lübeck was burned by British incendiary bombs in March 1942, and Exeter in Devon, a Roman city described by many contemporaries as more beautiful than York, was hammered by the Luftwaffe in response. Accidental fire destroyed medieval London in 1666; an earthquake toppled medieval Lisbon in 1755; and building projects everywhere have replaced the iconic lean of medieval timber and lath construction with the straight lines of cast-concrete block and rolled-steel beams. Where once we saw a leaning building as a threat to our health and a symbol of backwardness, we now see it as a rare and charming symbol of the past, something to be preserved.

> **Lisbon Earthquake (1755)** One of the most powerful European earthquakes in history and one of the world's deadliest natural disasters. Historians believe that up to 100,000 died in the quake and the three immense tsunamis that followed.

DISABILITY

The sense of guilt for failing to cherish and respect the past is also a theme that runs strongly through another history of the lean: the *human* lean. In the collections of the National Maritime Museum in London is a wonderful cache of visual imagery which survives as a record of the Greenwich Pensioners.

These were men who had served in the Royal Navy and who, either through age, infirmity or disability, were unable to continue their active service. In 1692 increasing attention came to be paid to these helpless men when the English queen, Mary II, witnessed injured sailors being taken ashore after the great

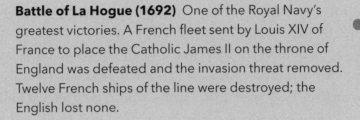

English naval victory over the French at La Hogue, a victory which, after years of Catholic invasion plots, finally secured the throne of her Protestant husband, William III. Mary took it upon herself to provide care for these men, who had given so much to secure the safety and wealth of the growing British empire, and she identified the Royal Palace at Greenwich, originally built for Charles II, as their future home.

After years of building work and fundraising it opened in 1705 and became a permanent residence for naval pensioners until 1869. The palace was converted into a hospital and the residential care was financed in an interesting way. More than half of the initial endowment came from funds paid by merchants caught and convicted of smuggling. Some more came from a public fundraising appeal and more still from a regular but small contribution from the treasury. Then, just before it opened, a payment that allowed the last works to be completed and Mary's seven-year-long vision of care finally to be realized came from the liquidated value of estates and treasure belonging to the recently captured and executed pirate, Captain William Kidd.

Very little imagery of any sort survives for these men before their queen began to take an interest in them but, once established in their new palace home, they became a fixture of London life for more than 150 years and a wealth of visual material was created that preserves their memory. The pensioners were highly distinctive. They wore a uniform – indeed they wore a uniform long before one was actually introduced into the Royal Navy in 1748 – and in the surviving depictions all are shown in their blue coats and tricorn hats and most are shown with walking sticks, some with crutches, many with wooden legs. Their age and infirmity are, more often than not, expressed with a lean to one side, forward or back. The lean that you see in images of the Greenwich Pensioners, therefore, is a particular type of lean of a particular group of people in a particular location at a particular time – people who had been saved by a caring sovereign and whose care was partly funded by smugglers and pirates. It is a lean of disability that was the result of, and also made possible by, the strength of the Royal Navy, and as such it was historically unique. However, these men were not your stereotypical elderly pensioners – far from it. Nicknamed 'Greenwich Geese' by the locals, these were tough navy men, many of whom returned to

A caricature of Greenwich Pensioners, c.1800

sea as cooks, and court records show them getting into fights and displaying other kinds of antisocial behaviour: do not be fooled by their lean.

THE WALKING STICK

As the images from Greenwich make clear, the stick was the material culture of the lean. Walking sticks or canes were commonly used by people with disabilities, as an orthopaedic prop that aided walking, but the walking stick had many other functions as well – practical, ceremonial, fashionable. Sticks or staffs were used by able-bodied pilgrims or travellers covering rough ground; they were used by bishops as part of religious ceremonies; they were used by the able-bodied as a fashion statement. The flamboyant Oscar Wilde was quite attached to a walking stick with an ivory handle, which had an intrinsic and aesthetic value. Throughout history famous figures have been associated with canes, many using them as a walking aid (connected to the lean), such as Franklin D. Roosevelt and Winston Churchill, who was said to be 'walking with destiny'.

Walking sticks as objects connected with disability and the able-bodied have a fascinating history, not least in their carvings, and often symbolic meanings attached to them. The famous biologist and naturalist Charles Darwin was particularly fond of walking, and owned a whalebone walking stick. Unusually the handle of the stick is carved into the shape of a skull, with two green glass eyes, and Darwin named the stick his 'morituri', a kind of memento mori.

Sometimes the sticks used weren't even walking sticks at all or at least served a dual purpose. Once the walking stick replaced the sword as the must-have accessory in the seventeenth and eighteenth centuries, it was also used as a weapon, sometimes with a sharp metal end. One of the most remarkable walking sticks-cum-weapons is on display at the Tower of London. What has become known as 'Henry VIII's walking stick' is a mean-looking wooden shaft, topped with a morning star mace, and concealed within it are no fewer than *three* matchlock pistols. This was nothing to do with faking disability, but a terrifying weapon of the deadliest sort. By the nineteenth century, the violence was increasingly concealed, as with sword sticks, which needed to be unsheathed for use, as well as with gun sticks, which incorporated the barrel of a gun and firing mechanism into the shaft and handle of the stick. The Remington rifle cane was an early example of this kind of stick gun. Manufactured between 1858 and 1888, only a few thousand of these artefacts were produced, and they are now much sought-after collectors' items. Designed with curved, carved handles, the sticks appear to the unsuspecting eye quite ordinary, which was presumably the whole point. The advertisement for the gun outlined 'Directions for Using':

> To load – unscrew the handle re breech from the body of the Cane: insert the Cartridge and replace the handle. Drawing back the lever will cock the piece ready for firing, when pressing upon the trigger knob underneath will discharge it.

These were straightforward, easy-to-use devices that played on the innocuous associations of the lean and the cane, only to deliver a deadly payload if challenged.

JAMES DEAN

Different from the lean of the old and infirm was the nonchalant lean of rebellious youth, as epitomized in the braggadocious slouch of Hollywood rebels such as James Dean and Marlon Brando. Jimmy Dean perfected the body language of cool: the

James Dean in *Rebel Without a Cause*, 1955

conceit of always leaning on something – a wall, counter, car or motorcycle – the sideways lean, the hand placed nonchalantly in the back pocket, leaning away while sitting so as to be almost horizontal rather than leaning forward during conversation in order to be heard. Who could forget the iconic images of a young leather-clad Marlon Brando leaning on his motorbike? For Dean and Brando, and many others like them, their ultra-cool body language was all very staged, very male. It was all quite different from the standing-to-attention of soldiers, or preppy types who lounged around the country clubs of the United States. This male, slouched lean was also very distinct from the kinds of upright posture that deportment manuals prescribed in ordering young women to stand up straight.

FEMALE ETIQUETTE

Florence Hartley's *The Ladies' Book of Etiquette* (1860) advised that a series of preparatory exercises were required to achieve a correct, upright posture. She advised that a young lady should

> successively learn to stand flat and firm upon both her feet, with her limbs quite straight, and the whole person perfectly upright, but not stiff; then to lift one foot from the ground, and to keep it so for some time without moving any part of her body.

The young lady was then advised to replace her foot on the ground, and to raise the other in the same manner. These actions were to be repeated until young women were quite familiar with them.

> They were then directed to keep the body quite erect, but not stiff, and bearing firmly upon one leg, to raise the other from the ground, gradually and slowly, by bending the upper joint of the limb, at the same time making the knee straight, and putting the toe to its proper extent, but *no more*.

In this way, these young women were trained to move and walk in an upright and dignified way: there was to be no slouching or leaning.

Finishing schools trained the daughters of the world's social elites for entrance into society. An upright posture with a straight back was synonymous with well-bred femininity, and photographs survive of women learning to walk with books on their heads in order to achieve the correct posture.

Of course precept was not the same as practice: just because women were told to act this way did not mean that they did so.

A woman balancing a book on her head during deportment classes, 1952

Just as there were rebellious men in Hollywood, so too were there legions of sassy and spirited women – women who could certainly strike a pose – such as Marilyn Monroe, Ava Gardner and Greta Garbo, women who were more than a match for their male counterparts, and could be seen leaning in movies on the big screen.

EXTORTION AND INTIMIDATION

There is also a fascinating history of people leaning on others, either for help or for its opposite: to put pressure on a person – to extract something from them or to force them to do something against their will. In this sense the history of the lean is the history of extortion, bullying and blackmail; it is the history of political persuasion, plots and back-stabbing.

The intimidating lean is beautifully demonstrated by the career of a fifteenth-century magnate, Sir John Cornewall (c.1364–1443), in the years preceding the Wars of the Roses. This was a period of internecine fighting and feuding in England between 1455 and 1485, effectively a civil war that saw the breakdown of royal authority and justice. Cornewall was an esteemed courtier, having served as a comrade in arms to the great English warrior king, Henry V, and was an uncle to the current king, Henry VI. His power rested on royal connections, success in wars in France, and marriage to Elizabeth of Lancaster, the widowed sister of Henry IV.

In 1432, Cornewall was created Lord Fanhope and purchased Ampthill Castle in Bedfordshire, from where he sought to extend his political influence throughout the county. This brought him into direct confrontation with another local landowner, Lord Grey of Ruthyn. To build support Fanhope tried to win over local justices of the peace, through fair means and foul. In 1439, the rival factions came to blows. Fanhope arrived in Bedford with over 140 armed retainers, interrupted court proceedings and insulted those justices of the peace allied to Grey, who then turned up himself – but with 800 men – and intimidated those favourable to Fanhope. In the ensuing ruckus, eighteen men were thrown downstairs and several jurors were 'accidentally' killed. The matter was then taken to the king's court, where Fanhope was pardoned, and the local justices purged of Grey supporters. In a patronage society, where personal connections and wealth roughly equated to power, and as a result of profits from an advantageous marriage, success in war and lavish royal patronage, he was able to buy a vast landed estate in Bedfordshire and the lordship of Ampthill.

TORTURE

In this kind of political world – which is not a far cry from the racketeering of later periods – success depended on influence, contacts and the ability to lean hard on those whose will you wished to bend. Such influence, however, often crossed the boundaries of what was legally or indeed morally acceptable.

Leaning on people connects to the history of torture, and along with the rack, waterboarding, bamboo under the fingernails, electric shocks, sleep deprivation and other devices and techniques, thumbscrews were a fairly effective way of leaning on people. Made out of cast iron, they were employed in medieval Europe as a very simple way of applying pressure and eventually breaking the thumbs, and were used throughout history by slave owners, by the Gestapo, and by mobsters.

One of the most fascinating pieces of historical evidence for such torture is the document signed by Guy Fawkes (1570–1606) in the aftermath of the Gunpowder Plot. Fawkes was arrested in a cellar under the House of Commons, surrounded by gunpowder. To see the full weight of a nation leaning on a single individual in the early seventeenth century, one only needs to compare Fawkes's signature before his interrogations with the barely legible scrawl after eight days of torture in the Tower of London, which included use of the rack. The history of leaning on people to act against their will thus brings us to the important question of the history of the signature...

·30·

THE SIGNATURE

——

The history of the signature is all about…
power, amputation, blame, leadership,
guillotines, brain damage and theft.

Has your signature always been the same? When did it first appear in its present form? When did it change? Why? These seemingly bland questions open up a world of the past, because your signature – in fact *any* signature – has its own history.

We both vividly remember practising ours as children, and interestingly were both influenced by the ways in which our fathers signed their names. James from an early age mimicked his father's rather formal and elegant signature 'R. J. T. Daybell', transposing his own initials to sign 'J. R. T. Daybell', with a flourish on the capital 'D', which he took as a sign of adult sophistication. This signature was fixed relatively early on in primary school, and has remained static ever since, though it does change on a day-to-day basis depending on the reason for signing – an official contract receives his best effort, a signature for the post just a scribble.

Sam was also inspired by his father's beautiful handwriting and particularly excellent signature. It was unique, cool and, crucially, it looked fun to write; a mixture of racing jagged lines and elaborate swirls, a signature that looked both modern and historic at the same time. The act of signing itself, moreover, was (and still is) a physical performance encompassing his personality and the way in which he desires to be seen in the world. This paternal inspiration formed the basis for his signature, therefore, but it was not until Sam was twenty-one that his signature settled. He remembers doodling or practising from the age of eight or so, which means that his signature has its own timeline – its own unexpected palaeographic history.

At some point in 2005 Sam was then faced with a pleasant problem. He published his first book and was frequently required to sign it. He saw this as a fun challenge and wanted to develop a more 'showy' version of his own signature for those who were kind enough to want a signed copy of one of his books. At the age of twenty-eight, then, Sam acquired a second signature – a sort of professional signature – which can be added to his signature's timeline.

ILLNESS

Sam and James's experiences are by no means unique but there are a variety of ways in which a person's signature changes throughout adulthood and a variety of reasons for that change. Ageing and frailty can alter handwriting, rendering it shakier and less controlled. By far the most common reason is illness, which, because of handwriting's requirement for fine motor control, clear eyesight and clear thinking, can quickly and easily affect handwriting in a number of ways. By far the most widespread and sudden impact on handwriting is caused by stroke, an illness that has affected many famous figures, including Churchill, Stalin, Bach, Nixon, Dickens, Grace Kelly and Woodrow Wilson.

Other illnesses that affected the hands might also impact on the writing of signatures. The Elizabethan aristocrat, George Talbot, Earl of Shrewsbury (1528–90), one-time keeper of Mary, Queen of Scots when she was prisoner in England, had atrocious handwriting and an almost illegible signature, so much so that it has been described by one scholar as an example of 'ugly-ography'. His tortuous handwriting was not down to upper-class disdain for the drudgery of composition, nor lack of practice, but due to a gouty hand, which on occasion was so painful that the earl employed a secretary to write on his behalf.

AMPUTATION

The most extreme form of physical impairment that might affect one's handwriting is amputation. One of the most famous historical examples comes from the eighteenth-century English naval hero Horatio Nelson (1758–1805). In late July 1797 Nelson took part in an attack on the port of Santa Cruz on the Spanish-held island of Tenerife in the Canary Islands. As he landed in a small boat and rushed ashore the humerus bone in his right arm was fractured in several places by a musket ball. He was taken back to his ship and his arm was immediately amputated. 'I have yet my legs left, and one arm,' he is reported to have said. 'Tell the surgeon to make haste and get his instruments. I know I must lose my right arm, so the sooner it is off the better.' His arm was taken off within thirty minutes and within just a few days he was writing letters but, being right-handed, was faced with the problem of having to relearn to write with his left hand. A significant part of this process was having to relearn his signature. On 27 July, just two days after the attack, he wrote to his commanding officer, John Jervis, the Earl of St Vincent.

The letter is full of self-loathing and misery: 'A left-handed admiral will never again be considered as useful, therefore the sooner I get to a humble cottage, the better... ' and it is signed in a clumsy but still impressive way considering the extremity of the operation he had so recently undergone. Underneath his name he writes: 'You will excuse my scrawl considering it is my first attempt.' Over time his ability to write with his left hand improved and his signature settled again to a more or less fixed state recognizable as his own.

Nelson is a particularly good example for the history of the signature because he was obsessed with his identity and, as his fame grew and European royalty bestowed upon him more and more titles and honorifics in the aftermath of his naval victories, his actual name also changed, causing him to rethink his signature yet again. The moment that caused him the greatest crisis was in the aftermath of the Battle of the Nile in the summer of 1798, a battle in which he annihilated Napoleon's fleet, which had been gathered together for the French invasion of Egypt.

Battle of the Nile (1798) The British admiral Nelson caught the French fleet, at anchor and unprepared, at the mouth of the Nile. It was one of the most decisive naval battles in history and catapulted Nelson to fame. The French lost thirteen ships, the British none.

The first change came as a result of being awarded an English peerage in the form of Baron Nelson of the Nile. This allowed him to style himself simply as 'Nelson', appropriate for an English peer and different from the 'Horatio Nelson' of his youth. The following summer, Ferdinand, the King of Naples, created Nelson the Duke of Bronte. This Sicilian dukedom was the grandest of the three peerages Nelson would receive in his life and it came with a 35,000-acre estate, a castle and a twelfth-century abbey – not bad for a priest's son from rural Norfolk. This led to something of an identity crisis. His simple 'Nelson' first changed to the confusing 'Bronte Nelson'. From there it changed to the narcissistic and elaborate 'Bronte Nelson of the Nile' before settling on the schizophrenic 'Nelson & Bronte', carefully and deliberately using the ampersand as part of the signature. His signature never changed again, though we know that he signed the last letter he wrote in his life, moments before the beginning of the Battle of Trafalgar, 'your father, Nelson & Bronte'. This was a letter to his daughter, Horatia, born from his love affair with Emma Hamilton, and it was the first time that he had ever, unequivocally, told her that he was her father.

It's safe to say that few of us will be lucky (or unlucky) enough to face the particular problems that Nelson faced, but the phenomenon of someone's signature changing over time is important to historians who can use that change as a window into exploring and explaining the past. It is also, however, something that has proved very useful indeed for the police.

FORGERY

In 1929 an American named Joseph Cosey (1887–1950), short of cash, went into the Library of Congress and stole a pay warrant signed by Benjamin Franklin in 1786. Cosey then tried to sell it but was refused, the dealer he approached believing it to be fake. This gave Cosey an idea. Several months later he returned to the same book dealer and sold him a scrap of paper with the words 'Yrs Truly, A. Lincoln' for $10 but this one really *was* a fake – Cosey had spent months practising the handwriting to make it perfect. His success launched a career in forgery that has led to Joseph Cosey being recognized as one of history's most influential forgers. As an American with easy access to American archives, he specialized in American male figures, including Thomas Jefferson, Mark Twain and George Washington. As he grew bolder he began to invent, rather than simply copy, historical texts, and this was his undoing: he used the writing of a healthy young man to fake a letter purporting to be by Abraham Lincoln in his fifties, by which time Lincoln's writing had begun to spider across the page due to illness. Cosey was arrested and imprisoned but his forged signatures are now collected and curated as valuable historical artefacts in their own right.

Mark Twain (1835–1910) The pen name of the American author Samuel Longhorne Clemens (1835–1910). Famous for *The Adventures of Tom Sawyer* (1876) and *The Adventures of Huckleberry Finn* (1885) in which he drew on his personal experience as a Mississippi riverboat pilot.

Cosey's arrest and imprisonment in 1937 is interesting. He was sentenced to three years but released in less than a year. Such punishment for forgery was remarkably lenient. In eighteenth-century England forgery was a capital offence and there was a notable crack-down between 1795 and 1804 when 66 per cent of those convicted of forgery were actually executed, as opposed to just 14 per cent of those convicted of burglary, which was also a capital crime. Forgery – essentially the theft and misuse of someone's identity – was thus treated with the utmost seriousness by the English justice system. Forgery was not considered the same as any old property offence; it was somehow more *sinister* than simple larceny. The reason was that in the eighteenth century signatures had a particular power in relation to property – they facilitated its ownership and transmission by authenticating legal documents. Without belief in, or perhaps faith in, the signature, the entire system of law, economics and politics at the end of the eighteenth century would have collapsed, and with France then in the grip of its Revolution, with heads rolling down the streets of Paris from the overflowing guillotine's basket, there was simply nothing more terrifying for the English than the theft of a signature.

LITERACY

This question of the signature as a means of identification, authentication or approval has its own history as well. The story of the signature as a means of identification begins with the pre-signature, or mark. For those unable to sign their name, it was common practice throughout the medieval world to authenticate documents with the use of symbols. This was a practice that continued into more modern times, and could simply be a cross or circle. In some cases, marks were far more elaborate, as in the case of merchants, where they functioned as symbolic representations of trades. Thus, a blacksmith might identify himself with a horseshoe, or a glover with a pair of gloves. John and Mary Shakespeare, whose grammar school-educated son William became one of history's greatest wordsmiths, both sealed documents with marks rather than signatures, testimony of their incapacity with pen and ink.

The signature is bound up with the history of education and literacy, which is also related to the surprising history of sand and chalk, both of which were used in early pedagogical environments to teach writing. The signature inscribed on paper and parchment indicated basic literacy ability. As literacy rates increased with the spread of education, the signature was ever more widely used as a form of identification and authority, with literates choosing to sign their names rather than rendering a mark. The signature has been taken up by social historians as a universal measurement of literacy, comparable across time and place.

The archives are littered with the historical signatures of people from all sections of society. Deponents in court and testators of wills were all required to endorse these legal documents, which are a veritable goldmine for historians interested in measuring literacy – itself fundamental to understanding the spread of ideas, which is why so many historians of the English Civil War period, the French Revolution and Colonial America have been interested in studying literacy, education and the book trade. They are interested in getting a broad picture of how many people could read and write and had access to radical ideas – and at the centre of these studies are humble signatures, which can be collected in their thousands from across countless archives.

One such trove of signatures for seventeenth-century England is the Protestation Oaths of 1641 to 1642. These were organized at a local level, and recorded the signatures of all adult males over eighteen who did or did not swear an oath of allegiance to 'live and die for the true Protestant religion, the liberties and rights of subjects and the privilege of Parliaments'. Similar protestation oaths were conducted throughout the sixteenth to eighteenth centuries in Britain, which map shifts in patterns of national literacy. Around the world different forms of collective documents have allowed historians to study literacy of a particular country or region, during specific periods as well as across time. In Russia, for example, paybooks among military records are an excellent source for literacy because soldiers had to sign to receive their pay. More generally, wills, paupers' letters, marriage registers and court records containing the signatures of litigants allow historians to explore the rank and file of society to assess popular literacy levels of both men *and* women.

HENRY VIII

The signatures of ordinary people provide a snapshot of levels of basic education and literacy of populations during different periods, but also the signature itself is meaningful depending on whose signature it is. Royal signatures, for example, carried authority, and there is no better example of the relationship between the signature and political power than the reign of Henry VIII (1491–1547), the sixteenth-century tyrant whose chief interests were war, women and religion. Unlike his bureaucratic father, Henry VII (1457–1509), whose handwriting and signature fill the pages of government documents, Henry VIII was famously allergic to the day-to-day grind of paperwork. Early in his reign, Henry's chief minister Cardinal Wolsey used to coax and distract the young king with toys and trifles, as he pushed on with the business of governing the realm and gaining the king's assent to policies, and personally attended to the paperwork rather than Henry.

In spite of Henry not liking to do routine paperwork in the early Tudor period, his was a distinctly personal monarchy. Henry was the fount of honour and political favour. All power was concentrated in the person and importantly in the 'hand' of the monarch. Henry was a reluctant writer, preferring instead to rely on secretaries and amanuenses for all but the most intimate and personal of writing tasks. Interestingly, his love letters to Anne Boleyn are among the only surviving examples of correspondence wholly in his own hand, and importantly declare that love with his signature 'Henry R.', the 'R' a short-form of Rex, Latin for king. These were powerful words indeed, with the full emotional authority of the royal hand.

The authority of the royal signature was demanded for all manner of pressing matters of state. In lieu of the monarch physically signing, the practice of using a 'sign manual' (or signature

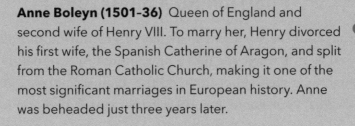

Anne Boleyn (1501-36) Queen of England and second wife of Henry VIII. To marry her, Henry divorced his first wife, the Spanish Catherine of Aragon, and split from the Roman Catholic Church, making it one of the most significant marriages in European history. Anne was beheaded just three years later.

stamp) had long been used to render the monarch's signature. In the example of Henry VIII's official signature, the sign manual appears to have been made with a crude wooden stamp (the 'wet stamp'), which was pressed first in ink and then applied to paper. After 1545, in the last years of his reign and with his powers waning, this system was replaced with the 'dry stamp', which was applied un-inked to the page, possibly with the use of a screw mechanism. This rendered an indentation of the king's signature on the page of the document, which was then inked over by a professional clerk to form a near-perfect facsimile of the royal signature.

Henry's signature was a key instrument of government, which was central to getting anything done during these savage and turbulent years. He was a man of wavering passions, likes and dislikes, and many a close friend or adviser, wife or near relative lost their head in the pressure-cooker of the Henrician court. Naturally, given the factionalized nature of the contemporary political scene, the jockeying for power among rival ministers and groups often involved tussles for control of the royal signature and therefore control over power. Power in early Tudor England was thus intricately bound up with the signature, because those who controlled the instrument of government – the king's signature – wielded authority in the name of the king.

POSITIONING A SIGNATURE

Throughout the sixteenth to eighteenth centuries, in England as well as in France, the meaning acquired by a signature was related to its physical position on the manuscript page. Where you signed your name, not just whether you signed or not, was crucially important in societies that were acutely conscious of status hierarchies. The significance of space is made explicit in William Fulwood's letter-writing manual *Enimie of Idlenesse* (1568), which outlines rules for the positioning and wording of the subscription and signature in a letter:

> which must be doone according to the estate of the writer, and the qualitie of the person to whom wee write: For to our superiors wee must write at the right side in the neither end of the paper, saying: By your most humble and obedient sonne, or seruaunt, &c. Or, yours to commaund, &c. And to our equals we must write towards the middest of the paper, saying: By your faithfull friend for euer, &c. Or, yours assured, &c. To our inferiours wee may write on high at the left hand, saying: By yours, &c.

One of the most fascinating examples of this form of meaningful signature relates to the poet John Donne (1572–1631). On leaving the University of Oxford as a young man, Donne was employed as a secretary by the Lord Keeper, Thomas Egerton, a role that destined him for a life as a government official or diplomat. His career took a turn for the worse, however, when he fell in love with Egerton's niece, Anne More, whom he married shortly before Christmas 1601, without the blessing of her uncle or her father George More, who was lieutenant of the Tower of London. Discovery of the clandestine match saw Donne incarcerated in the Fleet Prison, along with Samuel Brooke, the minister who married the couple, and the witness of the event.

It was during this period that Donne sent a series of letters to his father-in-law and former employer begging for clemency. Alongside the supplicatory rhetoric, Donne registered his contrition and self-abasement by leaving a gap of blank space between the main body of the letter and signature, which was crammed in the bottom right-hand corner of the page. As we have seen, letter-writing guides of the period recommended the significant use of manuscript space for a letter's signatory as a display of deference towards the recipient. Placement of the signature was thus part of what might be described as the material politics of the manuscript page: in other words, letters communicated by a series of visual cues.

MUTINY

One of the most powerful examples that *where* you sign a document has its own significance and even its own history comes from 1627 in the shape of a sailors' 'round robin'. This was a document created by a ship's crew designed to express dissatisfaction with their superiors. It was a fine line to tread as, technically, such a communication was mutiny, and mutiny was punishable by death. The crew's difficulty was that they wanted to demonstrate solidarity with each other and yet no one wanted to act as a ringleader and risk the wrath of authority. The solution was to compose a type of petition, but rather than being in the form of a list where the first name would carry added significance, perhaps identifying that person as the originator of the authority-challenging document, they signed it in a circle [*see fig. 41*].

This is the historical *opposite* of what we know today as 'signing on the dotted line'. In this example the sailors have not been paid and their ship has run out of food. There are seventy-six signatures in the circle and the central text reads:

> Good captain to your wordes wee all give eare
> But they unpleasing seame as wee doe heare...
> If that ower lowanse [our allowance] wee receive not dulye
> And allso staying heare wee victule newlye [victual newly –
> i.e. receive more food]
> The shipe shall ride whilst cables they be rotten
> Soo longes wee are whare victules maye be gotten
> Unto which saying wee will all applye
> Before wele yeld wee one and all will dye
> God blesse the kinge and send him longe to rayne...

This extraordinary signed circular petition not only stands as evidence of the literacy of these sailors – since most of them appear to have been able to sign their names – but also emphasizes the way in which the basic act of putting a name on a piece of paper can have huge significance for the historian. The many hands – in the sense of handwriting – adding signatures to this petition raises the important question of the history of the hand... Please turn to Chapter 1.

JOIN IN!

We believe passionately that everyone – not just professional historians – can effectively exercise their historical imagination. If you have a great idea for a *Histories of the Unexpected* subject fill in one of these forms, photograph it and send it to us

on Twitter **@UnexpectedPod**

or by email to **info@historiesoftheunexpected.com**

and we might dedicate a podcast episode to you and your historical imagination!

The history of _____ is all about…

_____

The history of _____ is all about…

_____

The history of _____ is all about…

_____

The history of _____ is all about…

_____

SELECTED FURTHER READING

CHAPTER 1. THE HAND

Alpenfels, Ethel J., 'The Anthropology and Social Significance of the Human Hand', http://www.oandplibrary.org/al/pdf/1955_02_004.pdf [accessed 16 November 2017].

Battersby, Matilda, '40,000-year-old cave paintings include "oldest hand stencil known to science"', *Independent*, 9 October 2014, http://www.independent.co.uk/arts-entertainment/art/news/40000-year-old-cave-paintings-include-oldest-hand-stencil-known-to-science-9783840.html [accessed 13 November 2017].

Bloch, Marc, *The Royal Touch: Monarchy and Miracles in France and England* (republished, London: Routledge, 2015).

Bremner, Jan A., *A Cultural History of Gesture* (Ithaca, NY: Cornell University Press, 1991).

Brogan, Stephen, *The Royal Touch in Early Modern England: Politics, Medicine and Sin* (Martlesham: Boydell and Brewer, 2015).

——, 'A Touch of Charles II', *History Today*, 66/5 (2016).

——, 'James I: The Royal Touch', *History Today*, 61/2 (2011).

Cunnington, P. E., and Catherine Lucas, *Costumes for Births, Marriages and Deaths* (London: Adam and Charles Black, 1972).

Daybell, James, *Women Letter-Writers in Tudor England* (Oxford: Oxford University Press, 2006).

Dowd, Marion, and Robert Hensey, *The Archaeology of Darkness* (Oxford: Oxbow Books, 2016).

Gardner, Arthur, *English Medieval Sculpture* (Cambridge: Cambridge University Press, 1951).

Gerard, John, *The Autobiography of an Elizabethan*, trans. and ed. Philip Caraman (London: Longmans, Green and Co., 1951).

Guthrie, R. Dale, *The Nature of Paleolithic Art* (Chicago: University of Chicago Press, 2006).

Karim-Cooper, Farah, *The Hand on the Shakespearean Stage (Arden Shakespeare)* (London: Bloomsbury, 2016).

Kellaway, Lucy, 'The Invention of the Career Ladder', excerpted from *History of Office Life*, Radio 4, 24 July 2013, http://www.bbc.co.uk/news/magazine-23419229 [accessed 13 November 2017].

Kendon, Adam, 'History of the Study of Gesture', *The Oxford Handbook of Linguistics*, ed. Keith Allan (Oxford: Oxford University Press, 2013), pp. 71–90.

Manhire, Anthony, 'The Role of Hand Prints in the Rock Art of the South-Western Cape', *South African Archaeological Bulletin*, 53/168 (1998), pp. 98–100.

Manning, John, *The Finger Book* (London: Faber and Faber, 2009).

Muir, Edward, *Ritual in Early Modern Europe* (Cambridge: Cambridge University Press, 2nd edition 2005).

Pettitt, P. B., 'Darkness Visible: Shadows, Art and the Ritual Experience of Caves in Upper Palaeolithic Europe', in *The Archaeology of Darkness*, ed. M. Dowd and R. Hensey (Oxford: Oxbow Books, 2016), pp. 11–23.

——, M. García-Diez, D. Hoffmann, A. Maximiano Castillejo, R. Ontanon-Peredo, A. Pike and J. Zilhao, 'Are Hand Stencils in Palaeolithic Cave Art Older Than We Think? An Evaluation of the Existing Data and Their Potential Implications', in *Prehistoric Art as Prehistoric Culture: Studies in Honour of Professor Rodrigo de Balbin-Behrmann*, ed. P. Bueno-Ramirez and P. Bahn (Oxford: Archaeopress, 2015), pp. 31–43.

Pike, A. W. G., D. L. Hoffman, M. García-Diez, P. B. Pettitt, J. Alcolea, R. De Balbín, C. González-Sainz, C. de las Heras, J. A. Lasheras, R. Montez and J. Zilhão, 'Uranium-Series Dating of Upper Palaeolithic Art in Spanish Caves. U-Series Dating of Paleolithic Art in 11 Caves in Spain', *Science*, 336 (2012), pp. 1409–13.

Poyatos, Fernadna, *Advances in Non-Verbal Communication: Sociocultural, Clinical, Esthetic and Literary Perspectives* (Amsterdam: John Benjamins Publishing Company, 1992).

Steane, John, *The Archaeology of the Medieval English Monarchy* (London and New York: Routledge, 1993).

Trumble, Angus, *The Finger: A Handbook* (New York: Farrar, Straus and Giroux, 2010).

Walter, John, 'Gesturing at Authority: Deciphering the Gestural Code of Early Modern England', *Past & Present*, 203 (2009), pp. 96–127.

Willemsen, Annemarieke, 'The Geoff Egan Memorial Lecture 2013: Taking up the glove: finds, uses and meanings of gloves, mittens and gauntlets in Western Europe, c. A D 1300–1700', *Post-Medieval Archaeology*, 49/1 (2015), pp. 1–36.

Withey, Alun, 'The Hand of History: Hands, Fingers and Nails in the Eighteenth Century', https://dralun.wordpress.com/2014/06/13/the-hand-of-history-hands-fingers-and-nails-in-the-eighteenth-century/ [accessed 16 November 2017].

CHAPTER 2. GLOVES

A Handful of History. Catalogue of the exhibition of decorative gloves from the Spence Collection, arranged by the Worshipful Company of Glovers and the Museum of London at Austin Reed, Regent Street, London (London: Austin Reed, 1980).

Author Archive, 'The White Glove Myth', *Forbes*, http://blogs.forbes.com/booked/author/raab/ [accessed 14 August 2107].

Baker, Cathleen A., and Randy Silverman, 'Misperceptions about White Gloves', *International Preservation News*, 37 (December 2005), pp. 4–16, https://www.ifla.org/files/assets/pac/ipn/ipnn37.pdf [accessed 14 August 2017].

Beck, S. William, *Gloves, Their Annals and Associations: A Chapter of Trade and Social History* (London, 1883).

Byrde, P., and P. Brears, 'A Pair of James I's Gloves', *Costume*, 24 (1990), pp. 34–42.

Collins, Cody, *Love of a Glove: The Romance, Legends and Fashion History of Gloves...* (New York: Fairchild Publishing Company, 1947).

Cuming, Valerie, *Gloves* (London: Batsford, 1982).

Doré, Judith, 'Elizabeth Hammond's Collection and the Kent Costume Trust: An Appreciation', *Costume,* 49/1 (2015), pp. 3–7.

Ellis, B. Eldred, *Gloves and the Glove Trade* (London: Sir Isaac Pitman and Sons, 1921).

Foster, Wanda, '"A Garden of Flowers": A Note on Some Unusual Embroidered Gloves', *Costume*, 14/1 (1980), pp. 90–94.

Hands & Their Handicraft: Gloves – Being a Brief Outline of the History & Manufacture of Fabric Gloves (London, n.d.).

Hull, Jr., William, *The History of the Glove Trade...* (London: Effingham Wilson, 1834).

Lawson, Jane A., *The Elizabethan New Year's Gift Exchanges, 1559–1603* (Oxford: Oxford University Press, 2013).

May, Steven W., 'Vavasour, Anne (fl.1580–1621)', *Oxford Dictionary of National Biography* (Oxford: Oxford University Press, 2004).

Pimlott, Jane, 'The use of white cotton gloves for handling collection items', https://www.bl.uk/aboutus/stratpolprog/collectioncare/publications/ videos/whitegloves.pdf [accessed 14 August 2017].

Redfern, William Beales, *Royal and Historic Gloves and Shoes* (London: Methuen, 1904).

Redwood, Mike, *Gloves and Glove-Making* (London: Bloomsbury Shire Publications, 2016).

Robinson, Claire, '"An old and faithful servand": A Pair of Early Seventeenth-Century Gauntlet Gloves Given by King Charles I to Sir Henry Wardlaw', *Costume*, 49/1 (2015), pp. 8–31.

Stallybrass, Peter, and Ann Jones, 'Fetishizing the Glove in Renaissance Europe', *Critical Inquiry*, 28/1 (2001), pp. 114–32.

Tittler, Robert, 'Freemen's Gloves and Civic Authority: the Evidence from Post-Reformation Portraiture', *Costume*, 40 (2006), pp. 13–20.

Willemsen, Annemarieke, 'The Geoff Egan Memorial Lecture 2013: Taking up the glove: finds, uses and meanings of gloves, mittens and gauntlets in Western Europe, c. AD 1300–1700', *Post-Medieval Archaeology*, 49/1 (2015), pp. 1–36.

CHAPTER 3. PERFUME

Ashenburg, Katherine, *The Dirt on Clean: An Unsanitized History* (New York: North Point Press, 2008).

Bembibre, Cecilia and Matija Strlič, 'Smell of heritage: a framework for the identification, analysis and archival of historic odours', *Heritage Science*, 5/2 (2017).

Chiang, Connie Y., 'The Nose Knows: The Sense of Smell in American History', *Journal of American History*, 95/2 (2008), pp. 405–16.

Classen, Constance, David Howes, and Antony Synott, *Aroma: A Cultural History of Smell* (London: Routledge, 1994).

de Feydeau, Elisabeth, *A Scented Palace: The Secret History of Marie Antoinette's Perfumer* (London: I. B. Tauris, 2006).

Dugan, Holly, *The Ephemeral History of Perfume: Scent and Sense in Early Modern England* (Baltimore, MD: Johns Hopkins University Press, 2011).

Friedman, Emily C., *Reading Smell in Eighteenth-Century Fiction* (Lanham, MD: Bucknell University Press, 2016).

Grossman Family Memories, 'Auschwitz: The Beginning, June 1944', United States Holocaust Museum, https://www.ushmm.org/ remember/the-holocaust-survivors-and-victims-resource-center/ benjamin-and-vladka-meed-registry-of-holocaust-survivors/

behind-every-name-a-story/grossman-family/grossman-familyaus-chwitz-part-3 [accessed 23 November 2017].

Jenner, Mark S. R., 'Follow Your Nose? Smell, Smelling, and Their Histories', *American Historical Review*, 116/2 (2011), pp. 335–51.

Kemp, Christopher, *Floating Gold: A Natural (and Unnatural) History of Ambergris* (Chicago: University of Chicago Press, 2012).

Kiechle, Melanie A., *Smell Detectives: An Olfactory History of Nineteenth-Century Urban America* (Seattle: University of Washington Press, 2017).

May, Steven W. and Arthur F. Marotti, *Ink, Stink Bait, Revenge, and Queen Elizabeth: A Yorkshire Yeoman's Household Book* (Ithaca, NY: Cornell University Press, 2014).

Morris, Edwin T., *Fragrance: The Story of Perfume from Cleopatra to Chanel* (London: Scribner, 1984).

Nobel Prize Committee, 'Press Release: The 2004 Nobel Prize in Physiology or Medicine to Richard Axel and Linda B. Buck', *Nobelprize.org*. Nobel Media AB 2014, http://www.nobelprize.org/nobel_prizes/medicine/laureates/2004/press.html [accessed 16 Aug 2017].

Oatman-Stanford, Hunter, 'Our Pungent History: Sweat, Perfume, and the Scent of Death', *Collectors Weekly*, 8 March 2016, http://www.collectorsweekly.com/articles/our-pungent-history/ [accessed 16 August 2017].

Ostrom, Lizzie, *Perfume: A Century of Scents* (London: Hutchinson, 2015).

The Perfume Society, 'Louis XIV: The Sweetest-Smelling King of All', https://perfumesociety.org/discover-perfume/an-introduction/history/louis-xiv-the-sweetest-smelling-king-of-all/ [accessed 23 November 2017].

Piesse, G. W. Septimus, *The Art of Perfumery, and the Method of Obtaining the Odors of Plants* (London 1857).

Pouy, Jean-Bernard, *Perfume: A Global History* (Somogy Editions d'Art, 2007).

Proust, Marcel, *The Remembrance of Things Past* [later *In Search of Lost Time*], 7 vols (1913–27), vol. 1 *Swann's Way* (first published 1913), translated by C. K. Scott Moncrieff and Terence Kilmartin, revised by D. Enright (New York: The Modern Library, 1992).

Reinarz, Jonathan, *Past Scents: Historical Perspectives on Smell* (Chicago: University of Illinois Press, 2014).

Saint Simon, Duc de, *Memoirs of Louis XIV and his Court and of the Regency* (London, 1958).

Schmidt, Louise Boisen, 'The Perfumed Court', This is Versailles blog, 28 April 2014, http://thisisversaillesmadame.blogspot.co.uk/2013/04/the-perfumed-court.html [accessed 23 November 2017].

Tullet, William, 'The Success of Sweet Smells', *History Today*, 65/8 (8 August 2015).

CHAPTER 4. THE BUBBLE

Barber, Malcolm, *The Two Cities: Medieval Europe 1050–1320* (London and New York: Routledge, 1992).

Barker, Nancy N., 'Let Them Eat Cake: The Mythical Marie Antoinette and the French Revolution', *Historian*, 55/4 (1993), pp. 709–24.

Beard, D. C., *The American Boys Handy Book: What to Do and How to Do It* (New York: Charles Scribner's Sons, 1882).

Bubble Blowers Museum, 'History of the Bubble Blower', http://www.bubbleblowers.com/history.html [accessed 21 September 2017].

Campbell, Gordon, *The Hermit in the Garden: From Imperial Rome to Ornamental Gnome* (Oxford: Oxford University Press, 2013).

Colegate, Isabel, *A Pelican in the Wilderness: Hermits, Solitaries, and Recluses* (London: HarperCollins, 2002).

Duby, Georges, ed., *A History of Private Life Volume II: Revelations of the Medieval World* (Cambridge, MA, and London: Harvard University Press, 1988).

E. F. A., 'Bubbles', *Journal of the Royal Society of Arts*, 88/4541 (1939), pp. 84–85.

Emmer, Michele, 'Soap Bubbles in Art and Science: From the Past to the Future of Math Art', *Leonardo*, 20/4, 20th Anniversary Special Issue: Art of the Future: The Future of Art (1987), pp. 327–34.

Eveleigh, David J., *Bogs, Baths and Basins: The Story of Domestic Sanitation* (Stroud, England: Sutton, 2002).

Fraser, Antonia, *A History of Toys* (London: Weidenfeld & Nicolson, 1966).

——, *Marie Antoinette: The Journey* (London: Anchor, 2002).

Geary, Patrick, ed., *Readings in Medieval History*, 3rd edition (New York: Broadview Press, 2003).

Gennes, Pierre-Gilles de, 'Soft Matter', Nobel Lecture, 9 December 1991, https://www.nobelprize.org/nobel_prizes/physics/laureates/1991/gennes-lecture.pdf [accessed 24 October 2017].

Gilchrist, John L., US Patent US1330701 for 'Bubble-Pipe', 1918, https://www.google.com/patents/US1330701 [accessed 21 September 2017].

Hollister, C. Warren, and Judith M. Bennett, *Medieval Europe: A Short History* (9th edition; New York: McGraw-Hill Press, 2002).

Kubota, Taylor, 'Engineers Stop Soap Bubbles from Swirling', Physics.org, 13 September 2016, https://phys.org/news/2016-09-soap-swirling.html#jCp [accessed 21 September 2017].

Kumar, David Devraj, 'Soap Bubbles: Not Just Kids' Stuff', *Chemist*, 88/2 (2015), pp. 36–37.

Mundy, John H., *Europe in the High Middle Ages, 1150–1300* (3rd edition; Addison-Wesley, 1999).

Quere, David, Françoise Brochard-Wyart, and Pierre-Gilles de Gennes, *Capillarity and Wetting Phenomena: Drops, Bubbles, Pearls, Waves* (New York: Springer, 2003).

Rousseau, Jr., Theodore, 'A Boy Blowing Bubbles by Chardin', *Metropolitan Museum of Art Bulletin*, 8/8 (1950), pp. 221–27.

Sitwell, Edith, *The English Eccentrics* (London: Faber & Faber, 1933).

Twain, Mark, *The Innocents Abroad* (Hartford, CT: American Publishing Company, 1869).

Waugh, Evelyn, *Brideshead Revisited* (London: Chapman and Hall, 1945).

CHAPTER 5. SHADOWS

Barrie, J. M., *Peter Pan* (London: Hodder and Stoughton, 1911).

Branch, J. E., and D. A. Gust, 'Effect of Solar Eclipse on the Behavior of a Captive Group of Chimpanzees (*Pan troglodytes*)', *American Journal of Primatology*, 11 (2005), pp. 367–73.

Chamberlain, Colby, 'Five O'clock Shadows', *Cabinet Magazine*, 24 (Winter 2006–2007), http://www.cabinetmagazine.org/issues/24/chamberlain. php [accessed 5 October 2017].

Classen, C., *Worlds of Sense: Exploring the Senses in History and Across Cultures* (London: Routledge, 1993).

Daniels, Cora Linn, and C. M. Stevans, *Encyclopedia of Superstitions, Folklore, and the Occult Sciences of the World*, vol. 3 (1903, reprinted Honolulu, Hawaii: University Press of the Pacific, 2003).

Elworthy, Frederick Thomas, *The Evil Eye: An Account of this Ancient and Widespread Superstition* (London: John Murray, 1895).

Fagan, Brian, 'Timelines: Dating by Solar Eclipse', *Archaeology*, 42/5 (1989), pp. 22–23.

Fiorani, Francesca, 'The Colors of Leonardo's Shadows', *Leonardo*, 41/3 (2008), pp. 271–78.

Gil-Burmann, C., and M. Beltrami, 'Effect of Solar Eclipse on the Behavior of a Captive Group of Hamadryas Baboons (*Paplo hamadryas*)', *Zoo Biology*, 22 (2003), pp. 299–303.

Grafton, Anthony, 'Some Uses of Eclipses in Early Modern Chronology', *Journal of the History of Ideas*, 64/2 (2003), pp. 213–29.

Gray, Richard, 'Eclipse Maps', *Journal of African History*, 6/3 (1965), pp. 251–62.

Henige, David, '"Day was of Sudden Turned into Night": On the Use of Eclipses for Dating Oral History', *Comparative Studies in Society and History*, 18/4 (1976), pp. 476–501.

Hsien-tzu, Wen, 'A Statistical Survey of Eclipses in Chinese History', *Popular Astronomy*, 42 (1934), pp. 136–41.

Jones, A., and G. MacGregor, eds., *Colouring the Past. The Significance of Colour in Archaeological Research* (Oxford: Oxford University Press, 2002).

Lloyd, S., P. Gouk, A. J. Turner, *Ivory Diptych Sundials: A Catalogue of the Collection of Historical Scientific Instruments* (Cambridge, MA: Harvard University Press, 1992).

Miller, Peter, 'Henry VIII's Lost Warship', *National Geographic*, 163/5 (May 1983), pp. 646–75.

Ozbey, O., M. H. Aysondu, H. Ozer, U. G. Simsek, 'The Effects of a Solar Eclipse on Animal Behaviour', *Turk Veterinerlik ve Hayvancik Dergisi* 28 (2004), pp. 55–61.

Rule, Margaret, *The Mary Rose: The Excavation and Raising of Henry VIII's Flagship*, 2nd edition (London: Conway Maritime Press, 1983).

Schechner, Sara, 'The Material Culture of Astronomy in Daily Life: Sundials, Science, and Social Change', *Journal for the History of Astronomy, 32/3* (2001), pp. 189–222.

Soreson, Roy, *Seeing Dark Things: The Philosophy of Shadows* (Oxford: Oxford University Press, 2008).

Stoichita, Victor I., *A Short History of the Shadow* (London: Reaktion, 1997).

Wheeler, William Morton, and Clinton V. MacCoy, Ludlow Griscom, Glover M. Allen and Harold J. Coolidge, Jr., 'Observations on the Behavior of Animals during the Total Solar Eclipse of August 31, 1932', *Proceedings of the American Academy of Arts and Sciences*, 70/2 (1935), pp. 33–70.

Young, D., 'The Colours of Things', in *Handbook of Material Culture*, ed. C. Tilley et al. (London: Sage Publications, 2006).

CHAPTER 6. BEARDS

Abassi, Lila, 'Beard Microbiology: Grubby Hipsters May Be On To Something', American Council on Science and Health, Blog, 13 February 2016, https://www.acsh.org/news/2016/02/13/beard-microbiology-grubby-hipsters-may-be-on-to-something [accessed 4 May 2018].

An English chapbook, 'The History of Blue Beard; or, the fatal effects of curiosity & disobedience (London: T. Evans, ca. 1805)', *Merveilles & Contes*, 5/2, Special Issue on Charles Perrault (December 1991), pp. 444–67.

Bacchilega,Cristina, *Postmodern Fairy Tales: Gender and Narrative Strategies* (Philadelphia: University of Pennsylvania Press, 1999).

Barzilai, Shuli, *Tales of Bluebeard and His Wives from Late Antiquity to Postmodern Times* (New York: Routledge, 2009).

——, 'The Bluebeard Barometer: Charles Dickens and Captain Murderer', *Victorian Literature and Culture*, 32/2 (2004), pp. 505–24.

Blow, Douglas, *On the Importance of Being an Individual in Renaissance Italy* (Philadelphia: University of Pennsylvania Press, 2015).

Bulwer, John, *Anthropometamorphosis – Anthropometamorphosis: Man Transform'd, or The Artificial Changeling* (London, 1653).

Church, Alfred John, William Jackson Brodribb and Lisa Cerrato, eds, *Complete Works of Tacitus* (New York: Random House, 1942).

'Danger Found in the Beard', *Star*, issue 7399, 10 May 1902, https://paperspast.natlib.govt.nz/newspapers/TS19020510.2.10 [accessed 8 September 2017].

Davids, Abu Muneer Ismail, *Getting the Best Out of Haj* (Darussalam, 2006).

Dickens, Charles, 'Captain Murderer', in *All the Year Round*, 8 September 1860.

Fisher, Will, 'The Renaissance Beard: Masculinity in Early Modern England', *Renaissance Quarterly*, 54/1 (2001), pp. 155–87.

Furbank, P. N., and W. R. Owens, *Defoe De-Attributions: A Critique of J. R. Moore's Checklist* (London: Hambledon Press, 1994).

Gowing, T. S., 'Philosophy of Beards: A Lecture Physiological, Artistic and Historic' (London, 1875).

Grimm, Jacob, and Wilhelm Grimm, 'Bluebeard' in *Kinder- und Hausmärchen* ('Children's and Household Tales') (Berlin: Erstdruck, 1812).

Hanks, Merry Wiesner, *The Marvelous Hairy Girls: The Gonzales Sisters and their Worlds* (New Haven, CT: Yale University Press, 2009).

Hawksley, Lucinda, *Moustaches, Whiskers & Beards* (NPG Short Histories) (London: National Portrait Gallery, 2014).

——, 'A Pogonophobe's View of Facial Hair in History', http://blog.wellcomelibrary.org/2015/11/a-pogonophobes-view-of-facial-hair-in-history/ [accessed 8 September 2017].

Hermansson, Casie, *Bluebeard: A Reader's Guide to the English Tradition* (Jackson, MS, University of Mississippi: Association of American University Presses, 2009).

Johnston, Mark Albert, *Beard Fetish in Early Modern England: Sex, Gender and Registers of Value* (Farnham: Ashgate, 2011).

Kim, Katherine, J., 'Corpse Hoarding: Control and the Female Body in "Bluebeard", "Schalken the Painter", and *Villette*', *Studies in the Novel*, 43/4 (2011), pp. 406–27.

Lovell-Smith, Rose, 'Anti-Housewives and Ogres' Housekeepers: The Roles of Bluebeard's Female Helper', *Folklore*, 113/2 (2002), pp. 197–214.

MacCulloch, Diarmaid, *Thomas Cranmer: A Life* (New Haven: Yale University Press, 1996).

Middleton, Jacob, 'Bearded Patriarchs', *History Today*, 56/2 (2006), pp. 26–27.

Oldstone-Moore, Christopher, *Of Beards and Men: The Revealing History of Facial Hair* (Chicago: University of Chicago Press, 2015).

——, 'The Rise and Fall of the Military Moustache', Wellcome Library Blog, 20 November 2015, http://blog.wellcomelibrary.org/2015/11/the-rise-and-fall-of-the-military-moustache [accessed 28 November 2017].

Parker, Patricia, 'Beards, Gender Ideology, Gender Change: The Case of Marie Germain', *Critical Inquiry*, 19/2 (1993), pp. 337–64.

Patel, Samir S., and Marion P. Blackburn, 'Blackbeard Surfaces', *Archaeology*, 61/2 (2008), pp. 22–27.

'Report of Committee on Industrial Pathology on Trades Which Affect the Eyes', *Journal of the Royal Society of Arts*, 112/3 (1855), pp. 119–27.

Rycroft, Eleanor, 'Facial Hair and the Performance of Adult Masculinity on the Early Modern English Stage', in H. Ostovich, H. Schott Syme and A. Griffin (eds), *Locating the Queen's Men, 1583–1603: Material Practices and Conditions of Playing* (Aldershot: Ashgate Publishing, 2009), pp. 217–28.

Toner, Jerry, 'Barbers, Barbershops and Searching for Roman Popular Culture', *Papers of the British School at Rome* 83 (2015), pp. 91–110.

Warner, Marina, *From Beast to the Blonde: On Fairy Tales and Their Tellers* (London: Chatto & Windus, 1994).

Withey, Alun, 'Beards in the Crimean', Florence Nightingale Museum, http://www.florence-nightingale.co.uk/2017/01/13/guest-post-dr-alun-withey-beards-in-the-crimean/?v=79cba1185463 [accessed 7 September 2017].

——, 'A Brief History of Beards', *BBC History Magazine*, History Extra (18 November 2016).

——, '5 things beards tell us about history', *BBC History Magazine*, History Extra (29 October 2014).

——, 'Shaving and Masculinity in Eighteenth-Century Britain', *British Society for Eighteenth-Century Studies*, 36/2 (2013), pp. 225–43.

Woodard, Colin, *The Republic of Pirates* (San Diego, CA: Harcourt, 2007).

Zipes, Jack, *Beauties, Beasts and Enchantments: Classic French Fairy Tales* (New York: New American Library, 1989).

——, *Why Fairy Tales Stick* (New York: Routledge, 2006).

CHAPTER 7. CLOUDS

Anderson, Katharine, *Predicting the Weather: Victorians and the Science of Meteorology* (Chicago: University of Chicago Press, 2005).

Aristotle, *Meteorologica*, trans. H. D. P. Lee (Loeb Classical Library: Cambridge, Mass.: Harvard University Press, 1952).

Burton, Jim, 'Howard, Luke (1772–1864)', *Oxford Dictionary of National Biography* (Oxford: Oxford University Press, 2004).

Das Gupta, N. N., and S. K. Ghosh, 'A Report on the Wilson Cloud Chamber and its Applications in Physics', *Reviews of Modern Physics*, 18/2 (1946), pp. 225–365.

Day, J. A., and F. H. Ludlam, 'Luke Howard and his Clouds', *Weather*, 27 (1972), pp. 448–61.

Dear, I. C. B., and Peter Kemp, *The Oxford Companion to Ships and the Sea*, 2nd edition (Oxford: Oxford University Press, 2006).

Dolan, E. F., *The Old Farmer's Almanac Book of Weather Lore* (Dublin, NH: Yankee Publishing Inc., 1988).

Gooley, T., *The Natural Navigator* (London: Random House, 2010).

The Great War, 1914–18, 'New German Weapon: the Gas Cloud', http://www. greatwar.co.uk/battles/second-ypres-1915/prelude/gas-development.htm [accessed 7 October 2017].

Haber, Ludwig Fritz, *The Poisonous Cloud: Chemical Warfare in the First World War* (Oxford: Oxford University Press, 1986).

Hamblyn, Richard, *The Invention of Clouds: How an Amateur Meteorologist Forged the Language of the Skies* (London: Macmillan, 2002).

Hibberd, D., *Wilfred Owen: A New Biography* (London: Weidenfeld & Nicolson, 2002).

Huth, J., *The Lost Art of Finding Our Way* (Cambridge, MA: Harvard University Press, 2013).

International Meteorological Committee, *International Cloud Altas, Published by the Order of the Committee by H. Hilderandsson, A. Riggensbach, L. Teisserence de Bort, Members of the Clouds Commission* (Paris: Gauthier-Villars, 1896).

Inwards, Richard, *Weather Lore: A Collection of Proverbs, Sayings, and Rules Concerning the Weather* (London: Elliot Stock, 1898).

Ludlum, David, 'Weather Lore', in *Encyclopedia of Climate and Weather*, 2nd edition, ed. Stephen H. Schneider, Terry L. Root and Michael D. Mastrandrea (Oxford: Oxford University Press, 2011).

McAdie, Alexander, *A Cloud Atlas* (Rand, McNally & Company, 1923).

McWilliams, James L., and R. James Steel, *Gas! The Battle for Ypres, 1915* (St. Catharines, Ontario: Vanwell Publishing, 1985).

Miller, Richard Lee, *Under the Cloud: The Decades of Nuclear Testing* (The Woodlands, TX: Two Sixty Press, 1991).

Mukharji, Projit Bihari, 'The "Cholera Cloud" in the Nineteenth-Century "British World": History of an Object-Without-an-Essence', *Bulletin of the History of Medicine*, 86/3 (2012), pp. 303–32.

Oxford University, 'The First World War Poetry Digital Archive', http:// ww1lit.nsms.ox.ac.uk/ww1lit/ [accessed 7 October 2017].

Pegis, Anton C., ed., *Basic Writings of Saint Thomas Aquinas*, vol. 1 (London: Random House, 1945; reprinted Indianapolis/Cambridge: Hackett Publishing, 1997).

Stallworthy, J., *Wilfred Owen: A Biography* (Oxford: Oxford University Press, 1977).

Thornes, John. E., *John Constable's Skies* (Birmingham: University of Birmingham Press, 1999).

Weart, Spencer R., *Nuclear Fear: A History of Images* (Cambridge, MA: Harvard University Press, 1989).

Wharton, W. J. L, *Captain Cook's Journal During his First Voyage Round the World Made in H.M. Bark 'Endeavour' 1768–81...* (London: Elliot Stock, 1893).

Williams, Daniel, 'Atmospheres of Liberty: Ruskin in the Clouds', *English Literary History*, 82 (2015), pp. 141–82.

CHAPTER 8. DUST

Amato, Joseph Anthony, *Dust: A History of the Small and the Invisible* (Berkeley and London: University of California Press, 2000).

Beal, Peter, *A Dictionary of English Manuscript Terminology, 1450–2000* (Oxford: Oxford University Press, 2008).

Bentlage, B. et al., eds, *Religious Dynamics under the Impact of Imperialism and Colonialism: A Sourcebook* (Leiden: Brill, 2017).

Day, Jasmine, *The Mummy's Curse: Mummymania in the English-speaking World* (London: Routledge, 2006).

Ertel, Patrick W., *The American Tractor: A Century of Legendary Machines* (Osceola, 2001).

Gallagher, Catherine, *The Body Economic: Life, Death, and Sensation in Political Economy and the Victorian Novel* (Princeton and Oxford: Princeton University Press, 2006).

Goudie, Andrew S., 'Desert Dust and Human Health Disorders', *Environment International*, 63 (2014), pp. 101–13.

Gregory, James Noble, *American Exodus: The Dust Bowl Migration and Okie Culture in California* (Oxford: Oxford University Press, 1989).

Holmes, Hannah, *The Secret Life of Dust: From the Cosmos to the Kitchen Counter, the Big Consequences of Little Things* (New York: John Wiley, 2001).

Horne, R. H., 'Dust; Or, Ugliness Redeemed', *Household Words*, vol. I (13 July 1850), pp. 379–84.

Hounsell, Peter, 'Dodd, Henry (1801–81)', *Oxford Dictionary of National Biography* (Oxford: Oxford University Press, 2004).

Jackson, Lee, *Dirty Old London: The Victorian Fight Against Filth* (New Haven: Yale University Press, 2014).

Library of Congress, 'Interview about dust storms in Oklahoma', 5 August 1940, 'Voices from the Dust Bowl: the Charles L. Todd and Robert Sonkin Migrant Worker Collection, 1940 to 1941', https://www.loc.gov/item/toddbib000091/ [accessed 14 September 2017].

——, 'Voices from the Dust Bowl: the Charles L. Todd and Robert Sonkin Migrant Worker Collection, 1940 to 1941', Washington, DC, https://www.loc.gov/collections/todd-and-sonkin-migrant-workers-from-1940-to-1941/about-this-collection/ [accessed 1 September 2017].

Lloyd, Helen, Katy Lithgow, Peter Brimblecombe, Young Hun Yoon, Kate Frame and Barry Knight, 'The Effects of Visitor Activity on Dust in Historic Collections', *Conservator*, 26/1 (2002), pp. 72–84.

Maidment, Brian, *Dusty Bob: A Cultural History of Dustmen, 1780–1870* (Manchester: Manchester University Press, 2007).

McIvor, Arthur, and Ronald Johnston, *Miners' Lung: A History of Dust Disease in British Coal Mining* (London: Routledge, 2007).

Marx, Karl, *Capital: Critique of Political Economy, vol. 1* (1867), ed. Ernest Mandel, trans. Ben Fowkes (London: Penguin, 2004).

Michelet, M., *History of France, From the Earliest Period to the Present Time*, vol. 1, trans. G. H. Smith (New York: D. Appleton & Co., 1895).

Middleton, N. J., and A. S. Goudie, 'Saharan Dust: Sources and Trajectories', *Transactions of the Institute of British Geographers*, 26/2 (2001), pp. 165–81.

'Oldest book jacket found in the Bodleian', Bodleian Library website, http://www.bodleian.ox.ac.uk/news/2009/2009_apr_27 [accessed 2 September 2017].

Poirer, David A., and Kenneth L. Feder, eds, *Dangerous Places: Health, Safety, and Archaeology* (Santa Barbara, CA: Greenwood Publishing Group, 2001).

Schrijver, K., and Schrijver, I., *Living with the Stars: How the Human Body is Connected to the Life Cycles of the Earth, the Planets and the Stars* (Oxford: Oxford University Press, 2015).

Steedman, Carolyn, *Dust* (Manchester: Manchester University Press, 2001).

Steinbeck, John, *The Grapes of Wrath* (New York: The Viking Press, 1939).

Winstone, H. V. F., *Howard Carter and the Discovery of the Tomb of Tutankhamun* (London: Constable, 1991).

Worster, Donald, *Dust Bowl: The Southern Plains in the 1930s* (Oxford: Oxford University Press, 1979).

CHAPTER 9. CLOCKS

Black, Jeremy, and Randall M. MacRaild, *Studying History* (Basingstoke: Palgrave Macmillan, 2007).

Bruton, Eric, *The History of Clocks and Watches* (London: Black Cat, 1989).

Cheney, C. R., and Michael Jones, *Handbook of Dates: For Students of British History*, 2nd edition (London: Royal Historical Society Guides and Handbooks, 2008).

Cipolla, Carlo M., *Clocks and Culture, 1300–1700* (London: Collins, 1967).

Clutton, Cecil, and G. H. Baillie, *Britten's Old Clocks and Watches and Their Makers: A History of Styles in Clocks and Watches and Their Mechanisms* (London: Bloomsbury, 1986).

Dean, Darron, Andrew Hann, Mark Overton and Jane Whittle, *Production and Consumption in English Households 1600–1750* (London: Routledge, 2004).

Dohrn-van Rossum, Gerhard, *History of the Hour: Clocks and Modern Temporal Orders* (Chicago: University of Chicago Press, 1996).

Duffy, Eamon, *Marking the Hours: English People and Their Prayers, 1240–1570* (New Haven, CT: Yale University Press, 2011).

Geary, Patrick J., *Readings in Medieval History* (4th edition; Toronto: University of Toronto Press, 2010).

Hale, J. R., *Renaissance Europe, 1480–1520* (Berkeley, Los Angeles and London: University of California Press, 1971).

Houlbrooke, Ralph A., *English Family Life, 1576–1716: An Anthology from Diaries* (Oxford: Blackwell, 1989).

Ladurie, Emmanuel Le Roy, *Montaillou: Cathars and Catholics in a French Village 1294–1324*, trans. Barbara Bray (first published in French 1978; London: Penguin Books, 1980).

McCrossen, Alexis, *Marking Modern Times: A History of Clocks, Watches, and Other Timekeepers in American Life* (Chicago: University of Chicago Press, 2013).

Moody, Joanna, ed., *The Private Life of An Elizabethan Lady: The Diary of Lady Margaret Hoby, 1599–1605* (Stroud: Sutton, 1998).

Sherman, Stuart, *Telling Time: Clocks, Diaries, and English Diurnal Form, 1660–1785* (Chicago: University of Chicago Press, 1997).

Thompson, E. P., *The Making of the English Working Class* (London: Victor Gollancz, 1963).

——, 'Time, Work-Discipline and Industrial Capitalism', *Past & Present* (1967), pp. 56–97.

Weber, Max, *The Protestant Ethic and the Spirit of Capitalism* (1905; 2nd edition: London and Boston: Unwin Hyman, 1930).

Webster, Tom, 'Writing to Redundancy: Approaches to Spiritual Journals and Early Modern Spirituality', *Historical Journal*, 39/1 (1996), pp. 33–56.

CHAPTER 10. NEEDLEWORK

Bell, Susan Groag, *The Lost Tapestries of the City of Ladies: Christine de Pizan's Renaissance* (Oakland: University of California Press, 2004).

Benberry, Cuesta, *Always There: The African-American Presence in American Quilts* (Philadelphia: University of Pennsylvania Press, 1992).

Bouet, Pierre, Brian Levy and François Neveux, *The Bayeux Tapestry: Embroidering the Facts of History* (Caen: Presses universitaires de Caen, 2004).

Browne, Clare, and Jennifer Wearden, *Samplers from the Victoria and Albert Museum* (London: V&A Publications, 1999).

Crawford, Patricia, '"The Only Holy Ornament of a Woman": Needlework in Early Modern England', in *All Her Labours II: Embroidering the Framework*, ed. by Jean Blackburn et al. (Sydney: Hale and Iremonger, 1984), pp. 7–20.

Frye, Susan, *Pens and Needles: Women's Textualities in Early Modern England* (Philadelphia: University of Pennsylvania Press, 2010).

——, 'Sewing Connections: Elizabeth Tudor, Mary Stuart, Elizabeth Talbot, and Seventeenth-Century Anonymous Needleworkers', in *Maids and Mistresses, Cousins and Queens: Women's Alliances in Early Modern England*, ed. by Susan Frye and Karen Robertson (New York and Oxford: Oxford University Press, 1999), pp. 165–82.

Henderson, A., and G. Owen-Crocker, eds, *Making Sense of the Bayeux Tapestry: Readings and Reworkings* (Manchester: Manchester University Press, 2016).

Jones, Ann Rosalind, and Peter Stallybrass, 'The Needle and the Pen: Needlework and the Appropriation of Printed Texts', in *Renaissance Clothing and the Materials of Memory* (Cambridge: Cambridge University Press, 2000), pp. 134–71.

Klein, L. M., 'Your Humble Handmaid: Elizabethan Gifts of Needlework', *Shakespeare Quarterly*, 50, 2 (1997), pp. 459–93.

McEwan, Cheryl, 'Building a Postcolonial Archive? Gender, Collective Memory and Citizenship in Post-Apartheid South Africa', *Journal of Southern African Studies*, 29/3 (2003), pp. 739–57.

Orlin, Lena Cowen, 'Three Ways to be Invisible in the Renaissance: Sex, Reputation, and Stitchery', in Patricia Fumerton and Simon Hunt, *Renaissance Culture and the Everyday* (Philadelphia: University of Pennsylvania Press, 1999), pp. 183–203.

Parker, Rozika, *The Subversive Stitch: Embroidery and the Making of the Feminine* (New York: Routledge, 1989).

Prichard, S., ed., *Quilts 1700–2010: Hidden Histories, Untold Stories* (London: V&A Publications, 2010).

Quilligan, Maureen, 'Elizabeth's Embroidery', *Shakespeare Studies*, 28 (2000), pp. 208–14.

Styles, John, *Threads of Feeling: The London Foundling Hospital's Textile Tokens 1740–1770* (London: Foundling Museum, 2010).

Summit, Jennifer, *Lost Property: The Woman Writer and English Literary History, 1380–1589* (Chicago and London: University of Chicago Press, 2000), ch. 4.

'Susan Strong's "Great Seal"', National Quilt Collection, National Museum of American History, http://americanhistory.si.edu/collections/search/object/nmah_556469 [accessed 22 November 2017].

Swain, Margaret, *The Needlework of Mary Queen of Scots* (New York: Van Norstrand Reinhold Co., 1973).

CHAPTER 11. THE ITCH

Arrizabalaga, Jon, John Henderson, and Roger Kenneth French, *The Great Pox: The French Disease in Renaissance Europe* (New Haven: Yale University Press, 1997).

Atherton, Ian, 'The Itch Grown a Disease: Manuscript Transmission of News in the Seventeenth Century', in Joad Raymond, ed., *News, Newspapers, and Society in Early Modern Britain* (London: Frank Cass, 1999), pp. 39–65.

Bain, Allison, 'Irritating Intimates: The Archaeoentomology of Lice, Fleas, and Bedbugs', *Northeast Historical Archaeology*, 33/8 (2004), pp. 81–90.

Brandão, José António, and Michael Shakir Nassaney, 'Suffering for Jesus: Penitential Practices at Fort St. Joseph (Niles, Michigan) during the French Regime', *Catholic Historical Review*, 94/3 (2008), pp. 476–99.

Coster, Will, *Family and Kinship in England 1450–1800* (London: Longmans, 2001).

Crawford, Patricia, and Laura Gowing, eds, *Women's Worlds in Seventeenth-Century England: A Sourcebook* (London: Routledge, 2000).

Crowley, John E., 'The Sensibility of Comfort', *American Historical Review*, 104/3 (1999), pp. 749–82.

Daybell, James, *Women Letter-Writers in Tudor England* (Oxford: Oxford University Press, 2006).

Ellison, David, and Andrew Leach, eds, *On Discomfort: Moments in a Modern History of Architectural Culture* (Abingdon: Routledge, 2017).

Ghesquier, D., 'A Gallic Affair: The Case of the Missing Itch-Mite in French Medicine in the Early Nineteenth Century', *Medical History*, 43/1 (1999), pp. 26–54.

Graunt, John, *Natural and Political Observations Made upon the Bills of Mortality* (London, 1662).

Houlbrooke, Ralph, *The English Family 1450–1700* (London: Macmillan, 1984).

Ingram, Martin, *Church Courts, Sex and Marriage in England 1570–1640* (Oxford: Oxford University Press, 1987).

Linehan, Peter, and Janet L. Nelson, *The Medieval World* (Abingdon: Routledge, 2001).

Montaigne, Michel de, *The Complete Essays*, ed. and trans. M. A. Screech (London: Penguin, 1993).

NHS Choices, 'Itching – Choices', http://www.nhs.uk/Conditions/Itching/Pages/Causes.aspx [accessed 10 October 2017].

Parascandola, John, *Sex, Science, and Sin: A History of Syphilis in America* (Santa Barbara, CA: Praeger Publishing, 2008).

Riello, Giorgio, *Cotton: The Fabric That Made the Modern World* (Cambridge: Cambridge University Press, 2013).

Roberts, Jennifer Sherman, 'Scratching "The Itch Infalable": Johanna St John's Anti-Itch Cure', The Recipes Project blog, https://recipes.hypotheses.org/5357 [accessed 10 October 2017].

Romm, Cari, 'A New Skeleton and an Old Debate About Syphilis', *Atlantic*, 18 February 2016, https://www.theatlantic.com/health/archive/2016/02/the-neverending-story-of-the-origins-of-syphilis/463401/ [accessed 24 October 2017].

Rouse, Lydia, 'The Flea Trap', Louth Museum blog, http://www.louthmuseum.org.uk/blog/louth_museum_opening_blog_2015.html [accessed 10 October 2017].

Rublack, Ulinka, *Dressing Up: Cultural Identity in Renaissance Europe* (Oxford: Oxford University Press, 2010).

Shakespeare, William, *Troilus and Cressida*, ed. Kenneth Muir (Oxford: Oxford University Press, 1982).

Shove, Elizabeth, *Comfort, Cleanliness and Convenience: The Social Organization of Normality* (Oxford: Berg, 2003).

Spooner, Thomas, *A Short Account of the Itch, Inveterate Itching Humours, Scabbiness and Leprosy: Plainly Describing Their Symptoms, Nature, Original Cause, and True Cure...* (London, 1718).

Stone, Lawrence, *Broken Lives: Separation and Divorce in England 1660–1857* (Oxford: Oxford University Press, 1993).

——, *The Family, Sex and Marriage in England 1500–1800* (London: Weidenfeld & Nicolson, 1977).

——, *Road to Divorce: England 1530–1989* (Oxford: Oxford University Press, 1990).

Tampa, M., I. Sarbu, C. Matei, V. Benea, and S. R. Georgescu, 'Brief History of Syphilis', *Journal of Medicine and Life*, 7/1 (2014), pp. 4–10.

Thomas, Keith, *The Ends of Life: Roads to Fulfilment in Early Modern England* (Oxford: Oxford University Press, 2009).

Thwaites R., ed., *The Jesuit Relations and Allied Documents*, 73 vols (Cleveland: Burrows Brothers, 1896–1901), vol. 39.

Weisshaar, Elke, et al., 'The Symptom of Itch in Medical History: Highlights Through the Centuries', *International Journal of Dermatology*, 48/12 (2009), pp. 1385–94.

White, Carolyn L., ed., *The Materiality of Individuality: Archaeological Studies of Individual Lives* (Reno: University of Nevada Press, 2009).

CHAPTER 12. HOLES

Campbell, James, ed., *The Anglo-Saxons* (London: Phaidon Press, 1982).

Caraman, Philip, *The Other Face: Catholic Life Under Elizabeth I* (London: Longmans, 1960).

Cowell, M., and Williams, G., 'Analysis of a gold mancus of Coenwulf of Mercia and other comparable coins' in *British Museum Technical Research Bulletin*, vol. 3 (2009), pp. 31–36.

Crawford, Patricia, and Gowing, Laura, eds, *Women's Worlds in Seventeenth-Century England: A Sourcebook* (London: Routledge, 2000).

Daybell, James, *The Material Letter: Manuscript Letters and the Culture and Practices of Letter-Writing in Early Modern England* (Basingstoke: Palgrave Macmillan, 2012).

Haward, Winifred I., *Hide or Hang: Priest Holes of North East England* (Clapham via Lancaster: Dalesman Publishing Company Ltd, 1966).

Hodgetts, Michael, 'Owen, Nicholas (d.1606)', *Oxford Dictionary of National Biography* (Oxford: Oxford University Press, 2004).

——, *Secret Hiding-Places* (Dublin: Veritas, 1989).

Hogge, Alice, *God's Secret Agents* (London: HarperCollins, 2005).

Keynes, Simon, 'The Discovery and First Publication of the Alfred Jewel', *Somerset Archaeology and Natural History* (1992), pp. 1–8.

Kilroy, Gerard, *Edmund Campion: Memory and Transcription* (Aldershot: Ashgate, 2005).

Kwakkel, Eric J., Medieval Book History Blog, Leiden University, http://erikkwakkel.tumblr.com/ [accessed 9 November 2017].

——, 'Parchment (the good, the bad and the ugly)', https://www.khanacademy.org/humanities/medieval-world/medieval-book/

making-medieval-book/a/parchment-the-good-the-bad-and-the-ugly [accessed 9 November 2017].

Laslett, B., 'The Family as a Public and Private Institution: An Historical Perspective', *Journal of Marriage and the Family*, 35 (1973).

Leahy, Kevin, and Roger Bland, *The Staffordshire Hoard* (London: British Museum Press, 2009).

Locke, John L., *Eavesdropping: An Intimate History* (Oxford: Oxford University Press, 2010).

Lodge, Edmund, *Illustrations of British History*, vol. 1, 2nd edition (John Chidley, 1938).

Morris, J., ed., *The Condition of Catholics Under James I: Father Gerard's Narrative of the Gunpowder Plot*, 2nd edition (London: Longmans, 1872).

Orlin, Lena Cowen, *Locating Privacy in Tudor London* (Oxford: Oxford University Press, 2007).

'Report of the Inter-Departmental Committee to establish the facts of State involvement with the Magdalen Laundries', February 2013, http://www.idcmagdalen.ie/en/MLW/Magdalen%20Rpt%20full.pdf/Files/Magdalen%20Rpt%20full.pdf [accessed 5 December 2017].

Smith, James M., *Ireland's Magdalen Laundries and the Nation's Architecture of Containment* (Manchester: Manchester University Press, 2007).

Stenton, Sir Frank, *Anglo-Saxon England* (Oxford: Oxford University Press, 1943).

Thomas, Keith, *The Ends of Life: Roads to Fulfilment in Early Modern England* (Oxford: Oxford University Press, 2010).

CHAPTER 13. THE BED

Aston, Margaret, *The King's Bedpost: Reformation and Iconography in a Tudor Group Portrait* (Cambridge: Cambridge University Press, 1995).

British Army War Diaries 1914–1922, http://www.nationalarchives.gov.uk/help-with-your-research/research-guides/british-army-war-diaries-1914–1922/ [accessed 8 December 2017].

Brawer, Nicholas A., *British Campaign Furniture: Elegance Under Canvas, 1740–1914* (New York and London: Harry N. Abrams, 2001).

——, 'Georgian Campaign Furniture', *Magazine Antiques*, 157/6 (2000), pp. 924–31.

——, 'Victorian Campaign Furniture', *Magazine Antiques*, 158/3 (2000), pp. 346–53.

Hamling, Tara, *Decorating the 'Godly' Household: Religious Art in Post-Reformation Britain* (New Haven: Yale University Press, 2010).

Handley, Sasha, *Sleep in Early Modern England* (New Haven: Yale University Press, 2016).

——, 'Sociable Sleeping in Early Modern England, 1660–1760', *History*, 98/329 (2013), pp. 79–104.

Harrison, William, *A Description of England, or a briefe rehearsal of the nature and qualities of the people of England...* (1577).

Hepplewhite, A., & Co., *The Cabinet-Maker and Upholsterer's Guide* (London: B. T. Batsford, 1897).

Hospital Records Database (Wellcome Trust/National Archives), nationalarchives.gov.uk/hospitalrecords [accessed 30 November 2017].

Houlbrooke, Ralph A., *Death, Religion and the Family in England, 1480–1750* (Oxford: Oxford University Press, 2000).

——, *English Family Life, 1576–1716: An Anthology of Diaries* (Oxford: Blackwell, 1989).

——, 'The Puritan Death-bed c.1560–c.1660', in Christopher Durston and Jacqueline Eales (eds), *The Culture of English Puritanism, 1560–1700* (Basingstoke: Macmillan, 1996), pp. 54–75.

Latham, Robert, and William Matthews, eds, *The Complete Diaries of Samuel Pepys*, 11 vols (London: G. Bell, 1973–83).

Metcalf, Priscilla, *The Halls of the Fishmongers' Company: An Architectural History of a Riverside Site* (London: Phillimore, 1977).

Moon, Iris, *The Architecture of Percier and Fontaine and the Struggle for Sovereignty in Revolutionary France* (London: Routledge, 2017).

Red Cross Society, *The County Branches [of the Red Cross]: Their Organization and Work During the First Months of the War, Volume I* (London, 1917).

Reports by the Joint War Committee and the Joint War Finance Committee of the British Red Cross Society and the Order of St. John of Jerusalem in England on Voluntary Aid rendered to the Sick and Wounded at Home and Abroad and to British Prisoners of War, 1914–1919 (London, His Majesty's Stationery Office, 1921).

Strong, Roy, *Tudor and Jacobean Portraits* (London: H. M. Stationery Office, 1969).

Stubbes, Philip, *A Chrystal Glasse for Christian Women. Containing a Most Excellent Discourse of the Godly Life and Christian Death of Mistris Katherine Stubbes* (London: Printed for John Wright, 1632).

Watson, Janet S. K., 'Wars in the Wards: The Social Construction of Medical Work in First World War Britain', *Journal of British Studies*, 41/4 (2002), pp. 484–510.

CHAPTER 14. DREAMS

Aikens, Kristina, *A Pharmacy of Her Own: Victorian Women and the Figure of the Opiate* (Ann Arbor, MI: ProQuest, 2008).

St Augustine, *The Confessions*, ed. Henry Chadwick (Oxford: Oxford's World Classics, 2008).

Berridge, Virginia, and Griffith Edwards, *Opium and the People: Opiate Use in Nineteenth-Century England* (London: Allen Lane, 1981).

Browne, Sir Thomas, *Collected Works of Sir Thomas Browne*, ed. Simon Wilkin (Norwich: Fletcher and Son, 1835–36).

Crawford, Patricia M., and Laura Gowing, eds, *Women's Worlds in Seventeenth-century England* (London: Routledge, 2000).

De Quincey, Thomas, *Confessions of an English Opium-Eater* (London: Taylor and Henry, 1822).

Dormandy, Thomas, *Opium: Reality's Dark Dream* (New Haven: Yale University Press, 2012).

Fellini, Federico, *The Book of Dreams* (New York: Rizzoli, 2008).

Freud, Sigmund, *The Interpretation of Dreams* (Leipzig and Vienna: Franz Deuticke, 1899).

Greene, Graham, *A World of My Own: A Dream Diary* (London: Viking, 1992).

Houlbrooke, Ralph A., *English Family Life, 1576–1716: An Anthology from Diaries* (Oxford: Basil Blackwell, 1989).

Kerouac, Jack, *Book of Dreams* (San Francisco: City Lights Books, 1961).

Levin, Carole, *Dreaming the English Renaissance: Politics and Desire in Court and Culture* (New York: Palgrave Macmillan, 2008).

Luther, Martin, *The Familiar Discourses of Dr. Martin Luther*, tr. by H. Bell (London, 1818).

MacFarlane, Alan, *The Diary of Ralph Josselin, 1616–1683* (first published 1976; paperback edition, Oxford: Oxford University Press, 1991).

Marinelli, Lydia, and Andreas Mayer, *Dreaming by the Book: Freud's 'The Interpretation of Dreams' and the History of the Psychoanalytic Movement* (New York: Other Press, 2003).

Ramaiah, G. Sundara and S. D. A. Joga Rao, 'Buddhist Interpretation of Dreams', *Tibet Journal*, 13/1 (1988), pp. 30–37.

Seaver, Paul S., *Wallington's World: A Puritan Artisan in Seventeenth-Century London* (Stanford: Stanford University Press, 1985).

The Second Part of the Secrets of Master Alexis of Piedmont (London: By Henry Bynneman for John Wyght, 1563).

Stott, G. S. J., 'Jerome before the judge: The dialogic nature of reports of dreams', *Dreaming*, 19/1 (2009), pp. 7–16.

Swedenborg, Emanuel, *Emanuel Swedenborg's Journal of Dreams and Spiritual Experiences* (trans. C. Th. Odhner, Bryn Athyn, PA: Academy Book Room, 1918).

Turner, David M., '"Secret and Immodest Curiosities?": Sex, Marriage and Conscience in Early Modern England', in Harald E. Braun and Edward Vallance, eds., *Contexts of Conscience in Early Modern Europe, 1500–1700* (Basingstoke: Palgrave Macmillan, 2004), pp. 132–50, 215–18.

CHAPTER 15. HAIR

Campbell, Sophie, *Nelson's Spyglass: 101 Curious Objects from British History* (Stroud: The History Press, 2016).

Carocci, Max, *Ritual and Honour: Warriors of the North American Plains* (London: British Museum Press, 2011).

Catlin, George, *Letters and Notes on the Manners, Customs and Condition of the American Indians,* 2 vols (London: By the Author, 1841).

Daybell, James, *Women Letter-Writers in Tudor England* (Oxford: Oxford University Press, 2006).

Good, Cassandra A., *Founding Friendships: Friendships between Men and Women in the Early American Republic* (Oxford: Oxford University Press, 2015).

Grass, Sean, 'On the Death of the Duke of Wellington, 14 September 1852', *BRANCH: Britain, Representation and Nineteenth-Century History*, ed. Dino Franco Felluga, http://www.branchcollective.org/?ps_articles=-sean-grass-on-the-death-of-the-duke-of-wellington-14-september-1852 [accessed 12 August 2017].

Griffin, Anastasia M., 'Georg Friederici's "Scalping and Similar Warfare Customs in America" with a Critical Introduction' (unpublished MA thesis, University of Colorado, 2008).

Hiltunen, Juha, 'Spiritual and religious aspects of torture and scalping among the Indian cultures in Eastern North America, from ancient to colonial times', *Scripta Instituti Donneriani Aboensis*, 23 (2011), pp. 115–28.

Iglikowski, Vicky, 'A Lock of Love', http://blog.nationalarchives.gov.uk/blog/lock-love (1 June 2015) [accessed 12 August 2017].

Le Faye, Deirdre, *Jane Austen's Letters* (Oxford: Oxford University Press, 2011).

Miller, Nancy K., 'Family Hair Looms', *Women's Studies Quarterly*, 36/1/2 (Spring–Summer, 2008), pp. 162–68.

Parker, Kenneth, *Dorothy Osborne: Letters to Sir William Temple, 1652–54: Observations on Love, Literature, Politics and Religion* (Aldershot: Ashgate, 2002).

Steele, Volney, 'Survivors of Scalping: The Frontier', *Journal of the West*, 44/1 (2005), pp. 72–7.

van de Logt, Mark, '"The Powers of the Heavens Shall Eat of My Smoke": The Significance of Scalping in Pawnee Warfare', *Journal of Military History*, 72/1 (2008), pp. 71–104.

Waters, Catherine, *Commodity Culture in Dickens's Household Words: The Social Life of Goods* (London: Routledge, 2008).

Wellesley, Jane, *Wellington: A Journey Through My Family* (London: Weidenfeld & Nicolson, 2008).

CHAPTER 16. THE PAPER CLIP

'Basic preservation for library and archive collections', Preservation Advisory Centre, British Library, https://www.bl.uk/aboutus/stratpolprog/collectioncare/publications/booklets/basic_preservation.pdf [accessed 8 December 2017].

Beale, Robert, 'A Treatise of the Office of a Councellor and Principall Secretarie to her Ma[jes]tie [1592]', printed in C. Read, *Mr Secretary Walsingham and the Policy of Queen Elizabeth*, 3 vols (Oxford: Clarendon Press, 1925), vol I, pp. 423–43.

Bell, H. E., *An Introduction to the History and Records of the Court of Wards and Liveries* (Cambridge: Cambridge University Press, 1953).

Breitman, Richard, Norman J. W. Goda, Timothy Naftali and Robert Wolfe, *U.S. Intelligence and the Nazis* (Cambridge: Cambridge University Press, 2004).

Bruce, Gary, *The Firm: The Inside Story of the Stasi* (Oxford: Oxford University Press, 2010).

Childs, David, *The Fall of the GDR* (Pearson Learning Limited, 2001).

——, and Richard Popplewell, *The Stasi: The East German Intelligence and Security Service* (New York: New York University Press, 1996).

Clanchy, Michael, *From Memory to the Written Record, England 1066–1307*, 3rd edition (Oxford: Wiley-Blackwell, 2013).

Daybell, James, *The Material Letter in Early Modern England: Manuscript Letters and the Culture and Practices of Letter-Writing, 1512–1635* (Basingstoke: Palgrave Macmillan, 2012).

Dennis, Mike, *The Stasi: Myth and Reality* (London: Pearson Education Limited, 2003).

Early Office Museum, 'History of the Paper Clip', http://www.officemuseum.com/paper_clips.htm [accessed 19 October 2017].

Farquharson, John, 'Governed or Exploited? The British Acquisition of German Technology, 1945–48', *Journal of Contemporary History*, 32/1 (1997), pp. 23–42.

Gimbel, John, 'German Scientists, United States Denazification Policy, and the "Paperclip Conspiracy"', *International History Review*, 12/3 (1990), pp. 441–65.

Gosnell, Harold, F., 'Symbols of National Solidarity', *Annals of the American Academy of Political and Social Science*, 223 (1942), pp. 157–61.

Hughes, Charles, 'Nicholas Faunt's Discourse Touching the Office of the Principal Secretary of Estate, & c.1592', *English Historical Review*, 20 (1905), pp. 499–508.

Hunt, Linda, *Secret Agenda. The United States Government, Nazi Scientists, and Project Paperclip, 1945 to 1990* (New York: St Martin's Press, 1991).

Jacobsen, Annie, *Operation Paperclip: The Secret Intelligence Program That Brought Nazi Scientists to America* (New York: Back Bay Books, 2015).

Koehler, John, *Stasi: The Untold Story of the East German Secret Police* (Boulder, Colorado: Westview Press, 1999).

Penn, Arthur, *The Home Library* (New York: D. Appleton and Company, 1883).

Petroski, Henry, *The Evolution of Useful Things: How Everyday Artifacts – from Forks and Pins to Paper Clips and Zippers – Came to be as They Are* (New York: Knopf Doubleday Publishing Group, 2010).

——, 'Polishing the Gem: A First-year Design Project', *Journal of Engineering Education*, 87/4 (1998), pp. 445–49.

Sander, Anna, 'Paper Clips', Balliol College Archives and Manuscripts blog, 15 April 2004, https://balliolarchivist.wordpress.com/tag/paper-clips/ [accessed 20 October 2017].

Schroeder-Hildebrand, Dagmar, and Peter W. Schroeder, *Six Million Paper Clips: The Making of a Children's Holocaust Memorial* (Minneapolis: Kar-Ben Publishing, 2004).

Smith, A. G. R., 'The Secretariats of the Cecils, c.1580–1612', *English Historical Review*, 83 (1968), pp. 481–504.

——, *Servant of the Cecils: The Life of Sir Michael Hicks* (London: Jonathan Cape, 1977).

Soll, Jacob, *The Information Master: Jean-Baptiste Colbert's Secret State Intelligence System* (Ann Arbor: University of Michigan Press, 2011).

Stewart, Alan, 'Familiar Letters and State Papers: The Afterlives of Early Modern Correspondence', in *Cultures of Correspondence in Early Modern Britain,* ed. James Daybell and Alan Stewart (Philadelphia: University of Pennsylvania Press, 2016), pp. 237–52.

——, *Shakespeare's Letters* (Oxford: Oxford University Press, 2008).

Sutton, Peter C., et al., *Love Letters: Dutch Genre Paintings in the Age of Vermeer* (Greenwich, CT, and Dublin: Frances Lincoln, 2003).

Tannhof, Angelika, 'The Stasi puzzle with 600 million pieces', Deutsche Welle, http://www.dw.com/en/the-stasi-puzzle-with-600-million-pieces/a-17039143 [accessed 20 October 2017].

Vivo, Filippo de, *Information and Communication in Venice: Rethinking Early Modern Politics* (Oxford: Oxford University Press, 2007).

Ward, James, *The Perfection of the Paper Clip: Curious Tales of Invention, Accidental Genius, and Stationery Obsession* (New York: Simon and Schuster, 2015).

Wingate, Charles F., and Andrew Geyer, *Who Makes It and Where: The Stationers' Book of Knowledge, 1916* (New York, 1916).

CHAPTER 17. LETTERS

Abelard, Peter, *The Letters of Abelard and Heloise*, ed. Michael Clanchy, trans. Betty Radice (London: Penguin Classics, 2003).

Ahrendt, Rebekah, and David van der Linden, 'The Postmasters' Piggy Bank: Experiencing the Accidental Archive', *French Historical Studies*, 40, no. 2 (2017), pp. 189–213.

Beal, Peter, *A Dictionary of English Manuscript Terminology, 1450–2000* (Oxford: Oxford University Press, 2008).

Beale, Philip, *England's Mail: Two Millennia of Letter Writing* (Stroud: Tempus, 2005).

Brant, Clare, *Eighteenth-Century Letters and British Culture* (Basingstoke: Palgrave Macmillan, 2006).

Constable, Giles, *Letters and Letter Collections* (Typologie des Sources du Moyen Age Occidental, 17, Turnhout, Belgium: Brepols, 1976).

Couchman, Jane, and Anne Crabb (eds), *Women's Letters Across Europe, 1400–1700: Form and Persuasion* (Aldershot: Ashgate, 2005).

Cressy, David, *Coming Over: Migration and Communication Between England and New England in the Seventeenth Century* (New York: Cambridge University Press, 1987).

Daybell, James, and Andrew Gordon, *Cultures of Correspondence in Early Modern Britain, 1580–1690* (Philadelphia: University of Pennsylvania Press, 2016).

Daybell, James, *Early Modern Women's Letter-Writing, 1450–1700* (Basingstoke: Palgrave Macmillan, 2001).

——, *The Material Letter: Manuscript Letters and the Culture and Practices of Letter-Writing in Early Modern England* (Basingstoke: Palgrave Macmillan, 2012).

——, and Andrew Gordon, *Women and Epistolary Agency in Early Modern Culture, 1450–1690* (London; Routledge, 2016).

——, *Women Letter-Writers in Tudor England* (Oxford: Oxford University Press, 2006).

Earle, Rebecca, ed., *Epistolary Selves: Letters and Letter-Writers, 1600–1945* (Aldershot: Ashgate, 1999).

Golden, Catherine, *Posting It: The Victorian Revolution in Letter Writing* (Gainesville: University Press of Florida, 2010).

Jardine, Lisa, *Erasmus, Man of Letters: The Construction of Charisma in Print* (Princeton, NJ: Princeton University Press, 1993).

Lerer, Seth, *Courtly Letters in the Age of Henry VIII: Literary Culture and the Arts of Deceit* (Cambridge: Cambridge University Press, 1997).

Mitchell, Linda C., and Susan Green, eds, *Studies in the Cultural History of Letter Writing* (Berkeley: University of California Press, 2005).

Moran, William L., *The Amarna Letters* (Baltimore, MD: Johns Hopkins University Press, 1992).

Rule, John C., and Ben S. Trotter, *A World of Paper: Louis XIV, Colbert de Torcy, and the Rise of the Information State* (Montreal: McGill-Queen's University Press, 2014).

Saint-Simon, Duc de, *Historical Memoirs of the Duc de Saint-Simon,* vols 1–3, 1691–1723, ed. and trans. Lucy Norton (London: Hamish Hamilton, 1967–72).

Schneider, Gary, *Culture of Epistolarity: Vernacular Letters and Letter Writing in Early Modern England, 1500–1700* (Newark: University of Delaware Press, 2005).

Stewart, Alan, et al., *Letterwriting in Renaissance England* (Washington, DC: Folger Shakespeare Library, 2004).

Stewart, Alan, *Shakespeare's Letters* (Oxford: Oxford University Press, 2008).

Sutton, Peter C., et al., *Love Letters: Dutch Genre Paintings in the Age of Vermeer* (Greenwich, CT, and Dublin, 2003).

Usher, Sean, *Letters of Note: Correspondence Deserving of a Wider Audience* (Edinburgh: Canongate Unbound, 2013).

Wall, Alison D., 'Elizabethan Precept and Feminine Practice: The Thynne Family of Longleat', *History*, 75 (1990), pp. 23–38.

——, ed., *Two Elizabethan Women: Correspondence of Joan and Maria Thynne, 1575–1611* (Wiltshire Record Society, vol. 38, 1982).

Wecker, Johann Jacob, *Eighteen books of the secrets of art & nature, being the summe and substance of naturall philosophy, methodically digested* (London: Printed for Simon Miller, 1660).

Whyman, Susan, *The Pen and the People: English Letter Writers 1660–1800* (Oxford: Oxford University Press, 2011).

CHAPTER 18. BOXES

Barrett, Michèle, and Peter Stallybrass, 'Printing, Writing and a Family Archive: Recording the First World War', *History Workshop Journal*, 75/1 (2013), pp. 1–32.

Campbell-Smith, Max, 'Letters and the Second World War' (unpublished BA dissertation, Plymouth University, 2016).

'Caring for Your Photographs', National Archives, http://www.nationalarchives.gov.uk/documents/archivesconservation_photo.pdf [accessed 4 August 2017].

Colvin, Clare, 'Forms of Documentation and Storage in the Tate Gallery Archive', *Archives*, 17/75 (1986), pp. 144–52.

Defoe, Daniel, *A Journal of the Plague Year* (London: Printed for E. Nutt at Royal Exchange; J. Roberts at Warwick Lane; A. Dodd without Temple Bar; and J. Graves in St James's Street, 1722).

Frye, Susan, *Pens and Needles: Women's Textualities in Early Modern England* (Philadelphia: University of Pennsylvania Press, 2013).

Hadgraft, Nicholas, 'Storing and Boxing the Parker Library Manuscripts', *Paper Conservator*, 18 (1994), pp. 20–29.

Honey, Andrew, 'Housing Single-Sheet Material: Fisherizing at the Bodleian Library, Oxford', *Paper Conservator*, 28 (2004), pp. 99–104.

Landers, J., *Death and the Metropolis: Studies in the Demographic History of London, 1670–1830* (Cambridge: Cambridge University Press, 1993).

Lindsay, Helen, and Christopher Clarkson, 'Housing Single-Sheet Material: The Development of the Fascicule System at the Bodleian Library', *Paper Conservator*, 18 (1994), pp. 40–48.

Moote, A. Lloyd, and Dorothy C. Moote, *The Great Plague: The Story of London's Most Deadly Year* (Baltimore, MD, and London: Johns Hopkins University Press, 2008).

Penfold-Mounce, Ruth, 'Corpses, Popular Culture and Forensic Science: Public Obsession with Death', *Mortality*, 21/1 (2016), pp. 19–35.

Pepys, Samuel, *The Diary of Samuel Pepys*, ed. R. Latham and W. Matthews, 11 vols (London: Bell and Hyman, 1970–83).

Quigley, Christine, *The Corpse: A History* (Jefferson, NC, and London: McFarland and Co., 1996).

Tebb, William, *Premature burial, and how it may be prevented, with special reference to trance catalepsy, and other forms of suspended animation* (London, 1905).

Wrigley, E. A., and Schofield, R., *The Population History of England 1541–1871* (Cambridge: Cambridge University Press, 2010).

CHAPTER 19. COURAGE

Anon., 'The Edward Medal', *British Medical Journal*, 1/2578 (1910), pp. 1310–11.

Avramenko, Richard, *Courage: The Politics of Life and Limb* (Notre Dame, IN: University of Notre Dame Press, 2011).

Byrne, Eugene, 'What is the Origin of the Phrase "Dutch Courage"?', BBC History Extra, http://www.historyextra.com/qa/dutch-courage [accessed 18 September 2017].

Clendinnen, Inga, *The Cost of Courage in Aztec Society: Essays on Mesoamerican Society and Culture* (Cambridge: Cambridge University Press, 2010).

Delap, L., '"Thus Does Man Prove His Fitness to Be the Master of Things": Shipwrecks, Chivalry and Masculinities in Nineteenth- and Twentieth-Century Britain', *Cultural and Social History*, 3/1 (2006), pp. 45–74.

Elinder, Mikael, and Oscar Erixson, 'Gender, Social Norms, and Survival in Maritime Disasters', *Proceedings of the National Academy of Sciences of the United States of America*, 109/33 (2012), pp. 13220–24.

Elizabeth I, *Elizabeth I: Collected Works*, ed. Leah S. Marcus, Janel Mueller and Mary Beth Rose (Chicago and London: Chicago University Press, 2000).

Evans, P. D., and D. G. White, 'Towards an Empirical Definition of Courage', *Behaviour Research and Therapy*, 19 (1981), pp. 419–24.

Ford, Worthington C., et al., eds., *Journals of the Continental Congress, 1774–1789* (Washington, DC, 1904–37), vol. II, p. 732.

Fowler, W. M., 'Esek Hopkins: Commander-in-Chief of the Continental Navy' in J. C. Bradford, ed., *Command under Sail: Makers of the American Naval Tradition* (Annapolis, MD: Naval Institute Press, 1985), pp. 3–17.

Frye, Susan, 'The Myth of Elizabeth at Tilbury', *Sixteenth Century Journal*, 23 (1992), pp. 95–114.

Garber, Megan, 'The "Leak" in the Age of Alternative Facts: From Ben Franklin to Uncle Tom's Cabin to H. R. McMaster, A Brief History of a Weaponized Word', *Atlantic*, https://www.theatlantic.com/entertainment/archive/2017/05/the-leak-in-the-age-of-the-alternative-fact/526914/ [accessed 20 September 2017].

Green, Janet M., '"I My Self": Elizabeth I's Oration at Tilbury Camp', *Sixteenth Century Journal*, 28 (1997), pp. 421–45.

Guthrie, Neil, *The Material Culture of the Jacobites* (Cambridge: Cambridge University Press, 2013).

Henderson D. V., *Heroic Endeavour: Complete Register of the Albert, Edward and Empire Gallantry Medals and How They Were Won* (London: J. B. Hayward, 1988).

Jones, Edgar, and Nicola T. Fear, 'Alcohol use and misuse within the military: A review', *International Review of Psychiatry*, 23 (2011), pp. 166–72.

Kamienski, Lukasz, *Shooting Up: A Short History of Drugs and War* (Oxford: Oxford University Press, 2016).

Larabee, Ann E., 'The American Hero and His Mechanical Bride: Gender Myths of the Titanic Disaster', *American Studies*, 31/1 (1990), pp. 5–23.

Mattingly, Garrett, *The Defeat of the Spanish Armada* (London: The Reprint Society, 1961).

Maxfield, Valerie A., *The Military Decorations of the Roman Army* (Berkeley: University of California Press, 1981).

Miller, William Ian, *The Mystery of Courage* (Cambridge, MA: Harvard University Press, 2000).

Mountain Rescue, 'The History of Mountain Rescue', https://www.mountain.rescue.org.uk/files.php?file=The%20Oracle/History%20and%20people/HistoryMREW.pdf [accessed 1 December 2017].

Osho, *Courage: The Joy of Living Dangerously* (London: Macmillan, 1999).

Pogăcias, Andrei, 'The Dacian Society – Fierce Warriors and Their Women, Sources and Representations', *Revista Hiperboreea*, 1 (2017), pp. 5–22.

Pury, Cynthia L. S., and Shane J. Lopez, 'Courage', in *The Oxford Handbook of Positive Psychology*, 2nd edition, ed. Shane J. Lopez and C. R. Snyder (Oxford: Oxford University Press, 2011), pp. 375–82.

Redmayne, R. A. S., 'Report on the Causes of and Circumstances attending the Explosion and Underground Fire which occurred at the Wellington Pit Whitehaven Colliery, on the 11th May 1910' (1911), http://www.dmm.org.uk/reports/5524-01.htm. [accessed 8 December 2017].

Saunders, Nicholas J., and Paul Cornish, eds, *Contested Objects: Material Memories of the Great War* (Abingdon: Routledge, 2009).

Scarre, Geoffrey, *On Courage* (London: Routledge, 2010).

Smith, Samantha, 'Unlocking *Cabala*, Mysteries of State and Government: the Politics of Publishing' (unpublished Ph.D. thesis, Birkbeck, University of London, 2017).

Spencer, William, *Medals: The Researcher's Guide* (Kew: National Archives, 2006).

Spink and Son Auctioneers, sales catalogue, 19 November 2015, https://www.aditnow.co.uk/documents/Wellington-Pit-Hugh-McKenzie.pdf [accessed 20 September 2017].

Tacitus, *The Agricola and Germania*, A. J. Church and W. J. Brodribb, trans. (London: Macmillan, 1877).

Tsur, Semyon, 'Nazis Attempted to Make Robots of Their Soldiers', *Pravda*, 14 February 2002, http://www.pravdareport.com/science/tech/14-02-2003/1872-nazi-0/ [accessed 20 September 2017].

Ulrich, Andreas, 'The Nazi Death Machine: Hitler's Drugged Soldiers', *Der Spiegel*, 6 May 2005, http://www.spiegel.de/international/

the-nazi-death-machine-hitler-s-drugged-soldiers-a-354606.html
[accessed 20 September 2017].

Willis, Sam, *The Fighting Temeraire: Legend of Trafalgar* (London: Quercus, 2009).

Woolf, Virginia, *A Room of One's Own* (London: Hogarth Press, 1929).

CHAPTER 20. MOUNTAINS

Bergh, Stefan, 'Transforming Knocknarea: The Archaeology of a Mountain', *Archaeology Ireland*, 14/2 (2000), pp. 14–18.

Bird, Isabella, *A Lady's Life in the Rocky Mountains* (Estes Park, CO: John Murray, 1879).

Braudel, Fernand, *The Mediterranean and the Mediterranean World in the Age of Philip II*, trans. Siân Reynolds (first published in French 1949; London: HarperCollins, 1992).

Carreño, Guillermo Salas, 'Mining and the living materiality of mountains in Andean societies', *Journal of Material Culture*, 22/2 (2017), pp. 133–50.

Debarbieux, Bernard, and Gilles Rudaz, eds, *The Mountain: A Political History from the Enlightenment to the Present* (Chicago: University of Chicago Press, 2015).

Edwards, Jacob, 'The Irony of Hannibal's Elephants', *Latomus*, 60/4 (2001), pp. 900–905.

Galop, Didier, and Norm Catto, 'Environmental history of European high mountains', *Quaternary International*, 353 (2014), pp. 1–2.

Green, Anna, and Kathleen Troup, *The Houses of History: A Critical Reader in Twentieth-Century History and Theory* (New York: New York University Press, 1999).

Gregorovius, Ferdinand, *Wanderings in Corsica: its history and its heroes, volume 1* (Edinburgh, Thomas Constable and Co., 1855).

Gunya, A., *Yagnob Valley: Nature, History, and Chances of a Mountain Community Development in Tajikistan* (Moscow: Scientific Press Ltd, 2002).

Hobsbawn, Eric, *Bandits* (London: Abacus, 2001).

Khromov, A. L., 'Idioms in Spoken Yaghnobian', *Acta Orientalia Academiae Scientiarum Hungaricae*, 23/2 (1970), pp. 189–203.

Ladurie, Emmanuel Le Roy, *Montaillou: Cathars and Catholics in a French Village 1294–1324*, trans. Barbara Bray (first published in French 1978; London: Penguin Books, 1980).

Loy, Thomas, *Yaghnob 1970: A Forced Migration in the Tajik SSR*, Central Eurasia-L Archive (18 July 2005).

National Park Service, Photographs of the Civilian Conservation Corps (CCC), https://www.nps.gov/media/photo/gallery.htm?id=C27A6BCE-1DD8-B71C-07E804E0164E3E31 [accessed 10 July 2017].

Nourzhanov, Kirill, and Christian Bleuer, *Tajikistan: A Political and Social History* (ANU Press, 2013).

Scullard, H. H., *The Elephant in the Greek and Roman World* (Ithaca, NY: Cornell University Press, 1974).

Shean, John F., 'Hannibal's Mules: The Logistical Limitations of Hannibal's Army and the Battle of Cannae, 216 BC', *Historia: Zeitschrift für Alte Geschichte*, 45/2 (1996), pp. 159–87.

Siehl, George H., *The Policy Path to the Great Outdoors: A History of the Outdoor Recreation Review Commissions* (October 2008), http://www.rff.org/files/sharepoint/WorkImages/Download/RFF-DP-08-44.pdf [accessed 10 July 2017].

Sims-Williams, Nicholas, 'The Sogdian Fragments of the British Library', *Indo-Iranian Journal*, 18/1&2 (1976), pp. 43–82.

Stewart, Elinore Pruitt, *Letters of a Woman Homesteader* (Boston: Houghton Mifflin Co., 1914).

Stoianovich, T., *French Historical Method: The Annales Paradigm* (Ithaca, NY: Cornell University Press, 1976).

Tarifa, Fatos, 'Of Time, Honor, and Memory: Oral Law in Albania', *Oral Tradition*, 23/1 (2008), pp. 3–14.

Wilson, Stephen, *Feuding, Conflict and Banditry in Nineteenth-Century Corsica* (Cambridge: Cambridge University Press, 1988).

CHAPTER 21. CHIMNEYS

Bailey Slagle, Judith, 'Literary Activism: James Montgomery, Joanna Baillie, and the Plight of Britain's Chimney Sweeps', *Studies in Romanticism,* 51/1 (Spring 2012), pp. 59–76.

Barton, D. Bradford, *A History of Copper Mining in Cornwall & Devon*, 3rd edition (Truro: Truro Bookshop, 1978).

Briggs, Katharine, *An Encyclopedia of Fairies, Hobgoblins, Brownies, Bogies, and Other Supernatural Creatures* (London: Penguin, 1977).

Burt, Roger, with Raymond Burnley, Michael Gill and Alasdair Neill, *Mining in Cornwall & Devon: Mines and Men* (Exeter: University of Exeter Press, 2014).

Clement C. Moore, *Twas The Night Before Christmas* (first published *New York Sentinel*, 23 December 1823).

Cornish Mining World Heritage, 'Working Conditions', http://www.cornish-mining.org.uk/sites/default/files/3%20-%20Working%20conditions.pdf [accessed 30 August 2017].

Craske, Matthew, 'Conversations and Chimneypieces: the imagery of the hearth in eighteenth-century English family portraiture', *British Art*

Studies, issue 2, https://doi.org/10.17658/issn.2058-5462/issue-02/mcraske [accessed 30 August 2017].

Crowley, John E., *The Invention of Comfort: Sensibilities and Design in Early Modern Britain and Early America* (Baltimore, MD: Johns Hopkins University Press, 2001).

Dresbeck, LeRoy, 'The Chimney and the Social Change in Medieval England', *Albion*, 3/1 (1971), pp. 21–32.

Foster, Donald, *Author Unknown: On the Trail of Anonymous* (New York: Henry Holt, 2000).

Great Britain Commissioners for Inquiring into the Employment and Condition of Children in Mines and Manufactories, *The Condition and Treatment of the Children Employed in the Mines and Collieries of the United Kingdom* (London: William Strange, 1842).

Hatcher, John, *English Tin Production and Trade Before 1550* (Oxford: Clarendon Press, 1973).

Houlbrook, Ceri, 'Home Is Where the Hearth Is', Concealed Revealed Project blog, University of Hertfordshire, 2 August 2016, https://theconcealedrevealed.wordpress.com/2016/08/08/home-is-where-the-hearth-is/ [accessed 30 August 2017].

Hutton, Ronald, ed., *Physical Evidence for Ritual Acts, Sorcery and Witchcraft in Christian Britain: A Feeling of Magic* (Basingstoke: Palgrave Macmillan, 2015).

Illes, Judika, *Encyclopedia of Spirits: The Ultimate Guide to the Magic of Fairies, Genies, Demons, Ghosts, Gods & Goddesses* (London: HarperCollins, 2009).

Jenkin, Kenneth Hamilton, *Mines and Miners of Cornwall*, 16 vols (Truro: Truro Bookshop, 1961–).

Lewis, Jim, 'Cornish copper mining 1795–1830: economy, structure and change', *Cornish Archaeology*, series 2, vol. 14 (2006), pp. 164–86.

Lynch, Alison, '91-year-old letter to Santa found up family's chimney, reveals the must-have toys of Christmas 1925', *Metro*, http://metro.co.uk/2016/06/06/91-year-old-letter-to-santa-found-up-familys-chimney-reveals-the-must-have-toys-of-christmas-1925-5926286/ [accessed 30 August 2017].

Mayhew, Henry, *London Labour and the London Poor* (London: George Woodfall and Son, 1851).

Miles, Clement A., *Christmas in Ritual and Tradition, Christian and Pagan* (Zhingoora Books, 2008).

National Library of Scotland, 'From rags to riches – restored map goes on display', https://www.nls.uk/news/press/2017/03/chimney-map-display [accessed 30 August 2017].

Nissenbaum, Stephen, *The Battle for Christmas: A Social and Cultural History of Christmas that Shows How It Was Transformed from an Unruly Carnival Season into the Quintessential American Family Holiday* (New York: Alfred A. Knopf, 1997).

Norton, George, 'William Blake's Chimney Sweeper poems: a close reading', British Library, Discovering Literature: Romantics and Victorians, https://www.bl.uk/romantics-and-victorians/articles/william-blakes-chimney-sweeper-poems-a-close-reading [accessed 31 August 2017].

'Report from the Committee of the... House of Commons on the employment of Boys in sweeping of Chimneys' (London, 1817).

Rule, J., 'The Misfortunes of the Mine: Coping with Life and Death in Nineteenth-Century Cornwall', *Cornish Studies*, 9 (2001), pp. 127–44.

Seal, Jeremy, *Nicholas: The Epic Journey from Saint to Santa Claus* (New York: Bloomsbury USA, 2005).

Shuffrey, L. A., *The English Fireplace: A History of the Development of the Chimney, Chimney-Piece and Firegrate with Their Accessories, from the Earliest Times to the Beginning of the XIXth Century* (London: B.T. Batsford, 1912).

Siefker, Phyllis, *Santa Claus, Last of the Wild Men: The Origins and Evolution of Saint Nicholas, Spanning 50,000 Years* (Jefferson, NC: McFarland and Co., 1996).

Stanier, Peter, *Mines of Cornwall and Devon: An Historic Photographic Record* (Truro: Twelveheads Press, 1998).

Strange, K. H., *Climbing Boys: A Study of Sweeps' Apprentices, 1772–1875* (London: Allison & Busby, 1982).

UNESCO, 'World Heritage List', http://whc.unesco.org/en/list/ [accessed 30 August 2017].

Willis, Sam, 'The Archaeology of Smuggling and the Falmouth King's Pipe', *Journal of Maritime Archaeology*, 4/1 (June 2009), pp. 51–65.

CHAPTER 22. TEARS

Ashton, John, *Curious Creatures in Zoology* (London: John C. Nimmo, 1890).

Astbury, Leah, 'Breeding Women and Lusty Infants in Seventeenth-Century England' (unpublished Ph.D. thesis, Cambridge University, 2015).

Bladen, Teri, '"Haile": A Discussion of Grief in Ethiopia', *Grief in a Family Context, HPER F460*, Summer 1999, Indiana University, http://www.indiana.edu/~famlygrf/culture/bladen.html [accessed 17 October 2017].

Brombert, Victor, 'Camus and the Novel of the "Absurd"', *Yale French Studies*, 1 (1948), pp. 119–23.

Brophy, Christina S., 'Keening Community: *Mná caointe*, Women, Death, and Power in Ireland' (unpublished Ph.D. thesis, Boston College, 2010).

Camus, Albert, *L'Etranger* (Paris: Gallimard, 1942).

Capp, Bernard, '"Jesus Wept" But Did the Englishman? Masculinity and Emotion in Early Modern England', *Past & Present,* 224/1 (2014), pp. 75–108.

Collier, Lorna, 'Why We Cry: New Research is Opening Eyes to the Psychology of Tears', *American Psychological Association*, 45/2 (2014), p. 47.

Dixon, Thomas, *Weeping Britannia: Portrait of a Nation in Tears* (Oxford: Oxford University Press, 2016).

Ford, Gina, *The New Contented Little Baby Book: The Secret to Calm and Confident Parenting* (Vermillion, 2006).

Gertsman, Elina, ed., *Crying in the Middle Ages: Tears of History* (London: Routledge, 2012).

Gildea, Robert, *Marianne in Chains: Daily Life in the Heart of France During the German Occupation* (London: Macmillan, 2002).

Halevi, Leor, 'Wailing for the Dead: The Role of Women in Early Islamic Funerals', *Past & Present*, 183/1 (2004), pp. 3–39.

Harvey, Katherine, 'Episcopal Emotions: Tears in the Life of the Medieval Bishop', *Historical Research*, 87/238 (November 2014), pp. 591–610.

Hook, Philip, *Breakfast at Sotheby's: An A–Z of the Art World* (New York: The Overlook Press, 2014).

Houlbrooke, Ralph, *Death, Religion and the Family in England, 1480–1750* (Oxford: Oxford University Press, 1998).

Hu, Elise, 'Campaign Trail Tears: The Changing Politics of Crying', *NPR*, 25 November 2011, http://www.npr.org/2011/11/25/142599676/campaign-trail-tears-the-changing-politics-of-crying [accessed 17 October 2017].

Lorpiola, Mia, and Anu Lahtinen, *Cultures of Death and Dying in Medieval and Early Modern Europe*, Collegium: Studies Across Disciplines in the Humanities and Social Sciences, 16 (2015).

Lutz, Tom, *Crying: The Natural and Cultural History of Tears* (New York: Norton, 2001)

Newton, Hannah, *The Sick Child in Early Modern England, 1580–1720* (Oxford: Oxford University Press, 2012).

Pease, Anna S., 'Swaddling and the Risk of Sudden Infant Death Syndrome: A Meta-Analysis', *Pediatrics* (May 2016), http://pediatrics.aappublications.org/content/pediatrics/early/2016/05/05/peds.2015-3275.full.pdf [accessed 17 October 2017].

Shaner, D., and K. Vliet, 'Crocodile Tears: "And Thei Eten Hem Wepynge"', *BioScience*, 57 (2007), pp. 615–17.

Sharp, Jane, *The Midwife's Book* (London: Printed for John Marshall, 1671).

'The Last Lap', *Punch* Digital Image Library, http://punch.photoshelter.com/
image/I00003dXyAKMf0Og [accessed 17 October 2017].
Viggiani, Carl A., 'Camus' *L'Etranger*', *Publications of the Modern Language
Association*, 71/5 (1956), pp. 865–87.

CHAPTER 23. LIONS

Arnold, Benjamin, 'Henry the Lion and His Time', *Journal of Medieval
History*, 22 (1996), pp. 379–93.
Attebery, Brian, *The Fantasy Tradition in American Literature: From Irving to Le
Guin* (Bloomington, 1980).
Baum, L. Frank, *The Wonderful Wizard of Oz* (Chicago, 1900).
Bolgiano, Chris, *Mountain Lion: An Unnatural History of Pumas and People*
(Mechanicsburg, PA: Stackpole Books, 2001).
Calder, William A., Jonas Bros, William S. Lackner, Anthony Stabinsky,
Lewis W. Steel, Ustavo Bronson and Frank Calcord, 'Man and the
Mountain Lion in the Early 1900s: Perspectives from a Wildcat Dump',
Journal of the Southwest, 32/2 (1990), pp. 150–72.
Cederlund, Carl Olof, *Vasa I: The Archaeology of a Swedish Warship of 1628*
(National Maritime Museums of Sweden, 2006).
Clark, Hugh, and J. R. Planché, *An Introduction to Heraldry*, 18th edition
(London: Bell & Daldy, 1866).
Durden, Robert F., *The Climax of Populism: The Election of 1896* (Lexington,
VA: University Press of Kentucky, 1965).
Fox-Davies, Arthur Charles, *A Complete Guide to Heraldry* (London: T. C. and
E. C. Jack, 1909; 2008 edition).
Geer, John G., and Thomas R. Rochon, 'William Jennings Bryan on the
Yellow Brick Road', *Journal of American Culture*, 16/4 (1993).
Gillingham, John, *Richard Coeur de Lion: Kingship, Chivalry and War in the
Twelfth Century* (London: Hambledon Continuum, 1994).
——, *Richard I* (New Haven: Yale University Press, 1999).
——, 'Richard I (1157–99)', *Oxford Dictionary of National Biography* (Oxford:
Oxford University Press, 2004).
Hocker, Frederick M., *Vasa, A Swedish Warship* (Stockholm: Medstroms
Bokforlag, 2011).
Jensen, Richard, *The Winning of the Midwest: Social and Political Conflict,
1888–1896* (Chicago: University of Chicago Press, 1971).
Kirby, David, *Northern Europe in the Early Modern Period: The Baltic World,
1492–1772* (London and New York: Longmans, 1990).
Littlefield, Henry M., 'The Wizard of Oz: Parable on Populism', *American
Quarterly*, 16 (1964), pp. 47–58.

Matz, Erling, *Vasa* (Stockholm: Vasa Museum, 2012).

McGee Morganstern, Anne, *Gothic Tombs of Kinship in France, the Low Countries, and England* (Philadelphia: Pennsylvania State University Press, 2000).

Magnusson, Magnus, *Scotland: Story of a Nation* (London: HarperCollins, 2001).

Parker, David B., 'The Rise and Fall of *The Wonderful Wizard of Oz* as a "Parable on Populism"', *Journal of the Georgia Association of Historians*, 15 (1994), pp. 49–63.

Ritter, Gretchen, 'Silver slippers and a golden cap: L. Frank Baum's *The Wonderful Wizard of Oz* and historical memory in American politics', *Journal of American Studies*, 31/2 (1997).

Roberts, Michael, *Gustavus Adolphus*, Profiles in Power, 2nd edition (London: Longmans, 1992).

——, *Gustavus Adolphus and the Rise of Sweden* (London: English Universities Press, 1973).

Rockoff, Hugh, 'The "Wizard of Oz" as a Monetary Allegory', *Journal of Political Economy*, 98/4 (1990), pp. 739–60.

Runciman, Steven, *A History of the Crusades*, 3 vols (Cambridge: Cambridge University Press, 1951–54).

Svanberg, Ingvar, *Svenska lejon* (Stockholm: Dialogos förlag, 2017).

Ziaukas, Tim, 'Baum's *Wizard of Oz* as Gilded Age Public Relations', *Public Relations Quarterly*, 43/3 (1998).

CHAPTER 24. RUBBISH

'Ancient Lives and the Zooniverse', https://www.ancientlives.org [accessed 18 September 2017].

Beckett, Andy, *When the Lights Went Out: Britain in the Seventies* (London: Faber and Faber, 2009).

Belolan, N., '"L'imagerie sucrée": Challenges in Cataloging and Researching Nineteenth-Century French Candy Wrappers' in *Art Documentation: Journal of the Art Libraries Society of North America*, vol. 29, no. 1 (Spring 2010), pp. 16–22.

Bowman, A. K., ed., *Oxyrhynchus: A City and Its Texts* (London: Published for the Arts and Humanities Research Council by the Egypt Exploration Society, 2007).

'Britain destroyed records of colonial crimes', *Guardian*, 18 April 2012.

Daybell, James, 'Gendered Archival Practices and the Future Lives of Letters', in *Cultures of Correspondence in Early Modern Britain, 1580–1690*, ed. James Daybell and Andrew Gordon (Philadelphia: University of Pennsylvania Press, 2016), pp. 210–36.

Eagan, Jane, 'An Unexpected Discovery: Early Modern Recycling', Merton College, Oxford website, https://www.merton.ox.ac.uk/library-and-archives/conservation/ream-wrapper [accessed 19 September 2017].

Emmerson, A., 'Repopulating an "Abandoned" Suburb: The Case of Pompeii's Tombs', paper given at the 2012 Archaeological Institute of America/American Philological Association Conference, http://www.uc.edu/news/NR.aspx?id=14812 [accessed 8 November 2017].

Feldman, Gerald D., *The Great Disorder: Politics, Economics, and Society in the German Inflation, 1914–1924* (New York: Oxford University Press, 1996).

Gonis, N., and D. Colomo, ed., *The Oxyrhynchus Papyri*, Graeco-Roman Memoirs, no. 92 (London: Published for the Arts and Humanities Research Council by the Egypt Exploration Society, 2008).

Grenfell, B. P., and A. S. Hunt, *Oxyrhynchus Papyri* (London: Egypt Exploration Society, 1914).

Hay, Colin, 'The Winter of Discontent Thirty Years On', *Political Quarterly*, 80/4 (2009), pp. 545–52.

'Hundreds of Liquor Bottles from World War I were exposed near Ramle', Friends of the Israel Antiquities Authority, http://www.archaeology.org.il/news/news.php?id=212 [accessed 8 November 2017].

Hunt, Arnold, '"Burn This Letter": Preservation and Destruction in the Early Modern Archive', in *Cultures of Correspondence in Early Modern Britain, 1580–1690*, ed. James Daybell and Andrew Gordon (Philadelphia: University of Pennsylvania Press, 2016), pp. 189–209.

Jarrin, W. A., *The Italian Confectioner; or, Complete Economy of Desserts, Containing the Elements of the Art According to the Most Modern and Approved Practice* (London: Printed for John Harding, 1820).

Lopez, Tara Martin, *The Winter of Discontent: Myth, Memory, and History* (Liverpool: Liverpool University Press, 2014).

Moon, Antonia, 'Destroying Records, Keeping Records: Some Practices at the East India Company and at the India Office', *Archives*, 33/119 (2008), pp. 110–21.

Nestlé Reminiscence Pack, https://www.nestle.co.uk/aboutus/history/reminiscence-pack [accessed 8 November 2017].

Orme, Nicholas, 'The Culture of Children in Medieval England', *Past & Present*, 148/1 (1995), pp. 48–88.

Oxyrhynchus Online, Papyrology at Oxford, University of Oxford, http://www.papyrology.ox.ac.uk/POxy/ [accessed 18 September 2017].

Petrie, Flinders, *Tombs of the Courtiers and Oxyrhynkhos* (London: British School of Archaeology in Egypt, 1925).

Rathbone, D. W., 'Grenfell and Hunt at Oxyrhynchus and in the Fayum', in P. Spencer, ed., *The Egypt Exploration Society – The Early Years* (EES, 2007), pp. 195–229.

Rathje, W., and Murphy, C., *RUBBISH! The Archaeology of Garbage* (New York: HarperCollins, 2001).

'Revealed: The Bonfire of Papers at the End of Empire', *Guardian*, 29 November 2013.

Shepherd, John, *Crisis? What Crisis?: The Callaghan Government and the British Winter of Discontent* (Manchester: Manchester University Press, 2013).

Smyth, Adam, *Autobiography in Early Modern England* (Cambridge: Cambridge University Press, 2010).

'Using banknotes as wallpaper during German hyperinflation, 1923', Rare Historical Photos blog, https://rarehistoricalphotos.com/banknotes-german-hyperinflation-1923/ [accessed 28 November 2017].

CHAPTER 25. SNOW

Appleby, Andrew B., 'Epidemics and Famine in the Little Ice Age', *Journal of Interdisciplinary History*, 10/4 (1980), pp. 643–63.

Arctic Miscellanies: A Souvenir of the Late Polar Search by the Officers and Seamen of the Expedition (London: Colburn, 1852).

Briggs, Raymond, *The Snowman* (London: Hamish Hamilton, 1978).

Dickert, D. Augustus, *History of Kershaw's Brigade, with Complete Roll of Companies, Biographical Sketches, Incidents, Anecdotes, etc.* (Newberry, SC: E. H. Aull Company, 1899).

Dixon, E. James, M. Callanan, A. Hafner and P. G. Hare, 'The Emergence of Glacial Archaeology', *Journal of Glacial Archaeology*, 1/1 (2014), pp. 1–9.

Eber, Dorothy, *Encounters on the Passage: Inuit Meet the Explorers* (Toronto: University of Toronto Press, 2008).

Eckstein, Bob, *The History of the Snowman: From the Ice Age to the Flea Market* (New York: Simon Spotlight Entertainment, 2007).

Eksteins, M., *Rites of Spring: The Great War and the Birth of the Modern Age* (Boston: Houghton Mifflin, 1999).

Engel, C. E., *Mountaineering in the Alps: An Historical Survey* (London: George Allen & Unwin, 1971).

Evelyn, John, 'An Abstract of a Letter from the Worshipful John Evelyn Esq; Sent to One of the Secretaries of the R. Society concerning the Dammage [sic] Done to His Gardens by the Preceding Winter', *Philosophical Transactions* (1683–1775), 14/155–166 (1684), pp. 559–63.

Fagan, Brian M., *The Little Ice Age: How Climate Made History, 1300–1850* (New York: Basic Books, 2001).

Gravino, Michelle, 'A Century Later, Relics Emerge from a War Frozen in Time', *National Geographic*, http://news.nationalgeographic.com/news/2014/10/141017-white-war-first-world-war-italy-austro-hungarian-mountains-history/ [accessed 2 October 2017].

Hudson, Roger, *London: Portrait of a City* (London: The Folio Society, 1998).

Keller, T., *Apostles of the Alps: Mountaineering and Nation Building in Germany and Austria, 1860–1939* (Chapel Hill, NC: University of North Carolina Press, 2016).

Ladurie, Emmanuel Le Roy, *Times of Feast, Times of Famine: a History of Climate Since the Year 1000* (Garden City, NY: Doubleday, 1971).

Mann, Michael, 'Little Ice Age', in Michael C. MacCracken and John S. Perry, eds, *Encyclopedia of Global Environmental Change, Volume 1, The Earth System: Physical and Chemical Dimensions of Global Environmental Change* (London: John Wiley, 2003).

Mergen, Bernard, *Snow in America* (London: Smithsonian Institution Press, 1997).

Morisini, S., *Sulle vette della patria: Politicia, guerra e nazione nel Club alpino italiano (1863–1922)* (Milan: Franco Angeli, 2009).

Neal, Avon, *Ephemeral Folk Figures: Scarecrows, Harvest Figures and Snowmen* (New York: Clarkson N. Potter, 1969).

Nobbs, Patrick, 'Six of the most catastrophic weather events in British history', *BBC History Magazine*, History Extra, 3 June 2015, http://www.historyextra.com/article/medieval/6-most-catastrophic-weather-events-british-history [accessed 2 October 2017].

——, *The Story of The British and Their Weather* (Stroud: Amberley Publishing, 2015).

Peverley, Sarah, 'Medieval Winter Sports', https://sarahpeverley.com/tag/snowballing/ [accessed 3 October 2017].

Pleij, Herman, 'Urban Elites in Search of a Culture: The Brussels Snow Festival of 1511', *New Literary History*, 21/3 (1990), pp. 629–47.

Simpson, St John, and Dr Svetlana Pankova, *Scythians: Warriors of Ancient Siberia* (London: Thames and Hudson for the British Museum, 2017).

Suchtelen, Arianne van, *Holland Frozen in Time: The Dutch Winter Landscape in the Golden Age* (Zwolle, Netherlands: Waanders Publishers, 2001).

Van Dam, Raymond, *Kingdom of Snow: Roman Rule and Greek Culture in Cappadocia* (Philadelphia: University of Pennsylvania Press, 2002).

Willemsen, Annemarieke, 'The Geoff Egan Memorial Lecture 2013: Taking up the glove: finds, uses and meanings of gloves, mittens and gauntlets in Western Europe, c. AD 1300–1700', *Post-Medieval Archaeology*, 49/1 (2015), pp. 1–36.

CHAPTER 26. CATS

Buglass, John, and Jennifer West, 'Pet Cats in Roman Villas: A North York-shire Candidate', *Archaeological Forum Journal: CBA Yorkshire* 3 (2014).

Darnton, Robert, *The Great Cat Massacre: And Other Episodes in French Cultural History* (New York: Vintage Books, 1984).

Davis, S. J. M., *The Archaeology of Animals* (London: Routledge, 1995).

Hoggard, Brian, 'The Archaeology of Counter-Witchcraft and Popular Magic', in Owen Davies and William Blécourt, eds, *Beyond the Witchtrials: Witchcraft and Magic in Enlightenment Europe* (Manchester: Manchester University Press, 2004).

Hollister, C. Warren, and Judith M. Bennett, *Medieval Europe: A Short History* (New York: McGraw-Hill Press, 2002).

Howard, Margaret M., 'Dried Cats', *Royal Anthropological Institute of Great Britain and Ireland*, 51 (1951), pp. 149–51.

Hu, Yaowu, Songmei Hu, Weilin Wang, Xiaohong Wu, Fiona B. Marshall, Xianglong Chen, Liangliang Hou, and Changsui Wang, 'Earliest evidence for commensal processes of cat domestication', *Proceedings of the National Academy of Sciences of the United States of America*, 111/1 (2014), pp. 116–20.

Lewis, Val, *Ships' Cats in War and Peace* (Shepperton: Nauticalia, 2001).

Luff, R. M., and M. Moreno-Garcia, 'Killing Cats in the Medieval Period: An Unusual Episode in the History of Cambridge, England', *Archaeofauna*, 4 (1995), pp. 93–114.

Marchini, Lucia, 'The archaeology of the domestic cat', *Current Archaeology*, 318 (5 August 2016).

Moran, N. C., and T. P. O'Connor, 'Bones That Cats Gnawed Upon: A Case Study in Bone Modification', *Circaea*, 9 (1992), pp. 27–34.

O'Connor, Terry, *The Archaeology of Animal Bones* (Stroud: Sutton Publishing, 2000).

Rothwell, Tom, J. D. Vigne and J. Guilaine, 'Evidence for Taming of Cats', *Science*, New Series, 305/5691 (2004), pp. 1714–15.

Swan, Madeline, *A Curious History of Cats* (Brentford: Max Press, 2015).

Tanner, Ron, 'Cats as Tuna', *Iowa Review*, 39/1 (2009), pp. 53–55.

Vocelle, L. A., *Revered and Reviled: A Complete History of the Domestic Cat* (Great Cat Publications, 2016).

Warner, Mark S., and Robert A. Genheimer, '"Cats Here, Cats There, Cats and Kittens Everywhere": An Urban Extermination of Cats in Nineteenth-Century Cincinnati', *Historical Archaeology*, 42, Living in Cities Revisited: Trends in Nineteenth- and Twentieth-Century Urban Archaeology (2008), pp. 11–25.

CHAPTER 27. THE SMILE

Bartie, Angela, 'Moral Panics and Glasgow Gangs: Exploring "the New Wave of Glasgow Hooliganism", 1965–1970', *Contemporary British History*, 24/3 (2010), pp. 385–408.

Davies, Andrew, *City of Gangs: Glasgow and the Rise of the British Gangster* (London: Hodder and Stoughton, 2013).

——, 'Glasgow's "Reign of Terror": Street Gangs, Racketeering and Intimidation in the 1920s and 1930s', *Contemporary British History*, 4 (2007), pp. 405–27.

Delaporte, François, *Anatomy of the Passions* (Stanford: Stanford University Press, 2008).

Ekman, Paul, 'Duchenne and Facial Expression of Emotion', *The Mechanism of Human Facial Expression*, ed. G. B. Duchenne de Boulogne (Cambridge: Cambridge University Press, 1990), pp. 270–84.

Finnegan, Cara A., 'Recognizing Lincoln: Portrait Photography and the Physiognomy of National Character', in *Making Photography Matter: A Viewer's History from the Civil War to the Great Depression* (Champaign, IL: University of Illinois Press, 2015), pp. 51–80.

Freitas-Magalhães, A., and E. Castro, 'The Neuropsychophysiological Construction of the Human Smile', in *Emotional Expression: The Brain and The Face*, ed. A. Freitas-Magalhães (Porto: University Fernando Pessoa Press, 2009), pp. 1–18.

Holzer, Harold, 'The "Gettysburg" Lincoln: The Back Story of a Full-Frontal Photograph', in *Lens of War: Exploring Iconic Photographs of the Civil War*, ed. J. Matthew Gallman and Gary W. Gallagher (Athens, GA: University of Georgia Press, 2015), pp. 7–16.

Jeeves, Nicholas, 'The Serious and the Smirk: The Smile in Portraiture', *Public Domain Review*, http://publicdomainreview.org/2013/09/18/the-serious-and-the-smirk-the-smile-in-portraiture/ [accessed 25 November 2017].

Jones, Colin, *The Smile Revolution in Eighteenth Century Paris* (Oxford: Oxford University Press, 2014).

Long, H. Kingsley, and Alexander McArthur, *No Mean City: A Story of the Glasgow Slums* (London: Longman, Green and Co., 1935).

McCarthy, Edwin, 'Reflections on the Rules of Christian Decorum and Civility', ed. William Mann, *AXIS: Journal of Lasallian Higher Education* 6, no. 1 (Institute for Lasallian Studies at Saint Mary's University of Minnesota: 2015).

Milano, Ronit, *The Portrait Bust and French Cultural Politics in the Eighteenth Century* (Leiden: Brill, 2015).

Parry-Giles, Shawn J., and David S. Kaufer, 'Lincoln Reminiscences and Nineteenth-Century Portraiture: The Private Virtues of Presidential Character', *Rhetoric and Public Affairs*, 15/2 (2012), pp. 199–234.

Pim, Keiron, *Jumpin' Jack Flash: David Litvinoff and the Rock'n'Roll Underworld* (London: Penguin Random House, 2016).

Simkins, Anthony, 'Sillitoe, Sir Percy Joseph (1888–1962)', *Oxford Dictionary of National Biography* (Oxford: Oxford University Press, 2004).

Trachtenberg, Alan, *Lincoln's Smile and Other Enigmas* (New York: Hill and Wang, 2008).

Trumble, Angus, *The Brief History of the Smile* (New York: Basic Books, 2004).

van der Pol, Lotte C., 'The Whore, the Bawd, and the Artist: The Reality and Imagery of Seventeenth-Century Dutch Prostitution', *Journal of Historians of Netherlandish Art*, 2/1–2 (Summer 2010).

CHAPTER 28. THE SCAR

Brady, Ciaran, ed., *A Viceroy's Vindication? Sir Henry Sidney's Memoir of Service in Ireland, 1556–78* (Cork: Cork University Press, 2002).

Camphausen, Rufus, *Return of the Tribal: Celebration of Body Adornment: Piercing, Tattooing, Scarification, Body Painting* (Rochester: Inner Traditions, 1998).

Gersons, B. P., and I. V. Carlier, 'Post-Traumatic Stress Disorder: The History of a Recent Concept', *British Journal of Psychiatry*, 161/6 (1992), pp. 742–48.

Hodge, Bernulf, *A History of Malmesbury* (5th edition; Friends of Malmesbury Abbey, Minety: 1990).

Knight, R. J. B., *The Pursuit of Victory: The Life and Achievement of Horatio Nelson* (London: Penguin, 2005).

Lévi-Strauss, Claude, *Structural Anthropology* (New York: Basic Books, 1963).

Lock, Margaret, and Judith Farquhar, eds., *Beyond the Body Proper: Reading the Anthropology of Material Life* (Durham: Duke University Press, 2007).

Luce, Richard H., *The History of the Abbey and Town of Malmesbury* (Friends of Malmesbury Abbey, Minety: 1979).

McAleer, Kevin, *Dueling: The Cult of Honor in Fin-de-siècle Germany* (Princeton: Princeton University Press, 1994).

Marshall, Alan, 'Bennet, Henry, first earl of Arlington (bap.1618, d.1685)', *Oxford Dictionary of National Biography* (Oxford: Oxford University Press, 2004).

Motley, John Lothrop, *Morton's Hope, or the Memoirs of a Provincial* (New York: Harper and Brothers, 1839).

Northup, Solomon, *Twelve Years a Slave* (Auburn, NY: Derby & Miller, 1853).

Rubin, Arnold, ed., *Marks of Civilization: Artistic Transformations of the Human Body* (Los Angeles: University of California Museum of Cultural History, 1988).

Scarry, Elaine, *The Body in Pain: The Making and Unmaking of the World* (New York: Oxford University Press, 1985).

Silkenat, David, '"A Typical Negro": Gordon, Peter, Vincent Colyer, and the Story behind Slavery's Most Famous Photograph', *American Nineteenth Century History*, 15/2 (2014), pp. 169–86.

Taylor, A. J. P., *Bismarck: The Man and the Statesman* (London: Hamish Hamilton, 1955).

Tomalin, Claire, *Samuel Pepys: The Unequalled Self* (London: Penguin, 2002).

Trimble, M. D., 'Post-Traumatic Stress Disorder: History of a Concept' in C. R. Figley, ed., *Trauma and its wake: The study and treatment of Post-Traumatic Stress Disorder* (New York: Brunner/Mazel, 1985), pp. 5–14.

Turner, Terence, 'Social Body and Embodied Subject: Bodiliness, Subjectivity, and Sociality among the Kayapo', *Cultural Anthropology* 10/2 (1995), pp. 143–70.

Whitehead, Colson, *The Underground Railroad* (New York: Doubleday, 2016).

Wolfe, Michael, 'Pain and Memory: The War Wounds of Blaise de Monluc' in *France and Its Spaces of War: Experience, Memory, Image*, ed. Patricia M. E. Lorcin and Daniel Brewer (New York: Palgrave Macmillan, 2009), pp. 105–19.

CHAPTER 29. THE LEAN

Abbate, Francesco, 'The Planning and Building of Architects in the Late Middle Ages', *Proceedings of the Second International Congress on Construction History*, 1 (2006), pp. 111–25.

Alcock, N. A., and Michael Laithwaite, 'Medieval Houses in Devon and Their Modernization', *Medieval Archaeology*, 17 (1973), pp. 100–25.

Bloom, Harold, *Oscar Wilde* (New York: Infobase Publishing, 2008).

Boehm, Eric H., *We Survived: The Stories of Fourteen of the Hidden and the Hunted of Nazi Germany* (Lucknow Books, 2015).

Boothroyd, A. E., *Fascinating Walking Sticks* (London and New York: White Lion Publishers, 1973).

Burka, Elliott L., 'Remington Rifle Cane', http://americansocietyofarmscollectors.org/wp-content/uploads/2012/11/85_burka_cane.pdf [accessed 13 November 2017].

Crawford, Patricia, and Laura Gowing, eds, *Women's Worlds in Seventeenth-Century England: A Sourcebook* (London: Routledge, 2000).

Dike, Catherine, *Cane Curiosa: From Gun to Gadget* (Paris: Les Editions de l'Amateur; Geneva: Dike Publications, 1983).

Ehrman, J., *The Navy in the War of William III 1689–97: Its State and Direction* (Cambridge: Cambridge University Press, 1953).

Forbes, A., 'Greenwich Hospital Money', *New England Quarterly*, 3/3 (1930), pp. 519–26.

Grenville, Jane, 'Out of the Shunting Yards – One Academic's Approach to Recording Small Buildings', in S. Pearson and B. Meeson, eds, *Vernacular Buildings in a Changing World* (York: Council for British Archaeology, 2001), pp. 22–24.

——, 'Urban and rural houses and households in the late Middle Ages', in M. Kowaleski and P. J. P. Goldberg, eds, *Medieval Domesticity* (Cambridge: Cambridge University Press, 2008), pp. 119–22.

Harris, Richard, *Discovering Timber-Framed Buildings*, 2nd edition (Aylesbury: Shire Publications, 1979).

Jones, Karen R., '"The Lungs of the City": Green Space, Public Health and Bodily Metaphor in the Landscape of Urban Park History', *Environment and History*, 24 (2018), pp. 39–58.

Jordan, David P., 'Haussmann and Haussmannisation: The Legacy for Paris', *French Historical Studies*, 27/1 (2004), pp. 87–113.

Klever, Ulrich, *Walking Sticks: Accessory, Tool and Symbol* (Atglen, PA: Schiffer Publishing Ltd., 1984).

Nevell, R., 'The Archaeology of Castle Slighting' (University of Exeter PhD, 2017).

Newell, P., *Greenwich Hospital: A Royal Foundation 1692–1983* (London, 1984).

Palliser, D. M., *Medieval York, 600–1540* (Oxford: Oxford University Press, 2014).

Payling, S. J., 'Cornewall, John, Baron Fanhope (d.1443)', *Oxford Dictionary of National Biography* (Oxford: Oxford University Press, 2004).

Quiney, Anthony, *Town Houses in Medieval Britain* (New Haven and London: Yale University Press, 2003).

Science Museum, London, 'Whalebone walking stick, owned by Charles Darwin, England, 1839–1881', http://www.sciencemuseum.org.uk/broughttolife/objects/display?id=92610 [accessed 8 September 2017].

Schofield, John, 'The Construction of Medieval and Tudor Houses in London', *Construction History*, 7 (1991), pp. 3–28.

——, 'Urban Housing', *The Oxford Handbook of Later Medieval Britain*, eds Christopher Gerrard and Alejandra Gutierrez (Oxford: Oxford University Press, forthcoming).

Sen, Sambudha, 'Hogarth, Egan, Dickens, and the Making of an Urban Aesthetic', *Representations*, 103/1 (2008), pp. 84–106.

Shelby, Lonnie R., 'Medieval Masons' Tools: The Level and Plumb Rule', *Technology and Culture*, 2/2 (1961), pp. 127–30.

Smith, Lacey Baldwin, *This Realm of England, Volume 2: 1399–1688*, 8th edition (Boston: Cengage Learning, 2001).

Stein, Kurt, *Canes and Walking Sticks* (York, PA: Liberty Cap Books, 1974).

Sutcliffe, Anthony, *Paris: An Architectural History* (New Haven: Yale University Press, 1993).

Taylor, Adam, 'It's Guy Fawkes Day – here's his signature before and after he was tortured', *Business Insider*, 5 November 2015, http://uk.businessinsider.com/guy-fawkes-signature-before-and-after-he-was-tortured-2015-11 [accessed 1 December 2017].

Taylor, Craig, 'The Disposal of Human Waste: A comparison between Ancient Rome and Medieval London', *Past Imperfect*, 11 (2005), pp. 53–72.

Thornwell, Emily, *The Lady's Guide to Perfect Gentility, in Manners, Dress, and Conversation... Also a Useful Instructor in Letter Writing...* (New York : Derby & Jackson, 1859).

Ubmach, Maiken, 'Memory and Historicism: Reading Between the Lines of the Built Environment, Germany c.1900', *Representations*, 88/1 (2004), pp. 26–54.

Wall, Cynthia, 'Novel Streets: The Rebuilding of London and Defoe's *A Journal of The Plague Year*', *Studies in the Novel*, 30/2 (1998), pp. 164–77.

Wilcox, Martin, 'The "Poor Decayed Seamen" of Greenwich Hospital, 1705–1763', *International Journal of Maritime History*, 25/1 (2013), pp. 65–90.

Willis, Sam, *The Admiral Benbow: The Life and Times of a Naval Legend* (London: Quercus, 2011).

Wilson, Van, 'Butchers, Bakers and Candlestick Makers: The Shambles and Colliergate' (York: York Archaeological Trust, 2014).

CHAPTER 30. THE SIGNATURE

Adamson, J. W., 'The Extent of Literacy in England in the Fifteenth and Sixteenth Centuries: Notes and Conjectures', *The Library*, 4th series, 10 (1929), pp. 163–93.

Collinson, Patrick, 'The Significance of Signatures', *Times Literary Supplement* (9 January 1981), p. 31.

Cressy, David, 'Literacy in Seventeenth-Century England: More Evidence', *Journal of Interdisciplinary History*, 8 (1977), pp. 141–50.

——, *Literacy and the Social Order: Reading and Writing in Tudor and Stuart England* (Cambridge: Cambridge University Press, 1980).

Daybell, James, 'Henry VIII's Sign Manual', in *The Pen's Excellencie: Manuscript Treasures at the Folger Shakespeare Library, A Festschrift on the Retirement of Laetitia Yeandle* (Washington, DC: Folger Shakespeare Library, 2002).

——, *The Material Letter in Early Modern England: Manuscript Letters and the Culture and Practices of Letter-Writing, 1512–1635* (Basingstoke: Palgrave Macmillan, 2012).

——, *Women Letter-Writers in Tudor England* (Oxford: Oxford University Press, 2006).

Fremantle, S., 'Nelson's first writing with his left hand', *Mariner's Mirror*, 36 (3) (1950), pp. 205–11.

Furet, F., and J. Ozouf, *Reading and Writing: Literacy in France from Calvin to Jules Ferry* (Cambridge: Cambridge University Press, 1982).

Gawthrop, R., and G. Strauss, 'Protestantism and Literacy in Early Modern Germany', *Past & Present*, 104 (1984), pp. 31–55.

Gilreath, James, 'Guilt, Innocence, Faith, Forensic Science, and the Lincoln Forgeries', *Journal of the Abraham Lincoln Association*, 17/1 (1996), pp. 27–38.

Goody, Jack, ed., *Literacy in Traditional Societies* (Cambridge: Cambridge University Press, 1968).

Graff, H. J., *Legacies of Literacy: Continuities and Contradictions in Western Culture and Society* (Bloomington, IN: Indiana University Press, 1987).

Hamilton, Charles, *Great Forgers and Famous Fakes: The Manuscript Forgers of America and How They Duped the Experts* (Lakewood, CO: Glenbridge Publishing Ltd, 1996).

Houston, R. A., *Literacy in Early Modern Europe: Culture and Education, 1500–1800* (London: Longmans, 1988).

——, 'The Literacy Myth? Illiteracy in Scotland 1630–1760', *Past & Present*, 96 (1982), pp. 81–102.

Kobler, John, 'Yrs. Truly, A. Lincoln', *New Yorker*, 25 February (1956).

Lang, Andrew, *Shakespeare, Bacon and the Great Unknown* (London: Longmans, 1912).

Lacqueur, T. W., 'The Cultural Origins of Popular Literacy in England, 1500–1850', *Oxford Review of Education*, 2 (1976), pp. 255–75.

——, 'Literacy and Social Mobility in the Industrial Revolution in England', *Past & Present*, 64 (August 1974), pp. 96–107.

McGowen, Randall, 'The Punishment of Forgery in Eighteenth-Century England', *IAHCCJ Bulletin*, no. 17, Processes of Criminalization and Decriminalization (Winter 1992/93), pp. 29–45.

Monaghan, Jay, 'Lincolniana: Autographs: Real and Forged', *Journal of the Illinois State Historical Society*, 42/1 (1949), pp. 80–83.

Munby, A. N. L., *The Cult of the Autograph Letter in England* (London: The Athlone Press, 1962).

Ong, Walter J., *Orality and Literacy: The Technologizing of the Word* (London: Methuen, 1982).

——, 'Writing is a Technology that Restructures Thought', in *The Written Word: Literacy in Transition, Wolfson College Lectures 1985*, ed. Gerd Baumann (Oxford: Clarendon Press, 1986), pp. 23–50.

Rylands, Paul J., 'Merchants' Marks and Other Mediaeval Personal Marks', *Transactions of the Historic Society of Lancashire and Cheshire*, 62 (1911), pp. 1–34.

Schofield, R. S., 'The Measurement of Literacy in Pre-Industrial England', in *Literacy in Traditional Societies*, ed. Jack Goody (Cambridge: Cambridge University Press, 1968), pp. 311–25.

Sisson, Charles, 'Marks as Signatures', *The Library*, 4th series, IX, 1 (1928), pp. 1–34.

Starkey, David, *The Reign of Henry VIII: Personalities and Politics* (London: Collins & Brown, 1985).

Sugden, John, *Nelson: The Sword of Albion* (London: Random House, 2012).

Thomas, Keith, 'The Meaning of Literacy in Early Modern England', in *The Written Word: Literacy in Transition, Wolfson College Lectures 1985*, ed. Gerd Baumann (Oxford: Clarendon Press, 1986), pp. 97–131.

Williams, Graham, '"My evil favoured writing": Uglyography, Disease, and the Epistolary Networks of George Talbot, Sixth Earl of Shrewsbury', *Huntington Library Quarterly*, 79/3 (2016), pp. 387–409.

ILLUSTRATION CREDITS

BLACK-AND-WHITE IMAGES

p. 4   Cueva de las Manos del Rio Pinturas, Argentina (*Iakov Filimonov/ Shutterstock.com*)

p. 11   Charles II performing the royal touch, engraving by Robert White (1684) (*Wellcome Collection*)

p. 36   Listerine advertisement, *The Sketch*, 21 May 1930 (*© Illustrated London News Ltd/Mary Evans*)

p. 42   Children blowing bubbles, sixteenth-century engraving (*Photo by Universal History Archive/Getty Images*)

p. 51   Eclipse of the Sun, 1842, from Emmanuel Liais, *L'Espace celeste et la nature tropicale, description physique de l'univers* (1866) (*Public Domain*)

p.61   Gem razor blade advertisement, USA, 1937 (*Public Domain*)

p. 64   Soldiers from the 72nd Highlanders, 1856 (*Military History Collection/ Alamy Stock Photo*)

p. 71   Illustration of Edward Teach (Blackbeard the Pirate), English School engraving, nineteenth century (*Hulton Archive/Getty Images*)

p. 75   Edward Lear's 'Old Man with a Beard', from *A Book of Nonsense* (1846) (*Public Domain*)

p. 83   Photograph of 'mammato-cumulus' clouds, from *The International Cloud Atlas* (Paris, 1896) (*Public Domain*)

p. 87   The atomic bombing of Nagasaki, 9 August 1945 (*U.S. National Archives and Records Administration*)

p. 95   *View of a Dust Yard*, from Henry Mayhew's *London Labour and the London Poor* (1851) (*Granger Historical Picture Archive/Alamy Stock Photo*)

p. 99   The Dust Bowl, Dallas, South Dakota, 1936 (*United States Department of Agriculture*)

p. 139 William Hogarth, *Harlot's Progress*, plate 5 (1731/32) (*Public Domain*)

FIRST COLOUR SECTION

SECOND COLOUR SECTION

18. Hole repaired with embroidery in fourteenth-century manuscript, C 371 (*University Library Uppsala*)
19. The Great Bed of Ware, c.1590 (© *Victoria and Albert Museum, London*)
20. Matteo di Giovanni (c.1430–1495), *Dream of St Jerome in 375* (1476), tempera on pane, 37.4 x 65.7 cm (*Art Institute Chicago*)
21. Hans Holbein the Younger, *Portrait of the Merchant Georg Gisze* (1532), oil on wood, 96 x 86 cm (*Staatliche Museen, Berlin*)

THIRD COLOUR SECTION

22. Seventeenth-century trunk containing 2600 unopened letters dating from 1689–1706 (*COMM – Museum voor Communicatie, The Hague*)
23. Gravestone of Marcus Caelius, c.9 CE (*Agnete*)
24. Edwin Landseer (1802–73), *Neptune, the Property of William Ellis Gosling, Esq.* (1824), oil on canvas (*Private Collection/Photo © Christie's Images/ Bridgeman Images*)
25. Sam Willis in the Zarafshan mountains, 2015 (*Courtesy of Sam Willis*)
26. Wheal Coates, Cornwall (*Ian Woolcock/Shutterstock.com*)
27. The King's Pipe, Falmouth (*Southimages/Alamy Stock Photo*)
28. Conservation of a seventeenth-century Dutch map at the National Library of Scotland (*Trina McKendrick, Written in Film*)
29. Giotto di Bondone (c.1266–1337) Cappella Bardi (c.1325), fresco (*Santa Croce, Florence, Italy/Bridgeman Images*)
30. Lion figurehead on Gustavus Adolphus's *Vasa* warship, Vasa Museum, Stockholm (*Courtesy of James Daybell*)

FOURTH COLOUR SECTION

31. Oxyrhynchus Papyrus 52 (*University of Glasgow Library, Special Collections*)
32. British advertisement for Rowntree's Clear Gums, 1929 (© *Illustrated London News Ltd/Mary Evans*)
33. Scythian tattoo on the skin of a child's arm, Russia, fifth century BCE (*Hermitage Museum, St Petersburg/Photo by CM Dixon/Print Collector/Getty Images*)
34. Snowman in the margins of a Book of Hours, c.1380 (*KB, National Library*)
35. Fresco depicting a snowball fight in January at Castello Buonconsiglio, Trento, Italy, c.1405–1410 (*The Picture Art Collection/Alamy Stock Photo*)
36. The Gayer-Anderson Cat, 664–332 BCE (*Adam Eastland/Alamy Stock Photo*)

37. Franz Hals, *Malle Babbe* (1633–1635), oil on canvas, 75 x 64 cm (*Gemälde-galerie, Berlin*)
38. Gerrit van Honthorst, *The Laughing Violinist* (1624), oil on canvas, 81.3 x 63 cm (*Private Collection/Johnny Van Haeften Ltd., London/Bridgeman Images*)
39. Corfe Castle, Dorset (*P. Phillips/Shutterstock.com*)
40. The Shambles, York (*D. K. Grove/Shutterstock.com*)
41. Sailors' Round Robin, 1620s, State Papers 16/88 fol. 110 (*The National Archives*)

INDEX

A NOTE ABOUT THE AUTHORS

Dr Sam Willis is one of the country's best-known historians. His work takes him on adventures all over the world. He has made twelve TV series for the BBC and National Geographic, including *The Silk Road*, and has written fourteen books, most recently *The Struggle for Sea Power: The Royal Navy vs the World, 1775–1782* and *The Spanish Armada*, a Ladybird Expert Book.

James Daybell is Professor of Early Modern British History at the University of Plymouth and a Fellow of the Royal Historical Society. He has written eight books and has appeared in a number of historical BBC TV documentaries.